WORLD COMMUNISM
AT THE CROSSROADS

WORLD COMMUNISM AT THE CROSSROADS:

Military Ascendancy, Political Economy, and Human Welfare

Steven Rosefielde, Editor
University of North Carolina, Chapel Hill

Martinus Nijhoff Publishing
Boston/The Hague/London

Distributors for North America:
Martinus Nijhoff Publishing
Kluwer Boston, Inc.
160 Old Derby Street
Hingham, Massachusetts 02043

Distributors outside North America:
Kluwer Academic Publishers Group
Distribution Centre
P.O. Box 322
3300 AH Dordrecht, The Netherlands

Library of Congress Cataloging in Publication Data

World Communism at the Crossroads.
  Bibliography: p.
  1. Communism—1945- —Addresses, essays,
lectures. 2. Russia—Military policy—Addresses,
essays, lectures. I. Rosefielde, Steven.
HX44.W685 1980   309.1'171'7   79-25750
ISBN 0–89838–041–3

Printed in the United States of America.

To Aleksandr Solzhenitsyn
whose unswerving realism
has alerted us all to
the perils of complacent ideology.

CONTENTS

PREFACE

The collection of essays presented in this volume grew out of a series of lectures given at the University of North Carolina during the academic year 1976–1977. The series was sponsored by the Soviet and East European Studies Program, which I chaired at the time, and the Curriculum of Peace, War and Defense, headed by James Leutze. In the ensuing years almost all the manuscripts have been redrafted at frequent intervals to reflect the changing state of knowledge in each respective discipline. The final version of the text that appears here is therefore the outcome of a long developmental process. It is up to date and embodies our individual views on world communism at the present juncture.

Although the recent Soviet invasion of Afghanistan occurred shortly after this volume was completed, that event has not impaired the book's timeliness. The findings of Rosefielde, Lee, Valenta, and Leutze all point toward a resurgence of Soviet expansionism, and Parker explicitly predicted the Afghan invasion in the first draft of his essay, June 1978 (see p. 32).

ACKNOWLEDGMENTS

First and foremost I wish to thank the numerous contributors for their patience and cooperation in bringing this book to fruition, as well as the many authors who submitted essays that could not be included because of space limitations imposed by the costs of publication. James Leutze, it must be acknowledged, was especially helpful in the early stages of this endeavor and assisted me materially with the editorial task. Francoise Uriot diligently prepared detailed indexes for each of the essays in the collection. To all these individuals I express my deep appreciation.

I also wish to acknowledge the following institutions for the financial assistance they provided in support of the publication of this volume: the office of the Dean of Arts and Sciences (University of North Carolina at Chapel Hill) through funds provided by the Paul A. Johnston Trust; the Curriculum in Peace, War and Defense through funds provided by the Z. Smith Reynolds Foundation (Winston-Salem); the University of North Carolina Research Council; and the Heritage Foundation.

Dean Samuel Williamson, James Leutze, Dean George Holcomb, and William Schneider were instrumental in helping me secure this assistance. To them and their institutions I also wish to express my deep gratitude.

Last, but not least, I reserve my most profound appreciation for my wife whose warm encouragement sustained my enthusiasm and lightened my task.

WORLD COMMUNISM
AT THE CROSSROADS

INTRODUCTION

Sometime during the late 1970s the military balance turned in favor of the communist bloc.[1] Startling improvements in the accuracy of Soviet strategic nuclear targeting,[2] the cumulative effect of two decades of double-digit procurement growth,[3] and a long succession of technical breakthroughs that revolutionized Soviet weapons systems[4] finally gave the communist bloc clear military superiority over the United States and its allies.[5]

The rapidity with which the Soviet Union has overcome its military inferiority and is now moving toward a posture of manifest strategic dominance has caught most of the American intellectual community by surprise. World communism, a phenomenon inextricably linked with the behavior of the Soviet Union, for the most part continues to be analyzed within the complacent and threadbare theoretical models of the past.[6] Instead of examining how and why the communist bloc has attained military preeminence or exploring the probable consequences of the new situation, many specialists seem content to recapitulate the reasons why a fundamental change in the status quo is unlikely.

The arguments put forward are familiar. The balance of power is durable because in the nuclear age total destruction is mutually assured. Supremacy, being unattainable, will not be frivolously sought because such a policy would be inherently irrational and might jeopardize the internal stability of

1

the communist political-economic system. Evidence for the latter proposition is found in the putative inefficiency of communist economies, in their slow growth, the pressures of consumerism, dependence on Western technology, agricultural failure, resource exhaustion, domestic dissent, fragile legitimacy, intra-elite discord, succession crises, Kremlin fears and complexes, and so on.

This inventory could be easily expanded, but such expansion would serve no purpose. The actions of the communist bloc, particularly those of the Soviet Union, belie the theories. Events have demonstrated that the communist world does not consider military supremacy irrational and that it has not been seriously constrained by domestic economic or political exigencies.

A reappraisal of the achievements, motivations, and potential of world communism is therefore clearly in order. World communism, despite all its deficiencies and contradictions, has arrived at a new crossroads. For the first time in history, its internal and external development will occur not in an environment in which it is menaced by the hostile forces of the West, but in one in which it is militarily ascendant.

Will the military preeminence of the communist bloc safeguard world peace, facilitate economic reform, and foster a major advance in the quality of human life under communism, as the optimists believe? Or will it encourage Soviet expansionism, increase the risk of war, and heighten domestic repression, as the pessimists predict? Or will the status quo simply remain intact because, as the adherents of mutually assured destruction contend, supremacy has no meaning when inferior powers can annihilate their adversaries?

These are the large issues raised by the recent change in the "correlation of forces."[7] They are certain to be hotly debated for a long time to come. Not only do they bear on narrow American domestic concerns; they also mark the beginning of an entirely new epoch in the theory and practice of world communism.

Although the collection of essays contained in this volume makes no pretense of systematically exploring all the critical themes posed by communist military ascendancy, it does join many of the central issues. Attention is focused in particular on understanding present communist reality in its various contradictory aspects. Military ascendancy, it will be readily understood, hardly implies the superiority of actual communist arrangements in other spheres, including economics, politics, and human welfare. Communist military power has grown despite formidable deficiencies in its political-economic systems, quite simply because the leadership of the Soviet Union has chosen to accept an economic burden of defense at levels that prevailed just before the outbreak of World War II — that is, 14 to 18 percent of GNP.[8] Coming to terms with the reality of contemporary communist societies therefore depends not so much on seeking the hidden mechanisms of their military ascendancy as on chronicling their recent achievements, assessing their intentions, analyzing the reasons why their political-economic systems function tolerably well despite the heavy burdens of defense, and probing the real conditions of communist existence against the foil of their unfulfilled ideological aspirations.

The collection of essays comprising the present work is devoted primarily to the study of these fundamental concerns. These concerns must be satisfactorily resolved before the larger questions regarding the prospects for world communism in the era of its military supremacy can be adequately addressed. The book is organized in three parts. Part I documents the astonishing growth of Soviet military power in the past two decades. It provides a detailed account of the quantitative and qualitative transformation of Soviet weapons systems (Parker), including an exhaustive analysis of Soviet accomplishments in the area of strategic nuclear targeting (Lee). Other topics assessed include an examination of the deficiencies of the CIA's estimates of Soviet defense expenditures, which significantly impeded an early recognition of the scope and momentum of the Soviet arms buildup (Rosefielde); a description of the assertive use of Soviet naval power in the Angolan crisis (Valenta); an assessment of Soviet intentions (Parker); and a proposal for restoring the strategic balance (Leutze).

Part II broaches the technical question of how contemporary communist societies work and respond to the challenges posed by their changing environments. Attention is directed here toward world communism not as an integrated system, but as a collection of highly differentiated political-economic regimes that share a common ideological objective: the attainment of a communist social order. This approach enables us to probe the sources of strength manifest in communist working arrangements, which have eluded those who see economic dysfunction as the Achilles' heel of communism. Although it is taken for granted that world communism is not monolithic and that each communist society will be affected in its own peculiar way by the "changing correlation of forces," it seems nonetheless imperative to emphasize that the viability of communism does not necessarily depend on the merit of any particular model. Borrowing from the experiences of others is hardly precluded in international relations, and during the postwar period a variety of communist models, including those of the Soviet Union, Maoist China, Yugoslavia, and Romania, have been successful in varying degrees. Part II focuses on successful examples of communist political economy drawn from four distinctly different communist regimes.

The specific topics explored in Part II include the rationale underlying Soviet urbanization policy (Ofer), the Yugoslav strategy for coping with international inflation (Neuberger and Tyson), Maoist agrotechnological innovation (Wiens), and political control structures in Romania (Fischer). Although this coverage is obviously circumscribed, it does provide a significant amount of evidence suggesting that the proverbial rigidity of the communist political-economic systems has been overdrawn. World communist development may be impaired by the deficiencies of its diverse working arrangements, but this should not be interpreted as evidence that its principal objectives cannot be attained.

Part III evaluates world communism from the standpoint of human welfare. It does not grapple directly with how communist military ascendancy will affect the future conditions of life in the East, but it does explore the deep contradictions existing between communist theory and practice at the present juncture. The first two essays appraise the merit of the two principal contending strategies for the construction of optimally functioning political economies. A detailed examination of the achievements of Soviet mathematical planning theory is provided in one (Ames), and a program for establishing workers' self-management in America is put forward in the other (Vanek). These theoretical pieces are followed by an evaluation of the disparities between the ideals and the actualities of Soviet and Maoist managerial practice (Rosefielde and Latané) and by an assessment of the intricacies of trying to advance the cause of human rights in the Soviet Union through international political intervention (Simes and Masterson).

The book concludes with some observations by the editor on the interrelationship between human welfare under communism and communist military ascendancy. It goes without saying that although the scholarly studies contained in Parts II and III help to illuminate important modalities of the present state of world communism, they in no way purport to resolve the larger issue of how world communism will evolve now that the military balance has turned in favor of the progressive camp. That has not been our intention. The contributors to this volume do not share a common point of view. Although substantial unanimity exists among those of us who have written on the growth of Soviet military power, it is especially important to emphasize that this does not mean the other contributors concur with this judgment. Under such conditions, any thought of putting together a unified treatise on the implications of military ascendancy for the evolution of world communism would have been frivolous.

The objectives of the present work have therefore been correspondingly delimited. We have sought to document the assertion that communist military ascendancy has created a new international climate in which world communism may unfold in novel ways. We have also sought to appraise some of the reasons why communist political economy has been more potent than commonly supposed and to examine some of the deep contradictions that continue to undermine its viability. The choice of topics selected in this regard largely reflects the special concerns of the authors and should not be interpreted as a judgment on the explanatory power that various other factors may have for the evaluation of the future development of world communism. A scientific assessment of the causal determinants of communist behavior is a formidable task that is best deferred until it is possible to observe how world communism adapts itself to its newly achieved military preeminence. In the interim, we believe the essays in this volume will establish the need for a comprehensive reappraisal of the world communist phenomenon and contribute in a modest way toward that accomplishment.

NOTES

1. Dating the precise moment when the military balance turned in favor of the communist bloc is, of course, controversial. The choice of the late 1970s is a subjective judgment on the editor's part and cannot be unambiguously confirmed on an objective, scientific basis. The reader may wish to note, however, that all the authors who have contributed essays to the first part of this volume concur that the strategic balance has shifted in favor of the communist bloc. Details concerning this transformation are provided in the text and are supported by the latest report issued by the Joint Chiefs of Staff.
2. See William Lee, "Soviet Nuclear Targeting Strategy and SALT" in this volume.
3. See Steven Rosefielde, "Real Soviet Arms Procurement Expenditures, 1960–1978" in this volume.
4. See Patrick Parker, "Soviet Military Objectives and Capabilities in the 1980s" in this volume.
5. The communist bloc encompasses the Soviet Union, the member states of COMECON, China, and such nations as Albania and Yugoslavia. Its dominant military component is the Warsaw Pact. Dissension within the communist bloc between China and the Soviet Union has been a weakening force, but it has not negated the newly achieved military ascendancy of the Warsaw Pact and the communist bloc as a whole.
6. The term *world communism* is employed here to designate the heterogeneous collection of modern nation-states that take the creation of a communist society to be their ultimate ideological objective and form what is often referred to as the world communist movement. This usage has obvious disadvantages. None of the states that profess a communist ideology has actually constructed a viable communist society in the Marxist sense, although the Soviets claim to have attained the first stage. Indeed, it is questionable whether these nations can even be considered socialist if judged by the ideals most socialists affirm. Moreover, the communist bloc is a fragile ideological association that is riven by internal dissension and that hardly constitutes a unified military force.

    Despite these deficiencies, we have chosen to use the concept of world communism to represent an incompletely actualized phenomenon that stands in observable opposition to an almost equally amorphous capitalist bloc, as well as to characterize the full dimensions of geopolitical shift in the world power balance that has recently taken place. The reader should be especially careful to note that in using the term *world communism,* the editor does not intend to imply that communism is a monolithic international movement, comprehensively bent on destroying the market institutions of the West, or that the military buildup in the Soviet Union has been matched in other communist nations.

7.   The *correlation of forces* is a Soviet term denoting the comparative military, political, and social power of the socialist and capitalist camps.

8.   See Steven Rosefielde, "Will the Rapid Growth of Soviet Armaments Be Curtailed by the Economic Burden of Defense?" testimony prepared for the U.S. Senate Arms Services Committee, November 8, 1979. The statement that Soviet defense expenditures today are at levels that prevailed just before the outbreak of World War II does not, of course, necessarily imply that World War III is just around the corner.

I MILITARY ASCENDANCY

1 SOVIET MILITARY OBJECTIVES AND CAPABILITIES IN THE 1980s

Patrick Parker

Few areas of U.S. public policy are characterized by greater controversy than national security, and this is especially true today. Views range all the way from the obsolescence of military force in the nuclear era to matching and surpassing all the military capabilities of our potential enemies and then having a substantial margin for error. Accomplished patriotic citizens can be found all across the spectrum, both inside and outside the government, and yet there is remarkable consensus about the underlying objections of national security: we seek to avoid war, especially nuclear war, and we seek to maintain the basic quality of life in the West, especially our extraordinary individual freedom and our unprecedented standard of living. Thus, to a considerable extent, the merit of one position or another depends on different assessments of the facts and different predictions about the consequences of alternative courses of action.

One of the main areas of disagreement is the nature of the Soviet Union — in particular, its global aspirations and its military capabilities,

I am greatly indebted to Lieutenant Richard Wright for helpful comments and thoughtful suggestions, especially on the Soviet view of the changing correlation of forces and the military balance. Steven Rosefielde, Thomas Rona, and William Van Cleave also read the paper and provided me with useful suggestions.

9

and the relationship between them. It is the theme of this paper that the Soviet Union continues to be expansionist, that its military buildup is directed at achieving a wide range of military power so obviously capable of winning in numerous local situations that it will be unopposed and so much more devastating in all-out nuclear war with the West that it will gamble on not being effectively opposed in that arena either. Russia will achieve this new military preponderance soon, in part as a result of that nation's own efforts and in part because the attention of the United States has been elsewhere. With our attention focused first on Vietnam and later on domestic issues, we have not made the continuing investment in our military forces and defense necessary to meet the rapidly growing Russian threat.

Russia became a military power of some consequence in World War II. Twice since then we have let our guard down: immediately after the war and today. In each period, Americans were sick of war and had high hopes for an era of peace, restraint, and world order. In the earlier period, those hopes were soon shattered. While the West was bringing its armies home and demobilizing, Russia moved. In the months immediately following the armistice, the Soviet Union established a number of repressive regimes and in most cases large military occupation forces as well. East Prussia and Poland were the first to fall, followed in 1946 by Albania, Bulgaria, and Romania, in 1947 by Hungary, and in 1948 by Czechoslovakia. By the summer of 1947, the growing Western awareness of the need to stop the spread of Russian dominion was signaled by the publication of George Kennan's famous "Mr. X" article in the July issue of *Foreign Affairs,* which articulated the policy of containment, George Marshall's speech of June 5 at Harvard proposing a plan for rebuilding a strong Western Europe, the Marshall Plan, and the announcement of the Truman Doctrine. Within the year, the West faced yet another attempt by the Russians to consolidate their hegemony in Eastern Europe — the Berlin Blockade. Less successful attempts were evidenced all along the Russian periphery in Finland, Yugoslavia, Greece, Turkey, and Iran, and a close relationship was established with the new communist regime in China. The need for a credible, united, coordinated, defensive force in Europe was recognized quickly in the West and acted upon decisively with the formation of NATO in 1949 — a remarkable four-year performance in the light of the glacial pace of U.S. reaction today.

But while the West achieved stability and containment in Europe and the Middle East, the signal was less than clear elsewhere. Complete recognition of the worldwide need to contain Russia's appetite was only fully achieved after the Korean War. The Korean conflict brought almost universal acceptance in the West of the proposition that without strong countervailing military power capable of worldwide application, the Soviet Union would continually expand its rule and influence throughout the world. There was also wide agreement that if the Soviets went unchecked, no coalition capable of confronting the Kremlin with greater strength could be assembled.[1] Had the current pace of U.S. reaction characterized our behavior during this brief period, the world would almost certainly be a very different place today.

Despite Russia's much larger ground forces, the U.S. nuclear monopoly was for a while thought to deter the Russians from any major direct confrontation with the United States. Even for a substantial period after the Soviets exploded their first nuclear weapon on August 29, 1949, the preponderant U.S. nuclear forces continued to play an important role in the deterrence of any direct Soviet military move that would bring them face to face with the United States in an all-out war that could include the use of nuclear weapons. The high-water mark of this U.S. nuclear preponderance was probably reached in the mid-1960s, and its importance evidenced in the working out of the Cuban missile crisis in 1962. However, as it became increasingly clear in the United States that our ability to damage the Soviets would soon be matched by their ability to damage us, the role of nuclear weapons in U.S. strategy changed. No longer did we regard our nuclear forces as playing a central role in containing any major military move, conventional or nuclear, on the part of the Russians. Instead, as belief in the inevitability of Russia's eventual nuclear equality became widespread, the top U.S. military planners came to view the principal role of nuclear weapons as one of making nuclear war so terrible that both sides would be deterred from their use. The realization of emerging nuclear parity came late to some. In an interview reported in the *U.S. News and World Report* of April 12, 1965, Robert McNamara stated:

> The Soviets have decided that they have lost the quantitative race, and they are not seeking to engage us in that contest. It means there is no indication that the Soviets are seeking to develop a strategic nuclear force as large as ours.

Nonetheless, starting in the mid-1960s, general nuclear-war fighting capabilities were progressively de-emphasized, and the doctrine of assured destruction began playing an increasingly important role. This heralded several important changes. First, the main military counter to continued Russian expansionism would be non-nuclear. Accordingly, expanded conventional forces and decreased reliance on nuclear weapons characterized U.S. military planning in the early and mid-1960s. Second, for the nuclear forces to play this new role, it was thought that the deterrent effect would be greatest if population and industry on both sides were hostage to the other and therefore that attempts to protect them, such as civil defense and area ballistic missile defenses, would be destabilizing and should be avoided. Similarly, since nuclear forces vulnerable to a first strike are obviously inviting targets in time of crisis, measures such as improved accuracy that make these forces capable of destroying those of the other side were considered undesirable.

However, to work, assured destruction depends on similar views being held by both sides. The danger is obvious if one side has largely embraced the doctrine of assured destruction and structures its forces accordingly, while the other has a more classic view of military force, including a doctrine of war fighting and a theory of victory, nuclear forces capable of a substantially disarming first strike, and facilities to defend and protect a large fraction of its population and industry. Advocates of the doctrine of mutual assured destruction assumed, and still do in many cases, that the Russians, being sensible, cannot fail to see the underlying logical imperative of mutual assured destruction, and if by chance they do not, they can be made to do so by careful tutoring in the ongoing dialogues between the two countries, especially regarding arms-limitation negotiations. However, no evidence that I am aware of supports the proposition that the Russians think of nuclear weapons in the same way that we do or that they have been influenced at all by our SALT tutorial. On the contrary, there is much to suggest that they view the whole spectrum of military force in a much more traditional way.[2]

This tendency to think we are looking at the Russians through a window, while actually looking at ourselves in a mirror, is common and dangerous. Moreover, certain rich bodies of material can provide a useful and necessary backdrop for understanding the role of the military in Soviet foreign policy and the way in which the Soviets may use military forces to help achieve foreign policy objectives. Soviet writings and information on major military procurement actions, budgetary emphases and trends, and military exercises and deployments are all accessible to varying degrees and frequently suggest foreign policy objectives and military doctrine and strategy in stark contrast to those of the West.

Soviet military writings represent a useful departure. Americans are accustomed to a free press and wide-ranging, divergent views vigorously and continually debated in public; we are also accustomed to frequent changes in government and associated changes in policy; we understand well that last year's posture statement may be a poor guide to next year's policy, especially if there is a presidential election in between. This experience naturally conditions our reaction to Russian writings and all too often leads us to give them a much more limited role than they deserve. In fact, since Russian public writings reflect national policy to a much greater degree than do ours, conformity and coherence characterize them on any particular issue, and the issues taken together tend to conform to a larger design and reinforce some particular part of the pattern. Changes and officially sanctioned debates do, of course, take place and receive articulation as new policies evolve or when the leadership changes, but this happens less frequently in Russia than in the United States. Thus, a coherent pattern can be discerned from serious study of Soviet writings on national security, especially those written for internal use.

Yet it is fashionable to debunk inferences drawn from Soviet speeches and writings, and we all too frequently seek out and hear what we want to hear. Sir Hugh Seton Watson has somewhat facetiously observed this trend:

> What 200,000 Communist Party officials, from Brezhnev down to the secretaries of the party branches in factories or collective farms, tell their subjects is all camouflage. The real views of the Soviet leaders are what some nice guy from the Soviet delegation at the UN said over a drink or what an itinerant Midwestern scientist heard from some friendly academician in Novosibirsk.[3]

Recent experience with détente is revealing in this regard. To Westerners, a period of détente is one of relaxation of cold war tension and of international dialogue and cooperation. Economic and social ties are strengthened and disputes are solved peacefully through negotiation and compromise.

Not so for the Russians. For them, détente represents the acceptance by the West of the principle of peaceful coexistence. Since the 1917 Revolution, the Soviets have most often referred to peaceful coexistence as the norm for Russian relationships with the West, particularly the United States. Lenin frequently referred to the ability of the capitalist and socialists systems to exist in close proximity to one another. But for the Soviets, closeness in no way precludes attempts to subvert and overcome the capitalist system. Soviet writer S. M. Maiorov addressed the question "What is peaceful coexistence?" in a July 1967 article in *Voprosy Istorii KPSS:*

> It presupposes an intense struggle between socialist and capitalist states in all realms of social life: politics, economics, and ideology. The specific nature of this kind of class warfare consists in its being waged by mutually hostile classes through the intermediary of their respective states, which represent opposite social systems. This class warfare is being waged without recourse to arms and while avoiding the risk of military conflicts.[4]

Thus, in advocating a policy of "peaceful coexistence," Nikita Khrushchev could at the same time promise to "bury" the United States. And Secretary

Brezhnev can argue strongly for détente while advocating greater military efforts at offensive readiness. Indeed, the Soviets believe that their greatly increased military capabilities since the 1962 missile crisis have been one of the primary factors making détente possible. Academician and director of the Institute of the USA of the Soviet Academy of Sciences, Dr. Georgiy Arbatov, asserted this in a 1973 article for *Kommunist:*

> Recent international events convincingly demonstrate the principal difference between socialism and imperialism is the political utilization of enhanced power. There is no doubt that any change in the balance of power in favor of imperialism would cause not detente, but rather a rise in tensions and would encourage aggressive intentions.[5]

In short, to the Russians, détente derives from the changed positions of the two superpowers in relation to each other and represents the forced acceptance by the West of the Soviet principle of peaceful coexistence. In turn, the Russians view peaceful coexistence as a method of carrying on the struggle between socialism and capitalism using all means short of war, a stark contrast to the Western view of détente.

Before turning to the role of the military in Soviet society and an examination of the implications of the qualitative and quantitative buildup in weapons systems and manpower since the mid-1960s, two terms to be utilized require further explanation: the Soviet expression *correlation of forces* and the Soviet concept of *strategic.*

Correlation of forces is a Russian expression seldom used in the West; it is fundamental to understanding the rationale behind the Soviet military buildup in an era of détente. The concept of a correlation of forces is a summation of all aspects of the Soviet Union's world power: its military might, its economic strength, the viability of its Eastern European bloc, its relationships with client states throughout the Third World, and its influence in the political councils of the world. The Kremlin believes that the correlation of forces is the major factor in international relations and that a correct assessment of it yields correct predictions of worldwide economic, political, and military trends and relationships. It is a concept that should not be confused with the traditional European "balance of power." The Soviets conceive of the correlation of forces as dynamic and ever-changing. A balance of power implies stability and maintenance of the status quo, something to which the Soviet state will not willingly acquiesce.

The predictive ability inherent in a proper understanding of the correlation of forces has led the Soviets to deduce that a final Armageddon between the socialist and capitalist systems is inevitable only if the Soviets fail to become overwhelmingly powerful. In *Soviet Military Strategy,* a standard text for all Soviet military officers, Marshal of the Soviet Union V. D. Sokolovskiy wrote:

> The XX Congress of the CPSU, on the basis of a Marxist-Leninist analysis of the radical change in the correlation of forces between the two world systems, and of the international situation as a whole, concluded that when the world socialist camp has been converted into a powerful political, economic and military force and the forces of peace over the entire world have been strengthened, war will not be a fatal inevitability.[6]

Thus, contrary to the Western view that an arms buildup is inherently unstable and heightens international tensions, the Kremlin's belief is that any strengthening of the world socialist camp can only serve as an agent of peace; such a strengthening will dissuade the capitalists from using military means to oppose the continuing change in the correlation of forces and the inevitable concomitant expansion of Soviet influence.

Finally, to understand the Soviet view of a military commitment, such as the Warsaw Pact in Eastern Europe, it is necessary to differentiate between the Western and Soviet views of *strategic* as that term applies to weapon systems. Any consideration of Soviet military thought must consider the legacy of World War II: the surprise German attack from Eastern Europe staging areas, the near defeat of the Soviet armies in European Russia, and the war's 20 million Russian dead, more than ten times the total number of Americans to die in combat since 1775. The United States, with thousands of miles of water separating it from the nearest unfriendly land forces, can afford to associate "strategic" weapons with those that can strike only from great distances. But planners in Moscow do not have that luxury: their perspective and their position in the Eurasian land mass have led them to develop a much different concept of "strategic" from that generally accepted in the West. "To the Soviets, 'strategic' begins at the Soviet border. From Moscow to Bonn, London, Paris, Rome and so forth, is a strategic distance to them . . . North America is not the measure of strategic distance, but only one of the more remote strategic areas."[7]

However, there is more than just Russia's belief in the inexorable worldwide expansion of socialism contributing to the underlying tension between the two powers. Russian political institutions are obviously quite different from our own. Their leaders maintain their position by suppressing opposing views. They are profoundly threatened by dissident internal criticism and equally so by the example provided by the West if it should become widely perceived within Russia. Propaganda, misinformation, secrecy, repression, coercion, and imprisonment all play roles both qualitatively and quantitatively different in Russian political life than they do in the United

States. These methods, together with the isolation of the Russian people from the example set by free institutions, are crucial to maintaining the grudging support necessary for the regime to maintain itself and operate effectively — thus, the iron curtain, the need for buffer states, and the intolerance for liberalization and reform both internally and in the satellites. Convergence, while viewed as an optimistic possibility in the West, can be regarded only with alarm by the Russian leaders. The existence of the Western democracies is a continual threat to the existence of the Russian leadership, not principally in a military sense, but because of the example provided by the contrasting quality of life in the West.

Reinforcing this threat is one of the fundamental predictions of Marxist-Leninist dogma: that capitalism will ultimately be brought down by a major economic cataclysm and that in its last dying gasps it may lash out at the socialist countries. Accordingly, the Russians believe that World War III must be planned for and survived.

In addition to these political considerations, Russia is increasingly driven to look outward to ameliorate its growing economic problems. Although there have been intermittent periods characterized by impressive growth rates, since 1959 the Soviets have been experiencing an increasingly serious decline in their economic growth, which many specialists believe will continue into the future, stabilizing at something less than 3 percent per year. A variety of reasons have been suggested for this decline. In the immediate postwar period, Russia, just like Germany and Japan, appeared to benefit from something of an economic miracle, but the circumstances that made that possible cannot be duplicated. The disruption and destruction resulting from the war engendered an overall reduction in economic activity. Because key pieces were missing, the productivity of much of the capital stock was reduced virtually to zero. Replacing these key pieces was much easier than building from scratch, and thus a relatively small investment had very large effects. At the same time, large quantities of industrial equipment were expropriated from the new Eastern European satellites, and extensive use was made of forced labor. After the war the Soviets arrested millions of their own returning soldiers who had been captured fighting in the West and interned them in forced labor camps. From 1945 to 1950, between 12 and 14 million Soviet citizens were in concentration camps, in addition to 7 million unrepatriated prisoners of war. By 1949 the situation was more normal, and Soviet economic growth required increases in capital, labor, or technological innovation on the usual scale.

Although technological innovation plays a role in economic growth for Russia, many observers have suggested that that role appears to be far smaller than in the West. Russian economic growth has generally depended heavily on a high rate of investment and increases in the industrial labor supply. However, population growth is declining, the composition of the Soviet population is changing, and there is little room to expand the labor force by increasing participation; at the moment, something over 92 percent of people of working age are employed. In sum, in the decade ahead, the labor force will grow more slowly, and the new entries will be drawn increasingly from the Soviet minorities rather than from the Great Russians. From the economic point of view, the increased proportion of minorities, many of whom do not even speak Russian very well, will require even greater capital investment, in this case in education, to bring the minorities to the same level of productivity as the Great Russians. Much education (i.e., investment in human capital) takes place in the home, but to a lesser extent for the minorities on balance than for the Great Russians. Therefore, bringing them to the same level of productivity will impose a burden on the state's scarce resources. A further problem is the very high percentage of the Soviet labor force that continues to be devoted to state agriculture. Roughly 23 percent of that labor force is so employed, producing about 72 percent of Soviet agricultural products; the bulk of the remaining 28 percent is produced on family plots. By comparison, about 5 percent of the U.S. work force is employed in agriculture, and we are net exporters. The comparative inefficiency of Soviet agricultural labor makes it difficult to shift this work force to more productive industrial occupations and so acts as a constraint on the achievable rate of aggregate Soviet economic development. The adverse trends will probably continue throughout the 1980s.

If indeed these considerations are important in explaining declining economic growth, they tell us that for the Soviets to maintain previous growth rates, they must make up the difference by increasing education; improving productivity; harnessing, developing, and absorbing imported technology better than they have in the past; increasing the capital budget to increase the capital-labor ratio; improving agricultural efficiency; importing more agricultural products; or using some combination of all these methods. However, for the Russians, much of this is difficult, if not impossible. Not only will they face qualitative and quantitative problems in maintaining their work force, but also the Soviet capital budget will come under great pressures over the next few years as it competes vigorously with the consumer sector and especially the defense sector for funds.

Some very interesting considerations relate to technology as a contributor to Soviet economic growth. On the one hand, the Soviets have not been particularly good at developing technology; on the other, one of the largest uncertainties we face is whether the Soviets will have a markedly better record in absorbing new technologies in the 1980s. The question of Soviet response to technological transfer is as yet poorly understood and is an area that needs a good deal of work. It may be that their problem is not only invention but absorption also. If that is the case, technological transfer will have less effect than we have thought in the past.

In summary, if the Soviets continue to do business as usual, their economic growth rates will decline in the next decade. The most promising conventional sources of amelioration for the decline are learning how to utilize technological innovation better than they have in the past and becoming more dependent on certain imports, especially agricultural imports, which would release labor to be used better elsewhere. A less conventional alternative is to become an increasingly imperialist power.

On that note, let me turn to the defense burden. We are all aware of the changing estimates of the size of the defense burden in the Soviet Union. There is a growing consensus that the percentage of Soviet GNP devoted to national security in the Soviet Union is between 13 and 20 percent, probably around 15 percent. Why is this number interesting at all? Mainly because it gives us some idea of how much the defense shoe pinches. However, it is at least as important to think about how the number is growing as it is to think about how big it is at any instant in time. It is equally important to consider the growth needs juxtaposed with the aforementioned trends in the economy as a whole. At the moment, the CIA's offical estimate is that the Soviet military budget is growing at about the same rate as the economy as a whole, but there can be little question that a high degree of uncertainty must surround present estimates. My own judgment is that the higher rates suggested by the studies of Lee[8] and Rosefielde[9] (8–10 percent) are probably closer to the mark.

If Lee and Rosefielde are correct, and they appear to be, their findings have profound implications for interpreting the Soviet military buildup and formulating U.S. policy for dealing with it. The Soviet defense burden is determined by the rate at which defense expenditures grow in relation to the growth of national income. With defense expenditures growing 8 to 10 percent and national income rising 3½ to 4 percent, the defense burden will increase very rapidly, and an obvious self-limiting process will be at work. With these growth rates superimposed on a defense budget of about 15 percent of GNP today, unless something changes, the Soviets will be spending between a quarter and a third of their GNP on defense in the mid-1980s. Obviously, such a situation cannot go on indefinitely; sooner or later these growth rates must converge.

Regardless of whether the defense burden is growing, it is clearly large. If there is a divergence between economic growth rate and defense expenditures, particularly one of this magnitude, it only reinforces some important nuances in interpreting Soviet behavior. First, if the military is getting a larger and larger share of the pie, they have probably persuaded their colleagues in the Politburo, the Secretariat, and the Central Committee that these expenditures have very great value. Second, there is likely to be more of a consensus at the top that military power is important and can be used to advantage. Third, bureaucratic inertia becomes a less credible explanation of Soviet actions because the costs of such inertia increase with the scale of the Soviet defense effort.

I have indicated previously that the expansion of Soviet socialism is driven by doctrine and politics. Economics may be important, too, for if Russian military power can be used to further expand Russian political influence, it can also be used to economic advantage, contributing to the solution of Russia's growing economic difficulties. While it is frequently argued that these economic difficulties will put increasing pressure on military spending, it is rarely argued that military forces can be used to overcome the difficulties and thereby ameliorate the pressure. Yet the divergent growth rates can be brought together not only by cutting back on military expenditures, but also by using military forces as instruments to improve the domestic economic situation.

How might this be done, and how well do the forces fit the task? What are they buying and why? To assess these issues, consider the recent trend in the comparative military power of the Soviet Union.

Quite clearly, the capabilities of Soviet military forces have been improving relative to those of the West. Sometime soon, if not already, the large Soviet military buildup will have substantially altered the military balance that has existed since World War II. Because new weapons and forces take a long time to develop and assemble, there is little that we can do until the second half of the 1980s to change this situation without a fundamental change in the way we normally do business in defense.

We can arrive at a rough measure of the current size of the U.S. and Soviet military forces by comparing the cost of U.S. forces with the cost of reproducing and operating the Soviet forces at U.S. prices and wages. Using this very crude measure and excluding military pensions, since they contribute nothing to overall capability, the dollar cost of Soviet defense activities as estimated by the CIA was about 40 percent larger than U.S. defense costs in 1976. Their overall active military manpower was about 4.8 million men, compared to about 2.1 in the United States.[10]

Past experience with the Soviets, together with the political and economic considerations that we have discussed, suggest that the Soviets may well
view the next few years as a time of significant opportunity. Soviet intercontinental nuclear forces and associated programs may have stalemated those
of the United States to a point where we can no longer pose a credible threat
to the Soviets and hence will neither deter Soviet military action at lesser
levels nor convince wavering allies to stand with us. Soviet theater forces
may have definite military superiority over the NATO central front; at the
same time, other Soviet forces will be able to achieve rapid superiority in a
growing number of areas worldwide.

Let me turn first to the strategic nuclear balance.

We have never fought a nuclear war. Yet, the typical analysis in the West
suggests that we understand nuclear war, especially intercontinental nuclear
war, and that we understand it well, certainly much better than conventional war. This is probably nonsense. We have a plethora of simple models.
They typically start with an attack by one side on the nuclear forces of the
other, which is followed by a return salvo at the other side's remaining
forces, and end with a comparative analysis of the ability of the surviving
forces to wreak "unacceptable damage" on each other. One step removed
from these models is an array of static measures, usually including warheads, total megatonnage, equivalent weapons, countermilitary potential,
and so forth.

Although familiarity with these measures and models must be considered
a necessary part of the kit bag of everyone who thinks seriously about
nuclear war, and although they can bring into focus some insights, such as
the important distinction between first- and second-strike capabilities, there
is profound uncertainty about how a nuclear war might start, how it would
unfold, and how best to avoid one. Until recently, the nuclear era has been
characterized by massive U.S. superiority over the Soviet Union, regardless
of how that superiority has been measured. The Defense Nuclear Agency
report "Measures and Trends — US and USSR — Strategic Force Effectiveness" shows forty-one different orderings, such as ICBM launcher numbers, ICBM throw weight, SLBM numbers, warheads, megatonnage, equivalent megatonnage, equivalent weapons, and countermilitary potential. At
the time of the Cuban missile crisis in 1962, virtually all these measures
favored the United States, and in most cases by a wide margin. Moreover,
at that time the Russians had virtually no capability to attack U.S. strategic
forces and could probably not have delivered more than twenty-five to fifty
nuclear weapons against the continental United States. Although even this
number would have inflicted substantial damage and loss of life, there was

no question about the ability of the United States to survive as a society and recover rapidly. By contrast, at that time the United States could not only inflict far greater damage on the Soviet Union (probably by several orders of magnitude) but could also achieve rapid military superiority with conventional forces throughout most of the world, especially Cuba. In 1962 the Russians had an object lesson in the meaning of strategic superiority and what one can do with it, a lesson apparently forgotten by the U.S. secretary of state a little over a decade later.[11]

Today the situation is very different. Of the forty-one static measures mentioned above, the Soviets are now ahead in all but eight, and in the next three to five years the U.S. advantage can easily disappear across all these measures, and probably will. In addition, the Russians have reportedly demonstrated the necessary ICBM accuracy to destroy virtually the entire U.S. land-based missile forces; this capability will probably be fully operational in the early 1980s. They can, of course, in a surprise attack also destroy about half the U.S. ballistic missile submarine force, which is normally in overhaul, repair, or routine maintenance, as well as a substantial fraction of the bomber force either on or near the bases.[12]

Although there is a high degree of uncertainty about trends in ASW, some analysts hold that the Russians may soon be able to mount a successful coordinated surprise attack on a substantial fraction of the older at-sea SSBNs. This issue is hotly debated. In any case, in the long run the Trident submarine, with its much larger operating area, will make the attackers' problem much more difficult. However, it must be obvious to the Russians that they can create serious problems for us that would inhibit the transmission of orders to the submarines if key vulnerable communication nodes are damaged or destroyed, and whatever their ability is to kill SSBNs at sea, the uncertainty about it must be much lower in their minds than in ours.

Although we do not know in detail what choices the Soviets are making about their intercontinental attack forces and thus do not know exactly what their force structure will be in five years, they have at the moment about 1,400 ICBMs, 950 modern SLBMs, and 200 bombers — an aggregate of 2,550 launchers. They currently have a vigorous modernization program underway and appear to have agreed in principle to the broad outlines of a SALT agreement that would provide for reductions to 2,250 launchers and a MIRV sublimit of 1,320 comprised of 820 ICBMs, 380 SLBMs, and 120 bombers with long-range ALCMs. Under such an agreement, Soviet forces in the mid-1980s would look at least as good as those shown in Table 1. The U.S. forces at the same time, allowing for the expected introduction of the Trident submarine, are shown in Table 2.

Table 1.   Mid-1980s Soviet Strategic Forces

	Number	Warheads per Launcher	Total Warheads	Yield MT	CEP[a]
ICBMs					
SS-18	320	8	2,460	1	.1
SS-19	400	6	2,400	1	.1
SS-17	100	4	400	1	.1
New	400	1	400	2	.1
	1,220		5,660		
SLBMs					
SS-N-8	530	1	530	1	.2
New MIRV	380	10	3,800	1	.2
	910		4,330		
Bombers					
Bear/Bison	120	4	480	1–5	.1
Total SAL	2,250		10,470		
Backfire	200	4	800	1–5	.1
Total	2,450		11,270		

Source: Data based on recent newspaper reports on the likely dimensions of a SALT agreement.

[a]Data from Clarence A. Robinson, Jr., "Soviets Boost ICBM Accuracy," *Aviation Week & Space Technology* (April 3, 1978):14–17.

If the SS-18 has a .9 reliability and if the Soviets can rapidly replace in-flight failures, 293 SS-18s could destroy 996 of the 1,000 Minutemen and essentially all the 54 Titan IIs, even using the highest published figures for Minutemen, 2300 psi. For a two-shot overpressure kill, the standard equations are:[13]

$$\text{SSPK} = 1 - .5^{\left(\frac{\frac{2.62}{2300^{1/3}}}{.1}\right)^2} \qquad \text{or} \qquad \text{for 2 shots, 2SPK} = 1 - .0652^2$$
$$= 1 - .0652 \qquad\qquad\qquad\qquad\qquad = .0042$$
$$= .9348 \qquad\qquad\qquad\qquad\qquad\quad = .9958.$$

The remaining 27 SS-18s, with 194 reliable warheads, would be adequate to target the 20 SSBNs in overhaul, repair, or maintenance, as well as key com-

Table 2.   Mid-1980s U.S. Strategic Forces

	Number	Warheads per Launcher	Total Warheads
ICBMs			
M^2-II	450	1	450
M^2-III	550	3	1,650
Titan II	54	1	54
	1,054		2,154
SLBMs			
5 Trident	120	10	1,200
5 Polaris A-3	80	3 MIRV	80
31 Poseidon	496	10	4,960
	696		6,240
Bombers			
B-52 ALCM	146	10	1,460
B-52 Bombs	154	4	616
FB-111	50	2	100
	350		2,176
Total	2,100		10,570

Source: Data based on current five-year defense plan.

mand and control centers. All the bomber bases could be covered by 160 SLBMs, which could destroy virtually all the nonalert bombers, presently about 70 percent of the force.

Thus, the residual forces on both sides after a Soviet strike could well be roughly as shown in Table 3. I have not calculated the situation for a U.S. first strike since we have only very limited ability to attack Russian nuclear forces successfully.

Although the residual forces shown in Table 3 are large, U.S. forces could be about one-third as large if approximately nine of the Polaris or Poseidon submarines at sea were destroyed and if bomber penetration were taken into account. Moreover, the Russian forces are much larger and effective than this simple numerical calculation suggests. Their weapons are on average about eight to ten times more powerful than ours, and they would be delivered against a country with very limited active defenses and

Table 3. Residual Forces after a Soviet Strike

U.S. Residual Forces:

	Launchers		Independently Targetable Warheads	
	No ASW or Air Defense	*50% Successful ASW and Air Defense*	*No ASW or Air Defense*	*50% Successful ASW and Air Defense*
ICBMs				
M^2	4	4	8	8
SLBMs				
Polaris (2 SSBNs)	32	16	32	16
Poseidon (16 SSBNs)	256	128	2,560	1,280
Trident (3 SSBNs)	72	72	720	720
Bombers				
B-52 ALCM	102	51	1,020	510
B-52	108	54	432	216
FB-111	35	18	70	36
TOTAL	609	343	4,842	2,786

Soviet Residual Forces:

	Number	*Warheads*
ICBMs		
19	400	2,400
17	100	400
New	400	400
TOTAL		3,200
SLBMs		
SSM-8	370	370
New MIRV	380	3,800
TOTAL		4,170
Bombers		
Bear/Bison	120	480
		7,850
Backfire	200	800
TOTAL	1,970	8,650

practically no civil defense. They could destroy at least two-thirds of the U.S. population and a high fraction of the capital stock. By contrast, U.S. bombers would have to penetrate over 12,000 surface-to-air missiles on launchers, as well as over 2,700 air defense aircraft. Whatever its capabilities, the Russians have a serious civil defense system. Their industry and population are more spread out than ours, and by 1985 they may have achieved a substantial ABM and ASW capability that could reduce the effectiveness of the SLBMs, the main residual U.S. capability. It is worth noting that although the United States dismantled its ABM system and for all practical purpose stopped ABM research and development following SALT I, the Soviets did not.

But perhaps the most important question is whether either the Russians or our allies believe that the president of the United States would fire under circumstances in which every measure he could take against his enemy, up to and including use of the entire force, would bring far greater retribution, if every Russian life cost ten American lives and every Russian factory five American factories. In the face of such second-strike capability, the American concept of deterrence through maintaining a second-strike assured destruction force could well result in deterring us far more than the Russians.

None of this suggests to me that the Russians will deliberately start a nuclear war, especially a large intercontinental one. The uncertainties are large and the probable damage, even under the most optimistic assumptions, great. Nonetheless, if by having sufficient intercontinental nuclear advantage under all circumstances, the Russians could essentially neutralize the U.S. nuclear threat, and if this neutralization were perceived by the rest of the world, it would have profound implications for the exercise of power everywhere. The U.S. nuclear umbrella no longer covers very well, and the safety of each country is far more dependent on the military balance in the region than on the strategic nuclear balance. Moreover, each country has greater incentive to go it alone, including even possible development of independent nuclear capabilities — an ironic twist given the present administration's great concern about nuclear proliferation. In the meantime, to the extent that intercontinental nuclear threats have bearing, they will, at least for the next decade, operate in favor of the Soviets since Soviet threats must be viewed as more believable than U.S. threats.

It is worth noting that the change in the strategic nuclear balance derives to a great extent from asymmetric vulnerabilities and that the most urgently needed programs are defensive, not offensive. If U.S. missile forces and bombers could once again be made highly survivable, the situation would be much improved. First, a major asymmetry in the relevant measure of force capability would have been repaired, and, second, the difference between the forces before and after a Soviet strike would again be small and stability in time of crisis much improved. Similarly, serious efforts to plan and implement steps to enhance U.S. ability to survive and recover from nuclear war would reduce the coercive power deriving from Soviet nuclear superiority without any buildup in offensive weaponry.

Taking all these factors into consideration, I believe it is useful to ask what key objectives Russia might pursue more vigorously in the future than they have in the recent past. A list is not particularly difficult to make. It would include further isolation of the Soviet people from those Western institutions that threaten the nation; improved access to foreign raw materials, technology, and markets (possibly including capture); enhanced ability to tax abroad one way or another (e.g., heavily subsidized credit terms where the obligations are renegotiated on more favorable terms or never paid); and expansion of Soviet ability to deploy and support its military forces worldwide. Although all particulars seem overdrawn before they occur, with these general guidelines, what comes to mind?

While West Germany and the NATO central front get most of the attention, this region is probably not the most likely trouble spot. A move in central Europe would bring the Soviets into direct conflict with the United States, with all the attendant risks of escalation to nuclear war in the theater and between the two powers. Nonetheless, the military balance of the central front strongly favors the East. Their forces are larger; they are better equipped and organized; they have paid much more attention to the details of war fighting; and their major reinforcements come relatively short distances over well-developed roads and railroads.

By contrast, NATO's reinforcements have to come across three thousand miles of ocean; the timely availability of shipping in adequate quantities is questionable; and the effectiveness of Russian submarines and mining is likely to be high against ships leaving ports on the U.S. East Coast, crossing the North Atlantic, and unloading in Western Europe. But, most important, NATO forces are not ready to fight the kind of war envisioned in Soviet doctrine and tactics. Maldeployment of forces; lack of a common logistics infrastructure; communications vulnerabilities and dependencies; limited electronic warfare equipment, training, and doctrine; absence of training and doctrine for fighting in a nuclear and chemical environment; and inadequate provisions for protecting, releasing, and issuing nuclear weapons — all are just part of a long list of the operational deficiencies of NATO that do not characterize the forces of the Warsaw Pact. Despite NATO's greater wealth, population, and comparable overall military and ground force manpower, no one could take a serious look at the NATO central front today and come away with any view other than that the Russian forces could occupy West Germany in a very few days.[14]

The same appraisal has been made for at least the past fifteen years. It has been accompanied by an assessment that NATO's main problem is not resources, but a general lack of seriousness about solving the bureaucratic and organizational problems that get in the way of mounting a credible, capable defense. This conclusion needs some qualification. Over the past fifteen years, the Department of Defense has conducted a number of studies that have concluded that NATO is very close to a credible conventional defense. These studies have a number of things in common. First, they count virtually all the national military forces of the central front, including the British forces in Northern Ireland and the French forces. Second, they assume massive, timely, and successful deployment of forces from the United States. Third, they assume conditions of warning and mobilization that allow the bulk of this reinforcement to take place unopposed. Finally, despite over 125 available Soviet and Warsaw Pact divisions, they assume that only about 85 divisions in Poland, East Germany, Czechoslovakia, Hungary, and the four Western military districts of the U.S.S.R. would be brought to bear and that actions would not have been taken to improve the readiness of these divisions and move them forward until thirty days before the beginning of the war. While these studies have served to draw attention to some important underlying aspects of the force structure and have highlighted important strengths and weaknesses on both sides, they contain one fundamental flaw, which is that the Soviets will use only 85 divisions when that is not enough to do the job. This implies either that the Soviets will miscalculate what they need or that they will start a war they do not intend to win. Make no mistake about it: they can marshall enough to do the job, and if they go to war, they will intend to win.

The Soviet military leaders are serious. A decision to attack NATO is likely to be made long before the outbreak of war and be surrounded with actions designed to cloud the Western perception of what is going on. The readiness of the forces will be raised, equipment modernized, gradual augmentation and forward movement of units will take place, and, above all, enough forces will be committed to ensure a high probability of victory. If enough are not available, the time will be taken to make them available. One could argue that such actions would result in Western mobilization. However, over the past few years we have observed substantial increases in the size and the quality, if not the number, of Soviet divisions facing the NATO central front without taking effective action, and we have observed very substantial qualitative improvement as well.

The developments are impressive, and they are not limited to the forces facing the NATO central front. Almost across the entire spectrum of land, sea, and tactical air forces, the military trends favor the Soviet Union. That is not surprising given the sustained margin in resources committed to research, development, and procurement that we have seen in the past few years. The West probably does retain both a qualitative and quantitative lead in some areas: we have more and better antitank weaponry, our tactical aircraft are more sophisticated, and the Soviets so far have not come close to matching the capabilities of our Airborne Warning and Control System. But they have larger numbers of tactical aircraft, and their quality has improved substantially over the past years. At sea, they have nothing comparable to the Navy's carrier strike forces; yet they have extensive land-based naval aircraft and have devoted large resources to developing anticarrier warfare. They have nothing qualitatively or quantitatively comparable to our amphibious assault forces, but their advanced research and development in this area, which is imaginative, may change all that in the next decade. The United States also enjoys a substantial qualitative advantage in submarines, despite the Soviets' substantially larger numbers, and there is little question that we maintain a lead of several years in electronics technology. However, this is a small list of advantages, and it is diminishing all the time. Table 4 shows the absolute size of key elements of the U.S. and Soviet force structures, as well as the percentage change since 1965.

Serious as these trends in the military balance are, in the long run it would be easy to reverse them if we wished to do so. NATO and its allies have almost three times the GNP of the Soviet Union and over one and a half times the population. Worldwide, the NATO and Warsaw Pact countries have approximately the same number of men under arms. But a loosely knit coalition of democratic states has difficulty in peacetime overcoming bureaucratic and organizational problems. Such a coalition has typically not been very good at responding to warning and has been inherently over-optimistic about its situation until very late in the day. It may be well that such a coalition simply has to have larger peacetime forces just to stay even.

In the past, U.S. nuclear superiority almost certainly played an important role in inhibiting a Soviet move against the NATO central front. But, again, the U.S. view of a nuclear Armageddon on the one hand (even if it is limited to Europe) and a conventional war on the other with nothing in between does not correlate with what we are learning about Soviet doctrine, tactics, and capabilities. The Soviets think about the use of nuclear weapons in war and have planned carefully for the nuclear transition. They can be expected to avoid cities except where overwhelming military advantage can be derived from such attacks, and they understand the difficulty of advancing through piles of radioactive rubble. Furthermore, they would like to capture something of value.[15]

However, the large uncertainty about how such a war would unfold; what fraction, if any, of the more than seven thousand NATO nuclear

Table 4.   Major Force Elements and Growth

	1976		10–12 Year Growth as of 1976	
	U.S.	*U.S.S.R.*	*U.S.*	*U.S.S.R.*
Manpower (millions of men)	2	4.4	− 32%	+ 20%
Ground force manpower (millions of men)	8	2.9	− 20%	+ 60%
Tanks (thousands)	10	45.0	0	+ 50%
APCs (thousands)	10	19.0	+ 20%	+ 100%
Helicopters (thousands)	9	3.5		
Artillery (thousands)	5	20.0	0	+ 100%
Major surface ships	170	230.0	− 44%	+ 15%
Nuclear attack submarines	75	90.0	− 20%	+ 80%
Tactical aircraft (thousands)	4	5.3	− 18%	+ 33%

Source: Data based on U.S. Congress, Congressional Budget Office, *Assessing the NATO/Warsaw Pact Military Balance* (Washington, D.C., December 1977), and on Central Intelligence Agency, *A Dollar Cost Comparison of Soviet and U.S. Defense Activities, 1966–1976* (SR77-1000166), (Washington, D.C., January 1977), p. 9.

Note: In estimating growth rates, an attempt has been made to exclude any distortion resulting from the Vietnam buildup.

weapons would come into play; whether the United States, despite the increasingly unfavorable strategic balance, would escalate the war — all are considerations that will probably inhibit the Soviets for some time to come, especially if there are more lucrative and readily accessible targets elsewhere. The current Soviet leadership is cautious. They understand that the most effective use of military power occurs when the outcome of war will be so disadvantageous that concessions are exacted without a shot being fired. They subscribe to the precepts of Clausewitz and Sun Tzu.

On the northern flank, Norway represents a particularly interesting case in point. A U.S. defense posture obviously incapable of effectively aiding in the defense of Norway and Iceland could gradually ease the Norwegians out of NATO. A close relationship with the Soviets or even the Soviets' capture of the northern countries would not only markedly improve the security of the northern fleet's deployment routes, but would also permit a defensible Soviet claim to a part of the North Sea oil. From a military point of view, a short local campaign would be easy, and it is difficult to design a U.S. or NATO response that would not worsen the situation. The likelihood of the United States actually using nuclear weapons under the threat of even more punishing retaliation must be seen as lower than in the central front. Under such circumstances, compliance and cooperation might become the preferred choice for Norway — if any choice were given.

A similar situation exists further south in Yugoslavia where Tito's leadership must soon end. There, careful exploitation of the succession process and judicious use of covert action forces could well set the scene for the introduction of a Soviet military presence. There is no Western treaty commitment to Yugoslavia, and its value to Russia, especially for the secure basing of Mediterranean naval forces, would be large.

Extensive documentation is available on the large buildup in Soviet naval capabilities and open ocean deployments over the past fifteen years.[16] Today in all categories of ships (except aircraft carriers) the Soviet Navy, in both numbers and tonnage, is as large as or larger than the U.S. Navy. The margin in tonnage is especially noteworthy since U.S. ships of equal capability must be larger to accommodate the greater habitability requirements of U.S. sailors. The Soviet fleet has, however, an Achilles' heel: lack of secure access to the ocean. The Barents, the Bosporus and Dardanelles, and the Kurils must represent a nightmare to Admiral Gorshkov, one that the Soviet leadership must place high value on fixing. Such straits and strategic points may not be important for peacetime presence or for a short nuclear war at sea, but for most conflicts in between they could be crucial. In addition to concerns about northern Norway and Yugoslavia, securing the Dardanelles and Bosporus and gaining an Indian Ocean port surely play a role in Soviet naval planning. In this regard, current U.S. policy in Turkey must be viewed as presenting a significant opportunity.

However, the great prize is further south and to the east. All Russian military spending since World War II would pay for itself if the Russians could bring Iran, Saudi Arabia, and the Persian Gulf states under the Red banner, and this cannot have escaped the notice of her leaders. Nor is it reasonable to believe that the Russian leaders have failed to think about it very hard, especially in the light of what is possibly a serious short-run energy problem in the early 1980s.

Although in the long run the Soviet Union may contain very large oil, coal, and natural gas reserves, the CIA has estimated that in the short run the Soviets will experience something of a shortfall, with production peaking around 1980 at no more than 12 million barrels of oil per day and then falling off rapidly by at least 10 to 15 percent by 1984.[17] At the moment, Russia supplies about three-fourths of Eastern Europe's oil and is also a substantial exporter to Western Europe. Oil is the single largest source of hard foreign exchange for the Soviets, currently accounting for 40 percent of the total. The extent and duration of the Soviet oil problem and the possibility of solving all or part of it with natural gas are as yet unclear. The Soviets have made extensive use of water infusion in their oil fields, a technique that results in lower total recovery and increasing pumping requirements per barrel of oil as the water-oil ratio rises. In doing so, they have progressively shortchanged new exploration in order to allocate their equipment to current production.

Thus, in the early 1980s control of major oil resources in the Middle East could do many things for the Soviets. It could help to solve their domestic energy problem, as well as provide badly needed hard currency. It could provide tremendous leverage with Western Europe and Japan, and it could be used to weaken and possibly destroy the NATO alliance. Finally, it could make increasing dependence on agricultural imports much less dangerous.

Only a fool would not take note of the Soviet threat to the Persian Gulf states and plan very seriously for their defense. But timing is important. Even if the United States were to act forcefully to repair its military weaknesses, many actions would not be felt directly until late in the 1980s. The Soviets probably cannot maintain their current military buildup indefinitely, but in the meantime they have large military forces that they can put to profitable use. If Russia changes from an oil exporter to a possible oil importer in the early 1980s, its foreign exchange problems will become acute; furthermore, its ability to use Middle East oil as an effective weapon against NATO and Japan may well not last long. Large new supplies of energy are coming into production, and growth in oil consumption is tapering off. In the late 1980s and beyond, the Persian Gulf oil will still be important but less so than today, and controlling it may have more modest effects. Thus, the Soviets may see the first half of the 1980s as unique, with their own relative military strength peaking and a major opportunity to use it fleeting.

I have left Asia and the Pacific out of this discussion. War with China, like war with NATO, poses high risks of major nuclear war for the Soviets, and Japan and potential Japanese rearmament can be influenced through oil. The Pacific is militarily more difficult for the Soviets, and the payoff less clear. In my view, they will turn their main attention there later.

So I suggest the main western security problem of the 1980s will be a series of events orchestrated by the Soviets to accelerate the change in the correlation of forces. These events may well include military initiatives, especially in the Gulf, preceded by possible flanking movements in the eastern Mediterranean, North Africa, and sub-Sahara Africa, as well as moves to secure direct access to the ocean.

In an early draft of this paper, I speculated on the moves we should worry about and their sequence. One speculation involved two steps: the first was a leftist takeover in Afghanistan; the second, a new outbreak of war between India and Pakistan, with Russia siding with India and eventually partitioning Pakistan. The former is now reality, but a divided Pakistan would be an even greater prize. It would provide the Soviets with secure access to the Indian Ocean, as well as the possibility of placing a military force on Iran's eastern border. This does not necessarily suggest that the Soviets would invade Iran or Saudi Arabia. The military problems in such an undertaking would be very difficult, especially for invading forces. Moreover, since the provocation to the United States would be large, the Soviets might instead try to foment an internal leftist revolution. The associated confusion and disruption would be a highly desirable prelude to military action, and an invitation from a new leftist government, no matter how fragile, would provide the appearance of legitimacy and possibly considerable tactical advantage as well. If carefully managed, the whole thing could be completed quickly and before we had time to react. In this regard, the Soviets currently enjoy a distinct advantage in clandestine operations, covert action forces, and the use of proxies — an advantage that comparisons of the capabilities of military forces do not capture. Whatever the merits of the case, the United States is at the moment clearly far more restricted in its ability to use these unconventional means than the Soviets. Even the term *unconventional* in this context is ironic since throughout history such tactics have been part of the conventional means of competition among nations, and effective competition without their use is frequently far more expensive and in some cases impossible.

In summary, a case can be made that there is more than bureaucratic inertia or even a general belief in the value of power behind the Soviet military buildup. Bureaucratic inertia cannot explain the overall size, growth, and modernization of Soviet military forces at a time when every ruble counts. Soviet military leaders must have to fight for their budget and persuade their colleagues of its value, especially if, as I believe is likely, the military share is increasing. Strategic superiority as a generality is not likely to be nearly as persuasive in the decision process as power detailed in its specifics: what you can do with it, where, when, with what risk, and to what advantage. Even if we have not asked these questions, the Soviet leadership almost certainly has, and the Soviet military will have had to answer them. Although rational explanations of bureaucratic processes are unpopular, it is useful to use rationality as one explanation of bureaucratic behavior, especially in a totalitarian state. The possibilities I have delineated represent attempts to do so. Of course, it can be argued that the general thrust outlined in this paper would not be rational for the Soviets — that the risk is too great, the chance of success too small, and the payoff too limited.

In 1979 that may have been so, but consider the world in 1982 under the following conditions:

1. The nuclear balance as outlined in this paper.
2. Continued Soviet military buildup at recent rates.
3. Stable or modest increases in United States defense expenditures as currently planned.
4. Increased Soviet military equipment inventories in the Middle East (e.g., Libya).
5. Improved access to the sea and larger Soviet naval presence in the Mediterranean and Indian oceans.
6. An increased military presence either to the east of Iran or on the east coast of Africa, or both.

These are not unreasonable conditions. If we allow them to come about, there may be no effective way to stop a general increase in Soviet influence and possibly a major Soviet military thrust, such as a move to the south, without bearing much greater costs than we can inflict in return.

I started this paper with the suggestion that different national security policies derive largely from different predictions about the consequences of different policies or about the state of the world. The propositions of this paper illuminate that point. If correct, they underline the need for serious changes in American defense policy. In any case, they imply the need for serious work to cast more light on the following questions: How fast is the Soviet defense budget growing compared to GNP? If it is growing faster, how much faster? And how much faster is cause for alarm? How large does the growth in defense spending and capability — taken together with Soviet rhetoric, dogma, and doctrine — have to be before we predict that the Soviets will try to use their power? If they use it, what will they do? Will they only try to persuade and coerce? Will they just continue to play around rather ineptly in the Third World, using Cuban soldiers, making friends here, and getting pushed out there, with no real political, military, or economic gains? If they have some larger purpose, what is it? If that purpose is not virtual control of Middle East oil resources, is it something larger, such as the NATO central front or China, or something smaller? If something smaller, how and where and to what extent does it affect vital U.S. interests? More important, what Western actions would affect the Soviets' perceptions and calculations by increasing the Soviets' costs and risks?

NOTES

1. "NSC 68: A Report to the National Security Council," *Naval War College Review* 27 (May–June 1975):51–108.
2. Richard Pipes, "Why the Soviet Union Thinks It Could Fight and Win a Nuclear War," *Commentary* (July 1977):21–34.
3. Leon Goure, Foy D. Kohler, and Mose L. Harvey, *The Role of Nuclear Forces in Current Soviet Strategy* (Coral Gables, Fla.: Center for Advanced International Studies, University of Miami, 1974), p. x.
4. W. W. Kulski, *The Soviet Union in World Affairs: A Documented Analysis 1964-1972* (Syracuse, N.Y.: Syracuse University Press, 1973), p. 67.
5. G. A. Arbatov, article in *Kommunist 3,* cited in Dimitri Simes, "Detente and Conflict: Soviet Foreign Policy 1972-1977," Washington Paper No. 44, 1977, p. 38.
6. V. D. Sokolovskiy, *Soviet Military Strategy,* 3rd ed., edited and with analysis and commentary by Harriet Fast Scott (New York: Crane, Russak, 1975), p. 184.
7. National Strategic Information Center, *Understanding the Soviet Military Threat,* Agenda Paper No. 6 (New York: National Strategic Information Center, 1977), p. 31.
8. William T. Lee, "Understanding the Soviet Military Threat: How CIA Estimates Went Astray," in National Strategic Information Center, *Understanding the Soviet Military Threat.*
9. Steven Rosefielde, Chapter 2, p. 43, this volume.
10. H. A. Kissinger, "What in the Name of God Is Strategic Superiority? What Is the Significance of It Politically, Militarily, and Operationally at These Levels of Numbers? What Do You Do with It?" Moscow press conference (July 3, 1974).
11. Ibid.
12. U.S. Congress, Senate, "American and Soviet Armed Services, Strengths Compared, 1970-76," *Congressional Record* (August 5, 1977):S14063-104.
13. Lynn Etheridge Davis and Warner R. Schilling, "All You Ever Wanted to Know about MIRV and ICBM Calculations but Were Not Cleared to Ask," *Journal of Conflict Resolution* 17, no. 2 (June 1973):207-42.

14. U.S. Congress, Senate, Committee on Armed Services, *NATO and the New Soviet Threat,* report of Senator Sam Nunn and Senator Dewey F. Bartlett, 94th Cong. 1st sess., January 24, 1977.
15. Joseph D. Douglass, Jr., "Soviet Nuclear Strategy in Europe: A Selective Targeting Doctrine?" *Strategic Review* 5 (Fall 1977).
16. Director of Naval Intelligence and the Chief of Information, *Understanding Soviet Naval Developments,* 3rd ed., NAVSO P-3560 (Washington, D.C.: Office of the Chief of Naval Operations, January 1978).
17. Central Intelligence Agency, *Prospects for Soviet Oil Production* (ER 77-10270, April 1977), and *Prospects for Soviet Oil Production, A Supplemental Analysis* (ER 77-10425, July 1977), Washington, D.C.: Library of Congress).

2 REAL SOVIET ARMS PROCUREMENT EXPENDITURES, 1960–1978

Steven Rosefielde

In 1976 the Central Intelligence Agency revealed that its ruble estimates of Soviet defense expenditures were substantially in error. The revised figure for total Soviet defense spending was 100 percent greater than previously supposed and 236 percent greater for procurements narrowly defined excluding construction and follow-on spares (see Figure 1).[1] The basis for this revision was also extraordinary. The new data were obtained from an informant who had transcribed them directly from the records of the Soviet Ministry of Defense.[2] Given these circumstances, one might infer that the quantitative procedures used by the CIA to compute Soviet defense expenditures in rubles were seriously deficient. The agency, however, has emphatically denied that this was the case and has attributed 90 percent of the discrepancy to the use of faulty ruble-dollar ratios.[3] This paper evaluates the cogency of the CIA's explanation and offers an alternative interpretation based largely on information from official CIA sources.

To avoid any unnecessary misunderstanding, it is important to emphasize from the outset that CIA sources provide an incomplete, and at times

The issues treated in this essay are developed more comprehensively in my book *Underestimating the Soviet Military Threat: An Appraisal of the CIA's Direct Costing Effort 1960–1975* (New York: Transaction Press, 1980).

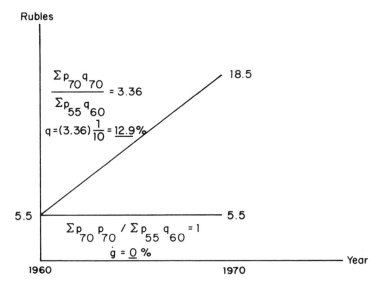

FIGURE 1. CIA Estimates of Soviet Procurement before and after the Revisions of 1976 (In billions of Current Rubles; 1960 Procurement in 1955 Prices and 1970 Procurement in 1970 Prices)

inconsistent, picture of Soviet defense expenditures. Despite agency claims to the contrary, the information available in the public domain is insufficient to allow independent analysts to evaluate the reliability of the CIA's work in a definitive way. This means that where lacunae in coverage, completeness, or conceptual foundation occur, allowance must be made for a range of error. Such allowances make the findings reported in this paper less certain than if the information made available by the CIA were more complete and consistent. These uncertainties, however, as the reader can confirm by replicating my calculations, are not especially large. It has therefore seemed preferable to publish my findings in their present form rather than allowing the CIA the sole authority to pass judgment on the credibility of its work.

REAL SOVIET ARMS PROCUREMENT
EXPENDITURES, 1960–1970

In appraising the rate and magnitude of real Soviet arms procurement expenditures since 1960, it is useful to begin by reviewing the evolution of the CIA's perception of these issues. Until the early 1970s CIA ruble estimates of Soviet procurement growth were computed in 1955 prices and prerevision 1970 prices.[4] Prices for 1955 were obtained from diverse sources, including official price handbooks for civilian goods thought to be reasonable proxies for weapons. These price data were supplemented from time to time with new information, much of it from the early 1960s. Nominal 1955 prices therefore more accurately characterize Soviet weapon prices circa 1960 than they do Soviet weapon prices in 1955. The prerevision 1970 price set was derived directly from 1955 prices. It constitutes a crude 6 percent upward adjustment for the change in industrial wholesale prices brought about by the 1967 Soviet price reform.[5]

The rate of Soviet procurement growth from 1960 through 1970 that the CIA calculated with these prices displays some very interesting properties.[6] The nominal annual compound growth rate for the 1960s is .6 percent. The Lespeyres real rate is:[7]

$$\frac{\Sigma r_{55} \Sigma q_{70}}{\Sigma r_{55} \Sigma q_{60}} = 1; 0 \text{ percent};$$

and the Paasche rate:[8]

$$\frac{\Sigma r_{70} \Sigma q_{70}}{\Sigma r_{70} \Sigma q_{60}} = 1; 0 \text{ percent}.$$

Around 1970 the CIA's own direct ruble-cost estimates therefore apparently showed that real Soviet arms procurement had not grown from 1960 to 1970 and that procurement price inflation, insofar as it existed at all, was minuscule.

If the agency believed its own numbers at the time, it must have been quite impressed by Soviet self-restraint. Instead of responding to the Vietnamese imbroglio by escalating their own defense expenditures, in the spirit of détente the Soviets held the line.

The CIA, however, had good reason to doubt the reliability of its ruble estimates. First, its own direct Paasche dollar-cost estimates indicated a higher rate of procurement growth, somewhat under 3 percent per annum.[9] This procurement growth rate not only exceeded the ruble Lespeyres rate but also violated the fundamental axiom that dollar growth rates should be less than, not greater than, ruble growth rates. Second, the official Soviet defense budget clearly showed that Soviet defense spending was rising rapidly during the 1960s — from 9.3 to 17.9 billion rubles valued in current prices.[10] While the CIA's direct cost estimate displayed zero procurement growth, official Soviet data showed nominal defense expenditures growing 6.8 percent per annum.[11]

These manifest contradictions intensified in the late 1960s and early 1970s when covert collection activities began to suggest that Soviet weapons were much more expensive than had been previously supposed. This information was ambiguous, lending itself to a variety of interpretations. It could have implied that the number of components in Soviet weapon systems were increasing, that Soviet weapons were improving qualitatively, or that production costs were being affected by inflation, which somehow was not reflected in the Soviet machine-building and metalworking price index.

These alternative explanations no doubt were heatedly debated within the agency. That they caused considerable consternation is plainly evidenced by the contradictory testimony that CIA Director William Colby gave to the Joint Economic Committee of Congress in 1974.[12] According to Colby, Soviet procurement expenditures valued in constant prerevision 1970 rubles grew during the 1960s at the same rate as all Soviet defense expenditures — that is, 4 percent per annum. This assertion, however, is strikingly contradicted elsewhere in his testimony where it is claimed that procurement expenditures in 1960 and 1970 were virtually the same: 5.5 billion rubles in constant 1970 prices.[13] Clearly, real Soviet procurement valued in constant ruble prices could not grow at 4 percent and remain unchanged at the same time.

Although Colby's testimony has now been repudiated in response to my criticisms,[14] it is easy to see in retrospect that his error was not fortuitous. It reflected a profound division of opinion within the agency. The agency's own direct ruble-cost estimates showed that Soviet procurement growth, whether valued in 1955 or prerevision 1970 prices, was zero in the 1960s.[15] The cost data collected covertly in the late 1960s and early 1970s, however, suggested a much higher rate of growth. The schism created by these disparate perceptions must have been very great because the evidence in the agency's possession was both contestable and portentous. The data were contestable partly for the conceptual reasons mentioned above and partly because they implied rates of real procurement growth far in excess of the 4 percent suggested in Colby's testimony.[16] If the 4 percent figure was actually derived with direct cost methods in 1973, that estimate must have been informal since it received no official sanction.[17] As a consequence, those who doubted the authenticity of the cost data could criticize the insurgents for drawing inferences from information that actually implied rates of Soviet procurement growth thought at the time to be completely implausible.

The data were portentous for the same reason they were believed to be implausible. If Soviet procurement had really been growing substantially faster than 4 percent since 1960, then everything known about Soviet defense expenditures and Soviet intentions would have to be called into question. Whereas it was formally believed that the Soviets had exhibited admirable self-restraint for the sake of détente, SALT I, and world peace, in this new light the possibility emerged that the Soviets had done no such thing. Whereas it had been thought that some impression of the Soviet defense effort could be gleaned from the official defense budget, it could now be surmised that the Soviets were deliberately manipulating their statistics to mask a formidable arms buildup. Whereas it had been firmly believed that the direct cost estimating method provided a reliable technique for measuring Soviet procurement growth, the possibility now had to be faced that the method failed even to determine the direction of the trend correctly.

The situation around 1973 was therefore fluid and riddled with contradiction. CIA estimates of total Soviet defense expenditures for 1970 were almost 40 percent higher than the figure stated officially by the Soviets,[18] but the agency's estimate of the growth of aggregate Soviet defense spending from 1960 through 1970 was 40 percent less than the rate reported in the Soviet defense budget.[19] The official CIA direct cost estimate of Soviet procurement growth during the 1960s was zero. However, new evidence, not yet formally validated by the direct costing method, suggested that Soviet procurement had been growing at least 4 percent per annum, and perhaps faster. If the latter view were confirmed, it would not only cast doubt on the reliability of the direct cost method but would also indicate that the Soviets were deliberately manipulating their reported defense expenditures, which were virtually unchanged between 1969 and 1973 and have remained unchanged ever since.[20]

To the best of my knowledge no coherent attempt has ever been made to come to terms systematically with these contradictions. Partial explanations, however, were tentatively put forward to rationalize two sensitive political issues. Highly placed defense department officials may not have known a great deal about index number theory, but they were bothered by the disparity between the arms growth they perceived in physical terms (confirmed partially by the CIA's dollar procurement growth rate) and the impression conveyed by both the CIA and the official Soviet defense budget that Soviet procurement growth in current ruble prices was zero.[21] How, they asked, could aggregate defense expenditures be constant between 1969 and 1973, as indicated by the Soviet defense budget, and how could the procurement share be declining, as indicated in Colby's testimony (from 40 percent to 20 percent between 1960 and 1970), if procurement were increasing? The answer widely circulated in the early 1970s was that the Soviet military machine-building sector was hyperproductive. Because the defense sector had priority in its access to the best resources, personnel, and technology, unit production costs were declining rapidly. As a consequence, while real procurement was rising, total procurement costs were not. The putative inconsistency therefore was not a real inconsistency; it was an illusion.[22]

At the time, this specious explanation gained broad currency because the facts needed to evaluate its merit were not generally known. Few knew that prerevision 1970 prices were really cosmetic adjustments of 1955 prices. Fewer still understood that the real ruble Lespeyres growth rate valued in 1955 prices was zero.[23] Ignorance of these facts made it easy, if nonetheless unpalatable, to accept on the authority of the CIA that the nominal cost of Soviet weapons was falling.

The other issue that demanded an answer was why the CIA believed that estimates of Soviet procurement growth in excess of 4 percent per annum were unthinkable when covert cost data indicated otherwise. The reason put forward was illuminating. Soviet procurement costs, it was contended, were rising because of hidden inflation.[24] The Soviet machine-building and metalworking sector was not hyperproductive; it was *hypo*productive. As a result, weapon prices paid by the Ministry of Defense were rising, not falling! Although this explanation of Soviet arms price behavior flatly contradicted the first rationale, no attempt was ever made to reconcile the inconsistency.

THE NEW INFORMATION

Had an informant who had personally inspected the expenditure data on the books of the Soviet Ministry of Defense not arrived on the scene in 1975, the standoff within the CIA between the contending factions would probably remain unresolved today.[25] Those who believed it unreasonable to suppose that Soviet procurement could significantly exceed levels supportable by the official defense budget would undoubtedly have continued to dispute the validity of covert cost data, while those who had confidence in the cost data would have found it politically inexpedient to challenge the prevailing orthodoxy that was based on direct cost estimates in constant 1955 and 1970 prerevision ruble prices.[26]

Be this as it may, the informant did arrive,[27] followed shortly thereafter by the discovery that weapon procurement costs were not included in the official Soviet defense budget after all. They were paid for out of the fund for the national economy.

The figures reported by the informant were entirely out of proportion to anything previously supposed. Instead of total defense spending for 1970 being 17.9 billion rubles, as officially claimed, or 25 billion rubles, as estimated by the CIA, it was 50 billion rubles.[28] Instead of procurement being 5.5 billion rubles, as stipulated in Colby's testimony, or 8.1 billion rubles, as implied by the covert cost data,[29] it was 18.5 billion rubles. The conclusion seemed inescapable. Some time in the early 1960s, the Soviets decided to embark on a massive arms buildup, concealing their intentions by publishing misleading information on their defense expenditures.

The CIA, however, found an escape. In May 1976 the agency published *Estimated Soviet Defense Spending in Rubles, 1970–1975,* in which it publicly admitted that Soviet defense expenditures were double those previously reported in Colby's testimony. But the agency unequivocally asserted that this change had no significant effect on its perception of real Soviet procurement growth:

> The revised estimate of the ruble costs of Soviet defense has had a major effect on some important intelligence judgments but not others. Specifically, because the changes are largely the result of estimates of higher ruble prices rather than discovery of larger programs, the revised estimate:
> — Does not affect our appraisal of the size or capabilities of Soviet military forces. Such estimates are based mainly on direct evidence.[30]

Did the agency therefore acknowledge that its direct cost estimate of Soviet procurement growth had been close to zero from 1960 through 1973? The CIA was more circumspect than that. Instead of analyzing the question of procurement directly, the agency focused on total defense expenditures. These expenditures, it asserted, grew 4 percent per annum from 1970 to 1975, which is in agreement with Colby's estimates for 1960 to 1970, and so "the revised estimate" was unaffected by the new information.[31] Only on page 13 in the section on resource analysis does the CIA's estimate of real procurement growth emerge. It is stated there that "investment, operating and RDT & E . . . has accounted for the same portion of the total" since 1970, implying that procurement grew at the same rate as the rest of Soviet defense expenditures: 4 percent per annum![32]

By burying its procurement revision inconspicuously in the text and confining the time frame to the period from 1970 through 1975, the CIA very cleverly and effectively contrived to bury the contradictions of the past. The fact that the agency's direct costing method indicated that real Soviet procurement did not grow at all during the 1960s and crept upward in pre-revision 1970 prices at about 1 percent per annum from 1970 to 1975 is completely ignored.[33] This is an omission of some moment. Not only did it conceal the real situation, but it also allowed the agency to establish the continuity of its estimates with Colby's testimony without having to acknowledge that Colby's testimony was internally inconsistent, that the direct costing methodology was unreliable, and that real Soviet procurement growth could be vastly greater than the agency was willing to admit publicly.

HIDDEN INFLATION

Although the CIA's attempt to cover its tracks was skillful, some formidable problems nonetheless remained embarrassingly visible. Figure 1, which illustrates Soviet procurement expenditures in current 1960 and 1970 prices, brings out several startling contradictions. According to the agency, the new information showed that Soviet procurement in 1970 was 236 percent greater than the prerevision estimate for 1970 and the direct cost estimate for 1960. This is a very large discrepancy, far greater than can be explained on the basis of a 4 percent real rate of growth. Other things being equal, had procurement in 1960 grown 4 percent annually during the 1960s, by 1970 it would have increased to 8.1 billion rubles, a figure 10.4 billion rubles less than the one actually observed. How can this gap be explained?

In view of the foregoing discussion, the agency's rationale is easily anticipated. The gap is attributable to hidden inflation. But can this hypothesis be sustained? The gap is very large. The hidden inflation rate implied is commensurately great. It can be computed by dividing the ratio of nominal procurement in 1970 and 1960 by the CIA's Paasche procurement growth index,

$$\frac{\Sigma r_{70}\Sigma q_{60}}{\Sigma r_{55}\Sigma q_{60}} = \frac{\Sigma r_{70}\Sigma q_{70}}{\Sigma r_{55}\Sigma q_{60}} \cdot \frac{\Sigma r_{70}\Sigma q_{60}}{\Sigma r_{70}\Sigma q_{70}}$$

$$= 18.5/5.5 \div 1.48$$

$$= 2.27,$$

and discounting this quotient for the number of years that hidden inflation is presumed to have been in effect. Remembering that a great many of the CIA's 1955 prices were actually collected in the early 1960s, a ten-year time frame can be employed for this purpose, which would yield an implied hidden rate of 8.6 percent.[34] Had the agency's Lespeyres procurement rate valued in constant 1955 prices been used instead of the Paasche rate, the implied rate of inflation would have been greater still:

$$\frac{\Sigma r_{70}\Sigma q_{70}}{\Sigma r_{55}\Sigma q_{70}} = \frac{\Sigma r_{70}\Sigma q_{70}}{\Sigma r_{55}\Sigma q_{60}} \cdot \frac{\Sigma r_{55}\Sigma q_{60}}{\Sigma r_{55}\Sigma q_{70}}$$

$$= 18.5/5.5 \div 1$$

$$= 3.36$$

and

$$\dot{P} = 100[(3.36)^{1/10} - 1] = 12.9 \text{ percent.}$$

Needless to say these rates of inflation are extremely implausible, especially so since the Lespeyres-Paasche relationship violates the usual pattern predicted by index number theory.

If the agency's implied hidden inflation rate is as dubious as has just been suggested, why has the CIA not acknowledged the problem? Part of the answer to this important question is explained by the index number phenomenon alluded to above. Because the CIA's ruble Lespeyres procurement growth rate is less than the corresponding Paasche procurement rate, the misleading impression is given that the agency's implied Lespeyres price inflation rate is an upper bound, rather than a lower bound. This perverse effect is compounded by a fifteen-year hidden inflation time horizon, used on the grounds that the agency's procurement prices pertain to 1955, even though a significant portion of these prices were actually collected in the early 1960s. The use of a fifteen-year inflation propagation period reduces the implied Lespeyres price inflation rate from 8.6 percent to 5.6 percent. Moreover, further reductions are easily achieved by employing alternative estimates of Soviet procurement in 1970. For example, if a figure of 15.3 billion rubles is chosen, the implied rate of hidden inflation can be reduced to 4.3 percent.[35]

The CIA itself actually favors a rate of hidden inflation slightly lower than 4 percent, which is putatively supported by two studies, one by James Steiner, the other by Rita Bricksin.[36] Bricksin's work is restricted to a single weapon system and is classified. Steiner's research, however, has been openly disseminated.[37] I have carefully replicated his calculations and have found them to be seriously in error. When these errors are corrected, his paper provides virtually no support for the agency's claims about hidden inflation. As a consequence, the CIA's position on hidden inflation appears to be more of a search for evidence to justify an arbitrary hypothesis than a firm inference rigorously deduced from a scientific determination of the facts.

The corollary is clear. The evidence at the agency's disposal can explain only 2.6 billion rubles of the 13 billion ruble discrepancy between its prerevision and postrevision estimates of Soviet procurement.[38] More than 10 billion rubles of the 18.5 billion rubles that the agency currently estimates the Soviets spent on procurement in 1970 cannot be accounted for, except by a gratuitous appeal to hidden inflation.[39] This figure may be reduced by 1 or 2 billion rubles to allow for a margin of error,[40] but the basic story is still the same. The new information strongly suggests that Soviet procurement during the 1960s grew two to three times faster than the 4 percent figure currently claimed by the CIA.[41] The new information may not have changed the agency's perceptions, but it should have.

THE RELIABILITY OF THE
DIRECT DOLLAR-COST METHOD

Since a substantial portion of the discrepancy of the CIA's ruble estimate has been shown to involve the real growth of Soviet weapons systems, the fundamental source of the CIA's miscalculation lies in the agency's direct dollar-cost estimates, which drive its ruble projections. To understand how the direct dollar-cost method could have been so grossly in error, it is necessary to review briefly the techniques that the agency employs and to appraise their intrinsic reliability. The four basic methods used are: stochastic parametric cost-estimating models derived for American weapons, analogue methods, engineering studies, and Soviet stochastic parametric estimating models.[42] The great majority of weapons systems are estimated by the first two approaches, which are known to be highly *un*reliable. As Timson and Tikhansky, the authors of the famous Rand airframe cost model, have pointed out, "Uncertainty bands are very wide regardless of the model form selected . . . the 95% prediction interval ranges from − 43% of predicted costs to + 75% of predicted costs."[43] The agency has countered lamely that the law of large number reduces the average variance of the sample population of all "estimated" weapons as the number of weapons systems increases. Assuming that the variance of the Rand airframe model is the highest in the sample of "estimated" weapons systems, that each weapon system is computed independently, and that each estimate is unbiased, it follows that aggregate variance will be reduced.[44] These assumptions, however, presume what needs to be proven. American stochastic parametric cost models seldom meet these requirements,[45] and the assertion that they yield unbiased estimates of weapons not in the underlying sample cannot be substantiated.

Moreover, since there can be no statistically justifiable adjustment of the underlying American ex-post production-cost data base for characteristics of Soviet weapons that could plausibly reduce the stochastic variance of the American models, stochastic parametric estimates either implicitly utilize a "least-dollar cost" production convention or entail arbitrary manipulation.

Matters are not any better with regard to engineering studies. In principle, any one of three conventions could be employed to estimate the cost of Soviet weapons systems:

1. Exact replication of Soviet procurement according to Soviet technical specifications with American fabrication methods (sometimes referred to as Chinese copy).

2. Exact replication of Soviet procurement according to Soviet technical specifications with Soviet fabrication methods.
3. Replication of Soviet performance characteristics using least-cost American designs and technologies.[46]

Reflection will quickly persuade the reader that none of these conventions is really unambiguous, especially in the absence of full information. Unless Soviet weapons are actually tested under diverse conditions, how can their performance characteristics be discerned? Suppose that in exactly replicating Soviet technology, costs rise far above alternative American substitutes; does it then make sense to insist on exactitude? In practice, because engineering studies require an enormous number of discretionary judgments, no one convention is rigorously applied. Yet CIA spokesmen appear to believe that whatever mix of conventions is utilized, ex post the aggregate estimate will be unbiased and will display small variance characteristics both in relation to ex-ante dollar engineering estimates and to real Soviet procurement as it appears on the books of the Soviet Ministry of Defense, computed with available ruble-dollar parities.

Surely all estimates cannot be unbiased indicators of Soviet procurement as it appears on the books of the Soviet Ministry of Defense adjusted for inflation since the agency does not calculate a different set of ruble-dollar parities for each costing convention. Worse yet, even if multiple sets of ruble-dollar parities were computed, the CIA's assertions regarding the reliability of its dollar-cost engineering estimates would remain invalid for the decisive reason that *the agency does not build Soviet weapons according to any convention whatsoever and so cannot be in a position to compare ex-ante cost-estimating predictions against realized ex-post cost.* As a consequence, all assertions about reliability are radically subjective and can have no basis in statistics or practical empirical experience.

What has been said for American cost-estimating procedures holds as well for Soviet cost-estimating models. There is no reason to assume that the reliability of Soviet stochastic parametric cost estimates is any greater than that of similar American estimates, especially if instead of using the "true" variable values in the underlying Soviet weapons sample, cost estimators have to estimate the characteristics of Soviet weapons subject to an unknown stochastic margin of error.

All these deficiencies pale, however, before the really fundamental defect of direct cost estimating. To determine the adequacy of the CIA's direct costing method, the accuracy of its weapons counts, the reliability of its dollar valuations, and the correctness of its ruble estimates, it is necessary to obtain information on actual Soviet arms production and actual procurement cost for several years. Without direct comparison of estimated and true values, an objective measure of reliability cannot be made. As is well known, the agency's weapons count, which is based on information gathered by technical means, has never been verified through a direct examination of Soviet books. All evaluations of the adequacy of direct costing therefore depend solely on whether procurements costs in Soviet rubles can be accurately computed from dollar estimates. If existing weapons counts, valuation conventions, and ruble-dollar parities generate estimates that correspond with true ruble procurement costs (allowing for adjustments in ruble-dollar parities over time that are justified on independent quantitative grounds), then the direct costing method can be convincingly, if not decisively, validated.

To perform such a test, however, numerous observations on the actual cost of Soviet arms procurement (adjusted for inflation) must be obtained so that estimated and actual costs can be compared. No amount of a priori reflection can substitute for these observations on true procurement costs. Without an adequate sample of true observations, the degree to which estimates approximate actual procurement costs cannot be ascertained. Since the CIA possesses only one direct observation of procurement as it stands on the books of the Soviet Ministry of Defense (1970), the real situation is plain. The CIA does not know, nor can it test, whether its direct cost method is reliable. No statistical assessment can ever be made on the basis of one observation. The agency's direct dollar-costing approach as it is currently employed cannot be proved false or unsound unless the Soviets open up their books to confirm whether estimated procurement costs approximate true costs or whether estimated weapons counts correspond with actual Soviet arms production.

Despite the fact that the Soviets have been noticeably reluctant to advance science by providing the necessary data, the CIA maintains that its direct cost estimates are reliable within 15 percent.[47] Such a posture is untenable because it implies that one can draw scientific inferences that do not require empirical verification and that cannot for all practical purposes be convincingly falsified. Not only does this attitude make direct costing objectively unscientific because empirical falsification is operationally infeasible, irrelevant, or both, but, perhaps even more insidiously, it also blinds the agency to the imponderables of its direct dollar-costing method. Thus, even when it is confronted with blatant contrafactual evidence, the agency fails to search out the inconsistencies in its own numbers, which it treats as transcendentally infallible (within 15 percent).

CONCLUSION

The discovery of a 236 percent error in the ruble estimate of Soviet procurement for 1970 has called into question the adequacy of the dollar-cost estimates of Soviet defense expenditures from which the ruble estimates themselves were derived. Rather than considering the possibility that its direct dollar-costing methodology could be wrong by more than 15 percent, the CIA has preferred to explain this enormous discrepancy in terms of disguised price inflation (a purely monetary phenomenon).

This paper has explicitly disputed that explanation and has argued that, as currently practiced, the CIA's direct dollar-cost method is unscientific since the empirical tests required to validate its claims for reliability are never performed and the estimates are treated as if they were transcendentally true — that is, verified — despite their contrafactual falsification by the covert evidence obtained from the books of the Soviet Ministry of Defense in 1970.

Moreover, it has been demonstrated that undetected increases in real Soviet weapons production may account for more than 10 billion rubles worth of the discrepancy in the CIA's prerevision and postrevision estimates of Soviet procurement. Since the agency's total estimate of real Soviet procurement in 1970 is only 8.1 billion rubles, it seems exaggerated to claim, as the CIA does, that the "new information" does not change our understanding of Soviet weapons production. All the evidence points in the same direction — that is, toward a massive and rapid Soviet arms buildup during the 1960s and early 1970s, which the Soviets effectively disguised by omitting weapons production from their official defense budget. This minor deception no doubt explains why the CIA did not recognize what was happening until very late, but it does not explain why the agency failed to forthrightly assess the facts after they were delivered to its doorstep by the informant. This failure, in my opinion, is a very serious matter and suggests that radical reforms are needed in the area of national economic intelligence analysis.

NOTES

1. Central Intelligence Agency, *USSR: Toward a Reconciliation of Marxist and Western Measures of National Income,* p. 14. The agency's "best estimate" using the residual method is 18.5 billion rubles. Transformed to the direct costing nomenclature, "This estimate ranged between 13 billion and 21 billion rubles with a best estimate of 17 billion." A 10 percent range of error suggests a lower limit of 15.3 billion rubles and an upper limit of 18.7 billion rubles. The

18.5 billion ruble estimate is John Pitzer's. See J. Pitzer, "Reconciliation of Gross National Product and Soviet National Income." Pitzer's estimate confirms William Lee's earlier calculations. See W. T. Lee, *The Estimation of Soviet Defense Expenditures for 1955–1975: An Unconventional Approach*, Table 4.3, p. 61.

I have chosen to use Pitzer's estimate for 1970 in the calculations that appear in the text because it is supported by Lee's estimates and until recently was the only number in the published literature that did not have to be derived from relevant, but imprecise, ancillary data. The 236 percent procurement error used in the text relies on the Pitzer-Lee estimate: 18.5/5.5 = 3.36. If the agency's best direct costing estimate is employed, the procurement error drops to 209 percent. The reader can easily compute other estimates from the range of estimates provided above.

2. "Assessing the Soviet Economy: The CIA's Giant Goof," *Business Week*, p. 97; U.S. Congress, Joint Economic Committee, *Allocation of Resources in the Soviet Union and China — 1976, Part 2*, p. 82; Joseph Alsop, "A Cautionary Tale."

3. The revised ruble estimates do not affect the agency's "appraisal of the size or capabilities of Soviet military forces" or "the dollar cost of reproducing Soviet defense programs in the U.S." because "the changes are largely the result of estimates of higher ruble prices rather than discovery of larger programs." Quoted from Central Intelligence Agency, *Estimated Soviet Defense Spending in Rubles, 1970–1975*, pp. 1–2. See also Joint Economic Committee, *Allocation of Resources — 1976*, pp. 14–20. The testimony is by George Bush.

4. Private letter from Donald Swain, Deputy Chief for Analysis Military-Economic Analysis Center, Office of Strategic Research, dated August 9, 1979.

5. Ibid. More than one ruble-dollar ratio were revised, but the effect on relative prices was negligible.

6. According to testimony provided by CIA Director William Colby, Soviet procurement in 1970 was roughly 20 percent of total Soviet defense expenditures, or 5 billion rubles. See U.S. Congress, Joint Economic Committee, *Allocation of Resources in the Soviet Union and China* (1974), pp. 68–69. In a letter dated February 21, 1979, Donald Burton, Chief of the Military-Economic Analysis Center, Office of Strategic Research, informed me that Colby's testimony was in error. The prices underlying the figures that he reported pertained to 1955. Adjusting Colby's estimate for this factor and allowing for some small error puts the estimate for 1970 at approximately 5.5 billion rubles. This figure is the same as Colby's estimate for 1960, a fact confirmed by Swain. It follows from this that nominal Soviet procurement growth from 1960 through 1970 was $\dot{g} = [100 \, (1.06)^{1/10} - 1] = .58$ percent.

7. Swain; see note 4.

8. Ibid.

9. Steven Rosefielde, "The Anomalous Behavior of the CIA's Indices of Soviet Procurement Growth 1960–1970," note 2.

10. *Narodnoe khoziaistvo, 1972*, p. 724.
11. $\dot{q} = 100[(1.92)^{1/10} - 1] = 6.76$ percent.
12. Joint Economic Committee, *Allocation of Resources* (1974).
13. See note 6.
14. Swain; see note 4.
15. Ibid.
16. Burton; see note 6. The CIA has vigorously denied my suggestion that the agency would not have revised its estimates as it did if the informant who saw the statistics on the books of the Soviet Ministry of Defense had not appeared. If Burton is correct, the data at the agency's disposal already indicated that Soviet procurement circa 1970 ranged between 15.3 and 18.7 billion rubles. Since the CIA's estimate for Soviet procurement in 1960 was roughly 5.5 billion rubles, it would have been easy to deduce that during the 1960s Soviet procurement had grown far faster than 4 percent.
17. Swain has indicated that the CIA ceased using the prerevision data at the beginning of 1974. See note 4.
18. The official Soviet figure was 17.9 billion rubles in 1970 prices. The CIA's estimate valued in its prerevision prices was 25 billion rubles. See Joint Economic Committee, *Allocation of Resources* (1974).
19. Ibid. The CIA has estimated that total Soviet defense expenditures grew 4 percent during the 1960s. The Soviets have stated that it grew 6.8 percent.
20. *Narodnoe khoziaistvo, 1977*, p. 559.
21. Stephen Enke probed this question with me at length in 1974.
22. Central Intelligence Agency, *Economic Impact of Soviet Military Spending*, pp. 6, 12. I have discussed this theory with Stephen Enke, Patrick Parker, and a host of other knowledgeable defense department officials. They all confirm its currency. Enke attributed the theory to Rush Greenslade, Chief of the Office of Economic Research of the CIA. I was never able to confirm this, although I was told it was so by others. I discussed the subject briefly with Greenslade at the First World Conference on Slavic Studies at Banff, Canada, in 1974. He supported the hypothesis but did not claim its authorship.
23. Almost no one in the defense department knows about these matters today.
24. The concept of hidden inflation predates the present controversy. The phenomenon was documented by Soviet scholars before World War II when hidden inflation was rampant. Many American scholars have commented on it in the postwar period. A revival of interest in the subject became manifest in the early 1970s. See Rush Greenslade, "Industrial Production Statistics in the USSR," and Abraham Becker, "The Price Level of Soviet Machinery in the 1960s."
25. Burton and Swain vehemently deny this. Their opinion should be given considerable weight. However, I personally remain skeptical. My impression is that the political pressures on the CIA to keep their estimates low are very strong.
26. Perhaps those who participated directly in CIA discussions will soon be stimulated to clarify the record and to correct any unintentional distortions that may blemish my account.

27. See note 2.
28. Central Intelligence Agency, *Estimated Soviet Defense Spending, 1970–1975,* p. 1.
29. $(1.04)^{10}$ 5.5 = 8.1 billion rubles.
30. Central Intelligence Agency, *Estimated Soviet Defense Spending, 1970–1975,* p. 1.
31. Swain indicated that the CIA switched to some form of revised 1970 prices in 1974; see note 4.
32. Central Intelligence Agency, *Estimated Soviet Defense Spending, 1970–1975.*
33. Rosefielde, "Anomalous Behavior of the CIA's Indices," notes 2 and 3. Swain's comment that the agency ceased using prerevision prices in 1974 raises some interesting questions about why the implied prerevision procurement growth rate was as low as I have calculated it to be. This problem, however, will have to be examined at a later date.
34. $\dot{p} = 100[(2.27)^{1/10} - 1] = 8.6$ percent.
35. See note 1. $\dot{p} = 100[(1.88)^{1/15} - 1] - 4.3$ percent.
36. Burton; see note 6.
37. James Steiner, *Inflation in Soviet Industry and Machine-Building and Metalworking (MBMW) 1960–1975.* For a detailed critique of this paper, see Steven Rosefielde, "Are Soviet Industrial Production Statistics Significantly Distorted by Hidden Inflation?"
38. $(1.04)^{10}5.5 - 5.5 = 2.6$ billion rubles.
39. $18.5 - 8.1 = 10.4$ billion rubles.
40. See note 1.
41. Without any hidden inflation, real procurement would have grown 12.9 percent. If machine-building and metalworking prices fell, as the official index suggests, 1.6 percent per annum from 1960 through 1970, then real procurement may have grown as much as 14.7 percent per annum.
42. For more information, see Central Intelligence Agency, "The Metaphysics of Dollar Estimates of Soviet Defense Activities," p. 7. This is a draft manuscript and does not constitute an official CIA position.
43. F. S. Timson and D. P. Tikhansky, *Confidence in Estimated Airframe Costs: Uncertainty in Aggregate Prediction,* p. 37.
44. According to the central limit theorem, whatever the distribution function, provided only that it has a finite variance, the sample mean will approximate the normal distribution for large samples. This implies that if the target population is the entire set of American weapons measured in terms of ex-post production costs, as the sample size increases, the relationship between the computed sample mean and the true target-population mean will coincide more and more closely. By extension, it would seem that if the sample, instead of containing observations on ex-post production cost, contains observations on the expected value of weapons not in the original sample (which are, however, normally distributed and unbiased), one could argue as before: as the sample size increases, the computed sample mean will approximate not only the target-population mean of expected weapons value, but also the true extended target-

population mean, which includes observations derived both from ex-post data and from unbiased estimates generated from stochastic cost-estimating models.

The validity of this inference depends critically on whether the projected estimates are in fact unbiased and accurate. That is unlikely to be the case and accounts for the familiar stricture that "statements about the target populations are not valid in a relative-frequency-population" (Alexander Mood and Franklin Graybill, *Introduction to the Theory of Statistics*, p. 142). Since Soviet weapons are never built in the United States, inferences drawn about Soviet weapons costs from American models are *not valid*, and it is impossible to ascertain how biased they might be on an a priori basis. Moreover, since any ultimate check on the accuracy of the agency's cost estimates (including its weapons count) requires that dollar estimates converted to constant rubles equal the constant ruble values on the books of the Soviet Ministry of Defense, no amount of juggling the American sample can lead to statistically meaningful inferences about the Soviet target population. See Mood and Graybill, *Statistics*, pp. 139–52.

45.   When I lectured on this theme to a seminar of cost-estimating experts at the U.S. Naval Postgraduate School, I received an unexpectedly cool reception; the audience could not understand why I wasted so much time belaboring the obvious. Of course, I was told, everyone knows American stochastic cost-estimating models are highly unreliable, and inferences drawn about Soviet costs from them are so much the worse! See also Alexander Callahan, "Industrial Engineering Estimates: Can They Be Used to Measure Procurement Costs of Operation Systems Built by a Foreign Economy?" and John Scott Redd, "An Examination of the CIA Economic Net Assessment of the United States and the Soviet Union."

46.   Central Intelligence Agency, "Metaphysics," pp. 4–7.

47.   National Foreign Assessment Center, *A Dollar Cost Comparison of Soviet and United States Defense Activities, 1967–1977*, p. 3. A somewhat weaker assertion is made with regard to ruble estimates. See also Central Intelligence Agency, *Estimated Soviet Defense Spending: Trends and Prospects*, pp. 13–14.

BIBLIOGRAPHY

Alsop, J. "A Cautionary Tale." *Washington Post*, no. 92 (March 7, 1977):A-21.

"Assessing the Soviet Economy: The CIA's Giant Goof." *Business Week* (February 28, 1977):96–103.

Becker, A. "The Price Level of Soviet Machinery in the 1960s." *Soviet Studies* 26, no. 3 (July 1974):363–79.

———. *Military Expenditure Limitation for Arms Control: Problems and Prospects*. Cambridge, Mass.: Ballinger, 1977.

Callahan, A. "Industrial Engineering Estimates: Can They Be Used to Measure Procurement Costs of Operational Systems Built by a Foreign Economy?" Unpublished manuscript, Naval Postgraduate School, September 1978.

Central Intelligence Agency. *Economic Impact of Soviet Military Spending* (ER-IR-75-3). Washington, D.C., April 1975.

————. *Estimated Soviet Defense Spending in Rubles, 1970-1975* (SR76-10121U). Washington, D.C., May 1976.

————. *A Dollar Cost Comparison of Soviet and U.S. Defense Activities: 1966-76* (SR77-100001U). Washington, D.C., January 1977.

————. *Estimated Soviet Defense Spending: Trends and Prospects* (SR78-10121). Washington, D.C., June 1978.

————. "The Metaphysics of Dollar Estimates of Soviet Defense Activities." Washington, D.C., 1978.

————. "Price Index Methodology Used for the 1978 Dollar Cost Comparison of U.S. and Soviet Defense Activities." Memorandum for the Record (CIA), July 28, 1978.

————. "USSR: Toward a Reconciliation of Marxist and Western Measures of National Income" (ER78-10508). Washington, D.C., October 1978.

Greenslade, R. "Industrial Production Statistics in the USSR." In V. Treml and J. Hardt, eds., *Soviet Economic Statistics*. Durham, N.C.: Duke University Press, 1972.

Lee, W. T. *The Estimation of Soviet Defense Expenditures for 1955-75: An Unconventional Approach*. New York: Praeger, 1977.

————. *Understanding the Soviet Military Threat: How CIA Estimates Went Astray*. New York: National Strategy Information Center, 1977.

————. "Soviet Defense Expenditures in the 19th FYP." *Osteuropa* (December 1977), reprinted in *Current News*, no. 322 (June 1, 1978):1-11.

Mood, A., and F. Graybill. *Introduction to the Theory of Statistics*. New York: McGraw-Hill, 1963.

National Foreign Assessment Center. *A Dollar Cost Comparison of Soviet and U.S. Defense Activities, 1967-1977* (SR78-1002). Washington, D.C., January 1978.

Pitzer, J. "Reconciliation of Gross National Product and Soviet National Income." Soviet Economy Branch USSR (Eastern European Division, OER*), December 1977. Paper presented at NATO Colloquium, July 1977.

Redd, J. S. "An Examination of the CIA Economic Net Assessment of the United States and the Soviet Union." Unpublished manuscript, Naval Postgraduate School, 1978.

Rosefielde, S. "The Anomalous Behavior of the CIA's Indices of Soviet Procurement Growth 1960-1970." In Rosefielde, *Underestimating the Soviet Military Threat*.

————. "Are Soviet Industrial Production Statistics Significantly Distorted by Hidden Inflation?" In Rosefielde, *Underestimating the Soviet Military Threat*.

————. *Underestimating the Soviet Military Threat: An Appraisal of the CIA's Direct Costing Effort 1960-1975*. New York: Transaction Press, 1980.

Steiner, J. *Inflation in Soviet Industry and Machine-Building and Metalworking (MBMW) 1960-75.* Washington, D.C.: Central Intelligence Agency, June 19, 1978.

————. "Price Deflators for the Output of Defense Oriented Industries." Unpublished manuscript, 1978.

Timson, F. S., and D. P. Tikhansky. *Confidence in Estimated Airframe Costs: Uncertainty in Aggregate Prediction* (R-903-PR). Santa Monica, Calif.: Rand Corporation, October 1972.

U.S. Congress, Joint Economic Committee. *Allocation of Resources in the Soviet Union and China.* Washington, D.C., 1974.

U.S. Congress, Joint Economic Committee. *Allocation of Resources in the Soviet Union and China — 1976, Part 2.* Washington, D.C., May–June 1976.

3 SOVIET NUCLEAR TARGETING STRATEGY AND SALT

William Lee

SALT is a political dialogue not only about how many and what kinds of weapons each superpower will have to deter the other, but also about the forces each would have if deterrence should fail. Both the United States and the Soviet Union reject initiation of nuclear war by a surprise attack "out of the blue" as an instrument of national policy. Both expect that if nuclear war occurs, it will arise out of a crisis. At the same time, each superpower suspects the other of harboring dark designs for a surprise attack should the circumstances appear propitious or if some desperate and reckless leader should come to power. In all cases, the "bottom line" is how each superpower proposes to "lay down" its weapons: What targets are to be attacked? What degree of damage is to be inflicted? What are the politico-military objectives, if any, of strategic nuclear strikes once deterrence has failed for whatever reason?

Public discussions of such matters in the United States are dominated by two images of how the Soviets would use their nuclear weapons. The first, and probably most prevalent, image is that the Soviets would use their weapons in a "mirror image" of the U.S. concept of assured destruction — that is, the Soviets would attack U.S. cities with their large weapons in order to inflict as many millions of casualties as possible (*countervalue* targeting). The second, less prevalent public image stresses the danger of a Soviet attack on U.S. strategic nuclear delivery systems — ICBMs, heavy bombers, and SLBMs in port (*counterforce* targeting). According to the second image, the Soviets would withhold strikes on our cities to see if we would capitulate or negotiate after losing most of our land-based strategic nuclear forces to the Soviet counterforce strike; thus, the fate of our cities would depend upon whether we chose to retaliate for the Soviet counterforce strike. However, in both images the Soviets are assumed to target the general population just as we have said we would do.

One of the U.S. objectives in SALT has been to constrain or reduce Soviet forces so that they could be used effectively only against U.S. population and urban infrastructures. For this reason, we have sought to limit the number of "heavy" Soviet missiles threatening our land-based missiles, while granting the Soviets numerical advantages in missiles that are effective only against U.S. cities and other soft targets. Meanwhile, we still have the advantage in the number of small MIRVed warheads, which also are effective only against "soft" targets, such as population and industry.[1]

This essay has three basic theses. First, Soviet targeting strategy differs from popular U.S. perceptions, more so from the purely countervalue perception than from the mixed counterforce-countervalue version. Second, Soviet strategic targeting strategy applies to both Eurasia and the United States. While we equate *strategic* with *intercontinental*, the Soviets do so only in the context of SALT, where acceptance of our definition of *strategic* is in Soviet interests. To the Soviets, Europe and adjacent areas in Asia are strategic dimensions of equal, if not greater, importance than the "transoceanic" dimension. Third, both Soviet targeting strategy and the Soviet concept of strategic dimensions have had much influence on the SALT process in the past and probably will continue to do so in the future.

Since World War II the Soviets have consistently argued that the defeat of the adversary's armed forces is the first and primary objective of military operations in a nuclear war. Two typical Soviet statements from the transition period between the death of Stalin, and of his "permanently operating factors," and the Soviet Union's entry into the nuclear-missile age are:

> The defeat of the enemy will be achieved above all by means of the annihilation of his armed forces."[2]

> Wars are won only when the enemy's will to resist is broken and that can only be broken, as the experience of history shows, when the armed forces of the enemy are destroyed. Therefore, *the objective of combat operations must be the destruction of the armed forces and not strategic bombing of targets in the rear.*[3]

The first statement was made in 1955, the second in 1957.

In 1962 the first edition of *Military Strategy*, edited by Marshal Sokolovsky, specified nuclear targets and priorities as follows:

> These troops (Strategic Rocket Troops) can, if necessary, be used to solve the main problems of war — destruction of the enemy's means of nuclear attack (the basis of his military might), the main formations of his armed forces, and his primary and vitally important objectives.[4]

> The main means of waging war will be massive nuclear-rocket strikes for the purpose of destroying the aggressor's nuclear weapons, for the simultaneous mass destruction of the vitally important objectives constituting the enemy's military, political, and economic potential, for crushing his will to resist, and for winning victory in the shortest possible time.[5]

One of the most authoritative public statements of Soviet targeting strategy was made by the commander of the Strategic Rocket Forces (SRF), Marshal Krylov, in September 1967.[6] (Krylov was commander in chief of SRF from 1963 until his death in 1972.) Consistent with the view that even a nuclear war should be conducted for positive ends, Marshal Krylov stated that the objective of such a war would be "victory" for the U.S.S.R. According to Marshal Krylov, the principal targets of the SRF would be the enemy's:

Delivery systems, weapons storage, and fabrication sites.
Military installations.
Military industries.
Centers of politico-military administration, command, and control.

As is readily apparent, this listing of targets, presumably in approximate order of priority, reflects a plan to fight a war rather than to retaliate against cities. It has nothing in common with "maximum-fatality" targeting and is not consistent with any simple "assured-destruction" objective.[7] The list is, however, consistent with the damage-limiting missions of Soviet forces and with the "victory" objective interpreted as national-entity survival.

Here is another typical example of Soviet views on the political nature of nuclear war, Soviet nuclear targeting principles, and the ultimate objective sought:

> Thus if the imperialist forces succeed in unleashing a war against the Soviet Union and other socialist countries then it will be a world war, a supreme armed conflict in which both sides will pursue extremely decisive objectives. In its socio-political essence it will be a war of two powerful coalitions of states.

The appearance and development of nuclear missile weapons determined the emergence of a completely new type of war — the nuclear war, which has as its main method of conduct the inflicting of nuclear strikes against the means of nuclear attack, enemy troop groupings and naval forces, his military objectives, and the centers of governmental and military control simultaneously over the entire territory of the probable enemy, *including the transoceanic enemy as well.*[8,9]

"Let everyone know," stated L. I. Brezhnev in his speech on the fiftieth anniversary of Soviet rule, "that in combat against any aggressor the Soviet country will gain a victory deserving of our great nation; worthy of the homeland of October."[10]

SOVIET DEFINITIONS OF THEATERS OF MILITARY OPERATIONS

These general principles of Soviet nuclear targeting strategy must be applied to specific geographic areas of strategic military operations. The targets located in each geographic area are not uniform, and Soviet politico-military objectives are not identical in all potential areas of conflict. Each area must be analyzed for differences in the targets located therein, as well as for the most vulnerable points of each target, in order to maximize the military effectiveness of the attack with the least collateral damage that is commensurate with Soviet politico-military objectives in that area.

Soviet concepts of strategic nuclear targeting in various geographic areas have had a significant impact on SALT negotiations thus far. They may have even greater influence on the effort to replace the Interim Agreement on offensive forces with a "permanent" agreement, particularly on any proposal to reduce the intercontinental strategic aggregate much below the ceiling of 2,400 delivery systems negotiated at Vladivostok. Because their targeting strategy requires large numbers of weapons, the Soviets are not likely to accept a much lower limit. For any ceiling under 2,400 ICBMs, SLBMs, and heavy bombers, they are likely to compensate themselves with such weapons as the SS-20 IRBM.

Whereas the prelevant U.S. concept of "strategic" nuclear operations is limited to intercontinental exchanges, the Soviets' concept of "strategic" operations begins at their borders. While this geographic definition of "strategic" may be a very natural result of Soviet history, geography, and physical juxtaposition of states that the Soviets regard as their "probable enemies" in the event of nuclear war, it has far-reaching consequences for the size and characteristics of Soviet strategic nuclear forces.

In the Soviet view, "The theater of military operations (TVD) is defined as the land or sea area within the limits of which armed forces during war execute a single strategic mission. The boundaries of probable theaters of war, along the front and in depth, are established in consideration of their political-economic and military-geographic conditions, and also the possibilities of deploying the forces and material on one or more fronts (fleets)."[11] Geographic theaters of military operations (TVDs) may be land or sea areas, or mixtures of the two. Politically, a TVD may include the territory of Soviet/Warsaw Pact countries and "that of the enemy as well," and "its boundaries may change in the course of the war."[12]

To the Soviets, NATO probably represents at least three, and probably four, TVDs (one or two in central Europe and one on the north and south flanks) for the conduct of strategic nuclear operations. China, Japan, Korea, and Okinawa probably constitute another TVD (or two). Finally, there is the "transoceanic" TVD: the United States and its military bases in the Atlantic and Pacific basins. To the Soviets, each of these TVDs is equally "strategic," although the central European TVD(s) may be *first* among equals in Soviet strategic force planning and resource planning. The Soviets have deployed, and continue to deploy, four basic types of strategic weapons systems for strategic nuclear operations in all of the prospective TVDs: IR/MRBMs, SLBMs, medium and heavy bombers, and ICBMs. In the Soviet scheme of things, all these strategic weapons systems are *equally* strategic.

APPLICATION OF SOVIET NUCLEAR TARGETING STRATEGY IN THE TVDs

Certain general factors affecting the conduct of strategic nuclear operations in the TVDs are stated in Soviet literature. Although these factors apply to all TVDs, variations probably exist because: (1) the Soviets recognize the differences in the target arrays found in each TVD; and (2) Soviet politico-military objectives vary somewhat among the prospective TVDs. The principal factors governing the application of targeting strategy to each TVD appear to be:

1. The political objectives set by the Soviet political leaders.
2. The nature and objectives of planned Soviet military operations in each theater.
3. The requirement to limit collateral damage to population, industry, and urban infrastructure commensurate with achieving miliary objectives.

4. The choice of the most vulnerable component(s) of the targets to be attacked.

Although these factors have been either explicitly stated or inferred from Soviet unclassified military and political literature for nearly two decades, they have not been widely accepted in the West. Several statements from *Military Thought,* the journal of the Soviet General Staff, deserve to be quoted at length:

> Political factors and the fact that both warring sides have nuclear weapons exert the main influence on the course of the war as a whole and also on the conduct of its basic operations. This is explained, first of all, by the fact that a modern world war, if the imperialists unleash one, will be a struggle between two opposed social systems in which the belligerents will pursue their own decisive political ends.[13]

> Theses of Soviet military strategy primarily reflect the political strategy of the Communist Party of the Soviet Union. It is in the interests of political strategy that military strategy makes use of the achievements of scientific-technical progress which materializes in weapons of varying power. Some of these weapons are capable of doing considerable damage to a continent. Others only to individual states. This would retard the social progress of their peoples for a long time. *Finally, still others lead to defeat of the enemy's armed forces without doing essential injury to the economy or populace of states whose aggressive rulers unleashed the war. Only political leadership can determine the scale and consistency of bringing to bear the most powerful means of destruction, in accordance with the interests of all mankind as a whole, the interests of the world communist movement and the national interests of Soviet citizens.*
>   Of all factors which affect military strategy, the most important are political factors, which determine the nature of armed forces. *This influence is due essentially to the role played by the military doctrine of the state, which officially consolidates specific principles, methods and forms of preparing for and waging war in case of an attack by imperialist aggressors.*[14]

Another good example of Soviet concern for limiting collateral damage is contained in the following statement:

> The most important task is to correctly determine economic objectives and targets and vulnerable points, and to deliver strikes to those targets where it will lead to disorganization of the enemy economy. *The objective is not to turn the large economic and industrial regions into a heap of ruins* (although great destruction, apparently, is unavoidable), *but to deliver strikes which will destroy strategic combat means, paralyze enemy military production, making it incapable of satisfying the priority needs of the front and rear areas and sharply reduce the enemy capability to conduct strikes.*[15]

This general principle of destroying only what is necessary to achieve Soviet political and military objectives is further expressed in discussions of what are the most vulnerable (i.e., vital) components of any given target array. Some of this discussion is related to contemporary economies; some of it appears in Soviet critiques of Allied strategic bombing operations in World War II.

In planning attacks on industrial target arrays, Colonel M. Shirokov stresses analysis of the regional distribution of industry and interindustry relationships; the destruction of plants and facilities engaged in the production of missiles, nuclear weapons, and other modern weapons; and determination of "the quantity of forces and means required for the destruction of the target and the capabilities of the enemy to rebuild."[16] He goes on to say that destruction of one or two key branches of transportation may be sufficient to sap or "significantly weaken" a country's military potential.[17] Similarly, it may not be necessary to attack all the plants and facilities engaged in missile production, since it is "sufficient to destroy a few enterprises producing transistors in order to extremely restrict the production of missiles for all branches of the armed forces."[18]

In general, Shirokov considers the following economic activities to be the most lucrative targets in terms of prohibiting the enemy from replacing the nuclear delivery systems, nuclear weapons, and other military assets to be destroyed as first priority targets. Targeting these activities also limits enemy capabilities to employ surviving military forces effectively.

Transportation.
Power stations.
Facilities producing liquid fuels.
Chemical industries.
Selected bottleneck facilities in other industries.[19]

As many other Soviet writers have done from time to time, Shirokov does not consider general attacks on all types of industrial targets to be either necessary or militarily effective, and he is particularly critical of the political and military futility of attacking population and cities.

Most of the latter arguments appear in Soviet critiques of Allied strategic air operations in World War II, for which the Soviets display considerable practical and moral disdain. Their analyses of the military effect of Allied bombing of German and Japanese industry and cities are not much different from the findings of the U.S. Strategic Bombing Survey, or from the observations of Albert Speer.[20] The Soviets also note that until nearly the very end of World War II when the Allies systematically concentrated on German facilities producing liquid fuel and on selected components of the rail and barge transport systems, German war production showed steady growth. At the same time, the Soviets give the Allied strategic bombing campaign no credit for tying down large German military assets for air defense. If all of those fighter aircraft and 88-mm guns had been deployed on the Eastern front, Soviet ground campaigns would have suffered greatly.[21]

As is generally agreed, bombing German cities did not break German civilian morale. Indeed, the bombing may have increased popular support for the German war effort. Shirokov comments at length about U.S. incendiary-bomb attacks on Japanese cities, concluding: "However, these barbarous bombings did not seriously affect enemy morale."[22] He then notes that Hiroshima and Nagasaki "were pointlessly destroyed and burned" and goes on to charge that the bombing of Japanese cities were designed to intimidate the Soviet Union rather than to break Japanese morale.[23] Other Soviets have made the same charge about the militarily pointless destruction of Dresden at the close of World War II in Europe.

Finally, Shirokov charges that the United States deliberately refrained from destroying Tokyo because it would have "impeded the U.S. negotiations with the Japanese reactionaries, with whom they proposed to find a common language."[24]

In these discussions on how to conduct nuclear war and target nuclear weapons, the Soviets conspicuously do not consider population and cities valid targets on political, military, and moral grounds. Rather, they consider such targeting concepts as "mutual assured destruction" to be yet another manifestation of the evils of "imperialism." After all, the Soviets want to promote "social progress," not inhibit it, as long as such progress meets their political and social criteria. On the other hand, this does not mean that the Soviets would not target some selected population groups, such as business and government elites — the "ruling groups" who are the "class enemy" — and possibly selected concentrations of "scientific-technical personnel" as well.[25] But any targeting of selected population groups evidently would meet specific political and military-industrial criteria and would not be extended to the general population, whom the Soviets prefer to preserve if possible.

POSSIBLE VARIATIONS IN TARGETING STRATEGY BY TVD

Just as individual TVDs present different target arrays, Soviet politico-military objectives are not uniform for every TVD. In the European TVDs, Soviet objectives are clear: to defeat and disarm NATO forces and occupy as intact a Western Europe as possible. The Soviets want to limit collateral damage to Western Europe for several reasons. Politically, they wish to bring their version of "social progress" to Western Europe in the wake of the next war, just as Eastern Europe was "liberated" after World War II.[26] The Soviets continue to express their belief that the next war will be the grave of capitalistic democracies everywhere and will usher in the era of world "socialism." However, they also believe that they can achieve the same objective without nuclear war and would much prefer to do so. As one of their leading military commissars put it recently:

> Peaceful coexistence between nations with a difference in social systems is an essential, mandatory condition for the upward movement of society, to secure progress and its main content — transition from a capitalist to a socialist socio-economic system. . . . The military might of the USSR constitutes a guarantee of peace, for our social system does not contain sources of war. On the other hand, there are constantly operating in the imperialist camp forces capable of disrupting the peace. Sources of war are to be found in the socio-economic system, in the very nature of "Imperialism."[27]

Whether they are to achieve their political objectives by "peaceful coexistence" or as the outcome of war, the Soviets need strategic nuclear forces commensurate with those objectives. This means forces that will accomplish the necessary military objectives but that will not destroy the human, social, and economic basis for the socioeconomic system that is to replace "imperialism."[28] They are not likely to negotiate away the right to acquire such forces in SALT.

There are two other very practical considerations guiding Soviet nuclear targeting in the European TVDs. First, the prevailing winds are westerly, so it is very much in the Soviet interest to target selectively, avoiding "overkill" with large weapons in order to limit fallout, not only on Eastern Europe and the Soviet Union, but also on the Soviet/Warsaw Pact occupation forces. Second, the Soviets could make good use of Europe's economic resources during the course of military operations, thereby helping to rebuild their own resources in the aftermath of a nuclear war:

> The destructive nature of modern warfare, the difficulty of transporting material means from the depth of a country and the great vulnerability of rear area organs make it necessary to devote serious attention to a study of the possibilities for acquiring local resources in theaters of military operations. For this purpose, *it is very important to determine which targets and enemy economic regions should be left intact or rapidly reconstructed and used in the interests of strengthening the economic potential of our own country and for supplying the troops.* It is also important to determine which, what, where and in what quantity the local resources can be stored and used in the interest of the troops.[29]

In the Far East, Soviet objectives probably would be more complex. They might wish to occupy sparsely populated regions outside the Great Wall, and possibly Manchuria, but they probably consider it quite infeasible to occupy China proper, where the population density would support a "people's war." In the latter area, the Soviets probably would use strategic nuclear force to disarm the country and to destroy sufficient industrial and transportation facilities to insure that China would not become a threat — nuclear or otherwise — to the Soviet Union for some time. Against Japan, on the other hand, Soviet targeting might be much more selective because Japan, like Europe, could contribute to Soviet postattack recovery.

Then there is the question of that other TVD — the "transoceanic" one. All the evidence known to this author explicitly or implicitly indicates that Soviet nuclear targeting strategy for the United States is the same as for other TVDs. On the other hand, since the Soviets have no ambition to occupy the United States, they must seek not only to destroy our existing military forces at the beginning of the war, but also to prevent us from reconstituting those forces. Hence, Soviet targeting of industry might be more extensive in the United States than in Europe and Japan. And if the Soviets target selected cities, then such targeting also could be more comprehensive against the United States than against Europe. In all TVDs, however, Soviet literature indicates that Soviet nuclear targeting would be selective with regard both to the targets attacked and to the degree of damage inflicted.[30]

ORIGINS OF SOVIET TARGETING STRATEGY

Despite his public statements denigrating nuclear weapons and the internal restrictions that he imposed on discussions of their military significance, Stalin probably understood their political and military potential quite well. He spared no effort to develop nuclear weapons as rapidly as possible and gave equal priority to the acquisition of strategic nuclear delivery systems. Soviet nuclear targeting strategy evidently was formulated in the late 1940s or early 1950s by Long Range Aviation in anticipation of having nuclear weapons.[31]

It is often forgotten that soon after World War II, the Soviets produced a large force of strategic bombers copied after the U.S. B-29 aircraft that came to earth in the Soviet Far East during U.S. bombing attacks on Japan. The medium and heavy jet bombers that shocked the United States when they appeared in the mid-1950s, and which precipitated the "bomber gap," were the result of programs initiated under Stalin.

Recent articles by General Tolubko, commander of Soviet Strategic Rocket Troops since 1972, throw fresh light on Stalin's appreciation of both nuclear weapons and strategic missile delivery systems, and on the participation of L. I. Brezhnev in associated developmental programs.[32] The first operational unit for future ballistic missile delivery systems was formed in 1946 on the basis of a tactical rocket regiment.[33] Research organizations and design bureaus for ballistic missiles were formed around a scientific-engineering cadre of people — S. P. Korolev, M. K. Iangel, V. P. Glushko, G. N. Babakin, and others — who became the "chief designers" of many contemporary Soviet strategic missile and space systems.[34] Shortly after World War II, a supraministerial organization charged with missile development was attached directly to the U.S.S.R. Council of Ministers.[35] Among those who served on that board of missile tsars were such prominent marshals of the Soviet Union as G. K. Zhukov and R. Ia. Malinovskiy, as well as Chief Marshals of Artillery N. N. Voronov and M. I. Nedelin.[36] Two nominal civilians who served as missile tsars are still prominent: L. I. Brezhnev, First Secretary of the Communist party since 1964 and marshal of the Soviet Union since 1976, and D. F. Ustinov, Central Committee member of the Military Industrial Commission (VPK) for more than a decade and marshal of the Soviet Union and minister of defense since 1976.[37]

As a result of the organizational efforts begun under Stalin, the Soviets were able to arm some of their missile units with nuclear weapons in the mid-1950s.[38] These units apparently included not only tactical missiles but also the first Soviet strategic missile, the MRBM designated as the SS-3 by the United States and NATO. Operationally, all the strategic missiles — the early SS-3 and later SS-4 MRBMs — may have been under Long Range Aviation before the Strategic Rocket Troops were formed as a new branch of service in 1960. Alternatively, the early strategic missile units may have been directly controlled by the Council of Defense.[39] In any case, from the beginning, the missile units evidently shared Long Range Avation's nuclear targeting strategy and carried it over to the Strategic Rocket Troops (SRT).

It is essential to understand that when formed in 1960, the SRT consisted entirely of MRBM units, with the possible exception of a handful of SS-6 ICBMs, and that the SRT had more IR/MRBMs than ICBMs until 1968–1969. Thus, early Soviet missile targeting focused on the European and Asian TVDs. The "transoceanic" TVD came later.

The relevance of this historical background for SALT lies in an awareness of the long intellectual and institutional lineage of Soviet nuclear targeting strategy and of the linkage of both Brezhnev and Ustinov to Soviet missile development and targeting. Any limit or reduction in total delivery vehicles or "heavy" Icbms would force the Soviets to reexamine their targeting and the political-military objectives they can achieve — or would be denied — under various limits. These are "gut" issues for both political and military Soviet leaders in the SALT process.

THE INFLUENCE OF SOVIET TARGETING STRATEGY ON SOVIET SALT POSITIONS

Having surveyed the necessary historical background, we now return to the question of how Soviet targeting strategy has affected the specifics of the SALT negotiations and agreements. It will be argued that several aspects of both the SALT I accords and the Vladivostok understanding were greatly influenced by the objectives of Soviet nuclear targeting strategy as previously outlined and by the strategic force requirements derived therefrom. Other factors, of course, were at work in the SALT process, not least of which was the Soviet fear of the consequences of the ten-to-fifteen-year lead the United States had in ABM technology when SALT began. Understanding the implications of Soviet nuclear targeting is not the only necessary and sufficient condition for understanding what has happened in the SALT process, but it is *one* necessary condition.

Specifically, Soviet nuclear targeting strategy appears to have played an essential role in the Interim Agreement on Offensive Forces signed by the two superpowers in May 1972 and in the negotiations leading to the agreement. That role was evidenced in the following ways:

1. The Soviet attempt to include in the U.S. strategic aggregate those U.S. tactical aircraft and missiles deployed in Europe that conceivably could deliver nuclear weapons in Soviet territory, the so-called forward-based (FBS) systems.
2. The relatively high ceilings — far more than required to destroy U.S. cities under the most adverse second-strike conditions — of about 1,600 launchers placed on Soviet Icbms and 740 to 950 launchers on Soviet SLBMs.[40,41]
3. The Soviet refusal to join in the U.S. unilateral declaration designed to limit the payload (throw weight) of all but the largest (the SS-18) of the four Soviet Icbms now being deployed.
4. The absence of any constraints on the development of the current generation of Icbms and SLBMs (the early prototypes of which were already at or en route to the flight-test range when the Interim Agreement was signed) or of the generation now under development.

Similarly, the limits agreed upon at Vladivostok, as well as Soviet insistence that the Vladivostok understanding serve as the basis for limits on offensive systems after October 1977, are intimately bound up in the requirements of Soviet targeting strategy. At Vladivostok it was agreed that both sides could have 2,400 "strategic" delivery systems, freedom to mix systems, and 1,320 MIRVed missiles, while the Soviets could retain just over 300 "heavy" ICBMs (308 seems to be the precise number of "heavy" ICBM silos, although 326 also is often mentioned).

VARIATIONS IN GEOGRAPHIC TVD TARGET CHARACTERISTICS AND THE EFFECTIVENESS OF SOVIET MISSILE FORCES

To demonstrate the relationship between past SALT agreements and Soviet reactions to U.S. proposals presented in March and April 1977 on new SALT agreements, some additional analysis of background is necessary. In the European TVDs generally, and in NATO particularly, most of the targets are relatively "soft," which is to say that nuclear weapons with sub-megaton, rather than multimegaton, yields are adequate even with relatively inaccurate missiles. As missile accuracy improves, even smaller weapons (in terms of yield) will suffice unless something is done to make the targets less vulnerable.

Between 1958 and 1964, the U.S.S.R. deployed a force of over 700 SS-4 and SS-5 IR/MRBMs, backed up by about 100 SLBMs, to deal with all classes of targets, mostly soft, in Eurasian TVDs. As further insurance, the Soviets maintained most of the Long Range Aviation medium and heavy bombers they had built in the late 1950s. Given the state of missile technology at that time, the SS-4 and SS-5 missiles were not particularly accurate. But since most targets in the Eurasian TVDs were (and still are) soft (i.e., 15 psi or less), these relatively inaccurate missiles were effective with warheads yielding kilotons (KT) rather than megatons (MT).

Table 1 shows the effectiveness of missiles of various accuracy (CEP for "circular error probable" — 50 percent) against targets in the 8-to-100 psi range (PVN 8 to 25).[42] Most targets in Eurasia TVDs fall in the 5-to-15 psi range. The low end of the CEP range, 0.25 nm, has been reported for the SS-20.[43] The upper portion of the range probably is an adequate approximation of the CEP of the SS-4 and SS-5 strategic missiles deployed fifteen to twenty years ago. As can be seen from the single-shot-probability-kill (SSPK) calculations in Table 1, most targets in the Eurasian TVDs could be destroyed with weapons in the 50-to-500 KT range if missile CEPs were in

Table 1.   Strategic Missiles' Effectiveness (SSPK) as Function of CEP, Yield, and Target Vulnerability for Targets in the Eurasian TVDs

	CEP 1.0 nm						
Megatons PVN	0.05	0.15	0.5	1.0	2.0	3.0	5.0
24.5							0.54
21						0.60	0.70
18			0.42	0.57	0.72	0.81	0.89
12		0.64	0.88	0.95	0.98+	0.99+	0.99+
8	0.73	0.91	0.98+	0.99+	0.99+	0.99+	0.99+
	CEP 0.7 nm						
Megatons PVN	0.05	0.15	0.5	1.0	2.0	3.0	5.0
24.5				0.42	0.54	0.66	0.77
21			0.43	0.58	0.73	0.82	0.90
18		0.60	0.65	0.80	0.90	0.94	0.97
12	0.64	0.91	0.97	0.99+	0.99+	0.99+	0.99+
8	0.90	0.98	0.99+	0.99+	0.99+	0.99+	0.99+
	CEP 0.25 nm						
Megatons PVN	0.05	0.15	0.5	1.0	2.0	3.0	5.0
24.5		0.67	0.90	0.96			
21		0.83	0.96	0.99			
18	0.81	0.95	0.99+	0.99+			
12	0.99	0.99+	0.99+	0.99+			
8	0.99+	0.99+	0.99+	0.99+			

the 0.5 to 1.0 nm range, which probably is the best the Soviets could have achieved with IR/MRBMs designed in the 1950s.

In the transoceanic TVDs, however, target vulnerabilities are much more varied. SAC airfields in the United States were as "soft" as tactical airfields in Europe until we built hangarettes designed to withstand direct hits from iron bombs for our tactical aircraft in Europe. Many military targets and virtually all industrial targets located in the United States are as soft as their Eurasian counterparts. Megaton weapons are as superflous against many targets in the United States as they are against most targets in Eurasia. But the United States contains a large number of really "hard" targets — over 1,100 ICBM silos and launch control centers, storage facilities for nuclear weapons, and command and control facilities — that have few, if any, counterparts in Eurasia. Destruction of these targets would require over-pressures of several hundred to several thousand psi. Given the CEPs of Soviet ICBMs, the hard targets located in the United States require multi-megaton weapons.

Table 2 illustrates this difference in vulnerability between most Eurasian targets and the missile silos and storage facilities for nuclear weapons located in the United States. Compared to Eurasia, first-priority targets in the United States, except for SAC airfields, are much "harder nuts to crack." For first- and second-generation Soviet ICBMs — SS-6, SS-7, SS-8, SS-9, and S-11 — very large yields (on the order of at least 5 to 25 megatons) would have been required to destroy the U.S. storage sites for

Table 2. Yield and Accuracy Relationships for Hard Targets in the U.S. (The "Transoceanic" TVD)

PVN	Yield MT (Megatons)			
	2	5	10	25
		CEP 1.0 nm		
37–38	0.28	0.41	0.57	0.76
41–42				0.60
		CEP 0.5 nm		
37–38	0.71	0.85	0.94	0.99+
41–42	0.54	0.74	0.87	0.98
45–46	0.37	0.56	0.72	0.82
47–49			0.60	0.75
		CEP 0.25 nm		
37–38	0.95	0.98	0.99+	0.99+
41–42	0.85	0.96	0.98	0.98
45–46	0.70	0.87	0.95	0.96
47–49	0.61	0.77	0.89	
		CEP 0.15 nm		
37–38	0.99+			
41–42	0.97	0.99+		
45–46	0.91	0.98		
47–49	0.86	0.94		

ICBM launchers and nuclear weapons because first- and second-generation Soviets ICBMs, like their IR/MRBMs, could hardly have had CEPs of less than 0.5 to 1.0 nm.[44] The same reasoning applied to the SS-N-6 and SS-N-8 SLBMs on Yankee- and Delta-class submarines.

Even if contemporary Soviet ICBMs have the same CEP to intercontinental ranges as the SS-20 to continental ranges (i.e., around 0.25 nm), multimegaton yields still are required to destroy U.S. missiles and weapons storage.[45] It will take the next generation of Soviet ICBMs to do the job, and even these ICBMs probably will require megaton weapons because until the CEPs of Soviet MIRVs are reduced to one-tenth of a nautical mile or less, the probability of killing hardened U.S. missile launchers with smaller weapons is too low for a planner's comfort.

When attacking soft targets, wider variations in CEP factors are tolerable since the probability of damage is not very sensitive to small differences in planned versus actual CEPs. But against hard targets, particularly ICBMs that can reach the Soviet Union in thirty minutes if not destroyed, Soviet planners probably want very high confidence factors. And because of the danger of fratricide and other characteristics of a nuclear-attack environment, multiple attacks on each ICBM silo are low confidence. For high confidence, one-to-one attacks must be effective, and this means megaton weapons until CEPs drop to less than 0.1 nm.

These requirements for large yields to compensate for the modest accuracy of Soviet strategic missile systems when attacking hard targets in all TVDs led the Soviets to develop large warheads in the 1950s and 1960s. Such development in turn led to the very questionable perception that since all Soviet strategic missiles could deliver multimegaton weapons, each and every missile in the Soviet inventory was armed with as much megatonage as the missile could carry. This perception, together with the popular "mirror image" that the Soviets target population masses, (a strategy that the United States proclaims in public but does not pursue in fact),[46] makes restraint of "overkill" of cities one of the perceived functions of the SALT process.

CAPABILITIES OF DEPLOYED SOVIET STRATEGIC MISSILES AND THE SALT PROCESS

As has been noted, by the mid-1960s the Soviets had enough strategic missiles to destroy targets in Europe and pave the way for the Soviet tactical nuclear offensive designed to defeat and disarm NATO forces and to occupy Europe. Only a few of these missiles needed warheads in the megaton range. The use of weapons for the most part in the 50-to-500 KT range and selective targeting according to the principles stated in the *Military Thought* articles cited earlier would make occupation feasible and worthwhile. Much European industry and most cities would be intact so that Europe could not only recover but could also aid Soviet recovery.

However, in the transoceanic TVD where most of the hard targets requiring large yields were located, Soviet forces fell far short of their requirements. Moreover, a large number of military bases and facilities in Asia and in the Pacific and Atlantic basins were out of range of Soviet IR/MRBMs. Thus, given the missile-guidance technology of the early 1960s, multimegaton yields were required for some 100 to 1,200 targets — U.S. missile launchers, nuclear-weapons storage sites, hardened command-control facilities — in the transoceanic TVD. At the same time, the large number of soft military and industrial targets located beyond IR/MRBM range required large numbers of ICBMs and SLBM launchers armed with the kiloton weapons that were adequate for most targets in the Eurasian TVDs.

Lack of understanding of Soviet targets strategy and requirements, plus failure to read what the Soviets say or to give Soviet literature any credence if in fact it is read, has created such Western perceptions of Soviet targeting as the following:

One of the most disquieting aspects of Soviet doctrine is its implication that something called "victory" could emerge from a full-scale theater nuclear war. The term presumably refers to the destruction of enemy forces and occupation of vital areas of territory. However, "mass employment of nuclear weapons" as the preferred means of realizing those objectives almost certainly would entail enormous civilian and military casualties as well as the utter ruin of much, if not most, of the territory to be occupied. Also not to be discounted is the probable transformation of large areas into radioactive "deserts" incapable of supporting human or plant life.

This judgment appears eminently realistic with respect to densely populated Europe, where an estimated 2,250 Soviet TNW confront a NATO deployment of some 7,000. Even a massive employment of Soviet TNW that did not provoke a nuclear response from NATO would deprive Europe of any industrial or agricultural value that might otherwise accrue to the USSR. Over two-thirds of Soviet TNW are believed to possess yields well in excess of the 13-kiloton Hiroshima bomb; more than 500 contain yields ranging from 1/2 to 3 megatons.[47]

In fact, inflicting such damage on Europe is the last thing the Soviets want to do since it would deny them the principal political and military objectives they wish to achieve in the event of war with NATO. And as far as can be determined, they do not desire to inflict the kind of damage that the above quote depicts either on Europe or on the United States. As has been noted, the Soviets might well plan to destroy more industry and transport facilities, and perhaps more selected population groups as well, in the transoceanic TVD than in the European TVDs because they do not plan to occupy the United States and do not expect to draw upon U.S. resources to aid their recovery. Otherwise, however, their targeting strategy appears to apply equally to all TVDs.

When the SALT negotiations started in 1969, the Soviets were far short of the forces they needed to satisfy their targeting requirements in the transoceanic TVD. By the middle of 1969, the Soviets had about 1,000 ICBMs, some (several operational) Yankee-class SLBMs, and many more of such missiles in process, but the force was still much too small and inaccurate to be effective.[48] Originally designed to immobilize the U.S. ICBMs by destroying the 100 launch control centers that controlled the 1,000 Minuteman ICBM launchers, the SS-9 deployments were frustrated by the U.S. airborne launch control system, which can launch missiles from each silo even if the control centers are destroyed. Building enough SS-9s to attack every Minuteman silo was not a feasible course of action. The Soviets experimented with a three RV version of the SS-9 that probably was an attempt to acquire a limited MIRV against the silos, which are relatively closely spaced.[49] But this approach either did not work or, more likely, was dropped in anticipation of achieving full MIRV technology.[50] However, the first generation of true Soviet MIRVed ICBMs, probably approved for development in 1966 and part of the military programs of the Eighth Five-Year Plan, were still three years from flight testing when SALT began. Even with improvements in accuracy, the current generation of new systems (SS-16 through SS-18) required much larger payloads (throw weight) to carry MIRVs with megaton yields.[51]

In 1969 Soviet requirements for hitting soft targets in the transoceanic TVD were also far from being satisfied. The new SS-11 ICBM and the SS-N-6 SLBM were effective against such targets, with warheads in the KT range in most cases, but there were so many targets. Although a complete list of U.S. and allied military bases and facilities located in Asia (beyond IRBM range), as well as in the Atlantic and Pacific basins and in the United States and Alaska, is hard to acquire, the number must be at least on the order of 600 and possibly over 1,000.[52] Some of these are large complex installations requiring several warheads to destroy all the facilities at each installation. In addition, there are all the industrial, transportation, communications, and administrative targets specified by Soviet targeting strategy.

It is no wonder, therefore, that the Soviets stretched out SALT until they had some 1,600 ICBMs; agreed only very reluctantly to a limit of just over 300 launchers for SS-9 type ICBMs ("heavy missiles" in SALT jargon); and insisted on an upper limit of 720 to 950 SLBMs.[53] Equally unsurprising, the SALT agreements were not concluded until the Soviets were nearly ready to start flight-testing their four new ICBMs in 1972, all of which have the MIRV system required to cover all the targets.[54] As has been noted, the United States tried to limit the throw weight of all new missiles, except the successor to the SS-9 "heavy missile," to roughly the throw weight of the SS-11. However, this was futile since the new liquid-fuel successors to the SS-11, the SS-17, and SS-19 were designed in 1965–1966 as heavy missiles, having throw weights approximately two to three times that of the SS-11[55] in order to carry enough MIRVed warheads to cover the entire target array in the transoceanic TVD and other areas outside the range of the IR/MRBMs.[56]

This is not to argue that the Soviets made no concessions at all in SALT. They may have intended to replace many, even all, of their IR/MRBMs with ICBMs, which began to be deployed with IR/MRBM units shortly after the SALT negotiations began.[57] On the other hand, they may have intended to replace most of the SS-4 and SS-5 missiles with the SS-20 from the beginning, inasmuch as the latter missile is the first two stages of the SS-16 ICBM.[58] Most important, they probably intended to build many more SS-9 type of silos than the some 308 launchers of this type to which they finally agreed.[59] Because the Soviets desperately wanted agreements to prohibit large-scale U.S. ABM deployment, which would have frustrated all their nuclear targeting ambitions and, in their view, would have given the United States a great military advantage,[60] the Soviets had to make some concessions. But the limit of the SS-9 type of silo is about the only concession that mattered since the unconstrained SS-20 will more than make up for ICBMs the Soviets may have planned as replacements for their SS-4 and SS-5 MR/IRBMs.

Although the SALT agreements permitted the Soviets to go ahead with their new ICBMs and placed no restrictions on the SS-20, which will be much more effective than the SS-4s and SS-5s for strategic operations in the Eurasian TVDs and will reduce collateral damage as well, satisfying the requirements of Soviet targeting strategy in the transoceanic TVD will require yet another generation of ICBMs.[61] The next generation of Soviet strategic missiles, which is now being developed,[62] will provide the large MIRVed force to cover all of the military and industrial targets.

The Vladivostok agreement limiting Soviet peripheral (i.e., transoceanic) strategic delivery systems to 2,400, without placing any limits on central So-

viet strategic systems for the Eurasian TVDs, was made to order for the Soviets.[63] Development of the next generation of Soviet ICBMs probably had
been approved in 1970–1971 as part of the Ninth Five-Year Plan's military
programs, and flight testing probably will begin in 1979–1980.

Anticipating the Vladivostok limits in 1975–1976, the Soviets approved
completion of development and initial deployments of the new systems as
part of the Tenth Five-Year Plan's military programs. Sometimes in the
early to mid-1980s, the combination of the current and next generation of
ICBM and SLBM systems should finally provide sufficient accuracy and
enough warheads to satisfy the transoceanic TVD requirements that Soviet
military planners have been struggling to meet since the late 1950s.

To be sure, two weapons systems continue to pose difficulties: the Soviet
Backfire bomber and the American cruise missile. Contrary to U.S. suspicions, the Soviets probably have been resistant to including Backfire in
SALT precisely because they *do* plan to use it primarily in Eurasia rather
than in the transoceanic TVD. Backfire's range probably was not designed
to employ the aircraft in the transoceanic TVD but, rather, to satisfy requirements of Soviet Naval Aviation for a longer-range, more effective medium bomber than the aging Badgers for attacks on U.S./NATO forces.

Cruise missiles pose a different set of problems. First, proposed U.S.
cruise missile launchers would vary from very difficult to impossible to target. Second, the cruise missile greatly complicates Soviet air defense problems. Contrary to all the logic of the ABM Treaty as understood in the
United States, the Soviets have continued to expand and modernize their air
defenses as part of their strategy to fight and win a nuclear war. But the
cruise missile is a tougher threat to defend against than a manned bomber;
hence, the greater Soviet concern about the cruise missile than the B-1
bomber.[64]

NEWLY RELEASED INFORMATION ON
SOVIET STRATEGIC MISSILERY

Data on Soviet strategic missile accuracies and yields released in the fall of
1977 provide the basis for a more realistic assessment of what the Soviets
have been doing and why. Figure 1 shows the trend in the accuracy of Soviet
strategic weapon systems. Note the sharply declining trend from the initial
systems deployed two decades ago to current and projected future systems.

Some might argue that the increase in Soviet missile accuracy is accidental — the result of bureaucratic inertia in the design bureaus, of engineers
doing their own thing without guidance or direction. There are three objec-

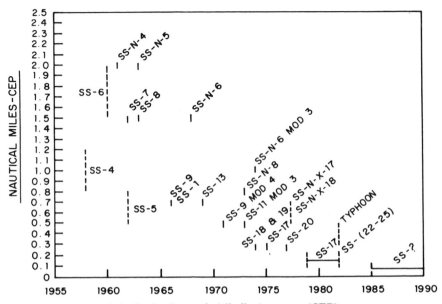

FIGURE 1.   Trends in Soviet Strategic Missile Accuracy (CEP)

Source: Estimates for all numbered ICBMs, except the SS-6, and for all SLBMs, except SS-NX-17 and SS-NX-18, are from John M. Collins, "American and Soviet Armed Services, Strengths Compared, 1970–1976," U.S. Congress, Senate, *Congressional Record,* no. 135, pt. 3 (August 5, 1977):S14072–73. Other systems shown in broken lines appear to be plausible estimates based on the general trend displayed by the systems for what Collins reports are the values. Each of the reported values has an unspecified range of uncertainty, but there is no question about the trend. The CEP of the SS-20 was reported by Henry S. Bradsher, "U.S. Offer Leaves Soviets Ahead in Blast Power," *Washington Star,* April 8, 1977. Later modifications of the SS-18 and SS-19 reportedly have achieved CEPs on the order of 0.1 nm; see John M. Collins, *American and Soviet Military Trends since the Cuban Missile Crisis* (Washington, D.C.: Center for Strategic and International Studies, Georgetown University, 1978), p. 120, note 69.

tions to this type of explanation. First, there appears to be no evidence to support it. Second, too many billions of rubles — representing the scarcest resources (except perhaps grain) in the Soviet Union — are involved. The Politburo, the VPK, the U.S.S.R. Gosplan, and the Ministry of Finance do not allow design bureaus and engineers such latitude with the state's resources.[65] Third, there is a more plausible interpretation: accuracy must be increased to achieve effective counterforce capabilities against hard targets and to damage soft targets to the degree desired while limiting collateral damage by using smaller warheads.

The latter point is illustrated in Table 3 where the accuracy data are combined with reported yields to compute the probability of target destruction (with one weapon).[66] Note that as accuracy increases and yields decline, effectiveness against most industrial and military targets — except missile silos, hardened command-control installations, and the like — holds constant or improves with each generation. As noted in the footnote to Table 3, the yields reported for the SS-17 and SS-19 MIRV may not be the maximum these missiles can carry, given their large throw weight. But 0.2 MT may well be a representative yield because it is effective up to 30 to 40 psi. (Most industrial and military targets are 5 to 15 psi).

The analysis in Table 3 also illustrates the Soviet requirement for future generations of strategic missile systems. As has been noted, even the SS-18 is marginal for its primary mission of destroying hard targets. The SS-17 and SS-19 MIRV versions apparently are effective only against soft targets (up to about 100 psi). For flexibility and greater effectiveness the Soviets probably want at least two of their ICBMs to be effective against hard targets. Meanwhile, the SLBMs still are relatively inaccurate in that the yields required are much larger than for the current ICBMs. Deployment of one or both of the two new SLBMs — the SS-NX-17 and SS-NX-18 — probably will improve force characteristics considerably. Development of the Typhoon system should make Soviet SLBM capabilities at least comparable to the current SS-17 and SS-19 ICBMs.[67]

Trends in Soviet ICBM and SLBM accuracy and yield therefore seem best explained as the product not only of institutional continuity and technological opportunity but also of Soviet strategic requirements to be able to destroy both hard and soft targets while limiting collateral damage in order to fight and survive a nuclear war. The Soviets apparently want to limit "overkill" of cities for their own political, strategic, and economic reasons. SALT is not particularly relevant to Soviet decisions on weapons characteristics and strategic objectives.

SOVIET STRATEGIC NUCLEAR FORCES AND RECENT U.S. SALT PROPOSALS

Against this background, the negative Soviet response to the U.S. SALT proposals of March and April 1977 becomes more understandable. A variety of factors were, of course, at work. The Soviets probably quite genuinely expected negotiations with the Carter administration to take place within the framework of the Vladivostok agreement. As much as they have tried to separate their anger over having civil rights in the Soviet Union made a public issue, there has been some linkage with SALT.[68] The Soviet

Table 3.   Trends in the Effectiveness of Selected Soviet Strategic Missile Systems (SSPK %)

Weapon System	CEP (nm)	Yield (MT)	PVN[a]				
			8	12	18	21	24.5
SS-7	1.5	5.0	0.99	0.97	0.66	0.44	0.30
SS-11 MOD 1	0.7	1.0	0.99+	0.99+	0.80	0.58	0.42
	0.7	2.0	0.99+	0.99+	0.90	0.74	0.57
SS-11 MOD 2	0.5	1.0	0.99+	0.99+	0.94	0.80	0.64
	0.5	0.5	0.99+	0.99+	0.85	0.65	0.48
	0.3	1.0	0.99+	0.99+	0.99+	0.97	0.92
	0.3	0.5	0.99+	0.99+	0.98	0.92	0.82
SS-17 MIRV[b]	0.3	0.2	0.99+	0.99+	0.93	0.79	0.64
SS-19 MIRV[b]	0.25	0.2	0.99+	0.99+	0.97	0.88	0.74
SS-17 or SS-19 MIRV[b]	0.2	0.2	0.99+	0.99+	0.99+	0.95	0.87
SS-20	0.25	0.5	0.99+	0.99+	0.99+	0.96	0.90
	0.25	0.2	0.99+	0.99+	0.97	0.88	0.74
SS-N-6	1.5	1.0	0.97	0.79	0.40	0.18	0.12
SS-N-8	0.8	1.0	0.99	0.98	0.72	0.49	0.34

Note: Yields for all systems, except the SS-20, are from John M. Collins, "American and Soviet Armed Services, Strengths Compared, 1970-1976," U.S. Congress, Senate, *Congressional Record*, no. 135, pt. 3 (August 5, 1977):S14072-73. CEP values are from the same source, except for those for the SS-20 and the lower limits of the SS-11 MOD 2 (0.3 nm) and the SS-17 or SS-19 (0.2 nm). The latter are estimates of the CEP of these systems to Eurasian TVD ranges—1,000 to 2,500 nm. Subsequently the International Institute of Strategic Studies (*The Military Balance 1978-1979*, pp. 80–81) has reported the SS-20 yield at 0.15 MT, which is near the lower limit of 0.2 MT shown in Table 3, to be more than adequate for most targets in the Eurasian TVDs. Given the throw weight of the SS-17 and SS-19, the maximum yield of these systems probably is higher, but 0.2 nm is adequate for most industrial and military targets. Based upon missile payload, the maximum yield for SS-17 and SS-19 RVs should be around 0.5 MT.

The SS-9 and SS-18 are not included because they clearly are hard target systems. The effectiveness of the SS-13 probably was comparable to that of the SS-11 MOD 1. Effectiveness of the SS-4 (MRBM) and SS-5 (IRBM) was discussed earlier.

[a]The PVN numbers are representative of soft urban-industrial and semihard military targets in the spectrum from about 5 to about 100 psi.

[b]These systems also are reported to have a single RV variant that presumably would have a yield of several megatons for use against hard targets.

leaders are not a group of total cynics. They believe in their social system and probably look upon their dissidents as ingrates, or worse. Being among the most self-righteous folk around these days, the Soviet leaders do not take kindly to U.S. candor on human rights.[69] But these factors aside, the proposals taken to Moscow by Secretary of State Vance represented arms-control measures that went against the grain of everything the Soviet political and military leaders have been doing, at great expense to the Soviet economy, for the last twenty-five years.

In this context, consider the U.S. proposals of March and April 1977, insofar as they have been released to the public, from a likely Soviet point of view. First, reduce the total number of ICBMs, "modern" SLBMs, and heavy bombers from 2,400 to 1,800. To the Soviets, that means scrapping either a lot of silos scheduled to be retrofitted with new missiles or recently built nuclear ballistic-missile submarines,[70] or some combination of the two. Second, reduce all ICBMs to 550 launchers from each side. Third, limit SS-9/18 "heavy" ICBMs to 150 launchers. Fourth, reduce MIRVed missiles to 1,100 to 1,200 for each side. The combination of these three provisions probably would make it impossible for the Soviets to satisfy their targeting requirements even when the next generation of ICBMs and SLBMs are deployed. Next, prohibit deployment of new or modified ICBMs and limit the number of flight tests per year. These last provisions would preclude development of future systems on which the Soviets already have spent millions of rubles and without which Soviet political and military leaders cannot possibly hope to achieve their strategic objectives.

Accepting all these points would have meant tearing out the Soviet's current Five-Year Plan, to say nothing of dissolving four or five missile-design bureaus and numerous supporting institutions. With such limits, the SRT would be playing second bureaucratic fiddle to the Red Navy. Moreover, had the Soviets accepted all the package proposed by the United States in March and April 1977, then all their efforts, all the sacrifices imposed on the economy over the past two decades for both strategic offensive and strategic defensive forces would have been rendered useless.[71]

Viewed in the context of Soviet nuclear targeting strategy, strategic force development, related strategic considerations, and bureaucratic constituencies that cross the formal lines of the party, military, and industrial bureaucracies, the Soviets' preference for the Vladivostok agreement is hardly surprising. Short of a U.S. threat to resort to unrestricted arms programs if a new agreement on offensive forces is not reached, or within reach, it is difficult to see why the Soviets will come down very far from the 2,400 limit and from freedom to mix mobile and fixed-based missile systems. They can always reduce their forces by a couple of hundred launchers as long as the "heavy" ICBM and MIRVed missile limits remain more or less intact. But it is difficult to discern any Soviet political, strategic, or bureaucratic interest in further reductions unless they are faced with the threat of unrestricted new U.S. strategic offensive and defensive weapons systems.

Moreover, the Soviets are not likely to be receptive to the U.S. proposal to cancel development of the U.S. MX ICBM if the Soviets cancel deployment of the SS-20 IRBM. The Soviets need the SS-20 to replace the SS-4s and SS-5s. They want the SS-20 because it will be more effective militarily and will further reduce collateral damage and fallout. Planned deployment of the SS-20 probably will make it possible to take out the entire NATO target array with no more megatons than the Soviets exploded in their atmospheric nuclear test series in the early 1960s. To quote Generals Semenov and Prokhorov, such an attack would not do "essential injury to the economy or populace of states whose aggressive rulers unleashed the war" in the sense that the shares of Europe's population killed and industry destroyed would be small.[72] Europe would be worth occupying and could help the Soviet Union rebuild if the United States retaliated.

In sum, the Soviets target counterforce rather than countervalue. They are selective in their choice of targets and tailor the yields of the weapons to the vulnerability of the target, given the CEP of the delivery systems, in order to reduce collateral damage. This means that neither Europe nor the U.S. would be turned into "radioactive deserts," at least not by the Soviets, in the event of nuclear war, and that the Soviets will reduce the inevitable collateral damage of a nuclear war as they improve the accuracy of their strategic missiles. On the other hand, because the number of counterforce, selective industrial, transport, and administrative targets in all of the TVDs is large, the Soviets need high ceilings in total launchers, MIRVed missiles, and "heavy" ICBMs. For clear and obvious military reasons, therefore, the Soviets are not likely to agree to more than token cuts in the ceilings specified by the Vladivostok accord. Meanwhile, they will expand and improve their strategic missile and aircraft forces assigned to strategic operations in the Eurasian TVDs.

CONCLUSION

The finishing touches are now being put on the SALT II agreement. The numerical limits on numbers of missiles and MIRVs apparently have been negotiated. As of this writing (April 1979), the two outstanding issues are definitions of what each side is permitted in the way of "new" missiles to be developed and deployed between now and 1985 and provisions governing encryption of missile telemetry.

As anticipated, the treaty provides the Soviets with more than enough warheads of the size needed to satisfy the requirements of their targeting strategy. With 308 "heavy" SS-18 missiles carrying 10 to 14 warheads each, the Soviets have a total of 3,000 to 4,200 warheads that yield roughly one MT each. If the accuracy of the SS-18 is nearing 600 feet as reported, the SS-18 force alone can destroy all U.S. ICBM silos, launch control centers, nuclear weapons stocks and manufacturing facilities, and the national command authorities that control use of U.S. nuclear weapons. Indeed, the SS-18 force can carry out a disarming strike either in a preemptive strike with no warning or in a second-strike scenario.

In addition to the 308 ICBMs officially recognized as "heavy" missiles, the treaty permits the Soviets to MIRV some 500 SS-17 and SS-19 ICBMs. With payloads of six to seven thousand pounds, these ICBMs also are "heavy" ICBMs by the standards of the unilateral declaration the United States attached to the Interim Agreement in 1972. Deployment of 500 MIRVed SS-17 and SS-19 missiles will add at least 2,500 warheads to the inventory — enough to take care of all military targets not destroyed by the SS-18s, all the selected industry the Soviets may wish to destroy, and then some. This leaves some 350 to 400 ICBMs that cannot be MIRVed but that can be equipped with multiple warheads (MRVs), which are very effective against soft targets. However, the Soviets may prefer to deploy only single RVs (of higher yield) on many of these missiles.

Then there are the 950 SLBMs, some 380 of which can be MIRVed. The number of warheads on the Soviet SLBM force will depend on the degree to which the Soviets fractionate the payloads of the SS-N-18 and the new Typhoon missile. Since SLBMs are intended primarily for soft targets and provide most of the Soviet secure reserve force, the Soviets may follow our example and go to large numbers of small warheads on the MIRVed SLBMs. The real range of uncertainty for 1985 is from 2,000 to over 5,000 warheads for the MIRVed SLBM force, plus another 600 to 2,000 for the remaining 570 SLBM launchers, depending upon whether the Soviets equip these with MIRVs or not. Thus Soviet targeteers who now have about 5,000 warheads on their ICBMs and SLBMs will have at least 8,000 to 9,000, and possibly more than 13,000, warheads on these missiles by the time the treaty expires in 1985.

Last but not least, there are all the strategic missiles and bombers not covered by the treaty: more than 500 IR/MRBMs and about an equal number of medium bombers, not including several hundred of the latter in the Soviet Naval Air Force. The Soviets probably will deploy at least 300 to 350 SS-20s; the upper limit will most likely depend on the progress of Chinese nuclear programs and what, if anything, NATO does to improve its long-range nuclear capabilities. Not counting refire missiles for the SS-20, Soviet strategic offensive forces not included in the SALT Treaty add something on the order of 2,000 additional nuclear weapons. Counting refires, the increment is on the order of 4,000 to 5,000 warheads. The total strategic warhead inventory allowed by the treaty is therefore on the order of 10,000 to 18,000 warheads in 1985, or roughly double the current Soviet inventory.

The Soviets have apparently conceded little on new ICBMs designed to improve the accuracy and effectiveness of the current generation (SS-17 through SS-19). Evidently, each side will be permitted one completely "new" ICBM. The other replacement missiles may be deployed as long as they do not differ from their predecessors by more than 5 percent in gross physical characteristics. This is quite a lot of leeway for good engineers who are free to change fuels and engine design in order to increase missile throw weight if that is desired.[73] Most important, constraining the gross size of the missile does nothing to constrain missile accuracy, which, after all, is the most important aspect of increasing missile effectiveness, given the large throw weights of existing Soviet missiles.

Soviet military and political leaders appear to be pleased with this treaty because it allows the Soviets everything they need in the way of strategic *offensive* forces to fight and "win" a nuclear war in almost any plausible scenario. Strategic offensive forces, however, can only provide so much in the way of war-fighting and damage-limiting capabilities; after that, it is up to the strategic defenses. Therefore, the principal thrust of future Soviet strategic programs probably will be to improve their strategic defenses — air, missile, and ASW. If Mr. Brezhnev and Mr. Carter can persuade the U.S. Senate to ratify this treaty, Mr. Brezhnev probably will get the place in Lenin's tomb that was denied to Stalin and not even considered for Khrushchev.

NOTES

1. Current U.S. MIRVed ICBMs and SLBMs are not effective against hard targets by design. For example, the current Poseidon missile does not have a stellar update component in the guidance system, which would have made it much more accurate. As currently proposed, the MX ICBM will have the combination of accuracy and yield required to attack missile silos. Whether similar proposals will be made for future SLBM designs remains to be seen.
2. Cited in Raymond L. Garthoff, *Soviet Strategy in the Nuclear Age* (New York: Praeger, 1958), p. 72.
3. Ibid., pp. 72–73; italics apparently in the original Russian language source.
4. *Voennaia strategiia* (Moscow, 1962), repeated on p. 235 of the 3rd ed. (1968).

5. Ibid., 3rd ed., p. 255.
6. *Nedeliia,* no. 36 (September 1967).
7. "Maximum-fatality" targeting is an optimization routine that maximizes the fatalities inflicted by the Nth weapon. Such optimization routines are feasible for computer simulations, usually described as "analysis," but are difficult to execute with missiles or aircraft actually deployed on either side. United States proponents of the "mutual-assured-destruction" (MAD) strategy usually have used the results of "maximum-fatality" computer simulations to show the outcome of the strategy in terms of the population losses on both sides.
8. General of the Army S. P. Ivanov, "Soviet Military Doctrine and Strategy," *Military Thought,* no. 5, 1969 (FPD no. 0116/69):47; italics added. For a more recent statement of these principles, except for the reference to the overseas adversary, see General N. A. Lomov (chief editor), *Nauchno-tekhnicheskii progress i revoliutsia v voennom dele* (Moscow, 1973), pp. 138–39. Lomov's book is written by a collective of line military officers and military commissars and is the latest volume in the Officers' Library Series.
9. Unfortunately, all references to the declassified issues of *Military Thought* are to U.S. translations because the originals were not available. Even the translations are difficult to acquire.
10. Ivanov, "Military Doctrine and Strategy," p. 48. (See note 9.) Soviet military writers routinely reference this statement by Brezhnev, like earlier statements by Khrushchev, as the political guidance for seeking "victory" in a nuclear war.
11. Rear Admiral V. Andreyev, "The Subdivision and Classification of Theaters of Military Operations," *Military Thought,* no. 11, 1964 (FPD no. 924, June 30, 1965):15. The acronym TVD used for convenience here is a transliteration of the Cyrillic letters. Translated, the acronym is TMO.
12. Ibid.
13. Colonel M. Shirokov, "Military Geography at the Present Stage," *Military Thought* (FDD no. 0730/67, no. 11, 1966):57.
14. General, Lieutenant G. Semenov and General Major V. Prokhorov, "Scientific-Technical Progress and Some Questions on Strategy," *Military Thought,* no. 2, February 1969 (FPD no. 60/69, June 18, 1969):23; italics added.
15. Shirokov, "Military Geography," p. 59; italics added.
16. Colonel M. Shirokov, "The Question of Geographic Influences on the Military and Economic Potential of Warring States," *Military Thought,* no. 4, April 1968 (FPD 0052/69):36.
17. Ibid., p. 34.
18. Ibid.
19. Ibid., pp. 37–40.
20. Albert Speer, *Inside the Third Reich* (New York: Macmillan, 1970), pp. 280–83.
21. Ibid., pp. 278–79, for Speer's observations not only on the ten thousand antiaircraft guns and hundreds of thousands of troops assigned to defending German cities, but also on the consequences of air defense demands on German electronic and optical industries.

22. Shirokov, "Geographic Influences," p. 38.
23. Ibid., p. 39.
24. Ibid.
25. Ibid., p. 36. None of this is to argue that the Soviets have not considered the alternative of targeting cities and population, nor is it to argue that no senior Soviet officers have proposed such targeting. The Soviets may well have considered such alternatives but do not seem to have adopted them.
26. As the Soviet leaders frankly said to the Yugoslavs:

> It is also necessary to emphasize that the services of the French and Italian CPs to the revolution were not lesser but greater than those of Yugoslavia. Even though the French and Italian CPs have so far achieved less success than the CPY, this is not due to any special qualities of the CPY, but mainly because after the destruction of the Yugoslav Partisan Headquarters by German paratroopers, at a moment when the people's liberation movement in Yugoslavia was passing through a serious crisis, the Soviet Army came to the aid of the Yugoslav people, crushed the German invader, liberated Belgrade and in this way created the conditions which were necessary to the CPY to achieve power. Unfortunately, the Soviet army did not and could not render such assistance to the French and Italian CPs. [*The Soviet-Yugoslav Dispute* (Royal Institute of International Affairs, 1948), p. 51]

This frank statement of what happened in Eastern Europe and, implicitly, what the Soviets would have done for Western Europe had they had the opportunity should not be dismissed as obsolete Stalinist rhetoric. Even today, the Soviets say essentially the same thing more subtly when they credit World War II with creating the "world socialist system". And as the postwar history of Hungary and Czechoslovakia has shown, the Red Army is prepared to "liberate" Eastern Europe more than once.

27. Colonel Ye. Rybkin, "XXV S'ezd KPSS i problema mirnogo sosushchestvovaniia sotsializma i kapitalizma," *Voenno-Istoricheskiy Zhurnal,* no. 1 (1977):3, 4.
28. For the typical Soviet view, expressed by another articulate military commissar, that nuclear weapons are instruments of political policy like any other weapon, see Colonel S. Tiushkevich, "Razvitie ucheniia o voine i armii na opyte Velikoi Otechestvennoi Voiny," *Kommunist Vooruzhennykh Sil,* no. 22 (1975):14. Tiushkevich writes: "The premise of Marxism-Leninism on war as a continuation of policy by military means remains true in a situation of fundamental changes in military affairs. The attempt of certain bourgeois ideologists to prove that nuclear missile weapons lead war outside the framework of policy and that nuclear war moves beyond the control of policy, outside the framework of policy, ceases to be an instrument of policy and does not constitute its continuation, is theoretically incorrect and politically reactionary."
29. Shirokov, "Military Geography," pp. 59, 60; italics added.
30. In Lomov, *Nauchno-teknichestii progress,* p. 139, the alternative objectives of nuclear targeting are given as "annihilation, destruction, neutralization," distinctions also found in *Military Thought* articles. The nature of the target probably determines the degree of damage in most cases. Thus, missiles in silos, or nuclear weapons in storage, must be annihilated or destroyed,

but airfield runways do not have to be cratered as long as the aircrafts are rendered inoperable and their crews killed. On the other hand, targets to be neutral-
ized in one theater could be destroyed in another depending on the politico-
military objectives of operations in the various TVDs.
31. Marshal S. A. Krasovskiy, ed., *Aviatsiia i kosmonavtika SSSR,* (M. 1968),
    p. 347.
32. General of the Army V. Tolubko, Raketnye voiska strategicheskogo nazna-
    cheniia," *Voenno-Istoricheskii Zhurnal* (*VIZ*), no. 4 (1975); and (same title)
    no. 10 (1976).
33. Ibid., no. 4, p. 54; no. 10, p. 21.
34. Ibid., no. 4, p. 54; no. 10, p. 20.
35. Ibid.
36. Ibid., no. 10, p. 20.
37. Ibid., p. 22, where Brezhnev is mentioned along with Ustinov and most of the
    military men previously cited, with the addition of Marshal A. M. Vasilevskiy
    and Marshal of Artillery N. D. Iakolev, as the political, state, and military
    leaders who directed missile development and the formation of the early mis-
    sile units. Marshal of the Soviet Union Brezhnev achieved one-star rank as a
    political officer in 1943, was promoted in 1953, and made four stars in 1975.
    Biographic information from William F. and Harriet F. Scott, *The Armed
    Forces of the USSR* (Boulder, Colo.: Westview Press, 1978). For Brezhnev's
    position as Chairman of the Military Council, probably since he became First
    Secretary in 1964, see Harriet Fast Scott, "The Soviet High Command," *Air
    Force* (March 1977).
38. Tolubko, *VIZ,* no. 10, p. 21.
39. The Council of Defense has existed, under one title or another, since
    1917–1918. During most, and probably all, of this period the Council has been
    headed by the reigning First Secretary of the Communist party, who probably
    approves or disapproves, funds or denies funding, for all major weapons sys-
    tem development and production deployment programs; see H. F. Scott, "So-
    viet High Command."
40. The upper limit of 950 total SLBM launchers and 62 "modern" ballistic mis-
    sile submarines is permitted only upon retirement of Soviet SS-7 and SS-8 laun-
    chers deployed before 1964. The Soviets are in the process of completing this
    trade-off; see statement to Congress by General George S. Brown, USAF,
    Chairman, Joint Chiefs of Staff, *On the Defense Posture of the United States
    for FY 1977* (prepared January 20, 1976), p. 37.
41. Just how many operational SLBM tubes in "modern" nuclear-powered sub-
    marines the Soviets had in May 1972 when the Interim Agreement was signed is
    difficult to determine precisely, but it probably was less than 500 tubes, com-
    pared to 656 tubes in the U.S. fleet. Nevertheless, the Interim Agreement cred-
    ited the Soviets with 740 SLBM tubes in May 1972. This number apparently in-
    cluded 48 Yankee- and Delta-class boats operational or under construction and
    the 10 Hotel-class boats, but that would have totaled some 742 tubes on these
    nuclear-powered classes without counting the tubes on diesel-powered Golf-

class boats. The whole question of where these SLBM numbers really originated and how, if at all, they were reconciled with U.S. intelligence is obscure and confusing. The reader may consult John Newhouse, *Cold Dawn; The Story of SALT* (New York: Holt, Rinehart and Winston, 1973), pp. 245-49; General George S. Brown, *U.S. Military Posture for FY 1977*, p. 36; Secretary of Defense Elliot L. Richardson, *Annual Defense Department Report FY 1974* (March 27, 1973), p. 32, which gives the total nuclear-powered Soviet SLBM operational force as 560 tubes as of mid-1973; Secretary of Defense Melvin R. Laird, statement before the House Armed Services Committee, *Fiscal Year 1972-76 Defense Program and the 1972 Defense Budget* (March 1, 1971), p. 45, which puts the Yankee-class *operational* force at that time at 17 boats, with another 15 boats "in various stages of assembly and fitting out," for a total of 512 tubes, plus the Hotel-class and diesel-powered boats. According to General Brown's statement (cited above), the Soviets did not reach the SLBM force credited to them in May 1972 until sometime in 1975.

42. In Tables 1, 2, and 3, psi values have been translated into PVN values for the purpose of calculations. The results shown are approximate, but adequate to illustrate the range of yields required, given the targets and the evolution of strategic ballistic missile CEPs. All calculations in these tables on the effectiveness of Soviet missiles were made on a hand computer; D. C. Kephart, "Damage Probability Computer for Point Targets with P and Q Vulnerability Numbers," RAND R-1380-PR, February 1974.

43. Henry S. Bradsher, "New Missile Key to Soviet War Strategy," *Washington Star,* March 22, 1977.

44. Robert Sherman, "A Manual of Missile Capability," *Air Force* (February 1977):39, which gives the CEP of the SS-11 as 1 nm and .3 nm for the SS-19. See also the subsequent discussion of newly released data of Soviet missile characteristics and calculations of their effectiveness.

45. Henry S. Bradsher, "U.S. Offer Leaves Soviets Ahead in Blast Power," *Washington Star,* April 8, 1977, gives the CEP of the SS-19 ICBM as .25 nm. More recent data are presented and analyzed in Figure 1 and Table 3.

46. Statement of Secretary of Defense James R. Schlesinger, *U.S. and Soviet Strategic Doctrine and Military Policies,* U.S. Congress, Senate, hearing before the Subcommittee on Arms Control, International Law, and Organization of the Committee on Foreign Relations, March 4, 1974 (Washington, D.C.: U.S. Government Printing Office, 1974), p. 8. Mr. Schlesinger's Soviet "counterdeterrent" appears to be a mirror image of the U.S. "overt public doctrine" of "only going against cities," while actual U.S. nuclear targeting has concentrated more on military targets and, presumably, industries in urban areas.

47. Jeffrey Record, "Sizing Up the Soviet Army," (Washington, D.C.: Brookings Institution, August 1975), p. 40. On pp. 6-7, Mr. Record cites "growing recognition of the unusability of strategic nuclear arms" as one of two reasons for the "restoration in 1967 of a separate command for Soviet ground forces." Nothing could be more at odds with the earlier citations from previously classi-

fied Soviet literature, the subsequent deployment of ICBMs at IR/MRBM sites, the growth of Soviet SLBM forces under the very generous SALT ceilings, and the development and deployment of the SS-20. The voluminous Soviet literature on military doctrine, strategy, combined-arms operations, and operational art also are at odds with Mr. Record's judgments. Last, but not least, several other political and military factors — the Brezhnev-Kosygin leadership, modification of Soviet doctrine to allow for a non-nuclear phase in a NATO-Warsaw Pact conflict, reevaluation of the role of aircraft, the middle East and Vietnam wars — appear to be much more plausible explanations for the resurgence of the Soviet ground forces in the late 1960s.

48. Statement by Secretary of Defense Melvin R. Laird before a joint session of the Senate Armed Services and Appropriations Committees, "Fiscal Year 1971 Defense Program and Budget" (February 20, 1970), pp. 35, 36. Secretary of Defense Clark Clifford, "The 1970 Defense Budget and Defense Program for Fiscal Years 1970-74," p. 42, gives U.S.S.R. forces as of September 1, 1968, as 900 ICBM and 45 SLBM launchers. The latter figure obviously included only the Yankee-class boats since, in American eyes, the 100 odd SLBMs deployed on Golf- and Hotel-class boats for strategic operations in the Eurasian TVDs were not really "strategic."

49. For some reflection of how the uncertainty concerning the capabilities and intent of the three-warhead version of the SS-9 affected SALT, see Newhouse, *Cold Dawn,* pp. 160-61.

50. Soviet MIRVs often are depicted as a response to U.S. MIRVs. The evidence does not support this contention. The concept obviously was clear to the Soviets by the mid-1960s since the SS-7 triplet was first flight-tested in 1968 at the same time as the MM III and Posiedon MIRV tests. The concept probably originated in the United States, although one cannot be sure even of that. The Soviets lagged in execution, as was to be expected, but the decisions to go ahead with the development of MIRVed missiles probably occurred at about the same time, and for quite different reasons, in the two countries.

51. The throw weight of the SS-11 has been reported at 2,000 pounds and that of the SS-19 with 6 RVs (MIRV) at 7,000 pounds by Sherman, "Missile Capability," p. 39. The SS-17 throw weight probably is in the same neighborhood, while the SS-16, being a solid propellant missile and a candidate for mobile deployment, probably is not much more powerful than the SS-11.

52. Some 400 U.S. military organizations are listed in the Pentagon phone book. Some are located at the same military installation, but more than one warhead must be delivered on large, complex installations.

53. Newhouse, *Cold Dawn,* p. 240, suggests that the Soviets only agreed to the limitation of SS-9 silos to avoid U.S. deployment of "hard-site" defenses to protect U.S. silos, which would make sense from the Soviet point of view. For the limitations on ICBM and SLBM launchers and the permitted substitution of new SLBMs for old ICBMs up to the 950 limit, see the protocol to the Interim Agreement in Newhouse, pp. 280-81. On p. 265, Newhouse says: "Moscow wanted an ABM treaty, but had little reason to negotiate on offensive weaponry, since the Americans were not building more strategic weapons.

Granted the Soviets didn't negotiate seriously until they had established a big enough lead in the number of offensive missiles they possessed.'' The first sentence is wide of the mark: the Russians could not negotiate too strenuously on offensive weaponry because the United States had started deploying their MIRVs some two years before the Soviets could begin to flight-test theirs. But the second sentence is very accurate.

54. For initial testing of the current family of Soviet ICBMs, see Schlesinger, *U.S. and Soviet Strategic Policies,* p. 4.

55. All this, of course, was well known to L. V. Smirnov who, as head of the Military Industrial Commission (VPK), had been managing the development of the new systems since their inception. His U.S. counterparts, who were surprised to meet Smirnov in the final stages of the negotiations (Newhouse, *Cold Dawn,* p. 251), did not know what was going on in Soviet missile development. U.S. intelligence was of little help (see Newhouse, *Cold Dawn,* pp. 244–45, 247–48). Even years after the current generation of Soviet ICBMs began flight testing, U.S. officials were still asking: "What are the Soviets up to?" The same question recurred when the SS–20 duly appeared on the scene. It is being asked again about the four new ICBMs now reported under development. The inability of U.S. officialdom to answer this question is exceeded only by the abundance of information, much of it unclassified, needed to answer the question.

56. Scheslinger, *U.S. and Soviet Strategic Policies,* p. 5.

57. Deployment of SS–11 ICBMs with IR/MRBM units has been reported by several sources, including Secretary of Defense Melvin R. Laird, "National Security Strategy of Strategic Deterrence," *Annual Defense Department Report for FY 1973,* pp. 36, 40, 45. This probably reflects the global targeting of Soviet ICBMs against targets in all TVDs, not merely the transoceanic TVD, in line with statements at the Twenty-fourth Party Congress in 1966 concerning Soviet capabilities to strike targets in any geographic quarter; see Leon Goure, Foy D. Kohler, and Mose L. Harvey, *The Role of Nuclear Forces in Current Soviet Strategy* (Coral Gables, Fla.: Center for Advanced International Studies, University of Miami, 1974).

58. Bradsher, "New Missile Key."

59. New house, *Cold Dawn,* pp. 201–202.

60. General Major V. Zemskov, "Wars of the Modern Era", *Military Thought,* no. 5, 1969 (FPD No. 0116/69):60.

61. For a discussion of SS–20 effectiveness, see William T. Lee, *Understanding the Soviet Military Threat: How CIA Estimates Went Astray,* Foreword by Eugene V. Rostow (New York: National Strategy Information Center, 1977), pp. 43–45.

62. Secretary of Defense Donald H. Rumsfeld, *Annual Defense Department Report, FY 1978,* January 17, 1977, p. 62 and Table 2.

63. The use of the words *peripheral* and *central* here is precisely the reverse of common U.S. usage, which applies the terms *strategic* and *central* only to those systems that can strike the U.S. and the U.S.S.R. respectively. This also was the Soviet definition for the purpose of SALT, so that the strategic forces they perceive as central, or at least equally strategic, would be outside the negotiations.

64. Although they would never say so publicly, the Soviets probably are very unhappy over the U.S. decision to drop the B-1 and deploy long-range, low-altitude cruise missiles instead; the Soviets have spent a great deal of money developing defenses against the bombers.

65. If anyone has evidence from Soviet sources to the contrary, the author would be most grateful to be informed of such evidence.

66. The SS-9 and SS-18 were not included because they are designed for hard targets and their effectiveness against such targets was discussed in connection with Table 2.

67. Development of this new SLBM has been reported in several sources — for example, Richard Burt, "Soviets Build Sub Designed to Fire Multiple Warhead Missiles," *Washington Star,* October 29, 1977.

68. After a number of denials, this linkage has been acknowledged by President Carter and other U.S. officials.

69. By citing the crime, unemployment, and poverty found in large U.S. cities, such as New York, the Soviets have gotten in a few licks of their own on the issue of human rights.

70. Presumably, some of the earlier Y-class submarines could be converted to other strategic missions in the Eurasian TVDs without being counted as "strategic" systems as defined in SALT. After all, the oldest Y-class subs were launched a little more than a decade ago, which is not exactly a scrapping age for major naval combatants.

71. In addition, the Soviets obviously were genuinely annoyed at the United States for, in effect, throwing out the Vladivostok agreements. The Soviets had put a lot of effort into those negotiations and probably had built their strategic force planning for the next five to ten years around the latitude offered to Soviet ambitions by the provisions of the Vladivostok agreements.

72. Semenov and Prokhorov, "Scientific-Technical Progress," p. 23.

73. U.S. estimates of Soviet missile characteristics have a range of uncertainty of at least ± 10 percent. In effect, Soviet designers can develop new missiles within a range of at least ± 15 percent before the U.S. can claim they are "new" missiles as defined in the treaty.

4 THE SOVIET-CUBAN INTERVENTION IN ANGOLA:
Politics, Naval Power, Security Implications

Jiri Valenta

The Soviet-Cuban intervention in Angola in 1975 and 1976 came as a surprise to many analysts of Soviet military strategy and politics. Here for the first time the Soviets deployed allied combat troops and naval warfare forces in a new and unprecedented way — at long distance, outside their sphere of influence. The intervention raised considerable doubt about Soviet intentions in strategic areas of the Third World and about the Soviet interpretation of détente.

A critical reappraisal of the intervention in Angola is now much needed. There is, for example, considerable disagreement among American analysts over the purpose, timing, and extent of the action.[1] More important, as a result of the successful intervention, Soviet and Cuban military involvement in Africa has been greatly extended. Many observers fear that the U.S.S.R.

An abbreviated version of this article was published in the April 1980 issue of the *U.S. Naval Institute Proceedings.* Copyright © 1980 U.S. Naval Institute. Reprinted by permission.

This study is based on a content analysis of Soviet, East European, Cuban, African, and Portuguese sources. In addition, it draws on information gained from interviews with several Portuguese officers who served in Angola in 1975 and with officials of several African governments. For one of my earlier works with a heavy focus on the origins of the Soviet involvement with the MLPA, see "The Soviet-Cuban Intervention in Angola — 1975," *Studies in Comparative Communism* 11, nos. 1 and 2 (Spring/Summer 1978):3–33.

and Cuba may one day try to exploit the opportunities available not only on the African continent (Zimbabwe-Rhodesia and Namibia) but also in other strategically important regions of the Third World — particularly along the "arc of instability" in the Middle East and Asia — and that the Soviet Navy will be used increasingly by the Soviet leadership as one of the most important instruments in pursuit of the forward strategy in these areas.

To understand this development, which has its roots in Angola, one must assess the elements of the Soviet decision on Angola in 1975: Soviet involvement in the civil war in that country, Soviet national security interests, the significant Cuban factor, the essence of Soviet decision-making processes, and the role of the Soviet armed forces, particularly the navy, in implementing the decision. The study of these factors offers the United States potentially important lessons.

THE SOVIET UNION AND CIVIL WAR IN ANGOLA

The collapse of the Portuguese dictatorship in April 1974 led to the decision of the new Portuguese government to end five hundred years of colonial rule in southern Africa, and to the complex problems involved in the transition of power. These were among the factors that precipitated the Angolan civil war and the subsequent Soviet-Cuban intervention. Angola was to obtain independence on November 11, 1975, but the national liberation movement there, unlike those in the other Portuguese African territories, was fragmented. It consisted of three competing submovements: the FNLA, or National Front for the Liberation of Angola; UNITA, or National Union for Total Liberation of Angola; and the MPLA, or Popular Movement for the Liberation of Angola.

The end of the Portuguese empire brought changes in the perceptions and behavior of many nations regarding developments in Angola, and several of these nations became actively involved in the arms race in that country. The U.S.S.R, Cuba, East Germany, Yugoslavia, Algeria, Guinea, and the People's Republic of the Congo actively supported the MPLA. The United States, China, South Africa, France, North Korea, Romania, Zaire, and Zambia supported the FNLA and UNITA. Thus, the triangular struggle among liberation movements that evolved within Angola along ethnic, political, and ideological lines was also greatly complicated from without. The arms race in Angola originated as a competition between the Soviet Union and China. The Soviets supported sporadically, with some ups and downs, the MPLA, led by Agostinho Neto, viewing the other movements — the FNLA, led by Holden Roberto, and UNITA, led by Jonas

Savimbi — with antipathy and suspicion because of their past ties with the United States and China. Indeed, in 1973, even before the coup in Portugal, the Chinese intensified military aid to their anti-MPLA clients in Angola, particularly the FNLA. The Chinese, President Mobuto Sésé Séko of Zaire (Roberto's principal African protector), and Roberto himself concluded a military assistance agreement providing for future training of the FNLA at bases in Zaire. A contingent of 112 Chinese military advisers arrived in Zaire to train the FNLA army shortly after the coup of June 1974 in Portugal. A month later, the CIA began covert funding of the FNLA. On January 22, 1975, the U.S. government authorized the CIA to pass $300,000 to the FNLA.[2]

The Soviets, after some hesitation and after awaiting the outcome of the factional struggle within the MPLA leadership (perhaps fearing Chinese and U.S. influence), renewed their support of Neto in October 1974. When fighting broke out between the rival liberation movements in March 1975, Soviet and East European ships began delivering arms to the MPLA on a massive scale. At least nine Soviet and East European deliveries were made in support of the MPLA in May and June of that year.[3] It is against this background — limited Chinese and U.S. military supplies delivered to the FNLA, massive Soviet military supplies making their way to the MPLA, and the power struggle among the three movements — that developments in Angola in 1975 should be viewed. In the spring of that year, the limited Cuban military intervention also began when upon request of the MPLA, the Cuban leadership decided to send 230 advisers to Angola to train the MPLA military cadres.[4] An additional 400 Cuban troops led by a Cuban general arrived in August.

Until August the Soviet leadership, while clearly concerned about the situation in Angola and intensifying its material support to the MPLA, did not view the situation as very serious. At the time, the MPLA was winning the undeclared civil war. The escalation of Soviet military aid and the arrival of a small number of Cuban advisers had given the MPLA an edge in its offensive. In May the MPLA forced the FNLA out of the suburbs of Luanda. In June the MPLA, gaining momentum, drove both rival organizations out of the capital of Luanda and on July 9 took control of the city, extending its authority to twelve of the fourteen provinces.[5]

From the Soviet point of view, the situation became dangerous in August. The main backers of UNITA and the FNLA, the United States and China, intensified their military support. On July 18, after urgings by Zaire and Zambia, the United States approved a $14 million paramilitary program for backing the FNLA and UNITA. In early August the U.S. covert military-aid program began by way of the airport in Kinshasa (Zaire).[6]

The Chinese, alarmed by the MPLA offensive, in mid-July authorized Zaire to release Chinese military equipment held by the Zairian Army. At about this time, Mobuto sent a few commando companies to Angola. By mid-August Soviet reports began to indicate concern about intensified Chinese and U.S. military aid, and by early September Soviet concern about coordination of Chinese and U.S. covert assistance was discernible.[7] The Chinese, however, had recalled their military personnel from FNLA bases in the summer. Nevertheless, they did not cease to support the FNLA and UNITA, at least politically.

From the Soviet standpoint, the South African intervention on August 8 in southern Angola, which had been requested by UNITA leader Savimbi, was most alarming. The limited intervention by a few hundred South African advisers and the increasing U.S. and South African military aid to the FNLA-UNITA coalition began to turn the tide in the civil war in late August and early September. At this time the MPLA forces had been halted and were being driven from a number of positions. A serious situation was meanwhile developing in the north, where FNLA forces came within twenty miles of the capital of Luanda. Although in early September the MPLA, with the help of Cuban military personnel, regained a brief initiative, the tide again turned in favor of the FNLA and UNITA. After the South African forces established a training base for the FNLA and two battalions of Zairian elite commandos joined the FNLA forces, the MPLA again began to retreat to Luanda.

Although for a while the vectors of the civil war moved from side to side, it was becoming clear that the presence of a few hundred Cubans was insufficient to stop the U.S.-South African-Zairian-backed counteroffensive of the FNLA-UNITA coalition before November 11, 1975, the day of Angolan independence. In August the Soviets resumed shipments of arms to the MPLA, and their reports began to describe the situation in Angola as being extremely critical because of "internal and external conspiracy."[8] The situation in Angola was fluid. By early September, then, the MPLA faced the possibility of defeat.

SOVIET NATIONAL SECURITY INTERESTS

Soviet leaders must have been aware of the strategic importance of the former Portuguese colonies, particularly Angola. Throughout the crisis they must have hoped to obtain strategic benefits, mainly by generating local support for use of port facilities by naval units. The Soviet Navy, as repeatedly stressed by its commander in chief, Admiral S. Gorshkov, is "one of the most important instruments of state policy." It is aimed at countering U.S. and other Western naval forces, at supporting Soviet policy offshore, and at offsetting the military and political presence of the Americans and Chinese in the Third World. There is evidence that the Soviet leaders were also aware of the economic potential of Angola's oil and minerals.[9] Moreover, the Angolan crisis provided the Soviets with an opportunity to weaken the presence of their two main rivals — China and the United States — by checking the growth of Chinese influence in Africa and by preventing the victory of the Chinese- and U.S.-backed forces of the FNLA and UNITA. Angola, because of its geostrategic position, mattered politically to the Soviets, who hoped to acquire a voice in southern African affairs. The Soviet leadership no doubt recognized as early as April 1974 that the collapse of the Portuguese empire would fundamentally alter the political situation in southern Africa. Geostrategically, Angola has potential in Soviet calculations as a springboard for a Soviet-backed guerrilla movement against the South African regime. The Soviets perceived an MPLA victory in Angola as being linked directly to operations of Soviet-supported liberation organizations in the region, such as Namibia's South West African People's Organization (SWAPO), which could intensify its guerrilla activities.[10]

The risks of an intervention on behalf of the MPLA were undoubtedly an important consideration in Soviet decision making. The main Soviet concern was to assess possible U.S. responses to such an action and the repercussions on U.S.-Soviet relations. Judging from Soviet analyses in the summer of 1975, Soviet U.S.-watchers were aware of the domestic constraints under which U.S. policymakers were operating after the collapse of South Vietnam in April 1975. Indeed, the Soviets viewed the outcome in Vietnam and the Watergate scandal as having far-reaching effects on the mood of the American public and the U.S. Congress. The fears of Congress and the public over "a repetition of Vietnam" were patent.[11] Also, the Soviet leadership must have noted that the U.S. government, caught up as it was in the post-Vietnam era, had taken no public notice of the initial Soviet-Cuban involvement in Angola in the spring and summer of 1975.

Moreover, the Soviets must have noticed that the U.S. program of covert paramilitary aid was, even in the summer of 1975, aimed primarily at *balancing* the power of the FNLA and UNITA in the face of MPLA advances during the summer offensive. A more extensive program of military aid, which might have brought victory to the FNLA-UNITA coalition, would have required congressional approval — a very unlikely possibility in the aftermath of Vietnam. Even this limited program of covert aid met with misgivings on the part of some U.S. government officials, such as Assistant Secretary for African Affairs Nathan Davis, who resigned in August 1975 because of his opposition to the program.[12]

Some powerful segments of the Soviet national security bureaucracies very likely saw the high stakes in Angola as offering unique opportunities for their organizational missions. This must have been the perception of the Soviet Navy, which was undoubtedly attracted by the strategic location of Angolan ports. To assure its mission, the Soviet Navy has tried to develop a network of naval facilities in the strategic areas of the Third World, and Angola provided a splendid opportunity. Also, the KGB (state security) and the GRU (military intelligence) may have perceived an MPLA victory as essential to intelligence operations in southern Africa. On the other hand, some reports suggest that elements in the Soviet Foreign Ministry and Ministry of Defense opposed the intervention because it threatened détente and might prove to be expensive.[13]

THE CUBAN "CONNECTION"

The Cuban factor is an important consideration in assessing the Soviet decision on Angola. Did the Soviets use Castro as a tool in the intervention, or, as some observers believe, did Castro put pressure on the Soviet leadership and convince them to support *his* policy of intervention?

The involvement of Cuban military personnel in Africa did not originate with the Angolan intervention. Its origins go back to 1964 when the Cubans began assisting Guinea and to 1965 when they fought briefly in the ex-Belgian Congo (now Zaire) against the incumbent government supported by the United States. In the late 1960s and early 1970s, particularly after the Chilean debacle of 1973, Castro appeared skeptical about prospects for revolution in Latin America. According to his own assessment, conditions in Africa, in contrast to those in Latin America, were ripe for revolutionary change.[14]

Thus, not surprisingly, having cut loose at least temporarily from Latin American revolution, the Cuban military became increasingly involved in Africa during the early 1970s. The African involvement was important to Castro for reasons of ideology and racial heritage.[15] It would be misleading, however, to view Castro's action in Angola solely in these terms. Castro had been a supporter of the MPLA and was a close friend of Neto. Cuba had given its support to the MPLA since the mid-1960s without the ups and downs characteristic of Soviet support for the same organization. Moreover, Angola in 1975 provided Castro with a unique opportunity to refurbish his image as a revolutionary leader and to increase the prestige and influence of his regime in the Third World before the Sixth Nonaligned Conference, scheduled to take place in Havana in September 1979.[16] Furthermore, it is possible that the Angolan situation gave Castro a chance to make adjustments in Soviet-Cuban economic relations. He may have expected that the Soviet Union would reward his "internationalism" with increased economic aid. It should be noted that in the aftermath of the Soviet-Cuban intervention, Cuba negotiated a highly favorable economic and scientific-technical agreement with the U.S.S.R. in April 1976 for the period 1976–1980.[17] Since the intervention, the Cuban armed forces have received more sophisticated weapons.

The Cuban military involvement in Africa was supported, if not advocated, by some Cuban bureaucracies, particularly the Revolutionary Armed Forces (RAF), which is overseen by Fidel's brother Raul. RAF went through a period of professionalization and improvement of its military capabilities in the early 1970s, and Cuban generals may have wanted to test their forces through a more ambitious, external mission in Africa. Cuban military personnel were actively involved on a limited scale in the ongoing Angolan civil war in the early summer, as confirmed by the Cuban leaders themselves, who, unlike their Soviet counterparts, could not keep the secret. This happened *before* the invasion by South Africa and before the U.S.S.R. had settled on the extent of its own involvement in Angola. In the spring and summer of 1975, and even in the initial stage of the intervention in the fall, Cuba appears to have been more eager than the U.S.S.R. to become vigorously involved on behalf of the MPLA, ironically at the very time when the United States seemed ready to normalize its relations with Cuba. Thus, it would be misleading to view Cuban policy on Angola as subservient to Soviet policy. The Cubans were not ordered into the war by the Soviets.

Still, it would be farfetched to think of Cuba as the main actor, or as bringing the Soviet Union into the Angolan conflict against its will. In the Angolan operation, the Cubans depended on the Soviets not only for logistics but also for politico-strategic cover and economic and military assistance. Although Cuban willingness to do the job provided an important input into Soviet decision making, Cuban and Soviet objectives in Angola seem to have coincided entirely only from late August through September 1975 onward, when the two countries began to function as allies. The Soviets, if they decided to intervene, needed to deploy combat troops capable of handling sophisticated weapons for the MPLA. The Soviets were cautious and hesitant to be involved directly in the civil war. Direct Soviet intervention, which might have elicited a firm response from the United States, could have been detrimental to Soviet interests in détente. The willingness of Castro to offer Cuban combat troops provided a convenient, if not superior, alternative. The Cubans were familiar with the physical environment of Angola, which is similar to that of Cuba. The fact that they could offer a substantial number of black and mulatto soldiers meant a fortuitous racial, as well as linguistic, affinity with the MPLA soldiers.

THE DECISION TO INTERVENE

In late August the Soviets viewed the MPLA situation as precarious, and a massive South African intervention as imminent. The stakes in Angola were high, the risks relatively low. The state of affairs was such that if the U.S.S.R. did not act, an intervention by South Africa backed by the United States (and, as the Soviets believed at the time, by China) would give victory to the FNLA and UNITA before Angolan Independence Day. This day became for all parties (both internal and external) a kind of deadline in the decision-making game on Angola. The Soviet Politburo was well aware of that day's significance. On November 11 the Portuguese armed forces would relinquish colonial rule in Angola to whatever national liberation movement, or coalition thereof, happened to be in control of the capital city of Luanda. Thus, from the Soviet point of view (as well as from that of the United States and other actors), the victor would be the faction that could muster sufficient support to win the battle of Luanda *before* this deadline. Since all three movements lacked modern equipment, a logistics system, and internal lines of communication, "sufficient support" meant in practical terms the right amount of sophisticated weapons and the right number of experienced soldiers capable of handling them. The MPLA would be able to defend Luanda and achieve total victory only if the U.S.S.R. provided bold and decisive support in terms of weaponry and sophisticated manpower.

With the deadline approaching, two options were open to Soviet decision makers: (1) to continue their policy of countering the FNLA and UNITA with limited military aid and the aid of a small number of Cuban advisers (with increasing risks of an MPLA military defeat), and (2) to intervene decisively and without restraint on behalf of the MPLA. The Soviets appear to have perceived U.S. policymakers as operating under multiplying domestic constraints; they probably believed that a Soviet-Cuban intervention would not provoke a strong U.S. response. In late August and September, those Soviet leaders who were advocates of intervention were able to convince their more hesitant colleagues that the massive deployment of Cuban troops was the only option left to the Politburo in preventing an MPLA defeat before November 11. In view of the perceived high stakes and low risks in Angola and current setbacks in Portugal (in late August the leftist government of Premier V. Concalvez collapsed), the Soviet leadership evidently decided that the situation warranted a massive deployment of Cuban combat units and Soviet advisers in support of the MPLA. Reports from Cuban prisoners indicate that the decision to intervene and the subsequent dispatch of forces probably took place before the South Africans decided on *their* military intervention in Angola.[18]

THE SOVIET-CUBAN INTERVENTION

The Soviet-Cuban intervention began in late September when the first Cuban ship, *Vietnam Heróico,* delivered a few hundred uniformed, regular Cuban soldiers to Pointe-Noire (Congo-Brazzaville). In early October Cuban ships began bringing in more units, and Cuban aircraft began airlifting additional units. The Soviets and East Europeans resumed shipments of military hardware to the MPLA and the Cubans in August and September. Initial air and sea deliveries, at least for a few weeks, were carried out primarily with Cuban civilian airliners (Britannias of Air Cubana) and Cuban merchant ships. The still cautious Soviets seemingly worked to preserve the image of not breaching international law and the status quo before Independence Day. Yet only a few weeks later, in late October, Soviet Military Transport Aviation (VTA) launched an emergency airlift of military equipment by medium and heavy logistic transport aircraft (An-12 and An-22). The Soviet-Cuban intervention came not a moment too soon for the MPLA, for on October 23, *almost simultaneously* with the Soviet-Cuban invasion, a large intervention by South Africa took place in southern Angola. It comprised two columns of armored cars and trucks, light planes, helicopters, and regular South African defense forces (roughly three thousand men, including logistic support troops around the borders) who were teamed with the forces of UNITA and Portuguese mercenaries. The main purpose of the intervention was to defeat the MPLA forces before Angolan Independence Day.

The South African intervention rapidly changed the military situation in southern Angola. On October 29 the South African column took Mocamedes in the south; by November 7 it had captured Benguela and Lobito. Meanwhile another column took Luso in the east. Both began pressing toward Luanda. In the north, the FNLA continued its cautious advances toward the capital's northern boundaries. The MPLA's position was becoming critical. As Independence Day drew nearer, the Cuban-MPLA forces were holding only Luanda, Cabinda, and three of the fifteen provinces — a narrow corridor stretching across north-central Angola. Even here the MPLA position became so tenuous that its panicky leaders actually began sending their families out of the country.[19] A Soviet eyewitness — Pravda's foreign policy analyst O. Ignatyev — reported that they even examined the possibility of proclaiming independence on November 5 instead of on November 11 as planned.[20] This earlier deadline would have made it easier to legitimize internationally the Soviet-Cuban intervention on behalf of the group in control of Luanda at that time — the MPLA. At this point Neto must have been desperately seeking speedy deployment of the

Cuban reinforcements. Indeed, as Castro pointed out, Neto "did not hesi-
tate" to ask for additional "assistance." In Castro's view, "Had Comrade
Neto hesitated, the Angolan revolution would have been crushed, tens of
thousands of Angolan revolutionaries would have been murdered and Comrade Neto would not be here among us because he himself would have died
in fighting."[21]

It is clear that the hurried Soviet-Cuban air and sea deliveries of additional Cuban regular units and Soviet advisers — essentially a rescue operation in its initial stage — saved the MPLA and Cuban units around
Luanda, which the South African invasion threatened to entrap, from
almost certain defeat. At about the time of Independence Day, the second
wave of Cuban troops and Soviet advisers arrived. There were approximately 2,800 Cuban troops and 170 Soviet military advisers in Angola at
that time, primarily involved in organizing and reinforcing the defense of
the capital. On November 12, only one day after a frightened MPLA leadership had declared the establishment of the People's Republic of Angola, the
FNLA army was halted by Cuban troops just short of Luanda. For a while
South African and UNITA forces continued to advance, managing to score
some temporary victories in late November and early December.

ESCALATION: THE ROLE OF THE SOVIET NAVY

The Soviet-Cuban military intervention escalated in both quantity and quality. In December and January, what had originally appeared to be a rescue
operation developed into a broad offensive. An important factor in the
escalation was undoubtedly a Soviet reassessment of the U.S. response.
This reassessment was probably made between December 9 and December
25, when the Soviets briefly halted the deployment of Cuban troops. It is
likely that the Soviet leadership was reevaluating, at least momentarily, its
policies in the light of U.S. public warnings that Soviet actions in Angola
threatened U.S.-Soviet relations. However, the vote of the U.S. Senate on
December 19 (the Tunney Amendment) to cut off covert aid to the FNLA
and UNITA apparently convinced Soviet leaders that domestic constraints
on U.S. policymakers were too strong to allow the United States any real
options. Subsequently, the Soviets and Cubans resumed their operation in
Angola. In December and January, the sealift and airlift were rapidly taken
over by the Soviets from the Cubans and transformed into a massive operation during which both the Soviet Air Force and the Soviet Navy were
operationally effective.

The Soviets had clearly learned from their experience in the early 1960s in the Congo (now Zaire), where poor coordination and shortages of sealift and airlift capabilities and experienced personnel had led to serious difficulties and ultimately to the failure of Soviet operations. This time the operation was executed perfectly, with substantial airlift and naval cover in adjacent waters being implemented in late November. Soviet VTA aircraft carried military equipment from the U.S.S.R. through Algeria and Congo-Brazzaville to Angola, and Soviet merchant ships carried arms to the Congolese port of Pointe-Noire and then to Angolan ports. Soviet arms included surface-to-surface missiles, the hand-held SAM-7 antiaircraft missile, the famous "Katyusha" 122 mm rockets, T-34 and T-54 tanks, PT-76 amphibious tanks, armored reconnaissance vehicles (BRDM-2), trucks, helicopters, gunships, heavy artillery, light aircraft, and eventually, in January 1976, MIG-21 aircraft. After Cuban aircraft (which could not fly to Africa without refueling) were denied landing rights in Barbados and the Azores, aircraft of the Soviet Aeroflot (I1-62s) assumed the role of transporting Cuban units from Cuba to Angola. The Soviet Navy played a significant role. From early December 1975 to February 1976, the U.S.S.R. deployed a number of warships in west African and south-central Atlantic waters, including amphibious landing ships manned with naval infantry and equipped with antitank- and antiair-missile vehicles, a cruiser and a destroyer armed with guided missiles, an intelligence collector, several auxiliaries, and possibly submarines. The Soviets kept additional ships in reserve, near the Strait of Gibraltar.[22]

In effect, as James McConnell and Bradford Dismukes pointed out, the Soviet Navy deployed at least one anticarrier warfare (ACW) task force in the central Atlantic in January 1976. This bold move seems to have been aimed at countering an anticipated U.S. carrier task group that did not show up.[23] Beginning in January 1976, the Soviet naval deployment was also supported by long-range naval reconnaissance aircraft (TU-95s) deployments over the Atlantic Ocean from bases in Havana and Conakry and by electronic intelligence satellites.

The Soviet deployment appears to have had several purposes. First, the Soviet naval presence provided physical and psychological support to the Cuban combat forces and the Soviet advisers. It played the role of what Admiral Gorshkov calls a "protector" of "progressive change" offshore. In addition, at least in the initial stages (late November and early December), deployment of the amphibious landing ships served to protect the Soviet-Cuban staging area at Pointe-Noire against local threats — primarily, small Zairian Navy warships positioned in Angolan waters — and provided a convenient instrument in case of an emergency for evacuating Soviet military and diplomatic personnel. (As late as early December, the South Africans scored some victories over the Cubans and the MPLA.)

The Soviet Navy also played the role of what Gorshkov calls "a deterrent to the aggressive inspiration of imperialist states." From early January onward, the deployment of a large Soviet task force served as a strategic cover for established Soviet-Cuban sea and air communications and as a deterrent against possible U.S. naval deployment. (It became obvious in late December, however, that the United States would not become involved militarily in Angola and that the deployment of a U.S. naval task force to Angolan waters was a very remote possibility indeed — although still a finite one, since such a response would not require congressional approval.) The fact remains, as pointed out by Charles Peterson and William Durch, that "Soviet Naval units were deployed in a way that suggested an effort to *anticipate* naval movements by the U.S., an action completely unprecedented before Angola."[24]

The military balance began to swing rapidly in favor of the Cuban-MPLA forces. The rate of Cuban troop deployment, 400 per week in December, jumped to 1,000 per week in January, eventually yielding a deployment total of 12,000 Cuban combat troops. Overall, during the war the Soviet Union supplied the MPLA with $400 million in arms and military assistance, compared with an estimated $54 million spent over the previous nineteen years.[25] In early February, the U.S. government, bending to the will of Congress (the Tunney Amendment passed the House of Representatives on January 27), discontinued its military aid to the FLNA and UNITA. South Africa likewise discontinued its intervention.

CONCLUSION

The Soviet-Cuban intervention was an action marked by vigorous exploitation of opportunities and reduction of risks. One cannot fail to recognize the new dimensions of the move: the deployment of Cuban regular combat troops, the well-orchestrated sealift and airlift under difficult conditions, and the bold deployment of naval warfare forces to further politico-military objectives. The intervention showed the Soviet Navy in its most mature, assertive deployment. Although the outcome of the war was decided mainly by the Cuban armed forces and Soviet advisers, the Soviet Navy and Air Force served as indispensable instruments in the action.

The intervention brought about important strategic gains for the U.S.S.R. In October 1976 the Soviets concluded a Treaty of Friendship and

Cooperation with Angola, which calls for "cooperation in the military field."[26] Since then, Soviet-Angolan cooperation has been extended to cover a wide range of military, security, and economic activities. The Soviet Navy now reportedly benefits from use of the strategic Angolan ports. Indeed, the Soviet Navy may be trying to establish permanent bases on the Angolan coast.[27] The Soviets have negotiated maritime and fishing agreements with the Angolans, whose small, but growing, naval force has become the beneficiary of hand-me-down Soviet ships.

Obviously, the Soviet involvement in Angola serves to further the U.S.S.R's national and strategic interests. First, it gives the Soviets better protection for their fishing fleet and maritime and oceanographic activities in the South Atlantic. The Soviet fishing fleet is the second largest in the world, and fishing in the South Atlantic is very attractive, particularly since the Soviets have been forbidden to fish off the coast of Latin America. Second, the deployment in Angola is an important step toward the development of a Soviet military presence in southern Africa, protecting the shipping routes from Soviet Europe to the Far East. (The alternative Northern Sea Route to the Soviet Far East is frozen two-thirds of the year.) Third, in strategic terms, deployment in Angola can facilitate the Soviet Navy mission to counter the U.S. nuclear deterrent and the deployment of Western naval forces in the South Atlantic, and can discourage movement toward closer naval cooperation among South Africa, Brazil, and Argentina in that area.

Although at the present time the Soviet military involvement in Angola is mainly of a defensive nature and has political consequences primarily for the southern African region, one cannot ignore the consequences of the Soviet effort to exploit the strategic value of Angolan naval facilities, where the Soviets are now flying antisubmarine (ASW) aircraft. From Luanda airport they are also conducting reconnaissance flights over the South Atlantic shipping lanes.[28] Obviously, if this trend continues, the mobility and flexibility of Soviet naval operations in the South Atlantic will be enhanced. The Soviet naval facilities in Angola may give advantage to the Soviet Navy because of their proximity to the Cape route — one of the prime strategic and trade sea-lanes in the world — increasing the Soviets' capability to interrupt the flow of oil to North America and Western Europe from the Persian Gulf. Although at the present time one can envision such activities only in an extreme case, such as war, the direct strategic advantage gained in Angola might serve as a very attractive example for the Soviets, to be followed in other countries of the western coast of Africa as well. Such facilities in Namibia, for example, combined with those in Angola and Guinea, and possibly in Ethiopia and South Yemen, could enable the Soviet Navy to patrol most of the African littoral effectively and could thereby pose a serious threat to U.S. naval activities in the South Atlantic and Indian oceans, as well as to Western sea-lanes of commerce.

What are the lessons and implications of the intervention in Angola for the future behavior of the Soviet Union and Cuba in the Third World? The Soviets and the Cubans will probably continue to exploit the opportunities available to them there, as demonstrated by the military intervention in Ethiopia, where they responded even more vigorously and boldly than before. Since early 1978, an estimated 20,000 Cuban combat troops, 3,000 Soviet advisers, and $2 billion worth of arms have been airlifted and sealifted to that country.[29] The intervention on the ground was managed by a group of Soviet and Cuban generals.

Overall, as a result of these successful outcomes in Angola and Ethiopia, Soviet and Cuban military involvement in Africa has been greatly extended. The U.S.S.R. now has strategic and political stakes in several countries of the Third World. Its naval deployment and security aid in this area are growing. Cuban involvement in strategic areas is growing as well. There are some 42,000 to 45,000 Cuban troops in Africa, stationed primarily in Angola and in the Horn of Africa in Ethiopia, with additional contingents of military advisory personnel in another nine African countries and in the Middle East in South Yemen.[30]

Obviously, future Soviet decision making in the strategically located regions of the Third World will be shaped by many factors, some of which may work for — and others work against — military involvement. Indeed, clear constraints on such involvement exist. One is the increasing number of Cuban casualties suffered in southern Angola from fighting Savimbi's UNITA guerrillas and in Ethiopia from fighting guerrillas in Eritria and the Ogaden region. Second, there is the potential danger of an entanglement similar to that of the United States in Vietnam. Third, the negative Soviet experiences in Egypt and, more recently, in Somalia are important reminders that the durability of the Soviet involvement in the Third World depends in part upon the interests of other parties.

Finally, one of the salient lessons of Angola is that the Soviet leaders are acutely conscious of the risks entailed in decision making vis-à-vis the Third World. It was their accurate assessment of the probable U.S. response that strengthened the arguments of those Soviet leaders who advocated low-cost military escalation in Angola. The Soviets behaved with restraint during the 1978 invasion of the Shaba province of Zaire by the Congolese National Liberation Front (an MPLA ally) in the light of the U.S.-backed French-Belgian counterintervention. American inaction, retreat, or vacillation tends to encourage Soviet assertive behavior and Soviet attempts to exploit opportunities in the Third World. The United States, it is suggested, should by diplomatic and other means — ranging from economic development to security aid and, if necessary, to direct presence — aim at a more determined, activist role in the Third World, thereby deterring the Soviet Union and its allies from resolving a crisis situation, such as the one in Angola, by use of military power.

NOTES

1. Thus, one school of thought sees the Soviet-Cuban involvement as a main factor in the escalation of the Angolan civil war and the role of the United States as that of a counterbalance. See Walter Hahn and Alvin Cottrell, *Soviet Shadow Over Africa* (Coral Gables, Fla.: Center for Advanced International Studies, University of Miami, 1976). Another school, represented by John Stockwell, former chief of the CIA's Angolan Task Force, interprets the intervention as a response to early U.S. and South African escalation of the Angolan civil war. See J. Stockwell, *In Search of Enemies: A CIA Story* (New York: Norton, 1978). Stockwell offers convincing data concerning the U.S. involvement in Angola; however, his analysis of Soviet and Cuban behavior in Angola is less convincing. For the Soviet interpretation, see Oleg Ignatyev, *Secret Weapon in Africa* (Moscow: Progress, 1977). Ignatyev, who is the most authoritative Soviet source on the subject, visited Angola twice (September 1974 and October to November 1975) in the capacity of foreign analyst for *Pravda*. Many observers assumed that the Cubans acted in Angola as Soviet proxies. For example, see Peter Vannemann and Martin James, "The Soviet Intervention in Angola: Intentions and Implications," *Strategic Review* 4, no. 3 (Summer 1976):92–103. So far the only exception to that view is found in William J. Durch, "The Cuban Military in Africa and the Middle East: From Algeria to Angola," Professional Paper No. 201, (Arlington, Va.: Center for Naval Analysis, September 1977).

2. John Marcum, "Lessons of Angola," *Foreign Affairs,* 54, no. 3 (April 1976): 414.

3. See Charles C. Peterson and William J. Durch "Angolan Crisis Deployments," in Bradford Dismukes and James McConnell, eds., *Soviet Naval Diplomacy: From the June War to Angola* (Arlington, Va.: Center for Naval Analysis, June 1978), p. 4-31, forthcoming from Pergamon Press.

4. *New York Times,* January 12, 1976. The CIA estimates were similar — 260 men by the summer of 1975. See Stockwell, *In Search of Enemies,* p. 170.

5. See Colin Legum, "The Soviet Union, China and the West in Southern Africa," *Foreign Affairs* 54, no. 4 (July 1976).

6. Assistant Secretary of State for African Affairs William E. Schaufele, Jr., "The African Dimension of the Angolan Conflict" (Washington, D.C.: Bureau of Public Affairs, February 6, 1976), p. 2.

7. Radio Moscow, August 16, 1975; Tass (Moscow), August 23 and 25, 1975. O. Ignatyev, "The True Face of Angola's Enemies," *Pravda,* September 9, 1975; B. Pilyatskin, "NCNA Covers Up the Traces," *Izvestiia,* September 9, 1975.

8. *Pravda,* August 18, 1975; V. Yermakov, "Portugal and Angola's Hour of Trial," *New Times,* no. 37 (September 8, 1975):14–15; Tass (Moscow), September 2, 1975.

9. M. Zenovich, "On the Road to Independence," *Pravda,* February 26, 1975; Radio Moscow, November 21, 1975. For a serious analysis of Angolan economic potential, see A. V. Pritvorov, "The Economics of Angola," *Narody Azii i Afriky,* no. 3 (March 1975):122–30.

10. V. Sidenko, "The Intrigues of Angola's Enemies," *New Times,* no. 30 (July 1975):14–15.

11. D. Kraminov, "A Skirmish at the Crossroads," *Za rubezhom* (June 13–19, 1975):12.

12. For a discussion of the U.S. covert program in Angola, see Stockwell, *In Search of Enemies,* pp. 40–56, 157–175. For Davis's version of decision making regarding these activities, see his article "The Angola Decision of 1975: A Personal Memoir," *Foreign Affairs* 57, no. 1 (Fall 1978):109–24.

13. Vannemann and James, "Soviet Intervention in Angola," p. 97; also their essay "The Lessons of Angola: A Global Perspective on Communist Intervention in Southern Africa," in Roger Pearson, ed., *Sino-Soviet Intervention in Africa* (Washington, D.C.: Council on American Affairs, 1977), pp. 10–37.

14. In an interview in Mexico City in January 1975, Castro stated that "we must be realistic. Changes similar to those of the Cuban revolution are not within sight in the Latin American countries," Radio Buenos Aires, January 10, 1975. See also an interview with Castro by Simon Alley, *Afrique-Asie* (May 16–29, 1977): 19.

15. Castro's speech at the Congress of the Cuban Communist party, Radio Havana, December 22, 1975.

16. In September 1975 Castro predicted that in the future "the prestige of our revolution will increase," and "we will be having more influence in the international revolutionary movement," Radio Havana, September 29, 1975.

17. See *Granma Weekly Review,* April 25, 1976.

18. Schaufele, "African Dimension of the Angolan Conflict," pp. 2–3.

19. For narratives describing military operations in Angola and the critical situation of the MPLA before November 11, see Stockwell, *In Search of Enemies,* pp. 164–68; and Ignatyev, *Secret Weapon in Africa,* pp. 155–74.

20. Ignatyev, *Secret Weapon in Africa,* p. 166.

21. Radio Havana, March 17, 1976.

22. In my discussion of the Soviet naval operation in Angola, I benefited immeasurably from the work of Peterson and Durch. See their discussion, "Angolan Crisis Deployments," pp. 4-29 to 4-47.

23. James M. McConnell and Bradford Dismukes, "Soviet Diplomacy of Force," *Problems of Communism* (January–February 1979):20, 24.

24. Peterson and Durch, "Angolan Crisis Deployments," p. 4-38.

25. Stockwell, *In Search of Enemies,* p. 232.
26. For the text of the treaty and the agreement between the CPSU and the MPLA, see *Pravda,* October 9 and 14, 1976.
27. *Marine Rundschau,* November 4, 1977, p. 270.
28. Here I benefited from a discussion of Geoffrey Kemp and Robert Legvold on the Soviet and American strategic interests in Africa. See Jennifer Seymour Whitaker, ed., *Africa and the United States Vital Interests,* (New York: Council on Foreign Relations, 1978), pp. 120–86.
29. Colin Legum, "The African Crisis," *Foreign Affairs* 57, no. 3 (1978):634.
30. *Expressen* (Stockholm), April 30, 1978; Radio Liberty Research (RL 62/79), February 23, 1979.

5 A NEW STRATEGY FOR NATO

James Leutze

In recent months there has been considerable discussion about the relative power balance between NATO and the Warsaw Pact Organization (WPO).[1] Some analysts also see a frightening Soviet buildup on the strategic level.[2] The undisputed evidence, and in these discussions that kind of evidence is rare, is that during the past several years (at least since 1973) relative strength of the WPO has increased dramatically. This increase in strength has faced NATO strategists with a number of challenges — few of which have been resolved. The same is true regarding the challenges at the strategic level. The easiest course would be to discuss only the buildup in Europe and thus avoid struggling with two troublesome issues. Unfortunately, the two issues are almost inextricable, and dangerously so, since there is realistic fear that a war in Europe with theater nuclear weapons (TNW) would quickly escalate into a strategic exchange. In fact, our present policy is so imprecise as to make blundering into such a disaster practically inevitable — if a war ever begins in Europe. Thus, while concentrating on the current situation in Europe, it is essential to think in terms that will be responsive to both the European and the worldwide danger.

CURRENT NATO STRATEGY

As is widely known, since 1967 NATO has relied upon a military doctrine enunciated in Military Committee Document MC 14/3, "Overall Strategic Concept for the Defense of the NATO Area"; this doctrine is commonly referred to as "flexible response." Flexible response calls for an initial attempt to counter an aggressive WPO move with conventional forces, then an escalation to TNW, and eventually a resort to strategic nuclear weapons. When this concept was adopted as NATO strategy, it was almost universally greeted with relief since it replaced the fearful "massive retaliation" doctrine.

Almost from the beginning, however, flexible response has been beset with problems. Some strategists doubted that the distinction between the tactical and strategic levels could long be maintained once the nuclear genie was out of the bottle; others, particularly Europeans, interpreted flexible response as a way of letting the United States off the hook by attempting to deter Soviet aggression with something short of a nuclear holocaust; others suggested that TNW made conventional forces unnecessary; while still others argued that the presence of TNW on the battlefield made larger conventional forces essential.[3] The Nixon administration spent years redefining the U.S. doctrine toward NATO. The result was a brilliant semantic and theoretical restructuring that essentially "evaded rather than resolved the ambiguity of the heart of flexible response."[4] Many American and European commanders felt better about the revised strategy and the projections, but, as one analyst put it, when Nixon left office, he left unresolved the central strategic issue of "how far NATO should be prepared to rely on non-nuclear forces to deter and if necessary, defend against aggression from the East."[5]

The recent buildup of strength in Eastern Europe has only made the task of resolving the dilemma more urgent. In the spring of 1977, after a lengthy study of the problem, Senator Sam Nunn (D., Ga.) speculated that the WPO forces might now be able to strike so fast and so hard that by the time NATO was ready to turn to TNW, WPO forces would be so deep into NATO territory that even the smallest nuclear action would destroy friendly territory and millions of our allies.[6] Furthermore, as will be related below, there is some fear that WPO forces, now well armed with TNW, might initiate their use and follow up that surprise with swift armored strikes aimed at our stockpiles and delivery systems — thus robbing us of a decisive TNW response. In sum, it would appear that while losing none of its dangers, a doctrine of gradually escalating warfare has become increasingly impractical. In short, it seems that the flexibility has gone out of our flexible response.

The most optimistic response to the recent developments is to point with confidence to the increasing effectiveness of defense weapons. Some would contend that the 1973 Arab-Israeli war proved that the pendulum has swung to the favor of the defense and that we therefore do not need to fear WPO armor. There are three responses to this argument: (1) It is theory not fact; it has yet to be tested on the central European plain. It reminds me of two famous theories before World War II: Churchill's declaration that the "problem" of the submarine had been "solved" and the widely held concept that "the bomber always gets through." (2) If the pendulum has indeed now swung to the defense, it is illusionary to assume that it will halt at that point in its course. The lessons of the last war regarding illusions that ignore the inevitability of change are too numerous and too well known to bear repeating. (3) Even were the defense to prove equal to stopping WPO armor, that does not eliminate the dangers of the battle going nuclear. Indeed it is possible that to avoid an ignominious defeat, the WPO might have its own escalatory ladder, and so stopping their armor might only be the prelude to their use of TNW. But these are all theoretical arguments based upon the theoretical possibility that one weapons system can counter another weapons system. The fact remains that the WPO is increasing its forces and that NATO has yet to enunciate its response, even though the specific issue has been under study since 1977. The issue is doctrinal as well as analytical.

The varying reactions to this doctrinal dilemma and to WPO advancements go beyond the usual hawk-dove bipolarity, with emotions ranging up and down the scale. As is not uncommon, the preferred way to attack the arguments of those concerned about recent developments is to discredit the group by accusing all members of holding the alarmist, anti-Soviet, aggressive, reductionist, inflexible views of the extremists. In an attempt to offset this criticism in advance, let us state some specific observations: (1) Nato does not need to match the WPO weapon for weapon or man for man; (2) it is not necessary that every increase in the Soviet defense budget should trigger a similar increase in our own; (3) it is not reasonable to assume that the Soviets are planning a first strike either against us or against Western Europe. In the broader sense, we do not even propose that we seek military superiority across the board, nor do we believe that we should limit ourselves to military solutions for East-West problems. On the other hand, recent trends are deeply troubling. It is hoped that NATO will continue to play its stabilizing, deterrent role in Europe — most preferably by conventional means; that the wisdom of maintaining military sufficiency will be recognized; and, perhaps most important, that the American public will be sensitized to the ramifications of current commitments, current strategies, and current deployments.

Out of all the discussion arise two seminal questions: Why has the WPO been building its forces and arming them with the tanks and tactical airpower that would appear ideally suited for an attack on Western Europe? And what should NATO's response be both in the short term and over the long haul? In this paper, we will not only explore those questions but also propose a strategy for NATO, which, if adopted, would trigger a crucial foreign policy debate.

WHY IS THE WARSAW PACT REARMING?

According to the latest *Military Balance*, published by the prestigious International Institute of Strategic Studies (IISS), in the critical northern and central European zones Moscow maintains the equivalent of 70 divisions and 21,100 tanks, while in the same zones NATO maintains 27 divisions backed up by 7,000 tanks. In the southern zone, not the most likely locus of attack, NATO has 37 divisions to 33 WPO divisions, but even there we are outnumbered in tanks: 6,800 Soviet to 4,300 NATO.[7] Some analysts come up with an even greater imbalance, but one very systematic student of the issue finds not the figures but the trends to be the most alarming aspect of the situation.[8] Considering only the central sector, which he regards as vital to NATO defense, John M. Collins notes that since 1970 the Soviets have increased their personnel by 90,000, which means the U.S. deployed forces are outnumbered by 569,000. The Soviets have also increased their tank strength by 1,200 so that our deficiency in tanks is now 6,980. Collins concludes that "NATO is quantitatively outclassed by the Warsaw Pact in almost every category." Furthermore, he believes that "emerging Soviet capabilities, with great stress on offensive shock power" have created "a new strategic environment" in which the "overall balance has not been so lopsided since the early 1950s." The IISS agrees, suggesting that "the pattern is one of a military balance moving steadily against the West."[9] This warning is given emphasis by the fact that the Soviets are outproducing us, and have been since 1972, in tanks, 6.5:1; in motorized infantry carriers, 5:1; and in artillery tubes, 7:1.[10]

The classic U.S./NATO response to Soviet/WPO conventional superiority has been to point with pride at our qualitative or technological superiority. Unfortunately, this response is not as reassuring as in the past. In its 1978 study, the IISS suggests that NATO's "qualitative superiority" is now being "eroded" by new additions to the WPO arsenal. The authors emphasize that while NATO has been modernizing, the Pact countries have been "modernizing faster and expanding" as well. Some Soviet weapons, such as surface-to-air missiles, armored personnel carriers, and artillery, are already superior to NATO's. Furthermore, the Soviets are closing the gap in an area of traditional NATO superiority, tactical aircraft. Collins, perhaps using some of the same data as the IISS, agrees that NATO not only is quantitatively outclassed by the Warsaw Pact but also "is losing its qualitative edge in several respects that count."[11] Part of the explanation for this phenomenon lies in the area of defense expenditures, discussed in detail elsewhere in this volume. Here it suffices to say that the Soviets have been progressively spending more as we have been spending less.

Ominously, the manner in which Soviet forces are deployed in the West as compared with their deployment on the Sino-Soviet border suggests that the Soviets anticipate offensive action in the West and defensive action in the East.[12] For instance, tank support for ground combat forces is some 50 percent greater on the European borders. Nuclear missile support in Eastern Europe is several times what it is in the Far East.[13] The Soviets also face NATO with a superior force of tactical surface missiles and medium bombers. The tactical airpower needed to advance an offensive strike is being improved rapidly, and although not yet judged as sophisticated as the tactical airpower available to NATO, giant strides are being taken. Only in the areas of antitank weapons, where NATO forces have a 5:1 advantage, and nuclear artillery, where NATO has 150 percent more weapons than the WPO, do we have a firepower advantage.[14]

Some professional students do not see these figures or dispositions as frightening and do not believe that WPO strength has increased dramatically enough to destabilize the European balance.[15] In some ways this is a difficult argument to counter. A balance between nations is not like a scale that can be read, and so in the absence of conflict one can claim that stability exists. On the other hand, the absence of conflict in the past is the best evidence that a balance previously existed. Thus, if the WPO has now increased its strength vis-à-vis that of NATO, it is logical to assume that the balance has changed, or is in the process of changing, and that that change is not in NATO's favor.[16] Whether the WPO will act upon its real or supposed advantage remains to be seen, but the whole issue of Soviet intentions has stirred a lively and unresolved debate within the U.S. intelligence community.[17]

Leaving aside for the moment the issue of the current state of balance, let us turn to the question of why the WPO has undertaken its current rearmament program. At the outset, we should accept the fact that we are venturing onto extremely boggy ground. Our record for anticipating or accurately analyzing Soviet defense policy or even gauging the amount the Soviets are spending on defense is extremely poor. In a recent article attacking those who are stirring up fear of Soviet advances, Daniel Yergin suggests seven possible reasons for why the WPO is presently arming: (1) a feeling of vulnerability; (2) bureaucratic momentum; (3) arms-race momentum; (4) a desire to establish a credible war-fighting capability as a deterrent or in case of war; (5) a desire to "overawe" their rivals politically; (6) a wish to project their power more effectively; (7) an interest in positioning for a first strike.[18] This list seems to be a reasonable starting point for exploring the WPO rearmament; it may be especially useful since Yergin is a member of the group that downgrades the Soviet threat. Yergin rejects the last reason on his list, and for the moment the issue of first strike can be dismissed. The first reason is probably true to an extent since almost everyone feels vulnerable to some degree in this dangerous world. The second and third reasons probably also contain some element of truth in that they accurately reflect things we know about bureaucracy and arms races. However, the most fruitful attention might be paid to the fourth, fifth, and sixth reasons.

Obviously the Soviets are trying to develop a credible war-fighting capability, and they are doing a very good job at it. They have not adopted the currently popular United States leaning toward sufficiency and are going for nothing less than superiority. If they are taking this course as a deterrent, one has to wonder, as a deterrent against what? Western capitalism, particularly as practiced in Western Europe, is not in one of its more dynamic, imperialistic, or even evangelical phases. Furthermore, as Mr. Yergin and many other critics of defense spending in this country contend, to have a credible deterrent, you do not need superiority. Hence, if deterrence is what the Soviets want, they are choosing a very wasteful way to achieve it. And if war were pressed upon them by the West, surely they can not imagine that we would send tank columns and massed troops, a la "Barbarossa," against the far more numerous WPO troops and tanks; theoretically it is the aggressor who needs the numerical advantage. It might just be possible for the Russians to imagine a demonic Dr. Strangelove attacking Mother Russia with nuclear missiles, but in that case why do they need superiority in tanks and artillery? Thus, it would appear that if they are building as a deterrent or to prepare for a defensive war, they are making some very costly and fundamental errors.

The fifth and sixth reasons (to "overawe" their rivals politically and to project their power) sound more plausible and fall into the "benign," or at least not actively hostile, category. In a sense, these reasons can be considered as one since in effectively projecting their power, they are also overawing their rivals. It seems plausible that the purpose of the Soviets' actions is to influence events; these actions obviously are not occurring in a vacuum. Judging from recent experience, it also seems likely that their intent is to use their weapons for influence, rather than for combat. An obvious area where these suggestions are applicable is international prestige. As is widely recognized, Soviet-style communism has been declining in attractiveness, largely for economic reasons, but in some instances because of sociological factors. Many leftists in undeveloped countries find Maoist ideology more applicable to their situations. Meanwhile, Eurocommunists, in an attempt to make themselves more palatable, are eagerly explaining the gulf that separates them from Muscovite ideologies. In this competition for attention and converts, there is still one thing the Soviets can do better than anyone else — they can play the power game with the major advanced countries. Thus, there is good reason to believe that the arms buildup is somehow related to the current struggle for converts within the communist world.[19]

Another area in which the benign "influence" explanation might be applicable is Western Europe. Leaving aside the question of whether the Soviets view Eurocommunism as a positive or a negative factor, they can hardly view the current problems of social democracy in Western Europe with displeasure.[20] The intensified arms buildup began at about the time the Western economies were struggling with the problems brought on by increases in the price of oil. In this context, the WPO rearmament can be seen as a step toward reinforcing trends that were already in progress. As Sir Edward Peck recently suggested, "The extent of the 'shove' which the Soviet Union thinks it can give to history already going its way is directly proportionate to Soviet military strength."[21] The Soviets might just be hedging their bets on historical inevitability by keeping the pressure on the weakened capitalistic systems. To paraphrase Lenin, they are increasing the length of the sword they are pushing into the mush of the Western democracies. If this reduces the risk of backsliding, all well and good, and if it should fail, little will be lost except the cost of the arms. In a society in which a high level of military presence is necessary anyhow, this cost may not be considered excessive.

There is another possible explanation not mentioned by Mr. Yergin. That is that the Soviets are increasing the size of their forces for no rational reason; instead, they are acting irrationally and without discernible aim or purpose.[22] One could argue more specifically that the buildup results from causes unrelated to defense issues between East and West. If this is the explanation, and debating whether it is or not is similar to debating the existence of infinity, it is unfortunate because nations and people react as readily to perceptions as to reality. In other words, it is reasonable for the West to react in a logical way to a perceived threat even when the provocation may have occurred for illogical reasons or when in fact no provocation was intended. However, in the real world the irrational model is of little value other than as a beguiling exercise. We must determine whether what we think is happening is actually happening and then act upon the assumption that there is conscious process behind the event. Furthermore, the Soviet Union must learn that that will be the case.

There is still another possibility that was not proposed by Mr. Yergin. It does not fall into the benign category; yet it does make considerable sense in a military context, which is, after all, where one might look for explanations of arms buildups. If the Soviets have been reading Western defense journals or listening to statements by U.S. or NATO defense chiefs, they must be aware that there have been many questions and considerable confusion about the doctrine concerning the use of TNW.[23] Recognizing the confusion, the Russians are acting to take advantage of either of the two extremes that may eventuate when the doctrinal debate is over. If, for instance, it is decided that it is simply too destructive and too dangerous to use TNW, the Soviets will wish to confront us with overwhelming superiority in conventional forces. On the other hand, if it is decided that the destruction of TNW simply must be accepted, the Soviets are acting on the theory that the nuclear battlefield requires more men and weapons, rather than less. In short, it is not unreasonable to deduce that the Russians are hedging their bets, partially because of confusion created by our side, but that their intention is to maintain superiority no matter how the issue is resolved. Unfortunately, this makes their actions no less destabilizing because the next move is up to us.

CAN NATO RESPOND EFFECTIVELY?

We are unlikely to arrive at a definitive answer to the question of why WPO has been rearming. What we can do with more assurance is to hypothesize about NATO's ability to respond successfully to any attack by the WPO forces. But why should NATO be concerned about such an attack when it is freely admitted that an attack is unlikely? One reason is that, as has just been suggested, we do not know why the WPO is arming at such a rapid rate. Unless we can be certain that an aggressive move can be discounted, we must be prepared for the worst. In defense matters, safety is earned only by those who are prepared to meet the possibilities as well as the probabilities, the unlikely as well as the certain. In a larger sense, NATO must prepare to counter a WPO offensive lest lack of preparation should signal a lack of will and thereby tempt a WPO miscalculation. Many critics feel, in fact, that one of the most dangerous things about the present imbalance is the confusing impression it creates within both the WPO and NATO.[24] What, then, should NATO be prepared to meet?

In the first place, it should be emphasized that the WPO has an abundance of TNW, and there is every reason to believe that they will use these weapons preemptively. As Colonel A. A. Sidorenko, one of the Soviet Army's leading strategists, wrote in 1970, "To attain the greatest effectiveness, it is recommended that the nuclear strike be launched at the start of firepower preparation. . . . Preemption in launching a nuclear strike is expected to be the decisive condition for the attainment of superiority . . . and the seizure and retention of the initiative."[25] Chief Marshal P. A. Rotmistrov, Soviet tank commander, echoes this theory by suggesting that "in battle, when an avalanche of attacking tanks follows immediately after nuclear strikes, the anti-tank weapons which have not been wiped out by these strikes will be quickly destroyed by the fire from those tanks as soon as they are located."[26]

Should war occur, these theories would no doubt be applied to the European battlefield. There are several good reasons why the Soviets might initiate the use of TNW: (1) Soviet weapons would be especially useful in destroying our TNW presently deployed in forward areas; (2) TNW are ideally adapted to blowing large holes in NATO defense lines through which WPO tanks could flow in approved blitzkreig fashion; and (3) TNW pose less threat to Soviet offensive forces than to the NATO defenders because the Soviets are trained to fight on a nuclear battlefield.[27] Hence, there is every possibility that the flexibility could be taken out of our flexible response at the very moment war begins.

All that is very interesting, some would say, but should the Soviets ever intend to act on any such diabolical theories, we would have adequate warning and could make defensive preparations accordingly. Moreover, the argument can be made that recent advances in technology give increased power to the defending forces. However, what some analysts find the most disturbing in the current situation is an apparently calculated attempt by the Soviets to balance those technological advances that favor the defenders by reducing the time required to launch an attack. Senator Nunn, for instance, believes that the Soviets are now capable of launching a "potentially devastating invasion of Europe with as little as a few days' warning."[28] If true, this is extremely worrisome because basic NATO doctrine has assumed a warning time of at least two weeks. In defense of such a theory, Nunn and others cite increased troop concentrations near the East-West boundary, higher concentrations of tanks and artillery, increased troop mobility con-

ferred by armored personnel carriers, improved TNW deployed within
range of NATO forward defenses, and increased numbers of tactical aircraft based in forward areas. Moreover, recent arms acquisitions make it
theoretically possible for WPO forces to neutralize, or at least decrease, the
effectiveness of one of NATO's most dependable defenses — tactical airpower. If WPO forces could move without giving NATO the warning time
our strategists have traditionally postulated and could counter or destroy on
the ground our tactical airpower, they might well be able to counterbalance
the advantage usually granted the defensive force. On that subject, the ratio
of three to one often cited as the requirement for an offensive force is totally irrelevant when the surprise gained by the initiator of a war is factored
in. German forces that attacked France in May 1940 and Japanese forces
that attacked Malaya in December 1941 were actually outnumbered by the
defenders. Other more geographically relevant instances were provided by
German forces fighting in central Europe in September 1939 and June 1941.
Although the degree of surprise achieved in those instances is probably not
possible today, it does appear that the WPO could achieve a significant degree of surprise and that new dispositions and weapons have enhanced that
possibility.[29]

In view of these speculations about the WPO's ability to launch a surprise attack, it is alarming to find that current Soviet doctrine emphasizes a
strategy intended to exploit surprise. According to this strategy, masses of
tanks supported by mobile artillery are to make breakthroughs on a narrow
front or on a series of narrow fronts. The swiftly moving tank columns are
to be followed by motorized infantry that will mop up the pockets of resistance. Theoretically, and this theory may be wildly optimistic, WPO forces
can cover 50 kilometers a day, which would put them on the Rhine within
five days. If the NATO forces should react quickly to the blitzkrieg and
swiftly go to TNW, the WPO forces would hope that the emphasis they
have given to fighting on a nuclear battlefield will pay off. WPO tanks are
provided with radiation shields, and their troops have practiced maneuver-
ing on contaminated terrain. One scenario would have WPO forces attacking swiftly across the northern German plain before U.S. forces could be
brought up from their bases in southern Germany and before reinforcements could be ferried in from Canada or the United States. By the time
NATO forces were capable of retaliation, WPO forces not only would be
on or close to the Rhine, but also would have overrun NATO supply bases,
cut communication lines, and at least partially occupied populous West
German cities.

That brings us to the other horn of the dilemma. We count upon the
more than 7,000 TNW that we have in Western Europe to counterbalance

the WPO conventional superiority, but how are we going to use those weapons? If we used only 10 percent of them, we would totally destroy the area where the battle took place — most probably West Germany. In 1955 a NATO war game involving simulated explosions demonstrated that 268 TNW explosions in West German territory would leave an estimated 1.5 million civilians dead and an addition 3.5 million wounded. This number is more than five times the casualties the Germans suffered from bombing in all of World War II. Many changes in weapons design and size have taken place since 1955, and even though the frightening estimate of 2 million to 20 million European lives made in the 1960s may be out of date, the fact remains that resort to TNW would extract a terrible toll on our friends.[30] Thus, a resort to TNW is a policy without a happy resolution. As testimony before several congressional committees has shown, even Defense Department officials have difficulty in proposing a scenario in which TNW can be used in a rational way.[31]

But if we should decide not to use TNW, the next step up the flexible ladder is hardly more reassuring — a resort to strategic nuclear weapons. Assuming that the French would not have already taken this determination out of our hands by launching their Pluton missiles, the United States, in a NATO forum, would have to decide if the situation warranted a resort to weapons that might result in mutual destruction. In the atmosphere that would surely exist after conventional defense had already unsuccessfully been attempted and with large areas of Western Europe occupied, an attack by U.S. missiles against counterforce targets within the Soviet Union would almost surely bring on a mutually destructive nuclear holocaust. The process of such decision making is in and of itself cumbersome and time-consuming, and NATO has shown an alarming tendency over the years to excel at intramural battling. But if these procedural problems could be overcome, would the United States really be willing to risk suicide to save a Western Europe already heavily penetrated by WPO forces? Would Western Europe want the United States to take such action?

Of obvious relevance on this last point is the growth in recent years of Eurocommunism. Most discussions of Eurocommunism and NATO have centered around the issue of maintaining security. In other words, can countries with strong Communist parties be trusted with plans and secrets relating to defense and war between East and West? Although opinions vary, many feel that on any critical issue nationalistic loyalties would outweigh loyalty to any international movement. That may or may not be the case, but let us take a situation in which a country would have to decide on risking some degree of nuclear destruction to ward off invading forces. Would a Social Democratic government with a strong and theoretically independent Communist party be able to reach consensus quickly on this question? Would not similar nationalistic loyalties militate against such a decision? Does the old "Red-or-dead" argument not lose all its tension if one is already Red? And what if the question were: Should France and Italy risk destruction to save Germany? Even if we accept totally the claims of independence of the Western European Communist parties, we know that the decision-making process incident to "going nuclear" is already shrouded in uncertainty; so the addition of Communist parties can only make the answer more problematic.[32]

Thus, NATO's defense in the face of a WPO attack is quite uncertain. The effectiveness of NATO's conventional forces against the kind of attack that WPO forces are capable of making is very questionable; once the defensive "forward shell" is broken, all may well be lost. It is far from certain that the various steps outlined under the "flexible" doctrine would be taken. This aspect of the problem has far-reaching implications for NATO's defense credibility. These same uncertainties, which must also be obvious to Soviet strategists, might tempt the Soviets into risk taking.

Furthermore, there is reason to fear that risk taking might extend all the way to strategic nuclear war. The following statement is from the November 1975 issue of *Communist of the Armed Forces,* the Soviet's foremost military publication: "The premise of Marxism-Leninism on war as a continuation of policy by military means remains true in an atmosphere of fundamental changes in military matters." In reference to the view expressed by many Western statesmen and strategists that there are no winners in modern major wars and that war is therefore unthinkable, the article goes on: "The attempt of certain bourgeois ideologists to prove that nuclear missile weapons leave war outside the framework of policy and that nuclear war moves beyond the control of policy and does not constitute its continuation is theoretically incorrect and politically reactionary."[33] In other words, the Soviets' view of the potential costs and benefits of nuclear war is fundamentally different from the Western view, or at least the Soviets say it is. They not only think differently about what we have traditionally regarded as Armageddon, but they also are preparing themselves to wage and survive a nuclear war. There is serious question about whether they are so prepared at the moment, but there can be no question that if the present trends in the strategic balance continue much further into the future, they will reach that point.

Survival, of course, is not the only objective of war; some analysts think that the Soviets conceive of themselves as winning. In a recent article in *Commentary,* Richard Pipes has provided an impressive array of data showing how Soviet strategists can, and do, argue that Russia can strike first, absorb a retaliatory strike, and still have enough power left to force the United States out of the contest.[34] Part of the reason is that civil defense and demography would presently insure them of casualities no more horrendous than those of World War II — a high price to be sure, but a price that in the earlier instance purchased victory. If all this sounds coldblooded, it is, but as Pipes and others point out, the Soviets have a different view of the way in which power influences relations between individuals and states. Power, strength, and force are valued above reason; principle, logic, and negotiations are not seen as a route to mutual concessions, but as another step toward getting one's own way. Harlan Cleveland has defined even détente as a "continuation of tensions by other means" and thus another psychological weapon in the Soviet arsenal. In this cosmos, one does not look for ways *not* to use the real weapons one has, but, rather, to find ways to use them in the most effective fashion.

Some will argue that the Soviets should be judged by their deeds and not their alarming words, and many will ask why we think the Soviets are telling us accurately what they propose to do. It is surprising that a closed society should be so open about something we tend to consider so secret. But in one of those curious paradoxes in which the Soviet Union excels, there does seem to be some compulsion to telegraph their punches. As Marshal of the Soviet Union A. A. Grechko writes in his recently published strategic overview, the Soviets never have and never will hide the fundamentals of their strategy or doctrine.[35] We may choose to ignore what they say, and since they have not started a nuclear war, there is no way to prove that they mean what they say, but it would be far more gratifying if Eastern strategists agreed with their Western counterparts about the "no-win" quality of nuclear war. In the West we have traditionally considered nuclear war unthinkable, while the Soviets have most emphatically disagreed. An interesting illustration of this difference is provided by comparing Henry Kissinger's view with that of a Soviet strategist, V. D. Sokolovskiy. Kissinger says, "The traditional mode of military analysis which saw in war a continuation of politics but with its own appropriate means is no longer applicable."[36] Sokolovskiy says, "It is well known that the essential nature of war as a continuation of politics does not change with changing technology and armament."[37] Surely there are those in the Soviet Union who disagree, but the number of prominent Soviet theorists and military officers who share the concept that nuclear war can be fought and won is profoundly disturbing.

Regardless of how this philosophical debate over the current applicability of Clausewitz's theories about war is resolved, it seems unarguably prudent to think of ways to insure that those who remain true to the master's teaching do not act upon their beliefs. This is especially true when our most likely potential adversary is designing his strategic arsenal in line with *his* theories, rather than *ours,* and is deploying his tactical forces in such a manner as to exploit our current deficiencies. One way to lose the argument is to lose the war — or is that winning?

The problems impeding the development of a credible alternative to the present ineffective policy of flexible response are that conventional forces are more expensive than nuclear weapons; developing and deploying arms for conventional forces take time; and the decision-making process required before these major expenditures are approved is equally time-consuming. Doubtless the time, energy, and expense of this endeavor is worthwhile if Western Europe is vital to our national defense posture. But what is needed is a stopgap strategy for the immediate future to counter the ongoing Soviet buildup. What follows is such a strategy, and while it certainly has inherent problems, it would seem to have significant advantages over the inadequate, improvisational, and seemingly irrational policy that we are presently pursuing.

AN INTERIM STRATEGY FOR NATO

To balance the defense posture of Western Europe and to provide time to prepare a conventional deterrent, the United States should encourage the NATO Defense Council to announce that for the next five years any offensive movement by WPO forces against any member of NATO will result in an immediate *strategic counterforce* by U.S. forces. During the five-year life of this policy, the United States would (1) remove most (perhaps three-quarters) of the TNW presently in Europe; (2) move with all possible speed to bring conventional force levels into balance; and (3) stand ready for meaningful discussions of mutual balanced force reduction (MBFR) leading to the denuclearization of the European continent. In his announcement, General Bernard W. Rodgers should make it clear that this policy was forced upon the United States by the threatening increase in WPO offensive forces. Moreover, it should be emphasized that this new policy is purely defensive and intended only as a deterrent.

At the same time, the United States should go forward with the development and deployment of the neutron bomb. As in the case of the major policy announcement, this should be presented as an *interim* action that the United States would willingly rescind in the face of a reduction in the conventional forces of the WPO. Moral and other questions aside, the neutron bomb is a weapon whose time has definitely come from NATO. It not only seems ideally suited for destroying WPO tank forces protected against regular nuclear weapons, but it also rescues us from, or at least appreciably assists us with, what is obviously an untenable TNW strategy. As has already been pointed out, TNW would produce more friendly than unfriendly casualties. The only function that these weapons now serve is to draw us into a strategic nuclear exchange. Therefore, our TNW remaining in Europe should be provided with neutron warheads as soon as possible.

What would be the implications of and the reactions to this proposed policy? There undoubtedly would be loud cries and protests that the West was acting irresponsibly, threatening the future of arms negotiations and undermining détente. There might even be Soviet saber rattling and a turn toward the bad old days of the cold war. It is doubtful, however, that the real cold war would be rekindled. Many of the bridges, cultural and economic, that have been built are self-supporting and are unlikely to be torn down in a fit of pique. Furthermore, the Soviets' need for Western technology is too pressing for them to wantonly cut off the flow.[38] In this instance, as in many others, détente is self-serving for the Soviets; it is not a favor they are according us. Moreover, the point should be explicitly stated that NATO and the United States were making these moves in reaction to WPO armament policies. We should clearly state that reduction of tensions must be mutual and that Soviet concessions or willingness to discuss seriously arms reduction in Europe would elicit Western reactions in support of détente and an immediate reevaluation of our nuclear strategy.

In this regard, let us consider a factor that must be basic to any East-West relationship. Westerners, and some Americans in particular, are very prone to apply a double standard in judging U.S. and Soviet behavior. We must not take provocative step A or deploy weapon B because it will alarm the Soviets and undermine détente, but the Soviets can deploy troops, increase the size of their strategic arsenal, or build heavier rockets, while we search for benign explanations. Has the increase in Soviet arms budgets deterred the United States from its pursuit of détente? In some ways, the increase has intensified that pursuit, even though many analysts are working overtime to explain why the Soviets feel they have to produce those tanks and artillery tubes. The same is true for those who argue against the deployment of the neutron bomb on the grounds that it may upset the Soviets and the prospects for arms-control negotiations. Do we have any evidence of similar restraint by the Soviets? Can anyone give any reliable evidence that the Soviets, when they master the secret of this weapon, and they may well have already done so, will have any compunctions about using it? And can anyone doubt that the neutron bomb, as effective as it would be in defense of Western Europe, would not be far more useful as an offensive weapon? Will the Soviets deny themselves a weapon that might give them Germany's industrial plant *sans* Germans unless we give them a good reason for so doing?

But to return to the Soviet reaction to the suggested policy announcement, what would the Soviets do in a tangible way to illustrate their displeasure? They hardly could build their strategic or conventional forces any faster than they are already doing. Nor could they be much more active in fermenting trouble in Africa or other places where opportunity beckons. In short, aside from considerable rhetoric and saber rattling, there are few actions the Soviets would be likely to take that are any more adverse to our interests than the things they are doing right now. And, given the buildup in their forces, any actions we intend to take, we had better take soon for the Soviet reactions are only going to become more potentially menacing. So, in addition to basing our policy on the firm ground that it is undertaken in direct reaction to Soviet policy, we would have to prepare to dig in and accept a barrage of denunciation.

It can also be anticipated that our policy would receive a mixed reaction within NATO. From what we can tell, NATO commanders would be heartened by this display of resolve by the United States. They would be especially pleased by the neutron-bomb decision and would also be impressed by United States willingness to accept the danger of a strategic nuclear exchange. However, as we have recently found, they would not "unanimously" accept the development of the neutron bomb, thus taking President Carter off the hook.[39] There would also be lamenting by some European leaders about the effect of our decision upon détente. We already have seen similar lamenting in reaction to President Carter's stance on human rights, and there undoubtedly will be more. This, too, we will have to accept, pointing out that we stand perfectly willing to continue seeking détente, but that détente bought at the price of capitulation is in no way a bargain.

To the cry that this proposed strategy makes nuclear holocaust more likely, the answer is that in fact all it does is to make the realities more obvious. Our *current* policy makes nuclear holocaust likely, primarily because of its serious lack of precision. The steps up the flexible ladder are very poorly defined, and the result could be miscalculation or blunder. And even if the process should defy its critics and work in ideal fashion, we would still move quickly to the brink of the inferno. Part of the logic behind this new strategy is that an assured nuclear exchange is a more sobering deterrent than a "ladder" intended in part to make confrontation more palatable.

What would be the reaction to this strategy within the United States? Undoubtedly there would be loud protestations by some members of Congress, and many others would be quick to point with alarm at our "provocative action. However, even these critics should be pleased by the opportunity — an opportunity that is central to this strategy — to debate the rationality of America's entire nuclear policy toward NATO.

Some will quickly point out that this is a return to the discredited "massive-retaliation" doctrine of the 1950s and 1960s. That suggestion would be correct; with a few additional refinements, this is an *ad interim* massive-retaliation policy. But that fact should not discredit it out of hand. First, it should be recalled that massive retaliation was adopted during a period of imbalance between Soviet and NATO conventional forces. It was changed not only because of its dangers, but also because NATO's conventional forces were achieving a rough parity. That same logic would apply in this case. Second, it can be argued that massive retaliation is not as reliable a deterrent as it was when we had nuclear superiority over the Soviets. That may be, but whether it is "as reliable" or not, it still should have a sobering effect on adventurism. Also it might be noted that massive retaliation is still accepted doctrine for any Soviet attack on the continental U.S. or direct national interest; if it is good for deterrence of direct U.S.-Soviet confrontation, why is it not equally acceptable as a deterrent to WPO-NATO confrontation? Third, massive retaliation has been opposed on the grounds that it is an unreasonable response to limited aggression and hence lacks credibility. However, the same argument can be made about TNW. The only "reasonable" response to aggression is response in kind, but if we balk at the expense and the complications of providing a conventional deterrent, we leave ourselves no alternative to an "unreasonable" response. That being the case, a well-defined, well-conceived, convincingly articulated policy is hardly less credible than a widely doubted, much debated, improvisational one.

The point will surely be raised that in actuality U.S. defense policy is a use-or-lose one that pays only lip service to TNW.[40] In other words the United States is already committed to a quick escalation to strategic nuclear war lest by delay we lose the opportunity to use nuclear weapons in an effective manner — for example, against communication centers in Eastern Europe or Russia. It also can be maintained that since the Soviets will probably start any offensive with an attack on our TNW capability, no one really believes in flexible response anyway. That may well be true, but how much better it would be to remove the layers of obfuscation and confront the issue head-on. It simply cannot be had both ways (i.e., we don't want a policy of massive retaliation, but we accept a policy of flexible response knowing it is illogical and likely to lead to nuclear holocaust). If we are all to be incinerated, it would be reassuring to know that all other options have been fully debated and discussed. If democracy can do nothing else, it should at least be able to assure its advocates that the manner and timing of their deaths have received the careful attention of competing minds, preferably in public forum. Moreover, it is at least theoretically possible that open examination of our dilemma would produce some fresh thought. Finally, the possibility must be admitted that the American public, if given the opportunity, would reject their commitment to NATO and a nuclear denouement. Even if that possibility is remote, our leaders owe us the opportunity to decide; that is why a debate at this time is so crucial.

One of the most disturbing aspects of the war in Southeast Asia, and something that continues to bedevil U.S. policy (e.g., in the Middle East), is the lack of debate and lack of definition in our commitments. Were we committed under SEATO to come to the aid of South Vietnam? Did Congress really understand the Gulf of Tonkin Resolution? Was Vietnam vital to U.S. interests? Can the American people be trusted with the facts, or should they be handled like adolescents? Those issues helped to poison the 1960s and early 1970s, but similar questions can be asked today. In the matter of NATO, the relevant question is: Would the United States really risk destruction in order to back up their commitment to Western Europe? Extended, serious, thoughtful discussion of that question is essential. Few things are worse than an uncertain or an outgrown commitment; it confuses one's friends and may lead one's enemy to make fatal miscalculations. A policy such as the one we have suggested here would provide the necessary fuel for a debate on national strategy. Despite the dangers of that debate, it would in the long run be desirable.

It would also be healthy to review the actions necessary to provide a conventional deterrent at the end of the five-year span of this policy. What is necessary if we really are going to have a conventional deterrent? For one thing, we will have to increase our defense budget. However, when President Carter promised our NATO allies a 10 percent increase in the U.S. spending on NATO, he was quickly attacked by critics who wish to cut our defense budget. Ironically, many of those same critics are the most vocal opponents of nuclear weapons. Conventional forces cost more than nuclear forces, particularly if those forces include a volunteer army. In fact, one aspect of the debate would be whether we can afford a volunteer army, or, at any rate, a volunteer army with the benefits and the retirement policy currently provided. Even if we could, how effective is the AVAF? Do we need the continued presence in Europe of large ground force units, or are we willing to accept vast expansion of our airlift capacity so that troops can be ferried swiftly to their battle stations when required? The size of the navy, as well as the size of our antisubmarine forces, would have to be increased so that we could reliably supply our forces in an extended land battle. Our NATO allies would also have to face some harsh realities concerning their budgets and their force levels. In short, the debate would be extended, basic, and long overdue. It might even have to encompass a basic examination of our doctrine concerning war and peace and the use of nuclear weapons.

Finally, we need to consider the ramifications of not reacting to the current WPO arms buildup. The most obvious danger is that of miscalculation. A lack of response or a continuation of our very low-key debate on "What does it all mean?" might well convince the Soviets that we are not serious about defending Western Europe. The Soviets also might read into a lack of reaction implications about our policy toward the rest of the world. These interpretations might be correct, or they might lead them to a policy of risk taking that would be neither in their interests nor in ours. At this point, we might take a lesson from recent history. Barbara Tuchman wrote movingly about the dangers of miscalculation and misinterpretation in *The Guns of August.* One of her readers, John Kennedy, applied his awareness of those dangers to his handling of the Cuban missile crisis, taking elaborate steps to avoid any misreading of America's intent. In the two major wars of the twentieth century, America's opponents were not so cautious and hence badly misread our intentions and our abilities. In 1917 the Germans were certain that they could win the war before the United States could become a factor in the conflict. Accordingly, they announced unrestricted submarine warfare, well aware that the Wilson administration would consider that action a virtual declaration of war. In 1941 the Japanese were confident that successful strikes in the South and Central Pacific would face us with a task of reconquest so formidable that we would accept the fait accompli rather than fight. On that basis, they attacked Pearl Harbor and the Philippines. It is also highly improbable that either North Korea or North Vietnam correctly estimated our reactions to their provocative moves.

It is extremely important that no similar miscalculation be made by the WPO. It is equally important that the United States debate and decide what its commitments and its limitations are. The strategy outlined here would elicit such debate and might allow us to undertake a rational — and we hope a conventional — defense of our national interests.

NOTES

1. The bibliography on this debate is really too lengthy to be quoted here; however, there are several useful sources that give the flavor of the argument. For the view that the buildup has not been significant or ominous, see George F. Kennan, *The Cloud of Danger* (Boston, 1977); and Arthur Macy Cox, *The Dynamics of Detente: How to End the Arms Race* (New York, 1976). For the opposite side, see Theodore Draper et al., *Defending America: Toward a New Role in the Post-Detente World* (New York, 1977). For a more polemical view, see the statements put out by the Committee on the Present Danger. The middle ground is intelligently taken by Jerome H. Kahan, *Security in the Nuclear Age: Developing U.S. Strategic Arms Policy* (Washington, D.C., 1975).

2. See especially the news stories covering the retirement of Major General George J. Keegan (U.S.A.F.) in January 1977. General Keegan, formerly chief of Air Force Intelligence, was a member of "Team B," which was appointed by the president's Foreign Intelligence Advisory Board to prepare an estimate of Soviet strategic objectives as an alternative to the one done by the CIA.

3. When the concept was initially established, General Maxwell Taylor, among others, pointed out that by their nature, nuclear weapons — tactical or strategic — would take a high toll, and hence the attrition rates would force manpower needs upward. See Maxwell Taylor, *The Uncertain Trumpet* (New York: Harper, 1960), p. 174.

4. Richard Hart Sinnreich, "NATO's Doctrinal Dilemma," *Orbis* 19, no. 2 (Summer 1975):475.

5. Ibid.

6. See the report of Senators Sam Nunn and Dewey F. Bartlett, "NATO and the New Soviet Threat," U.S. Congress, Senate, *Congressional Record*, 95th Cong., 1st sess., pp. 1411-17.

7. International Institute for Strategic Studies (IISS), "The Military Balance 1978-79," (IISS, 1978), pp. 108-13. For a study that gives much higher figures for the Soviet side, see William Schneider, Jr., "General Purpose Forces: Army and Air Force," in William Schneider, Jr., and Francis P. Hoeber, eds., *Arms, Men, and Military Budgets* (New York: National Strategy Information Center, 1977).

8. John M. Collins, "American and Soviet Military Strength; Contemporary Trends Compared, 1970-76." This study was done when Collins was at the Library of Congress in the Legislative Reference Service. It is most easily available in U.S. Congress, Senate, *Congressional Record*, 95th Cong., 1st sess., pp. 14064-104.

9. IISS, "Military Balance 1978-79," p. 122.

10. See Chart 2 in Bruno Augenstein, "Military RDT and E. Raison D'Etre and Policy Background," in Schneider and Hoeber, *Arms, Men, and Military Budgets*, p. 226.

11. Collins, "American and Soviet Military Strength," p. 14097.
12. S. T. Cohen and W. C. Lyons, "A Comparison of U.S.-Allied and Soviet Tactical Nuclear Force Capabilities and Policies," *Orbis* 19, no. 1 (Spring 1975):72–92.
13. Ibid., p. 80.
14. Ibid., p. 81.
15. Kennan argues that point well in *Cloud of Danger;* see especially pp. 150–74.
16. See John Erickson, "Trends in the Soviet Combined Arms Concept," *Strategic Review* (Winter 1977):38–53.
17. See announcement at time of Keegan's retirement, *New York Times,* January 3, 1977, p. 3; rebuttal by Senator Proxmire and Joint Chiefs of Staff, *New York Times,* January 31, 1977, p. 6. Also see Keegan's explanation of his views, *Strategic Review* (Spring 1977):6–11.
18. Daniel Yergin, "The Arms Zealots: On the System Devoted to Defending America's Defense Budget," *Harpers* (June 1977):74.
19. See Lawrence L. Whetten, ed., *The Political Implications of Soviet Military Power* (New York: Crane, Russak, 1977).
20. For a discussion of the destabilizing effect of Eurocommunism and reasons for Moscow's lack of enthusiam, see Charles Gati, "The 'Europeanization' of Communism," *Foriegn Affairs* (April 1977):539–53; and James O, Goldsborough, "Eurocommunism after Madrid," *Foreign Affairs* (July 1977): 800–14.
21. "Soviet Military Power and Political Influence," *NATO Review* (April 1979):17.
22. For the classic statement of the irrational model, see Graham Allison, *Essence of Decision: Explaining the Cuban Missile Crisis* (Boston: Little, Brown, 1971).
23. See most particularly James R. Schlesinger, *The Theatre Nuclear Force Posture in Europe,* (Washington D.C.: U.S. Department of Defense, Spring 1975), pp. 25–30.
24. See, for instance, Walter Laqueur, "Perils of Detente," *New York .Times Magazine,* February 27, 1977; and Walter F. Hahn, "NATO's Quiet Crisis," *Strategic Review* (Summer 1977):26–39.
25. A. A. Sidorenko, *The Offensive, A Soviet View* (Moscow, 1970), p. 115.
26. P. A. Rotmistrov, *Nauchnaia zhizn'* (Moscow, 1968); quoted in Cohen and Lyons, "Tactical Nuclear Force Capabilities and Policies," p. 80.
27. For a fuller explication of this theory, see Joseph D. Douglass, Jr., *The Soviet Theatre Nuclear Offensive* (Washington, D.C.: U.S. Government Printing Office, 1976).
28. Nunn and Bartlett, "NATO and the New Soviet Threat," reprinted in part in *Atlantic Community Quarterly* (Spring 1977):21.
29. During NATO war games in the fall of 1977, the friendly forces spent the opening days of the exercise retreating. See *Time* (October 3, 1977):42–47.

30. Barry R. Schneider, "U.S. Tactical Nuclear Weapons: A Controversial Arsenal," in David T. Johnson and Barry R. Schneider, eds., *Current Issues and Defense Policy* (New York: Praeger, 1976), p. 176. See also Helmut Schmidt, *Defense or Retaliation* (London: Oliver and Boyd, 1962).

31. See Schlesinger, *Theatre Nuclear Force Posture in Europe.*

32. As one very familiar with NATO's moods and methods recently wrote, "The difficulties of assuring prompt and unanimous NATO decisions on the use of nuclear weapons are so nebulous and complex as almost to defy solution." Quote from Captain John H. Morse, "Questionable NATO Assumptions," *Strategic Review* (Winter 1976):26.

33. Quoted in Paul H. Nitze, "Deterring our Deterrent," *Foreign Policy* (Winter 1976–77):197. A similar statement was made by V. D. Sokolovskiy, *Soviet Military Strategy* (Santa Monica, Calif.: Rand Corporation, 1963).

34. Richard Pipes, "Why the Soviet Union Thinks It Could Fight and Win a Nuclear War," *Commentary* (July 1977):21–34.

35. A. A. Grechko, *The Armed Forces of the Soviet Union* (Washington, D.C.: U.S. Government Printing Office, 1977).

36. In Michael Howard, ed., *The Theory and Practice of War* (New York: Praeger, 1966), p. 291.

37. Sokolovskiy, *Soviet Military Strategy,* p. 99.

38. For a knowledgeable dissent on this issue, see Steven Rosefielde, "East-West Trade and Postwar Soviet Economic Growth," unpublished manuscript, October 1, 1976. For yet another point of view, see William Kintner and Harvey Sicherman, *Technology and International Politics* (Lexington, Mass.: Lexington Books, 1975).

39. For discussion among NATO leaders, see the *Washington Post,* October 12, 1977, p. 15. An interesting aspect of this debate is the contention that the neutron bomb has a lower threshold and is therefore more likely to be used. Can one assume from that that some NATO commanders prefer defensive weapons because they will not be used or will not be used until WPO forces are deep within Western territory? If we do not intend to use TNW, we should admit it and remove them.

40. It is already widely suspected that the "NATO elite" considers flexible response a "useful fiction." See Hahn, "NATO's Quiet Crisis," p. 35. General Maxwell Taylor believes that the use of tactical nuclear weapons is highly "uncertain." See Maxwell Taylor, *Precarious Security* (New York: Norton, 1976), p. 96.

II POLITICAL ECONOMY

6 INDUSTRIAL STRUCTURE, URBANIZATION, AND SOCIALIST GROWTH STRATEGY:

A Historical Analysis, 1940–1970

Gur Ofer

This paper compares the structural changes that took place in the economies of seven socialist, centrally planned countries in East Europe with similar changes in market economies. The comparisons are for the period 1950 to 1970, the formative years of the socialist regimes, with references to 1940. The purpose of these comparisons is, first, to demonstrate that the patterns of structural changes of these two groups of countries are different and, second, to link those differences to specific aspects of the growth strategy of the socialist countries (SOC).

Since this is the fourth paper by the author on this general topic and some of its implications, it is necessary to carve a place for it by summarizing the main findings and arguments of its predecessors and by better defining its specific tasks.[1]

Two of the earlier papers (1974, 1977) established that contrary to whatever the apparent image of their growth strategy, socialist countries employ a larger proportion of their labor force in agriculture than do equally developed market economies. Likewise, it was found that despite a very rapid industrialization drive, at growth rates higher than in most market economies, the socialist urban sectors are relatively smaller. The apparent contradiction is resolved by showing that the urban deficiency in SOC is due in part to an abnormally low level of economic activity in the service industries, which are located mostly in cities, and in part to economizing on the size of rural to urban migration by using a highly capital-intensive production technique in manufacturing and highly labor-intensive modes of production in agriculture. This policy will henceforth be called the "input-substitution" policy. So while the industrial production structure of SOC in 1960 reflected the emphasis on manufacturing and related industries, as well as the notorious "neglect of agriculture" and of the service industries, the industrial distribution of the labor force and of investment strongly reflected policies in line with the input-substitution hypothesis.

A historical investigation of the industrial structure of the Eastern European countries during the presocialist period revealed, however, that similar phenomena of smaller than "normal" urban sectors and abnormal concentration of labor in agriculture prevailed long before the socialist takeover. It is possible that the snapshot of the industrial structure of SOC in 1960 presented in the 1976 paper may simply reflect legacies of the past that were being "corrected" over time but that, as of 1960, had not fully converged with the normal course. Nonetheless, a study of the dynamic changes of the urbanization process and the ratio of rural to urban migration (1973) showed that migration flows and the rate of growth of the urban sector were indeed slower than one would expect on the basis of similar processes in comparable market economies.[2] Further investigation has shown that while the structural anomalies in the industrial distribution of labor in SOC are similar to those of the presocialist period, the explanations are quite different for the two periods. In the presocialist period, the abnormal structure reflected a combination of economic stagnation and a comparative advantage in agriculture; in the socialist period, the abnormal structure existed amid dynamic growth and a drastic shift in apparent comparative advantage, combined with an overall structural shift and a decline in trade. The 1979 paper presents evidence on the quite extreme shift in the structure of trade and the decline in its relative size following the socialist takeover, along with the implication that the industrial structure of output must have also shifted from agriculture toward manufacturing.[3]

The high initial concentration of economic activity, including labor, in rural areas and in agriculture made economizing on urbanization both a more obviously needed and a more rational policy. With the then backward and undeveloped urban infrastructure, these countries were confronted with a need they could not afford — to invest a very high proportion of their scarce investable funds in urban construction and to move people to cities. For this reason, the policies of economizing on urbanization and input substitution were used to a somewhat lesser extent by such countries as Czechoslovakia and East Germany, and perhaps Hungary, which were more developed in the late 1940s when the socialist regimes started.

As stated, the policy of input substitution is recognized as one aspect of the socialist tendency to neglect agriculture. In previous papers we developed a similar argument in support of input substitution as part of a rational policy of economizing on urbanization. A possible offsetting result of such a policy is that input substitution could be instrumental in lowering the relative overall efficiency of agricultural production — that is, if input substitution is not merely a movement *along* a given isoquant of agricultural production, but also causes a movement of this isoquant to a less efficient location. In the 1979 paper we focused on the price that SOC may have paid for their "neglect-of-agriculture" policies. We showed that it may well be profitable for at least some of the less developed SOC to follow a more traditional strategy and specialize in agricultural production in a market (COMECON) where agricultural products are considered "hard" goods and are in short supply. We were able to establish that Bulgaria, which seems to have followed such a strategy, did benefit from it, but that in doing so, it did not follow the policy of input substitution, which may indicate a causal relationship between such a policy and low general efficiency in agriculture.

The question of whether SOC indeed followed a policy of economizing on urbanization, especially in its input-substitution aspect, has not been directly tested in a dynamic context through the study of the pattern of changes over time in the industrial composition of the SOC economies.[4] That is what we set out to accomplish in this paper in the context of a comparison with similar changes in market economies.

In view of the apparent realization by planners of SOC that "neglect-of-agriculture" policies did cause economic difficulties as early as the 1960s, it may be interesting to find out to what extent these policies may have shifted in the latter part of the socialist period.

In the next section we present, in a nutshell, the argument in favor of "economizing on urbanization" and of input substitution. We also set up a framework of relationships between the various aspects of the industrial structure by which one can test for the existence of a certain set of "as-if" policies. The following section contains the main argument of the paper. In the concluding section we try to point to possible policy changes in the second part of the period under investigation.

A CASE FOR "ECONOMIZING ON URBANIZATION" AND HOW TO TEST FOR IT

The case for economizing on urbanization in the context of a socialist system is based on the following propositions:

1. The socialist growth strategy is one that attempts to maximize growth (investment) and keep consumption levels at the attainable minimum. This goal is to be achieved through an intensive self-industrialization drive.

2. Industrialization needs urban development, but the extent of urbanization needed depends more on the number of people that have to be moved to cities than on the amount of capital invested in new plants. To minimize that cost and the number of people to be moved, the planning authorities have tried to maximize the number of workers among the migrants (all women should work); to minimize the number of those employed in servicing the urban population (let services be self-supplied during off-work hours); and to plan for a high capital-labor ratio in manufacturing and other urban industries.

3. A centrally planned system can take into consideration all the social costs involved in urbanization, while in a market economy some of these costs are neglected and too much urbanization is created at various stages of development. An authoritarian regime can also better prevent individuals from "irrational" migration (from country to cities), which often happens in countries where no such controls are exercised.

4. Urbanization raises consumption levels on two counts. First, services and some goods (housing, retailing, etc.) that are self-supplied in rural areas by the peasants during dead seasons and off-work hours have to be provided in the cities from public funds that might otherwise be productively invested. Second, the way of life in cities creates pressure to raise consumption levels, which socialist planners consider to be additional costs rather than product. Thus, the minimum attainable level of consumption is simply raised.

This gives us three reasons why SOC should urbanize less than a market economy at a given level of development. They internalize social costs of urbanization, they are more effective in preventing overurbanization, and they consider additional consumption that may be created as cost rather than benefit. If one adds to these reasons a starting point of low-level urban development and a bias against "nonproductive" investments, one has a complete case.

The argument for economizing on urbanization in the socialist growth context can be presented in a stereotyped form using the following model: Assume a three-sector socialist economy that attempts to minimize the product of the manufacturing (M) sector (assumed to be entirely investment), while keeping constant the product of the agricultural (A) sector (i.e., per capita consumption level). The product of the service (S) sector is considered as an input, or cost, necessary to produce M. More specifically, the cost of S is associated with the transfer of labor to the city to work in M. The cost of S can be conceived of as an addition to the wages paid to M workers or it can be subtracted from the value of their marginal product. Formally, the optimal equilibrium conditions can be stated as follows:

$$\frac{Y_L^A}{Y_K^A} = \frac{w}{r} < \frac{w(1 + v)}{r} = \frac{Y_L^M}{Y_K^M} \tag{1.1}$$

$$\frac{Y_L^A}{Y_K^A} = \frac{w}{r} = \frac{Y_L^M \left(\frac{1}{1 + v}\right)}{Y_K^M} \tag{1.2}$$

where A and M stand for the sectors; L for labor and K for capital; w and r for wage and rental rates, respectively; Y_L^A, etc., for marginal products; and v for the proportion (as percent of w or as percent of the value of the marginal product of labor in M) of total urbanization costs per urban M worker, including moving expenses, investment in infrastructure, and the cost of services. The assumption is that v is smaller in the market economy than in the socialist one. In the Edgeworth box diagram (Figure 1 drawn on the basis of equation 1.2) we have three situations: E_p is the optimum production point as seen by private agents in a market economy; E_s, drawn for the same level of A production (AA isoquant), is the optimum point of a market economy with the social costs of moving labor to cities taken into account; S is the socialist equilibrium point where the extra consumption expenditures considered as costs are also taken into account. All these extra costs are embodied in the diagram as a decline in the marginal productivity of M labor and thus as a counterclockwise shift of the MM isoquant. The M isoquants MM, $M'M'$, and $M''M''$ correspond to the three positions where $M''M''$ represents the lowest level of $Y_L^M/(1 + v)$, that is, that of a socialist economy. The socialist shift in the factor proportions used in A and M is seen by observing that $\alpha_s < \alpha_{E_s} < \alpha_{E_p}$ and that $\beta_s > \beta_{E_s} > \beta_{E_p}$, where α_i and β_i are the K to L ratios in the A and M sectors under the three situations.

In view of all this, what kind of deviations should be expected in the industrial structure of SOC as compared with that of a market economy (ME)? An underlying assumption is that there is some regularity in the pat-

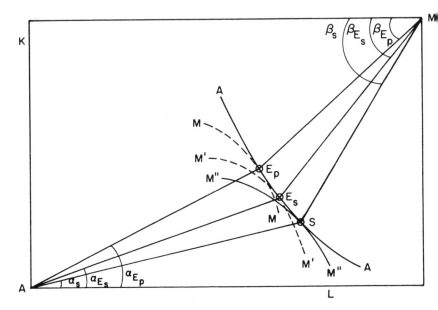

FIGURE 1.   Urbanization Costs in Market and Socialist Economies

terns of change in the industrial structure of countries during their process
of economic development. That is the theoretical base for this analysis.
Indeed, for a comparison of this kind to be valid, one has to compare countries at similar stages of economic development.[5]

The comparison of industrial structures is carried out for three sectors of
the economy: A (agriculture), M (manufacturing and related industries,
such as construction and transportation), and S (all the service industries).
Three measures of the size of each sector are used in the analysis: the proportion of the total labor force employed in the sector (L_i); the share of the
sector in total output (GNP) in current prices (P_i) or "value-i"; and the
share of the sector in total output valued in "constant" prices (Q_i) or
"real-i" where i stands for one of the sectors. We also discuss the same
measures for nonservice parts of the economy. The share of agriculture in
this $A + M$ economy is designated as A' and that of manufacturing as M'.
The purpose of the discussion in terms of A' and M' is to focus on the
input-substitution aspect without having to account for the size of the S sector.

Assuming for a moment that at any given level of development the relative intersectoral prices are the same for SOC and ME, one would expect
SOC, compared to ME, to have a smaller S sector, a larger M sector, and a
similar or somewhat smaller A sector.[6] This would be a direct result of the

growth strategy of SOC, including policies of economizing on urbanization. But it is precisely those latter policies, and especially that of input substitution, that may cause differentiation in the patterns of deviations of the various shares, as well as in the relative intersectoral prices. Figure 2 presents the main aspects for the A and A' sectors.

Figure 2 is drawn in an ordinary production space for the A sector except that the quantities of inputs and outputs are measured in *relative terms* as the proportions of the entire stock of the respective input and the total output of the economy under consideration. Thus, point N may indicate that with 25 percent of total labor (L_0) and half of the entire capital stock (K_0), the A sector is able to produce 30 percent of total output (Y), which is the real-output share of A. To accommodate economies of different sizes, we have to assume constant returns to scale, which, for an entire sector and in the long run, is not so restrictive. Let point N and the Y isoquant represent a normal situation in a market economy at a given level of development. Also assume that the real-output share of the A sector in a socialist country at the same level of development is Y. As we have seen, this is plausible in view of the expected larger real-M share and lower real-S share.

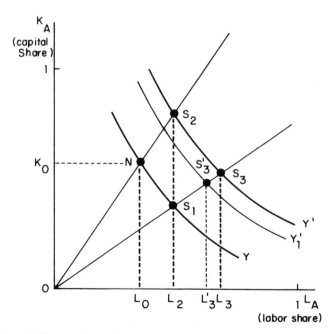

FIGURE 2.   Differences in the A and A' Employment and Output Shares between Socialist and Market Economies

We can now think of three alternative positions for the socialist economy. The socialist economy will be in position S_1 when there is only input
substitution and no loss in relative efficiency on the part of the A sector. In
such a case, there will be a positive gap in the A labor share $(L_2 - L_0)$ and
no gap in the value-A share. As pointed out above, it is likely that the input
substitution will be accompanied by lower overall relative efficiency in A.
Isoquant Y' represents the same real-A share produced at lower relative
efficiency — that is, with higher labor and capital shares and thus a higher
value-A share. SOC position in S_2 means that there is no input substitution,
only lower efficiency; this will manifest itself in positive gaps in L, K, and
value-A share, all of them of approximately the same relative size. If, however, SOC position is in S_3 where there are both input substitution and
lower efficiency, then we will have a larger labor gap (than in both S_1 and
S_2), now larger than the value-A share gap, while it is not clear if there will
be any gap in capital or in which direction it will go.

If, in addition, the real-A share of SOC is also lower, not much is
changed: SOC will be now on Y'_1 (point S'_3) with the same efficiency as on
Y', but with a somewhat lower real-A share. At S'_3 the SOC gaps of the
value-A share and of labor will be somewhat smaller, but still the first will
be smaller than the second, and both will be larger (more positive) than the
real-A gap (which is assumed to be negative).

If instead of A the diagram depicts the A' sector in an $A + M$ universe,
then the real-A' share in SOC will be lower than normal, the value-A' gap
will be larger, and that of labor larger still.

The analysis with respect to the M or M' sectors is the mirror image of
that for A and A', and so we would expect the real-M (or M') share to be
larger than normal, the gap of the value-M share to be smaller, and that for
labor the smallest.

So much for the expected SOC pattern of deviations at a time when a
socialist system is fully established. This static analysis has to be developed
into a dynamic one that must take into account two additional factors: the
"normal" structural *changes* during a process of economic growth and the
initial industrial structure of SOC when socialism took over.

STRUCTURAL CHANGES, 1950–1970

The main goal of this paper is to test in a dynamic setting the validity of the
economizing-on-urbanization hypothesis, especially its input-substitution
aspect, by identifying the effects of these policies on the structural changes
that took place in SOC between 1950 and 1970. To identify these effects,

one must distinguish between the different structural changes that occurred: (1) those resulting from historical legacies; (2) those caused by the normal development process; and (3) those particular to the socialist system and growth strategy. The last category of changes is further divided into general changes and changes specifically due to economizing-on-urbanization policies.

A vigorous growth effort following long periods of stagnation should change the industrial structure of both output and inputs in a direction converging with the normal pattern by correcting previous misallocations created by the stagnation. We would expect the previously underemployed labor concentration in the A sector to be absorbed rather fast and previously neglected industries and services to develop. There is some evidence in the literature that if deviations from normal structure exist initially and the reasons for them are removed, a convergence trend is set in motion.[7] The logic for such an occurrence is obvious. It should be emphasized that by *convergence,* we mean that changes toward a typical structure will be more intensive than the normal unit of *growth* in per capita GNP. If growth rates in SOC are also higher, then obviously the structural changes per unit of *time* should be further enhanced. The tendency to converge should be strengthened, or even result in overconvergence, if we add to the mere dynamic growth element the socialist emphasis on manufacturing and high rates of investment (and low consumption levels), and the marked shifts of trade policies from agricultural specialization toward partial autarky combined with M specialization.[8] Such policies should reduce the product and inputs shares of the A sector and increase those of M beyond what is necessary for typical development.

On the other hand, all the factors connected with the policy of economizing on urbanization have the exact opposite effect on the evolution of some of the major structural shares of SOC; they affect those various shares in a direction divergent from typical trends. Specifically, they hold back the convergence (or overconvergence) of urbanization, of the S inputs and output shares, and, most important for our argument here, of the A and M *labor* shares. The economizing-on-urbanization policies should not lower or alter the wider than typical decline that is expected in the real-output share of the A (and A') sector and the increase in the real-output share of the M sector.

Overconvergence in changes in the real-output A (and A') and M shares and underconvergence of the corresponding labor shares should also result in a typical change in the corresponding *real* relative labor productivities.[9] That of the A sector should not increase as fast as expected, while that of the M sector should increase faster than normal.

The force of the economizing-on-urbanization factors can thus be tested by examining how much the relevant parameters of the industrial structure of SOC actually converged. The smaller the convergence, the larger the impact will be judged, and vice versa. To put it differently, only definite and strong economizing-on-urbanization policies can produce a pattern of labor-share gaps not much different from that of the presocialist period.

The statistical analysis is carried out using two somewhat different methods. First, we estimate typical patterns of structural changes, and SOC deviations therefrom, on the basis of the equations

$$\Delta X_i = \alpha + \beta \ell n Y_0 + \gamma \ell n \Delta Y + \delta \ell n N_0 + u \qquad (2.1)$$

and

$$dX_i = \alpha' + \beta' \ell n Y_0 + \gamma' \ell n dY + \delta' \ell n N_0 + u \qquad (2.2)$$

where ΔX_i and dX_i stand for absolute (Δ) and relative (d) changes in the structural variables under investigation; $\ell n Y_0$ and $\ell n N_0$ respectively represent the logs of GNP per capita and population size in the initial year of the period over which changes are estimated; and $\ell n \Delta Y$ and $\ell n dY$ respectively represent the logs of the absolute and relative changes in GNP per càpita over that period. We include the dynamic change in the income variables in order to standardize for differences in structural changes resulting from different rates of growth. By keeping initial income levels in, we allow for differences in the impact of structural changes per unit of growth alòng different segments of the income range. Initial population is kept as a (static) size variable.

The second statistical method used is to compute normal structural *changes* for market economies on the basis of "static" structural equations for all observations (1950, 1960, and 1970) of the general form

$$X_i = a + b \ell n Y + [c(\ell n Y)^2] + d \ell n N_0 + D_1 + D_2 \qquad (3)$$

where the variables are as in equations 2.1 and 2.2 and D_1 and D_2 are two time-dummy variables signifying 1950 and 1960, respectively. The deviations of SOC from typical patterns are estimated both for individual countries and for the group as a whole, the latter by adding the dummy variable SC of "being a socialist country" to the various equations and the observations of SOC to the sample of countries.[10]

All the estimates are for the entire period from 1950 to 1970 and for two subperiods, 1950–1960 and 1960–1970. The disruptions of World War II and the following reconstruction period, as well as the bad quality of some of the data, preclude estimating the equations for a period starting in 1940. Instead, qualitative observations are used to link 1940 to 1950 and to evaluate the differences in the results created by choosing the 1950, rather than the 1940, industrial structure as the initial presocialist position. The ME group consists of twenty-three countries for which data were available. They range from the United States with the highest GNP per capita to Portugal with the lowest. The nature and sources of the data are given in the notes to Table 1.

Finally, a distinction should be made between a "large" or "converging" change in the gap structure and what should be considered a small change — small enough to sustain the hypothesis. Here, differences between the results based on relative changes and results based on absolute changes in the various shares can be used.[11] When the initial shares of SOC differ from the norm — as in the present case — what is estimated as normal *relative* change may be either an above- or below-normal *absolute* change. Specifically in our case, since the initial SOC labor A (or A') shares are above normal, an above-normal absolute decline in the share may turn out to be just normal or even below normal in relative terms. The opposite relation holds with respect to the M shares where an initial below-normal SOC level can turn a below-normal absolute change into an above-normal relative one. Since there is no firm theoretical base for preferring one form of change to the other, these differences can be used as one test for convergence. Conditions for a given share to converge might be that none of the two changes be smaller than normal, and preferably that both be above normal, the latter certainly when overconvergence (that is, without economizing-on-urbanization effects) is assumed. The size of the initial presocialist gaps can serve as a second supporting criterion by which to evaluate the extent of the convergence tendencies: the wider the initial gap, the greater the change should be — over and above the normal change.

Some of the estimated normal equations are presented in Table 1. As may be observed there, most of the coefficients have the "right" or expected signs and are statistically significant. Thus, as income rises, there is a general decline in the A (and A') shares and increases in the M and S shares. Similarly, whenever significant, the scale variables (ℓnN) have positive signs with respect to the M shares and negative ones with respect to the A and S shares — a manifestation of the relative large-scale advantages of the M sector. However, at least with respect to the S output shares, the normal equations do not produce the commonly expected results. For 1950 through 1970 (and for the subperiods), the normal equations estimate an overall decline in the S real-output shares. In the static equations, this is a result of a downward time trend in the shares picked up by the dummy coefficients D_1 (1950) and D_2 (1960), which is strong enough to overturn the positive effects of quite significant growth in GNP per capita. In the dynamic equa-

Table 1. Structural Equations: Market Economies, 1950–1970

Dependent Variables	Constant	ℓn Y	ℓn N	D_{50}	D_{60}	ΔY	δY	$R^{2\,a}$	SEE^b
"Static" eqs. 1950–1970									
L_A	172.95 (13.07)	−20.12 (−11.58)	−1.73 (−2.17)	−0.77 (−0.28)	−1.69 (−0.69)			.80	7.0
$L_{A'}$	215.20 (12.22)	−24.15 (−10.44)	−2.66 (−2.50)	−2.55 (−0.71)	−2.52 (−0.77)			.76	9.3
L_M	−34.98 (−2.64)	10.29 (5.92)	0.70 (0.88)	3.91 (1.44)	2.83 (1.15)			.46	7.0
L_S	215.20 (12.22)	−24.15 (−10.44)	−2.66 (−2.50)	−2.55 (−0.71)	−2.52 (−0.77)			.76	9.3
Q_A	89.94 (13.25)	−9.97 (−10.96)	−1.91 (−4.74)	−1.35 (−1.05)	−0.47 (−0.41)			.82	3.2
$Q_{A'}$	147.09 (11.92)	−16.37 (−9.90)	−2.92 (−3.99)	−1.50 (−0.64)	−0.51 (−0.25)			.79	5.7
Q_M	−3.00 (−0.22)	6.99 (3.77)	0.44 (0.53)	−2.26 (0.86)	−1.78 (−0.76)			.37	6.4
Q_S	13.10 (1.20)	2.97 (2.03)	1.48 (2.27)	3.60 (1.74)	2.24 (1.21)			.23	5.1
Dynamic eqs. 1950–1970									
ΔL_A	−59.15 (−4.74)	8.36 (4.25)	0.409 (0.41)		−0.0132 (−3.65)			.61	4.7

142

$\Delta L_{A'}$	−57.96 (−4.97)	8.20 (4.47)	0.017 (0.02)	−0.0139 (−4.10)			.66	4.4
ΔL_M	65.02 (5.39)	−10.38 (−5.46)	0.340 (0.35)	0.0081 (2.31)			.69	4.6
ΔL_S	−6.37 (−0.47)	2.07 (.96)	−0.725 (−.66)	0.0052 (1.31)			.26	5.2
ΔQ_A	−28.89 (−4.54)	3.24 (3.18)	1.400 (3.31)	−0.0031 (−1.54)			.74	1.8
$\Delta Q_{A'}$	−60.99 (−5.27)	7.04 (3.79)	1.630 (2.12)	−0.0027 (−0.74)			.73	3.2
ΔQ_M	53.23 (5.74)	−6.83 (−4.59)	0.0034 (0.01)		0.0017 (0.58)		.73	2.6
ΔQ_S	−24.22 (−2.58)	3.57 (2.37)	−1.395 (−2.23)		0.0014 (0.48)		.55	2.6
dL_A	319.43 (5.30)	−46.88 (−6.44)	−5.37 (−2.19)			−0.835 (−4.25)	.81	11.4
$dL_{A'}$	255.28 (3.22)	−36.32 (−3.80)	−5.87 (−1.82)			−0.696 (−2.70)	.63	15.0
dL_M	88.95 (1.73)	−14.85 (−2.39)	0.60 (0.29)			0.296 (1.77)	.77	9.7
dL_S	−144.81 (−1.28)	17.93 (1.65)	−4.04 (−1.11)			0.507 (1.73)	.20	17.0
Dynamic eqs. 1950–1960								
$L_{A'}$	−9.34 (−0.80)	1.23 (0.71)	−0.97 (−1.02)	−0.0143 (−2.14)			.35	4.5
$Q_{A'}$	−30.10 (163.55)	3.50 (2.86)	0.22 (0.38)	−0.0003 (−0.07)			.50	2.3

	Constant	ℓn Y	ℓn N	D_{50}	D_{60}	ΔY	·δY	R^{2a}	SEE^b
Dynamic eqs. 1960–1970									
$L_{A'}$	−55.71	7.47	0.49			−0.0104		.63	2.9
	(−5.61)	(4.82)	(0.82)			(−2.95)			
$Q_{A'}$	−53.84	6.50	1.24			−0.0037		.83	1.8
	(−6.62)	(4.48)	(3.10)			(−0.98)			

Source: The main sources for the data for nonsocialist countries are as follows:

Labor force shares: Data are mostly from two sources, International Labor Organization, *Yearbook of Labor Statistics* (Geneva, 1953 and later years); United Nations, *Demographic Yearbook* (New York, 1964 and later years). An attempt was made to use consistent data of "active employed population." However, in some cases, the data are of "total active population"; in other cases, they are of civilian labor data only.

Product shares: The industrial distribution by sector of origin is in most cases of GDP at current factor cost. In a few cases, GNP or current market price is used. The source is United Nations, *Yearbook of National Accounts Statistics* (New York, 1966 and later years).

Income per capita: Data are mostly GNP of factor cost per capita at 1964 U.S. dollars. The source is International Bank for Reconstruction and Development, *World Tables* (Washington, D.C., 1971), Table 4, column 17.

Growth rates: Growth rates for 1950–1960 and 1960–1970 were calculated on the basis of the above figures.

The following are the sources for all socialist East European countries and dates, except for cases specifically mentioned.

Labor force shares: Data for East European countries, 1950–1970, are from Andrew Elias, *Estimated Employment in Seven East European Countries, by Branch and Sector: Circa 1950 to 1970, Statistical Tables* (Washington, D.C.: Foreign Demographic Analysis Division, U.S. Department of Commerce, March 1973).

Product shares: Most data (GNP at factor costs in constant prices) are from Thad P. Alton, "Economic Growth and Resource Allocation in Eastern Europe," in U.S. Congress, Joint Economic Committee, *Reorientation and Commercial Relations of the Economies of East Europe* (Washington, D.C., 1974), Table 2, pp. 256–57. Data for the Soviet Union are at 1955 factor costs and are from Norman Kaplan, *The Record of Soviet Economic Growth 1928–1965* (Santa Monica, Calif.: Rand Corporation, 1969). The 1955 weights are from Table A-6.1, p. 123, column 14, and the sectoral production indices (1955 = 100) are from Table 1, p. 5, columns 2, 4, 5, 6.

GNP per capita: For most countries and years, data are based on growth rates in Alton, "Economic Growth and Resource Allocation," Table 10, p. 270, and on GNP per capita levels for 1960 as derived from Gur Ofer, "Economizing on Urbanization in Socialist Countries: Historical Necessity or Socialist Strategy?" in A. A. Brown and Egon Neuberger, eds., *Internal Migration: A Comparative Perspective* (New York: Academic Press, 1977), Appendix Table 1, pp. 298–303.

Growth rates: Growth rates for the Soviet Union are based on Abram Bergson, *The Real National Income of Soviet Russia since 1928* (Cambridge, Mass.: Harvard University Press, 1961), p. 265, Table 55, and on Rush Greenslade, "The Real Gross National Product of the USSR, 1950–1975," in U.S. Congress, Joint Economic Committee, *Soviet Economy in a New Perspective* (Washington, D.C., 1976), Table 6, p. 276. Soviet population data are from TsSU *Narodnoe Khoziaistvo SSSR*, various years.

Note: Figures in parentheses are *t* values. Space considerations prevent the presentation of the data used in estimating the equations and gaps. The author will be glad to send it personally to those interested.

tions, the offsetting factor is a very large and negative intercept, which probably captures the time-trend effect. Since the accepted wisdom calls for real-output S shares to increase with the level of economic development, one has to treat this specific decline with a degree of caution. It may result from statistical and definitional problems of estimating S output and prices or from their changes over time.[12] Such problems, if indeed they exist, also affect the estimates of the A and M shares, only the A' share being immune to them.

The estimated SOC gaps from the normal patterns are presented in Tables 2 to 4. To set the stage for the discussion on the convergence hypothesis with respect to the labor-force shares, we first present the estimated changes and SOC deviations therefrom of the real-output shares (Table 2). A few words of explanation on the nature and power of the ME-SOC comparisons in this category are needed. First, at this point we renounce estimate and test changes of the value-output shares, mainly because of difficulties in establishing what the static and dynamic relations between actual sectoral prices and true factor costs in SOC are. Second, an ideal cross-country comparison of real-output shares should use the same set of prices for all the countries in the sample. At the moment this is unrealistic. The second-best method possible is to use different sets of prices for each country over the entire period. This procedure introduces into the comparisons various biases of the index-number-problem type. It also eliminates the possibility of meaningful comparison of the *levels* of, and by implication the relative changes in, the output shares at any one point of time.[13] That is why Table 2 only gives results for absolute changes, which are the least affected by the biases. The data used for SOC, which are Alton's, are at constant prices for unspecified years.[14] Estimated *absolute changes* in real-output shares and the corresponding SOC residuals are based on the dynamic and static equations as explained above (see left-hand column of Table 2).

First let us observe the quite wide differences between typical and actual changes in the real-output shares of the S sectors in SOC (see table 2, panel d). In view of the above discussion, we prefer the normal figures of the "static" equations, which estimate smaller and statistically nonsignificant declines in the Q_S shares in all SOC. But even on the basis of the dynamic equations, the SOC deviations certainly point to a strong tendency to minimize S output. This is demonstrated by the very large negative individual residuals, which show much stronger declines than the estimated ones in the SOC Q_S shares. This is also true for all SOC together where statistically significant negative coefficients are estimated for SC, -3.7 points in the dynamic equation and -7.2 points in the static one (Table 2, column 9). The deviational nature of the findings is further strengthened by the fact

Table 2. Actual and Estimated Changes in the Real-Product Shares of Socialist Countries, 1950–1970

	Czechoslovakia	East Germany	Soviet Union	Hungary	Poland	Bulgaria	Romania	SEE[a]	SC[b]
	(1)	(2)	(3)	(4)	(5)	(6)	(7)	(8)	(9)
a. Q_A: Gap in 1950	8.5	-3.2	21.4	8.3	17.5	14.3	18.1		
(1) Dynamic: estimated	-6.0	-7.0	-3.3	-7.3	-5.3	-9.4	-7.5		-5.9
(2) residual	-6.0	1.7	-11.4	-5.6	-11.6	-9.4	-11.6	1.8	(-3.0)
(3) Static: estimated	-5.8	-8.1	-7.7	-6.5	-5.2	-10.0	-8.2		-6.6
(4) residual	-6.2	2.8	-7.0	-6.4	-11.7	-8.8	-10.9		(-2.27)
b. Q_A: Gap in 1950	6.8	-6.8	28.4	6.2	20.7	17.8	18.1		
(1) Dynamic: estimated	-11.1	-13.5	-9.5	-14.6	-12.4	-18.7	-16.2		-7.3
(2) residual	-6.6	3.0	-17.1	-5.2	-14.3	-14.2	-14.9	3.2	(-2.4)
(3) Static: estimated	-10.2	-13.9	-13.2	-11.4	-9.2	-17.2	-15.7		-10.5
(4) residual	-7.5	3.5	-13.3	-8.4	-17.5	-15.7	-16.8		(-2.42)
c. Q_M: Gap in 1950	5.0	6.1	-10.9	1.2	-8.2	-11.6	-7.4		
(1) Dynamic: estimated	8.0	10.8	10.7	11.2	10.8	14.7	13.6		9.6
(2) residual	9.9	3.3	15.3	6.6	11.9	13.9	17.6	2.6	(4.3)
(3) Static: estimated	7.1	8.9	8.4	7.6	6.5	10.1	8.8		14.0
(4) residual	10.8	5.2	17.6	10.2	16.2	18.5	22.4		(3.74)
d. Q_S: Gap in 1950	-13.5	-2.8	-10.5	-9.5	-9.4	-2.8	-10.7		
(1) Dynamic: estimated	-1.9	-3.7	-7.3	-3.9	-5.4	-5.3	-6.1		-3.7
(2) residual	-4.0	-5.1	-4.0	-1.0	-0.4	-4.5	-4.2	2.6	(-2.5)
(3) Static: estimated	-1.3	-0.8	-0.6	-1.2	-1.5	-0.1	-0.6		-7.2
(4) residual	-4.6	-8.0	-10.7	-3.7	-4.3	-9.7	-9.7		(2.31)

Note: For sources and explanations, see Table 1.

146

that the initial 1950 Q_S levels of most SOC were already much below normal. For reasons mentioned above, and ME-SOC comparison of service output shares at any point in time might be completely meaningless. Still, for what it is worth, our general notion that service activity in SOC in the early 1950s was very low is also supported by such a comparison. Q_S in both current 1950 prices and in "constant" prices of later years shows negative gaps, sometimes very large, for almost all SOC.[15]

That SOC did not catch up dynamically with the level of activity in the service industries is also supported by evidence on the changes in the S labor share between 1950 and 1970 (see Table 3, panel d) and on urbanization as shown in another paper.[16] In both cases, it is shown that while SOC L_S and urbanization levels increased over the period, and in many cases *relatively* faster than in ME, the absolute changes fall short of parallel changes in ME, and the initial 1950 gaps were not narrowed.

All this evidence on the various S shares and urbanization levels is in line with the economizing-on-urbanization strategy. Most of the following discussion is aimed at testing the particular argument about input substitution.

Panels a to c in Table 2 present the evidence for real-output shares of the A, A', and M sectors. As hypothesized earlier, we indeed find large above-normal declines in the real-output A and A' shares of all SOC (except East Germany), collectively estimated at 6.6 points for A and 10.5 points for A' (column 9), and much larger than normal SOC increases in the M shares — collectively estimated at 14 points above normal. All collective deviations are highly significant, and most individual ones are much larger than the standard error of estimate of the relevant equations (shown in column 8). In fact, in most cases, the declines in Q_A and $Q_{A'}$ and increases in Q_M are more than double the corresponding normal change. Unfortunately, we were not able to include in the analysis real-output changes since the late 1930s. However, given that by 1950 most SOC had already undergone structural changes in the "socialist" direction, it can be deduced with certainty that the 1950–1970 comparisons underestimate the extent of SOC deviational behavior with respect to the above variables. Some fragmentary information on changes in real-output shares between the 1930s and 1950 supports that conclusion. Specifically, according to Alton, the real-output shares declined over that period for Hungary from 37.3 to 29.7 percent in the A sector and from 55.4 to 42 percent in the A' sector; for Bulgaria from 55.1 to 39.4 percent in the A sector and from 78.6 to 57.1 percent in the A' sector; and for Czechoslovakia from 28.9 to 23.9 percent in the A sector and from 40.5 to 32.9 percent in the A' sector.[17] This strongly overconvergent behavior with respect to Q_A, $Q_{A'}$, and Q_S clearly reflects the socialist growth policies of industrialization and autarky discussed above. Under

Table 3. Actual and Estimated Changes in the Industrial Distribution of the Labor Force of Socialist Countries, 1950–1970

A. Dynamic Equations

	Czechoslovakia (1)	East Germany (2)	Soviet Union (3)	Hungary (4)	Poland (5)	Bulgaria (6)	Romania (7)	Yugoslavia (8)	SEE[a] (9)	SC[b] (10)
a. L_A: Gap in 1950	8.9	−15.6	15.0	7.7	15.4	23.9	27.0	20.2	7.0	
(1) Changes: absolute: estimated	−13.3	−17.5	−14.3	−13.9	−11.0	−18.8	−15.9	−19.9	4.7	5.3
(2) residual	−7.1	8.7	−9.3	−10.6	−7.9	−22.5	−8.7	−0.3		(4.3)
(3) relative: estimated	−71.2	−73.8	−77.1	−49.7	−43.1	−47.8	−45.5	−58.6	11.7	2.2
(4) residual	−0.4	22.0	13.3	−16.6	1.3	−26.9	6.2	25.3		(0.3)
b. $L_{A'}$: Gap in 1950	8.0	−20.5	15.8	8.5	12.4	16.5	20.4	12.0	9.8	
(1) Changes: absolute: estimated	−14.9	−19.2	−16.7	−15.0	−12.4	−19.7	−17.1	−22.2	4.4	−5.6
(2) residual	−7.7	8.9	−7.3	−15.0	−7.0	−20.3	−5.5	4.6		(−1.8)
(3) relative: estimated	−54.9	−58.7	−64.7	−38.1	−33.9	−37.6	−36.4	−47.7	15.0	−0.3
(4) residual	−6.4	14.1	14.1	−25.1	−2.0	−25.2	4.5	23.4		(−0.0)
c. L_M: Gap in 1950	0.2	17.0	−5.2	−6.2	−5.0	−15.2	−15.8	−9.4	8.1	
(1) Changes: absolute: estimated	2.4	7.3	6.8	5.4	4.2	11.0	9.0	12.1	4.6	7.6
(2) residual	9.2	−4.1	5.8	16.3	9.6	18.8	8.9	−0.1		(2.7)
(3) relative: estimated	8.4	21.0	20.3	18.2	14.1	33.9	27.9	36.4	9.7	21.1
(4) residual	16.2	−15.3	11.3	35.9	22.0	64.4	43.6	7.5		(2.7)
d. L_S: Gap in 1950	−9.0	−1.4	−9.8	−1.4	−10.4	−8.6	−11.1	−10.8	5.5	
(1) Changes: absolute: estimated	10.9	10.3	7.5	8.4	6.8	7.7	6.8	7.8	5.2	−0.8
(2) residual	−2.1	−4.2	3.4	−5.7	−1.7	3.8	−0.1	0.4		(−0.4)
(3) relative: estimated	31.7	34.5	20.2	26.5	15.2	32.5	23.9	33.1	17.0	15.1
(4) residual	4.5	−12.1	26.7	−14.9	15.6	43.9	30.4	34.1		(1.8)

B. Static Equations

	(1) Czechoslovakia	(2) East Germany	(3) Soviet Union	(4) Hungary	(5) Poland	(6) Bulgaria	(7) Romania	(8) Yugoslavia	(10) SC^b
a. L_A: Gap in 1950	8.9	−15.6	15.0	7.7	15.4	23.9	27.0	20.2	
(1) Changes: absolute: estimated	−13.4	−18.4	−16.9	−14.9	−11.8	−21.9	−18.1	−24.1	
(2) residual	−7.0	9.6	−6.7	−9.5	−7.1	−19.4	−6.5	3.9	−6.6
(3) relative: estimated	−58.0	−66.2	−66.7	−44.0	−35.3	−53.5	−46.6	−62.8	(1.3)
(4) residual	−13.6	14.4	2.9	−22.3	−6.4	−21.3	7.3	29.5	
b. $L_{A'}$: Gap in 1950	8.0	−20.5	15.8	8.5	12.4	16.5	20.4	12.0	
(1) Changes: absolute: estimated	−14.6	−20.4	−18.8	−16.3	−12.6	−24.8	−20.3	−27.4	
(2) residual	−8.0	10.1	−5.2	−13.8	−6.8	−15.2	−2.3	10.8	−3.6
(3) relative: estimated	−44.2	−53.0	−55.1	−35.4	−28.1	−45.3	−39.2	−53.6	(0.6)
(4) residual	−17.0	8.5	4.5	−27.8	−7.8	−17.5	7.3	29.4	
c. L_M: Gap in 1950	0.2	17.0	−5.2	−6.2	−5.0	−15.2	−15.8	−9.4	
(1) Changes: absolute: estimated	3.3	5.9	5.1	4.1	2.4	7.7	5.7	8.7	
(2) residual	8.3	−2.7	7.5	17.6	11.4	22.1	12.2	3.3	9.8
(3) relative: estimated	7.7	14.6	12.4	10.9	6.4	22.7	16.4	24.8	(2.2)
(4) residual	16.9	−8.9	19.3	43.3	29.7	77.6	55.1	19.2	
d. L_S: Gap in 1950	−9.0	−1.4	−9.8	−1.4	−10.4	−8.6	−11.1	−10.8	
(1) Changes: absolute: estimated	10.1	12.5	11.8	10.8	9.3	14.3	12.4	15.3	
(2) residual	−1.3	−6.4	−0.9	−8.1	−4.2	−2.8	−5.7	−7.1	4.2
(3) relative: estimated	29.7	39.4	35.2	37.8	32.0	57.1	47.1	57.6	(1.8)
(4) residual	6.5	−16.9	11.7	−26.1	−1.2	19.3	7.1	9.6	

Note: For sources and explanations, see Table 1.

[a] Standard error of estimate in relevant equation.

[b] Figures in parenthesis are t values.

normal development process, it calls for similarly large overconvergence in the corresponding labor shares.

It may be somewhat difficult to decide whether this overconvergent behavior is really happening on the basis of findings on changes in the labor shares shown in Table 3. Still, we believe that with few exceptions, the findings fail to indicate a clear overconvergence. True, in most SOC, especially the less developed among the group, the *absolute* decline in the labor *A* shares over the period were significantly above normal, but with Bulgaria being the only significant exception, such declines amounted to just normal or even below-normal *relative* changes. Similar results are shown for the collective SOC deviations (Table 3, column 9). Since the *S* labor shares did not grow faster than normal, the absolute changes in their *A'* labor shares (panel b) show smaller excesses over normal changes, and the corresponding relative negative gaps are typically even larger than corresponding changes in the *A* shares.

Changes in the *M* labor shares give an even stronger impression of overconvergence (Table 3, panel c). Here many *absolute* changes are twice as large, or larger, than the normal ones, which, considering the below-normal initial 1950 levels, translate into much larger than normal *relative* increases. Let us mention a number of points that qualify this strong impression of convergence. First, the very low presocialist levels of the *M* shares in many of these countries and the rather large corresponding gaps call for a movement toward convergence that is greater than normal. Second, we have some reservations in this case concerning the "normality" of the normal equations. Specifically, the estimated normal changes in the *M* share are heavily influenced by the tendency in most of the highly developed countries in the ME group to *reduce* their *M* labor shares, or at least not to increase them after a certain level of income is obtained.[18] Had the more developed countries been removed from the sample, the estimated increase in the *M* labor shares would have gone up (in relevant income range) by a number of points and thus seriously cut into the "excessive" SOC increases. Finally, the SOC changes in the *M* labor shares are only slightly above normal when estimated within the *A* + *M* sectors. This was already observed when overconvergence was found in the changes of the *A'* shares.[19]

Two comments on the findings for periods other than the 1950–1970 period are warranted. First, the above results hold for 1940 through 1970 with no major differences; the gaps in the labor shares for the Eastern European countries in 1940 are similar enough to those in 1950.[20] Second, as we shall see in the concluding section in somewhat greater detail, a high proportion of the excessive changes of labor shares in SOC is concentrated in the second decade of the period under investigation; between 1950 and 1960, convergence or overconvergence tendencies were much weaker.

A more direct way to estimate the existence and extent of different degrees of convergence between real-output and labor shares and to test the validity of the input-substitution hypothesis is to compare the size of the SOC deviations in real-output shares with those in the labor shares. The crucial result is that in all sectors and for almost all countries, the deviations from normal in the changes of the output shares exceed by far the corresponding deviations in the labor shares. That this is so can be seen by comparing corresponding lines in Tables 2 and 3 or by examining Table 4, where we present ratios of actual to estimated changes of the various shares of the A' sector.[21] The focus on A' is warranted, first, because of the precarious nature of the real-output shares of S and, second, because we concentrate on the A to M input substitution. As can be seen from lines 1 and 2 (the dynamic estimate) or 3 and 4 (the static estimate) in Table 4, the excessive decline in the real-output A' shares overtakes (for some countries, by wide margins) the corresponding excessive decline in the labor A' shares. There are, however, important exceptions to this finding. For Hungary (for both the dynamic and static estimates) and Bulgaria (the dynamic estimate only), the deviations in the changes of the $L_{A'}$ shares between 1950 and 1970 are larger than the corresponding deviations in the $Q_{A'}$ shares. Similar deviations of both shares in the dynamic estimates are also found in Yugoslavia. These exceptions are quite disturbing since it is in the less developed countries among SOC that we should look for input substitution if it exists.

However, it turns out that at least with respect to Hungary and Bulgaria, the findings as shown in Table 4 are somewhat misleading since in these two cases the 1950 $Q_{A'}$ shares are already much lower than the prewar shares. Exact calculations of these figures are impossible, but approximations on the basis of a reasonable set of assumptions will show that the ratio of actual to estimated changes in $Q_{A'}$ (also in $Q_{A'}$, of course) between 1940 and 1970 is around 3:0 for both dynamic and static estimations for Bulgaria. For Hungary, the ratio for the dynamic estimate is around 2:3 (and higher than that for labor — 2:0), and the ratio for the static estimate is around 2:9.[22] If this correction is accepted, we can conclude that in all SOC over the period from 1950 (1940) to 1970, the decline of both the output and the labor shares of the A' (or the A) sector was much faster than the "normal" decline in ME for a similar development process. Under the same condition, we can also conclude that the excessive decline of the real-output shares was typically higher than that of the labor share, a strong indication for A to M input substitution as defined in this paper.

Table 4. Ratios of Actual to Estimated Changes in the Labor and Product Shares of the A' Sector, 1950–1970

	Czechoslovakia	East Germany	Soviet Union	Hungary	Poland	Bulgaria	Romania	Yugoslavia
(1) 1950–1970 Dynamic: L	1.51	0.54	1.44	2.01	1.56	2.03	1.32	0.78
(2) Q	1.59	0.78	2.81	1.35	2.15	1.76	1.92	0.77[a]
(3) Static: L	1.55	0.50	1.28	1.85	1.54	1.61	1.11	0.61
(4) Q	1.74	0.75	2.01	1.74	2.90	1.91	2.18	0.72[a]
(5) 1950–1960 Dynamic: L	1.57	0.29	0.84	1.97	1.37	2.34	0.86	1.16
(6) Q	1.03	1.02	2.68	1.59	2.03	1.50	0.98	0.56
(7) Static: L	1.62	0.24	0.85	1.46	1.36	1.24	0.58	0.76
(8) Q	1.09	0.77	2.46	2.09	3.70	1.70	1.30	0.77
(9) 1960–1970 Dynamic: L	1.33	1.12	2.23	1.82	1.24	1.89	1.53	0.56
(10) Q	2.16	0.56	2.20	0.88	1.52	1.62	2.22	0.72[a]
(11) Static: L	1.38	1.33	1.92	2.49	1.78	2.11	1.83	0.49
(12) Q	2.48	0.71	1.47	1.38	2.29	2.11	2.95	0.69[a]

Note: For sources and explanations, see Table 1.

[a] Assuming that P_A declined by the same proportion as L_A over the 1960–1970 period, then $Q_{A70} = 29.0$ [$Q_{A50} = 42.6$, $Q_{A60} = 37.5$].

MORE HIGHLY DEVELOPED SOC
AND RECENT CHANGES

It is interesting to note that even the more highly developed SOC that did not originally have large labor reserves in the countryside have followed the policy of input substitution. This is true even of East Germany, which started out with a smaller than normal A sector and was overurbanized and overindustrialized back in the 1930s. But since the normal process of economic development calls for a decline in the A sector shares, even East Germany, in which this decline for both the labor and the output shares was lower than normal for market economies, removed fewer people from agriculture than the decline in the A (or A') output shares required. Only during the second part of the period did East Germany turn around, as did some other SOC, to reestablish more balanced ratios of labor to output in its A and A' sectors.

Czechoslovakia and Hungary, which had moderate positive A and A' gaps in the late 1930s and an overall structure not very different from the normal structure of other SOC,[23] also followed input-substitution policies, albeit not as intensively as other SOC. The strange thing about Czechoslovakia is that — in contrast to the picture presented by other countries — this policy was concentrated in the second period and absent during the early socialist years. This may be explained by the relative overall shortage of labor, especially in agriculture, resulting from the loss of the German population of the Sudeten region and the Bulgarian migrant workers.

As can be seen from Tables 2 and 3, the more highly developed SOC also followed other policies of economizing on urbanization related to changes in the S sector. Like the less developed SOC, they (including even East Germany) experienced declines over time in the labor and output shares of their service industries. Czechoslovakia and Hungary had an initial negative S gap, which further widened during the socialist period. In East Germany a very small initial gap developed into a larger one over the same period (see Tables 2 and 3, panels d).

In the introduction to this paper (and in previous ones), we argued that countries that had embarked on the socialist growth strategy at a later stage of economic development may have both less reason and less opportunity to engage in policies of economizing on urbanization and input substitution. However, we find that such policies are indeed pursued, even if not with such force as in the less developed countries. Two explanations are possible. First, since normal economic development calls for a decline in the A and A' shares and an increase in the M and S shares, these policies can abstain from shifting labor from agriculture to the urban sectors and can restrict the growth of output of the S sector. Since socialist economic strategy calls for an even smaller than normal A share output, there is additional room for such policies, even when this share was at the outset normal or lower than normal (as in East Germany). The second explanation is that the more developed SOC simply followed the strategy designed by the Soviet Union, regardless of whether it fully or partially fitted their needs and situation. Most analysts consider the shift in Czechoslovakia from the traditional prewar emphasis on light industry to an emphasis on heavy industry to be a grave strategic mistake that was the result of emulation of Soviet policies. Emulation caused similar errors to occur in other aspects of the growth strategy as well. It thus may have happened with respect to urbanization policies, which can be rationalized at least to some degree even for these countries.

That brings us to a consideration of why the Soviet Union embarked on such policies in the first place. Such a consideration cannot be conducted on the basis of data for the 1930s and 1940s, when the Soviet Union was already pushing its growth strategy at full tilt. To get to the origins of that Soviet strategy, we have to go back to the 1920s.

Indeed on the eve of the Soviet Five-Year-Plan period (or in 1913), conditions were conducive to incorporating the policy of economizing on urbanization into the growth strategy. With income per capita of between \$150 and \$200 in both 1913 and 1928, the Soviet Union had a level of urbanization about 15 points below normal, a surplus of A labor share of between 15 and 20 points or more, and deficiencies of M and S labor shares of about half as much each.[24] Gaps in the same direction are estimated for the output shares.

It was during this period that the Soviet growth strategy was formed. In line with Marxist tradition and Lenin's writings, the official plan for agriculture called for turning the backward labor-intensive sector into a collectivized or nationalized industry, characterized by large-scale, highly mechanized (and electrified) units of production.[25] Such policies seem to imply the opposite of input substitution as defined here. It is not very clear if these were also the immediate goals of Stalin when he decided on mass collectivization in the late 1920s. It is very clear, however, that he was faced with an extreme shortage of capital, a large deficiency of urban infrastructure, and a majority of the population living in rural areas — all, given the basic growth decisions, highly conducive for a policy of economizing on urbanization. And, indeed, either through a positive decision or by yielding to pressures and following priorities, a policy of economizing on urbanization was followed in the Soviet Union for a long period *despite* the collectivization. It is in this way that historical conditions affected and reshaped the socialist growth strategy.

ʼ

From 1929 to 1960 and beyond — despite the cruelty of the collectivization drive and the size of rural-urban migration, which, especially during
the earlier Five-Year Plans, was greater than planned[26] — the Soviet Union
maintained the same deviant industrial structure of low urbanization level,
low S shares, surplus A labor shares, and no surplus M labor shares. All this
occurred despite a very marked increase in the real-output M share (see
Tables 2 and 3).

CONCLUSION

Was this socialist urbanization policy successful? Was its input-substitution
aspect a good policy? This is not the place to engage in a full cost-benefit
analysis. But one of the merits of the policy of input substitution seems to
emerge from this paper's analysis. Looking back on the SOC experience,
one finds a series of failures in agricultural production for all countries.
Clearly such failures are the outcome of many flaws in the planning and
management systems. They are also the result of making the A sector the
main buffer to absorb unfulfilled plans in high-priority sectors. However,
they may also be a result of an overestimation of the production potential of
what was intended to be just a change in the factor proportions. What the
planners may have overlooked is the extent of the complementarity between
factor proportions and efficiency, or, rather, between the amount of capital
invested and potential changes in technological level and thus productivity.
What was intended as a movement along a given isoquant may have resulted
in a retreat to a lower one. So, for this or other reasons, the neglect of agriculture seems to have been overdone. The results have manifested themselves in minimum consumption levels that have been lower than planned
and in a lower than warranted contribution of agricultural production to exports, with the possible end result of slower growth even in the noncon-
sumption parts of GNP. There is no question that the acute periodical
shortages of food and agricultural crises have affected productivity
throughout the economy in a variety of ways. The fact that agricultural
goods are "hard goods" in the trade relations of the East European bloc
(i.e., goods for which hard currency can be received) and machinery is considered "soft" indicates the growth potential embodied in a more productive agricultural sector.[27] This could be a major reason for the apparent
change of direction that took place in some SOC after 1960, as can be observed from data on subperiods presented in Table 4.

A comparison of the figures in lines 5 to 8 with those in lines 9 to 12 in
Table 4 reveals that while the main finding for 1950 to 1970 is even more
evident in 1950 to 1960 (with Yugoslavia and Czechoslovakia as excep-

tions), the picture is quite different between 1960 and 1970. We find that the A' labor shares of East Germany, the Soviet Union, Hungary, and Bulgaria were not only falling at a pace faster than normal (as always), but were also overtaking the normal rates by a wider margin than were the corresponding A' output shares. Such a shift in the size of the gaps between the labor and output shares (which nevertheless also continued to shrink) indicates that the relative overall productivity in agriculture started to turn upward in these countries and/or that the policy of input substitution was eased or even reversed. It also indicates that these countries increased the share of capital invested in agriculture over that of the early socialist period. There is much evidence that indeed this has been happening in the Soviet Union and in Hungary, and the author has observed this phenomenon in Bulgaria. Bulgaria (and possibly Hungary as well) has been taking steps to renew the role of its agricultural sector as a foreign exchange earner.[28] It might be revealing that such changes did not take place by 1970 in Romania, the most ideologically unorthodox of the group, and in Poland (and possibly Yugoslavia), where agriculture is not nationalized and is even more neglected by the government. A closer look at the return to agriculture in at least some SOC and its implications for the industrial structure and the growth strategy must be deferred to another study.

NOTES

1. The other papers were written in 1976, 1977, and 1979 (see Bibliography). The present paper is based in part on a draft written in 1974, which appeared only in draft form. References are made to sections in this last paper that are not included in the present one or elsewhere.
2. Gur Ofer, "Economizing on Urbanization in Socialist Countries."
3. See also Gur Ofer, "Industrial Structure, Urbanization and Socialist Strategy" (1974), pp. 18-25.
4. The pattern of development of the urban sector and of trade were discussed in the papers mentioned in note 1.
5. See, for example, Hollis B. Chenery and M. Syrquin, *Patterns of Development, 1950-1970.*
6. See Gur Ofer, "Industrial Structure, Urbanization and the Growth Strategy of Socialist Countries," pp. 220-22.
7. Hollis B. Chenery and Lance Taylor, "Development Patterns," pp. 401-03.
8. Gur Ofer, "Industrial Structure" (1974), pp. 18-25, and "Growth Strategy, Specialization in Agriculture and Trade."
9. Relative to the average in the economy. Clearly one would expect increases in labor productivities in all sectors.

10. In the "static" equation (equation 3), the normal deviation of changes in SOC is estimated by adding SC time and SC interaction dummy variables DS_1 and DS_2 signifying SOC differences from normal in 1950 and in 1960 as distinct from that in 1970. The estimated values for DS_1 with opposite signs give us the deviation of SOC *changes* from normal changes over the 1950–1970 period.

11. An absolute change is defined as the number of percentage points by which a given share increased or declined over the period. A relative change is the ratio of the absolute change to the corresponding share at the beginning of the period.

12. We do get an overall increase through growth and time of the value-output shares reflecting the expected increase of the relative prices of services.

13. That the relative changes in the shares are affected much more than the absolute changes was established by simulating a number of cases that are quantitatively in the range of the actual changes in SOC.

14. Thad P. Alton, "Economic Growth and Resource Allocation in Eastern Europe," Table 2, pp. 256–57.

15. In "current" prices there are two exceptions: East Germany and Bulgaria, which have small positive deviations.

16. Ofer, "Economizing on Urbanization," Table 16.1, p. 281.

17. Thad P. Alton, "Economic Structure and Growth in Eastern Europe," Table 8, p. 54.

18. This is the case for almost all ME with GNP per capita at or above that of most SOC; see Table 1.

19. This results because by definition the *absolute* change in any A' share is equal to the negative of the absolute change in the corresponding M' share.

20. In the case of Romania and Hungary, the labor gaps in 1940 and 1950 are almost identical. The smaller gap in postwar Poland represents the major change in its territory and population as a result of the war; it relinquished the heavily rural regions in the east to the Soviet Union and gained (from Germany) the much more developed regions to the west and north. Only in the case of the A labor share for Bulgaria is the prewar gap smaller than the 1950 gap, but even if the prewar A share is used, the decline in the share up to 1960 is still very large — larger than for any other SOC.

21. The ratios are $\Delta X_{ij} / \Delta Z_{ij}$, where Δ stands for change (in points), X and Z for the actual and estimated shares respectively, i for the specific share, and j for an individual country.

22. No other ratios are critically affected by the shift of the starting point to 1940 for all cases where 1940 information is available.

23. See Tables 16.1–16.3 in Ofer, "Economizing on Urbanization." See also lines called "Gap in 1950" in Tables 2 and 3 in this chapter.

24. See the related discussion in Ofer, "Economizing on Urbanization," pp. 144–47, 185–90. The normal equations used to estimate the Soviet structural deviations in 1928 or before are those for ME in 1940 and 1950.

25. Vladimir I. Lenin, "The Tasks of the Proletariat in the Present Revolution,"

p. 23; N. Bukharin and E. Preobrazhensky, *The ABC of Communism*, pp. 352–57.
26. See Ofer, "Industrial Structure" (1976), pp. 243–44.
27. Alan Brown and Paul Marer, "Foreign Trade in the East European Reforms," pp. 160–62.
28. Ofer, "Growth Strategy."

BIBLIOGRAPHY

Alton, T. P., "Economic Structure and Growth in Eastern Europe." In U.S. Congress, Joint Economic Committee, *Economic Development in Countries of Eastern Europe*. Washington, D.C., 1970.
————. "Economic Growth and Resource Allocation in Eastern Europe." In U.S. Congress, Joint Economic Committee, *Reorientation and Commercial Relations of the Economies of East Europe*. Washington, D.C., 1974.
Bergson, A. *The Real National Income of Soviet Russia since 1928*. Cambridge, Mass.: Harvard University Press, 1961.
Brown, A., and P. Marer. "Foreign Trade in the East European Reforms." In M. Bornstein, ed., *Plan and Market: Economic Reform in Eastern Europe*. New Haven, Conn.: Yale University Press, 1973.
Bukharin, N., and E. Preobrazhensky. *The ABC of Communism*. Baltimore: Penguin Books, 1969.
Chenery, H. B., and L. Taylor. "Development Patterns: Among Countries and over Time." *Review of Economics and Statistics*, L, no. 4 (November 1968):391–416.
Chenery, H. B., and M. Syrquin. *Patterns of Development, 1950–1970*. London: Oxford University Press, 1975.
Elias, A. *Estimated Employment in Seven East European Countries, by Branch and Sector: Circa 1950 to 1970, Statistical Tables*. Washington, D.C.: Foreign Demographic Analysis Division, U.S. Department of Commerce, March 1973.
Greenslade, R. "The Real Gross National Product of the USSR, 1950–1975." In U.S. Congress, Joint Economic Committee, *Soviet Economy in a New Perspective*. Washington, D.C., 1976.
International Bank for Reconstruction and Development. *World Tables*. Washington, D.C., 1971.
International Labor Organization. *Yearbook of Labor Statistics* (various volumes). Geneva.
Kaplan, N. *The Record of Soviet Economic Growth 1928–1965* (Memorandum RM-6169.) Santa Monica, Calif.: Rand Corporation, 1969.
Lenin, V. I. "The Tasks of the Proletariat in the Present Revolution: Theses (April 1917)." *Collected Works*, vol. 24. London, 1964.
Organization for European Cooperation and Development. *Labor Force Statistics 1958–1969*. Paris, 1971.
Ofer, G. "Industrial Structure, Urbanization and Socialist Strategy: A Historical Analysis 1940–1967." (Draft.) Jerusalem, March 1974.

————. "Industrial Structure, Urbanization and the Growth Strategy of Socialist Countries." *Quarterly Journal of Economics* 40 (May 1976):219–44.

————. "Economizing on Urbanization in Socialist Countries: Historical Necessity or Socialist Strategy?" In A. A. Brown and E. Neuberger, eds., *Internal Migration: A Comparative Perspective.* New York: Academic Press, 1977.

————. "Growth Strategy, Specialization in Agriculture and Trade: A Comparison of Bulgaria with the Rest of Eastern Europe." In P. Marer and J. M. Montias, eds., *East European Integration and East-West Trade.* Bloomington: University of Indiana Press, 1979.

Soviet Union, Tsentralnoe statisticheskoe upravlenie. *Narodnoe khoziaistvo SSSR 1967* (The National Economy of the USSR). Moscow, 1968.

United Nations. *Demographic Yearbook* (various issues). New York.

————. *Statistical Yearbook* (various volumes). New York.

————. *Yearbook of National Accounts Statistics* (various volumes). New York.

7 THE IMPACT OF INTERNATIONAL INFLATION ON YUGOSLAVIA

Egon Neuberger and Laura Tyson

This paper utilizes a particular conceptual framework, called the "impact model,"[1] to analyze the effects of the worldwide price increases in fuel and raw material on Yugoslavia between 1973 and 1975. We begin by providing a very brief description of this framework and of the data required for its application to a specific economy.

The impact model identifies four separate processes — generation, transmission, propagation, and containment — by which world price increases influence economic conditions in a particular country. The generation process focuses on the events and policies that give rise to external inflationary pressure. The transmission process examines the manner by which world price increases are transmitted to domestic wholesale or producer prices of tradable goods. The propagation process refers to the vari-

This paper represents a revised and expanded version of the Yugoslav case study by Zbigniew Fallenbuchl, Egon Neuberger, and Laura Tyson, "East European Reactions to International Commodity Inflation," in John P. Hardt, ed., *East European Economies post Helsinki,* Joint Economic Committee of Congress Compendium, 1977; University of Windsor Discussion Paper Series No. 45; Stony Brook Working Paper No. 176, April 1977. This paper was partially supported by the Ford Foundation International Competition on Research on the Soviet Union and Eastern Europe in 1975.

ous ways in which increases in the domestic prices of tradables cause further domestic inflation. Finally, the containment process identifies all the policies and changes in the economic system introduced specifically to prevent both the transmission and the propagation of the effects of externally generated inflation on the domestic economy.

The efficiency of the transmission and propagation processes — the facility and speed with which external events affect the internal economic situation — is a function of the nature of the existing economic system, of the development strategy that determines the structure of the country's imports and exports, of existing government policies, and of the efficacy of the containment process. A useful way of examining the containment process is to consider three major potential insulation layers — that is, points at which the containment of imported inflation can best be accomplished: (1) the foreign trade and exchange sector, where changes in world market prices can be prevented from causing changes in domestic wholesale prices of tradables; (2) the consumer and producer trade networks, where changes in the domestic wholesale prices of tradables can be prevented from causing changes in retail prices of both tradables and nontradables; and (3) the labor market, where changes in retail prices of consumer goods, which raise the cost of living, can be prevented from causing increases in wages, thereby breaking the price-wage-price spiral.

Yugoslavia represents an exception to the other East European socialist countries with respect to all aspects of the impact model.[2] Whereas these other countres attempt to insulate their domestic price levels from changes in world market prices, Yugoslavia permits domestic prices to be affected by externally generated inflation to a significant extent. Yugoslavia is therefore much more comparable to a developing market economy than to a planned Soviet type of economy in the manner and extent to which it is influenced by such inflation.

THE IMPACT ON FOREIGN TRADE: STATISTICAL EVIDENCE

In Yugoslavia the balance of payments has always constituted the ultimate constraint on expansion in output and employment, and, as will be shown below, this was again true in 1975. The Yugoslav balance of payments has been affected by many factors, but the key ones to be discussed in this paper are the perennial deficit in the trade balance, shifts in the terms of trade, differential growth in the volume of exports and imports, and changes in the invisibles account.

As shown in Table 1, the deficit in the trade balance was very large between 1971 and 1975, ranging from 44 percent of total Yugoslav commodity exports in 1972 to 98 percent in 1974, the year that the impact of increased world commodity prices was the greatest. Given this large trade deficit, even if worldwide inflation had caused both Yugoslav export and import prices to rise at the same rate, leaving the net barter terms of trade unchanged, Yugoslavia's trade deficit in current prices would have risen in absolute terms.

The trade deficit was also increased by the much faster growth of imports than of exports, even when measured in constant prices in 1973 and 1974, the two years when the impact of externally generated inflation was greatest.

The combination of these two factors — the superimposition of rising international prices on the large trade deficit existing even in 1972 (the year with the lowest absolute and relative deficit) and the growing gap between the real volume of imports and the real volume of exports — caused the trade deficit to increase by about two-thirds between 1972 and 1973 even though there was a slight improvement in the Yugoslav terms of trade. Thus, it is not surprising that the roof caved in during 1974, when a 10.5

Table 1. Yugoslavia's International Trade

	1970	1971	1972	1973	1974	1975
Millions of current dinars[a]						
Imports	48,857	55,284	54,957	76,689	127,837	130,844
Exports	28,544	30,845	38,033	48,494	64,678	69,228
Balance of trade	− 20,313	− 24,439	− 16,924	− 28,195	− 63,159	− 61,610
Balance as % of						
exports	71.2	79.2	44.5	58.1	97.7	89.0
Rates of growth (%)						
Imports						
(current prices)		13.2	− .6	39.5	66.7	2.4
Exports						
(current prices)		8.1	23.3	27.5	33.4	7.0
Imports						
(constant prices)[b]		9.3	− 6.1	16.9	14.4	− 2.9
Exports						
(constant prices)[b]		3.8	17.3	6.3	1.0	− 2.0
Balance of trade						
(current prices)		+ 20.3	− 30.7	+ 66.6	+ 224.0	− 2.4

Source: SZS, Statisticki Godisnjak, 1976.
[a]$1 = 17 dinars.
[b]1975 prices = 100.

percent deterioration in the terms of trade exacerbated the existing trade imbalance (see Table 2). The combination of these three factors caused the trade deficit to rise from 17 billion current dinars in 1972 to 63 billion in 1974. The 1974 deficit was 3.7 times that in 1972 and was almost as large as total Yugoslav exports. As indicated below, the situation was further aggravated by the slowdown in earnings in the invisibles account attributable to the stagnation in Western Europe.

Table 2. Yugoslavia's Export and Import Prices and Terms of Trade, 1971–1975 (Annual Percentage Changes)

	1971	1972	1973	1974	1975
Export price index	5.3%	5.0%	20.6%	31.6%	9.0%
Food	4.6	14.7	30.8	− 2.0	4.0
Raw materials	8.5	3.9	64.2	14.9	− 2.1
Fuels	9.8	2.2	23.9	75.4	8.0
Chemicals	4.3	4.1	5.9	85.2	3.0
Machinery and equipment	12.9	2.8	16.7	19.1	24.0
Processed materials	− 3.5	1.8	17.9	51.5	4.0
Import price index	3.8	7.4	17.2	47.1	5.0
Food	3.3	0.0	40.3	14.9	7.0
Raw materials	− 4.2	8.7	26.0	58.7	0.0
Fuels	28.6	0.0	29.6	285.7	4.0
Chemicals	− 1.7	1.7	17.2	47.0	2.0
Machinery and equipment	8.1	13.4	11.8	17.6	11.0
Processed materials	− 1.6	1.6	16.1	38.9	11.0
Terms of trade	1.4	− 2.2	2.9	− 10.5	3.8
Food	1.3	14.7	− 6.8	− 14.7	− 2.8
Raw materials	13.3	− 4.4	30.3	− 27.6	− 2.1
Fuels	− 14.6	2.2	− 4.4	− 38.6	3.9
Chemicals	6.1	2.4	− 9.6	26.0	1.0
Machinery and equipment	4.4	− 9.3	4.4	1.3	11.7
Processed materials	− 1.9	.2	1.6	9.1	− 6.3

Source: SZS, Statisticki Godisnjak, 1976, pp. 232–33.

The Yugoslav trade deficit has traditionally been offset in part by two items in the invisibles account: earnings from tourism and remittances from workers temporarily employed abroad. Between 1971 and 1975, receipts from these sources equaled about 63 percent of receipts from total merchandise exports. As a result of earnings from these two items, the current account deficit has been significantly smaller than the balance of trade deficit, as the figures in Table 3 illustrate. The importance of these items in Yugoslavia makes them potential channels through which international economic disturbances influence the domestic economic situation.

Table 3.   Yugoslavia's Indicators of Macroeconomic Performance, 1971–1976

	1971	1972	1973	1974	1975	1976
Annual rates of growth (%)						
Real social product[a]	8.1	4.3	4.9	8.5	3.3	
Nonagricultural[b] production	8.2	6.2	3.9	10.0	6.2	0.0
Industrial[c] production	10.3	8.1	5.8	10.9	5.4	3.8
Balance of trade[d] (millions U.S. $)	-1268	-727	-1299	-3184	-2907	-1711
Current account[d] balance (millions U.S. $)	-388	415	491	-1226	-925	330[e]
Remittances[d] (millions U.S. $)	708	889	1326	1469	1639	
Tourism[d] (millions U.S. $)	392	463	638	714	748	
Changes in holdings[d] of convertible foreign exchange (millions U.S. $)	47	543	647	-342	-210	
Increase in long-term capital[d] (millions U.S. $)	583	489	614	496	823	

[a]1971–1975 growth rates calculated from data in *Statisticki Godisnjak,* 1976, Table 106–9.
[b]Figures calculated from data contained in various issues of *Indeks;* 1976 is a January–June estimate of growth over same period of previous year.
[c]Figures calculated from data contained in various issues of *Indeks;* 1976 is a January–September estimate of growth over same period of previous year.
[d]International Monetary Fund, *Balance of Payments Yearbook.*
[e]Estimate, January–September, 1976, cited by B. Sefer in an interview with *Borba,* October 27, 1976, p. 9.

The significant slowdown in world price inflation in 1975 and the turn-about in Yugoslav terms of trade, combined with government policies to control imports (causing a decline in the real volume of imports), brought about a slight improvement in the trade balance, which dropped from 63.2 billion to 61.6 billion dinars and from 98 percent to 89 percent of total exports.

As shown in Table 2, the 1973–1974 inflation hit different commodity groups in a highly differentiated pattern. Not surprisingly, prices of imported fuels rose most rapidly, by 30 percent in 1973 and by almost 300 percent in 1974. The prices of raw materials, food, processed materials, and chemicals all experienced increases of more than 50 percent in these two years, with only machinery and equipment prices rising at a slower rate. With all prices rising more slowly in 1975, the trend was reversed, with somewhat slower increases of prices in the commodity groups whose prices had risen most dramatically in 1974, and faster increases in other categories.

During the 1973–1974 period, the Yugoslav terms of trade deteriorated for food and fuels, were about even for raw materials, and improved for chemicals, machinery and equipment, and processed materials. However, as indicated earlier, the overall terms of trade deteriorated during this period.

The overall impact of worldwide inflation on Yugoslav export and import prices can be seen in Table 2. After two years of relatively stable foreign trade prices, export prices rose by 21 percent and import prices by 17 percent in 1973. In 1974 the full impact of worldwide inflation hit Yugoslavia, with export prices rising by 32 percent and import prices by a dramatic 47 percent, resulting in a 10.5 percent decline in the net barter terms of trade. Taking 1972 as the base year, the export price index rose to 158 by 1974, and the import price index to 174. These changes contributed to the two-thirds increase in the balance of trade deficit in 1974.

The data in Table 4 indicate the effects of changes in world prices on the commodity composition of Yugoslav imports and exports. The increased cost of essential fuels and raw materials in 1974 contributed to a decline in the share of food and machinery imports. The relative decline in machinery imports was quickly reversed in 1975, when the line was held on the value of fuel imports and there was a significant drop in the value of raw material imports, due in part to government contractionary policies discussed later in this paper.

The impact of the worldwide price inflation on Yugoslavia was somewhat moderated by the fact that well over half of both Yugoslav imports and exports consisted of machinery and equipment and other manufactured products, whose prices moved at a slower rate than did fuel prices. Other raw material and fuel categories accounted for over one-quarter of Yugo-

Table 4. Yugoslavia's Commodity Composition of Import and Export (Standard International Trade Classification, Current Prices)

	Millions Dinars					% of Total				
	1971	1972	1973	1974	1975	1971	1972	1973	1974	1975
Imports										
Food, beverage, tobacco	5,036	5,249	8,636	11,323	7,133	9.1	9.6	11.3	8.9	5.5
Raw materials	5,299	5,715	8,260	17,073	12,558	9.6	10.4	10.8	13.4	9.6
Fuels	3,274	2,998	6,092	16,169	16,030	5.9	5.5	7.9	12.6	12.3
Animal and vegetable oils	826	715	367	912	1,779	1.5	1.3	0.5	0.7	1.4
Chemicals	5,054	5,930	7,650	13,787	14,177	9.1	10.8	10.0	10.8	10.9
Machinery and equipment	17,299	17,317	24,060	33,298	44,456	31.3	31.5	31.4	26.0	34.0
Other manufactures	18,496	17,033	21,624	35,275	34,711	33.5	30.9	28.1	27.6	26.3
Total	55,284	54,957	76,689	127,837	130,844	100.0	100.0	100.0	100.0	100.0
Exports										
Food, beverage, tobacco	5,418	6,659	7,805	7,008	8,132	17.6	17.5	16.1	10.8	11.8
Raw materials	2,523	3,135	4,668	6,122	4,799	8.2	8.2	9.7	9.5	6.9
Fuels	337	302	370	693	511	1.1	0.8	0.8	1.1	.7
Animal and vegetable oils	72	19	47	135	26	0.2		0.1	0.2	
Chemicals	2,197	2,430	2,998	6,522	6,450	7.1	6.4	6.2	10.1	9.3
Machinery and equipment	7,558	9,292	11,975	15,010	19,406	24.5	24.4	24.7	23.2	28.0
Other manufactures	12,740	16,196	20,631	29,188	29,904	41.3	42.7	42.4	45.1	43.3
Total	30,845	38,033	48,494	64,678	69,228	100.0	100.0	100.0	100.0	100.0

slav imports only in 1974 when prices of these goods rose dramatically. Before 1974, and again in 1975, these two crucial categories accounted for less than 25 percent of total imports.

When we look at Yugoslav exports, we see that machinery and other manufactured goods play an even more dominant role in Yugoslav trade. In every year included in Table 4, these two categories accounted for over two-thirds of Yugoslav exports. On the other hand, raw materials and fuels played a much smaller role in Yugoslav exports than in imports, accounting for only about 10 percent of total exports. When this observation is combined with the fact that Yugoslavia runs a large trade deficit, it becomes clear why Yugoslavia was not able to benefit from the pattern of commodity price increases in world markets.

There is a specific geographic pattern to Yugoslav exports, imports, and the trade balance. As shown in Table 5, between 60 and 66 percent of Yugoslav imports come from OECD (Organization for European Cooperation and Development) countries, between 23 and 25 percent from planned economies, and only 10 to 16 percent from less developed countries (LDCs). This pattern was quite steady between 1971 and 1975 and was affected only marginally by world price inflation. The rise in the share of imports from less developed economies from 9.8 percent of total imports in 1972 to 16.2 percent in 1974 was the consequence of the rise in oil and raw material prices; it was compensated by a drop in the share of imports (primarily

Table 5. Yugoslav Foreign Trade, by Geographical Area

	1971	1972	1973	1974	1975
Exports (% of total)					
OECD countries	52.9	56.9	55.7	46.6	35.7
Planned economies[a]	36.7	36.1	34.0	41.6	47.2
LDCs	10.4	7.0	10.3	11.8	17.1
Imports (% of total)					
OECD countries	65.8	65.4	62.5	60.5	60.8
Planned economies[a]	23.9	24.8	24.8	23.3	24.8
LDCs	10.3	9.8	12.7	16.2	14.4
Trade Deficit (% of total)					
OECD countries	82.0	84.5	74.3	74.6	89.0
Planned economies[a]	7.8	−0.5	8.9	4.7	−0.5
LDCs	10.2	16.0	16.8	20.7	11.5

Source: Table L, Appendix, OECD, Yugoslavia, 1976.
[a]Planned economies include CMEA, China, and Albania.

manufactured goods) from the OECD countries from 65.4 to 60.5 percent of the total.

The impact of stagnation in the OECD countries and the ban on Yugoslav beef exports to the EEC (European Economic Community) in 1974 actually caused a much more noticeable reorientation of Yugoslav exports than the reorientation of imports caused by external inflation. The share of the OECD countries in total exports dropped from 56.9 percent in 1972 to 35.7 percent in 1975. This decline was compensated by significant increases in exports to the planned economies, whose share in total Yugoslav exports increased from 36.1 to 47.2 percent, and to the less developed economies, whose share increased from 7 to 17.1 percent.

The Yugoslav trade deficit also has a specific geographic pattern. The major share of the deficit arises in trade with Western industrial countries. For example, in 1973, 1974, and 1975, the shares of the overall trade deficit arising in this segment of Yugoslav trade were 74, 75 and 89 percent, respectively. Trade with centrally planned economies is generally balanced, with only minor net surpluses or deficits in any given year. The same conclusions apply to trade with developing countries. Only in 1974 and 1975 did the deficit in trade with developing countries increase sharply, primarily because of increases in the price of oil. Even in these years, the magnitude of the deficit was small as compared to the deficit in trade with the industrialized West.

The data in Table 6 indicate the important role that CMEA (Council for Mutual Economic Assistance) countries play in Yugoslav imports of some of the fuels and raw materials whose prices rose sharply on world markets in 1974. Yugoslavia depended on CMEA sources for dominant shares of its imports of coal, coke, and chemical fertilizers and for significant shares of its imports of crude oil and cotton fiber. As an observer rather than a full member of CMEA, Yugoslavia was unable to purchase these imports at intra-CMEA prices, which lagged behind world prices. Nonetheless, the figures in Table 6 suggest that the prices that CMEA sellers charged Yugoslav buyers for coke and cotton fiber did not rise nearly as fast as the prices charged by non-CMEA sellers. In addition, the CMEA price for coal exports to Yugoslavia did not rise as fast as the world price of coal, as measured by the cost per short ton of U.S. coal (which rose by about 70 percent in 1974). On the other hand, CMEA and non-CMEA prices for oil and fertilizer imports in Yugoslavia increased at roughly the same rate.

These results suggest that at least for imports of coke and cotton fiber, and possibly also for imports of coal, Yugoslav dependence on CMEA sources acted to mitigate the effects of the worldwide commodity price in-

Table 6.   Yugoslavia's Important Raw Material and Fuel Imports, 1973 and 1974

| | Share of CMEA Sources | | | |
| | Total Volume | | Total Value | |
	1973	*1974*	*1973*	*1974*
Crude oil	27.7	28.3	26.9	27.3
Coal[a]	92.5	100.0	89.2	100.0
Coke	81.3	81.3	74.5	68.8
Cotton fiber	46.7	43.6	45.0	39.5
Fertilizer				
Natural phosphate	1.5	1.6	1.8	2.0
Chemical	93.7	91.0	87.6	83.2

| | %Increase in Import Unit Price in 1974 | |
	CMEA Sources	*Non-CMEA Sources*
Crude oil	345.6	348.0
Coal[a]	48.7	
Coke	58.4	209.2
Cotton fiber	77.7	95.7
Fertilizer		
Natural phosphate	290.8	283.4
Chemical	78.4	75.0

Source: *Statistika Spoljne Trgovine SFR Jugoslavyi,* 1973 and 1974.
[a]Coal includes anthracite, coking pit coal, and gas coal.

flation in 1974. The data indicate, however, that the benefit to Yugoslavia of slower increases in import prices from CMEA sources was limited. Yugoslavia was apparently not able to substitute lower-priced CMEA goods for higher-priced Western materials to any significant degree, since the share of CMEA in the total volume of Yugoslav imports remained roughly constant between 1973 and 1974. Only in the case of coal did the CMEA share increase noticeably, from 92.5 percent in 1973 to 100 percent in 1974. In evaluating the evidence presented in Table 6, we must be careful to take account of possible differences in the quality or the nature of imports from the two sources. These differences cannot be captured by the comparison of unit values presented in the table.

THE TRANSMISSION PROCESS

According to the impact model, transmission is the first part of the process by which inflation from abroad exerts influence on a specific country. The transmission process begins with changes in international prices and works through the foreign trade and exchange network to cause actual or potential changes in domestic wholesale prices and/or quantities of imported and exported goods. Therefore, an understanding of how this process operates in a particular country requires an analysis of its foreign trade and foreign exchange systems.

East European socialist countries attempt to insulate their domestic wholesale prices from changes in world prices by using a system of taxes and subsidies and by negotiating long-term trade agreements at fixed prices (generally an average of world market prices in past years). Yugoslavia, on the other hand, not only does not attempt to impede the transmission process but also actually facilitates it by means of a special policy of price control that administratively links the domestic wholesale prices of many tradable goods to their prices on the world market. In accordance with this policy, the domestic prices of a significant number of commodities are administratively and automatically linked to international prices by formulas that use world prices, the prevailing rate of foreign exchange, and existing taxes and subsidies to calculate the appropriate domestic wholesale (producer) prices.[3] By using formulas of this type, the Yugoslav authorities have, in effect, replaced the market mechanism with a system of controls designed to keep domestic relative prices in line with world relative prices.

In the administrative linking of domestic to world prices, the official exchange rate plays an important role. From 1971 to the middle of 1973, the dinar followed the dollar as it depreciated vis-à-vis the currencies of Yugoslavia's major Western trading partners in the OECD. Then, just as world market prices began their sharp ascent in mid-1973, the Yugoslavs, in an attempt to realize a proper market relationship between the dinar and Western European currencies, removed the peg to the dollar, and the dinar appreciated relative to it. Since mid-1973, the dinar exchange rate in Yugoslavia has been set on a managed foreign exchange market, tightly regulated by the National Bank. The rate has been determined by the supply of and demand for foreign currency by authorized buyers and sellers, but within limits established by the National Bank. Thus, this new system is best understood as a managed flexible or floating exchange rate system. The data in Table 7 indicate that the rate has been kept within fairly narrow limits for protracted periods of time, with a major devaluation occurring in October 1974. The devaluation was one of the many policy responses of the

Table 7.   Dinar-Dollar Exchange Rate

Year	Qtr.	Rate	Year	Qtr.	Rate
1971	I	15.00	1974	I	15.94
	II	15.00		II	15.21
	III	15.00		III	15.59
	IV	17.00		IV	16.91
1972	I	17.00	1975	I	17.02
	II	17.00		II	17.00
	III	17.00		III	17.63
	IV	17.00		IV	17.89
1973	I	17.00	1976	I	18.04
	II	17.00		II	18.19
	III	15.32		III	18.25
	IV	15.44			

Source: International Monetary Fund, *International Financial Statistics,* November 1976.
Note: Until mid-1973, the rates shown are official dinar-dollar exchange rates agreed upon with the International Monetary Fund. The National Bank of Yugoslavia was obliged to maintain these rates within 1 percent of par. After July 1973, the rates shown are period averages of market rates.

Yugoslav government to the deterioration in its balance of payments caused by the worldwide inflation.[4]

As opposed to the other East European countries, which exercise varying degrees of centralized control over decisions on foreign trade, Yugoslavia provides freedom for individual enterprises to engage in foreign trade. In this decentralized system, the foreign exchange rate and tariffs and subsidies exert significant influence on foreign trade decisions. This is certainly not the case in the other East European countries. Yugoslavia, like many developing market economies, has formulated a strategy to influence decentralized foreign trade decisions by a number of selective policy tools. In addition to export subsidies (usually in the form of tax reductions or tariff rebates), the Yugoslavs have used retention quotas, which allow enterprises to retain a certain portion of their foreign exchange earnings for their own use, and preferential rediscount credits to finance the production and sale of exports. On the import side, in addition to tariffs and surcharges, the Yugoslavs have used quantitative restrictions and foreign exchange quotas to limit imports. To finance imports of certain crucial commodities, they have used selective credit policy.

Government trade and exchange policies of this type are aimed at keeping enterprise decisions, which are based on profitability criteria, consistent with broader social goals. They are generally not designed to prevent the transmission of changes in world market prices to domestic prices, although they can be used for this purpose under extreme circumstances. For example, in 1974, import duties and import taxes on oil, gas, ferrous metallurgy products, and some other raw materials were lowered in an attempt to reduce the impact of the rise in world prices on domestic wholesale prices.

THE PROPAGATION PROCESS

Through the transmission process, price increases on the world market cause increases in the domestic wholesale prices of tradable goods. The importance of this "first-round" effect of the worldwide commodity inflation on producer prices in Yugoslavia in 1974 and 1975 is suggested by the figures contained in Table 8. The propagation process begins with these increases in domestic wholesale prices and works through the consumer and producer trade and production networks, the labor market, and the household and financial sectors to raise retail prices and wages.

The commodities whose prices increased most dramatically on world markets from 1973 to 1975 were raw materials and fuels, commodities that are important inputs in the production of a very large number of goods. Therefore, a crucial step in the 1974–1975 propagation process in Yugoslavia, as in other countries importing these commodities, was the pass-through of the cost increases of these commodities to the wholesale prices of other goods. Although a pass-through of this type is typical of market economies, its operation in Yugoslavia was unique. Cost pass-throughs worked through the price control system, which covered about 80 percent of industrial products and most basic food items in the 1973–1975 period.

The system required that enterprises that wished to raise prices obtain approval from the appropriate price control agency.[5] Two of the key criteria used by these agencies in deciding whether to approve a request for a change in price were changes in world market prices and changes in the cost of production. Enterprises whose input prices rose were virtually certain to consider this a sufficient reason for requesting price increases, and price control authorities were very likely to agree.

Between 1973 and 1975, when input prices rose dramatically, the price control system allowed cost increases to be passed on very quickly to the wholesale prices of many domestic commodities. To the extent that retail margins, transportation costs, and turnover taxes remained constant, in-

Table 8.   Yugoslavia's Prices and Wages: Annual Rates of Growth (%),
1971–1976

	1971	1972	1973	1974	1975	1976[b]
Industrial producer prices	14.8[a]	9.7	13.2	29.9	22.0	7.2
Raw materials	18.4	10.3	12.5	38.9	23.0	8.2
Investment goods	13.2	5.2	9.9	12.4	22.0	13.7
Consumption goods	12.3	12.5	13.9	22.0	21.0	5.1
Industrial retail prices	14.3	17.9	16.7	29.9	26.0	8.2
Agricultural retail prices	17.3	16.4	21.1	16.3	23.0	17.3
Retail prices of services	14.3	10.9	16.9	20.5	26.0	15.8
Cost-of-living index	15.7	16.9	20.3	20.5	24.0	13.3
Nominal wages	23.4	17.2	14.7	28.2	24.0	14.9[c]
Real wages	6.5	1.0	−5.1	6.4	−1.0	

[a]Year-to-year annual growth rates calculated from data in Tables 122-2 through 122-6, *Statisticki Godisnjak,* 1976.

[b]Rate of growth measured from January through July 1976, over the same period of the previous year; figures calculated from data in *Indeks,* August 1976, p. 34.

[c]January through May 1976, relative to same period of previous year; figures calculated from data in *Indeks,* August 1976, p. 43.

creases in wholesale prices led to proportionate increases in retail prices. There is no reason to assume that retail margins declined; if anything, transportation costs increased because of higher fuel costs; and only for a few commodities (including gasoline, other fuel products, and a few basic consumer goods) did turnover taxes decrease, which was the result of government efforts to moderate retail price increases (see the section on containment). The one-to-one pass-through of wholesale price increases to retail prices of industrial products is consistent with the data in Table 8. Wholesale and retail price indexes for these products both increased by 29.9 percent.

So far, the argument indicates why wholesale and retail prices of tradables, and of those goods that use tradables as inputs in production, rose in 1974. However, this argument does not in itself prove that these passthroughs led to an increase in the aggregate price level or in the overall rate of inflation.[6] In fact, under conditions of constant or constantly growing nominal aggregate demand, these pass-throughs would have been offset by reductions in prices or in rates of inflation of other commodities, leaving the overall rate of inflation unchanged. However, these conditions were not satisfied in Yugoslavia, just as they were not satisfied in many market economies, because of the presence of nominal and real wage rigidities and consequent price rigidities. The causes of such rigidities in Yugoslavia lie in the institutional system of wage and price determination.[7]

Under the Yugoslav system of worker self-management, the members of each enterprise are given the authority to allocate net enterprise revenue to personal incomes, collective consumption, and investment.[8] Personal incomes combine the returns to labor (wages) and a share of the returns to entrepreneurship and capital (profits and interest). Both anecdotal evidence and empirical data suggest that workers attempt to achieve a target rate of growth in the real value of their personal incomes or, at the very least, try to prevent a drop in real incomes. In this way, the self-management system acts like the collective bargaining system of Western market economies to build in what Hicks has called "real wage resistance."[9]

A key difference between the capitalist firm and the self-managed firm is evident when either market conditions or price controls preclude the possibility of price increases. In this case, management and labor in the capitalist firm will struggle over their respective income shares. In the self-managed firm, no conflict need arise since the members of the enterprise constitute both its labor force and its management.[10] When output prices can be increased, the self-managed firm, like the capitalist firm, usually raises its price to cover an increase in labor incomes. For the self-managed firm, the alternative of allowing enterprise savings to absorb the burden of increases in personal income is frequently not desirable because it thwarts enterprise saving and investment objectives.

In the presence of nominal wage rigidity, a fall in real income occasioned by a deterioration in the terms of trade must take place by prices rising relatively faster than nominal incomes as import costs are passed on. The magnitude of this "first-round" inflationary impact of the shift in the terms of trade on Yugoslavia has been estimated by two Yugoslav economists, Sekulic and Babic. They use an input-output table for 1972 to calculate sectoral price increases caused by the simple pass-through of increases in import prices at constant nominal wages. Their technique allows them to capture both the direct and indirect effects of the rising prices of raw material and fuel imports used as inputs in production and the direct effects of increases in the prices of final product imports. Assuming no change in value added or in its distribution between labor and nonlabor incomes, Sekulic and Babic conclude that the overall rate of inflation caused by import prices was about 12 percent in 1974.[11] This represents about 40 percent of the increase in domestic industrial producer (wholesale) prices that actually occurred in that year.

These first-round effects can be amplified by the existence of real wage resistance. For example, the Yugoslav input-output calculations indicate that if real, rather than nominal, labor incomes are held constant, then the 1974 import-induced inflation rate rises to 16.8 percent.[12] On the basis of the data in Table 8, it seems reasonable to argue that real wage resistance was probably a factor in Yugoslavia in 1974. During that year, there was a sharp acceleration in nominal wages to make up for stagnant and declining real wages in 1972 and 1973, which were caused in part by poor harvests and rising food prices and in part by a partial wage freeze during the first half of 1973. Efforts to restore real wages to their target growth path fostered a 7.1 percent increase in real wages in the first half of 1974 and a further 3 percent increase in the second half of the year.

In analyzing real wage resistance, it is necessary to specify the price index according to which real wage calculations are made. In Yugoslavia, as in many Western market economies, workers tend to regard the cost-of-living index as the appropriate deflator. Since this index includes services and non-tradables, especially many food items not involved in foreign trade, there is no reason to anticipate a one-to-one relationship between increases in producer prices caused by increases in import prices and increases in the cost of living. In fact, as the data in Table 8 reveal, in 1974 — partly because of a good harvest and partly because of a moderate increase in the prices of services — the Yugoslav cost-of-living index increased by 20.5 percent, while producer prices increased by 29.9 percent. The significance of this difference lies in the fact that worker pressure for increases in nominal wages was less intense in 1974 than it would have been if the wholesale price index had been considered the relevant wage deflator. Consequently, the second-round effects of import-induced inflation were moderated somewhat.

THE CONTAINMENT PROCESS

The containment process encompasses all the policies designed to moderate the transmission and propagation of external price increases, as well as any changes in the economic system designed to accomplish the same task. In Yugoslavia in 1974, the containment process was extremely weak, which was a consequence of three elements in the Yugoslav economic strategy for that year. First, since the 1965 reform, a key policy goal had been the creation of a rational price system that would serve as a guide to efficient resource allocation. A crucial component of this policy was an attempt to link domestic prices of tradables to world market prices in the manner discussed above. A containment policy aimed at interfering with the transmission process was clearly inconsistent with this goal. Second, the strong commitment to the expansionary policy pursued from mid-1973 to mid-1975 made it impossible to adopt demand-reducing measures to control inflation.[13] Third, given the reduction of real wages in the 1972–1973 period, the Yugoslav government was reluctant to depress real wages for a third year in a row. Therefore, a very strict incomes' policy to control inflationary pressures was not a realistic policy option.

Given these limitations, the Yugoslav government was willing to adopt only relatively weak containment policies, such as reductions in tariffs and small reductions in turnover taxes on a few commodities.[14] These measures were too weak and too isolated to have any major impact on the aggregate rate of inflation.

CONCLUSION

The Yugoslav economic system and development strategy were structured to achieve several specific policy objectives. These objectives did not include insulating domestic prices from changes in world market prices. Thus, it is not at all surprising that there existed very few systematic barriers to the transmission of these externally generated price changes or to their propagation throughout the economy. For the same reasons, the Yugoslav leaders did not choose to adopt any major containment policies to interfere with either the transmission or propagation of external price increases, and none of the three possible insulation layers operated at all effectively. Because of their commitment to a rapid growth policy, which had been introduced coincidentally with the initiation of sharp increases in world market prices in mid-1973, Yugoslav leaders were particularly reluctant to fight domestic inflation by adopting measures to reduce domestic aggregate demand. Their reluctance, combined with downward rigidities in wages and prices, permitted external price rises to add to the already significant rate of domestically generated inflation.

The results of the Yugoslav economic strategy are evident from the data in Tables 3 and 8. First, the Yugoslavs accomplished their primary objective of achieving a rapid growth rate in 1974 and through the first half of 1975. Second, the overall rate of inflation increased sharply between 1973 and 1974. Third, the combination of rapid inflation and rapid growth, along with a deterioration in the aggregate terms of trade (over which the Yugo-slavs had little control), caused a sharp deterioration in the balance of trade and consequent reserve losses. The situation was aggravated, of course, by stagnating markets in Western Europe and by the fact that Yugoslavia's in-flation outpaced the inflation realized by many of its Western industrial trading partners. Ironically, a major factor behind these differential rates of inflation was the Yugoslav decision to maintain an expansionary policy de-spite the unexpected loss in terms of trade, while other countries accepted the demand-constraining effects of this loss to varying degrees. If Yugo-slavia's trading partners had responded as Yugoslavia's own leaders did, its situation with regard to balance of trade would have been somewhat less critical.

Stagnating conditions in Western Europe also affected earnings from tourism and remittances from workers temporarily employed abroad. The' annual rate of growth of earnings from tourism declined from an average of 29 percent in 1971–1973 to 11.9 percent in 1974. For the same periods, the annual rate of growth of worker remittances declined from an average of 39.2 percent to 10.6 percent. Slowdowns in these receipts aggravated the problem of financing the growing trade deficit. In addition, slowing growth in Western Europe stemmed the net outflow of Yugoslav workers and gen-erated a net return of between 50,000 and 100,000 workers in 1974.[15] The net inflow of labor worsened the unemployment situation in Yugoslavia and provided yet another channel by which the international economic situation influenced domestic economic conditions.

The Yugoslavs' first major policy response to the growing current ac-count and trade deficits took the form of a devaluation of the dinar by ap-proximately 8 percent relative to the dollar in October 1974. In addition, direct controls or quotas on imports of many commodities were gradually introduced. In response to these policy measures, the trade deficit declined somewhat between the second half of 1974 and the first half of 1975, but its absolute size remained intolerable. Reserve losses continued, and Yugo-slavia's net long-term indebtedness to the rest of the world climbed sharply in the first half of 1975. In the longer run, because of low price elasticities of demand for Yugoslav imports and exports and the gradual upward adjust-ment of domestic wages and prices to the higher prices of tradable goods, the devaluation promised little in the way of a permanent reduction in the trade deficit.

Under these circumstances, in the second half of 1975, the Yugoslav leaders were finally forced to adopt contractionary aggregate demand policies to cut imports and thereby to reduce the trade deficit. As the data in Tables 3 and 8 indicate, this attempt was successful, but only at the expense of a marked deceleration in real growth. Ultimately, then, the external inflation, combined with the adverse shift in the terms of trade and aggravated by stagnation in Western Europe, compelled the Yugoslavs to sacrifice their expansionary output and employment goals, at least temporarily.

The Yugoslav experience between 1973 and 1975 clearly attests to the trade-offs between external balance and price stability, domestic employment, and output targets that exist in a market economy with wage and price rigidities. As the simple Keynesian model predicts, in such a system an adverse shift in the terms of trade generates overall inflationary pressure. That is true as long as the import-induced inflation of certain commodity prices is not offset by deflation of other commodity prices caused either by the contractionary effects of the real income loss resulting from this shift or by restrictive government policies. This conclusion applies whether the economy operates under fixed or flexible exchange rates.

Under fixed exchange rates, if the government pursues an aggregate demand policy that is inconsistent with price stability, the balance of trade will deteriorate, as it did in Yugoslavia during 1974 and 1975. This situation can be sustained only as long as the government is willing to reduce its foreign exchange reserves or is willing and able to add to its foreign indebtedness. At some point, these two avenues of escape will be closed. Assuming the government is still unwilling to sacrifice domestic output and employment targets, devaluation of the currency becomes necessary, as it did in Yugoslavia in October 1974. Given real wage resistance, however, the effects of a devaluation on the balance of trade are likely to be small, since devaluation will gradually be followed by an upward adjustment of domestic wages and prices. In addition, devaluation is relatively ineffectual when price elasticities for exports and imports are low, as they are in Yugoslavia and in many import-dependent developing countries.

The substitution of flexible exchange rates for fixed exchange rates does not eliminate the conflict between domestic price stability and domestic output targets occasioned by deterioration in the terms of trade. Under a system of flexible exchange rates, government efforts to maintain aggregate demand in the face of import-induced inflationary pressure result in a declining exchange rate and subsequent rounds of domestic inflation that are fueled by workers' efforts to prevent declines in their real wages.

Since wage and price rigidity lies at the root of the conflict between inflation, external balance, and growth, an incomes' policy suggests itself as a useful addition to government policy instruments. An effective incomes' policy in 1974 would have undoubtedly reduced the inflationary impact of the import price increases at given levels of output and employment. This is not to say, however, that such a policy could have eliminated that impact completely. Given the magnitude of the import price rises in 1974 and the primary nature of the particular commodities involved, there was no way for the Yugoslavs to offset the import-induced inflation completely. The use of either an incomes' policy or a contractionary fiscal and monetary policy sufficient to accomplish this task would have required a politically unacceptable contraction in employment, output, and real incomes.

NOTES

1. A. A. Brown et al., "The Impact of International Stagflation on Systemic and Policy Changes in Eastern Europe: Theoretical Reflections," in Simon McInnes, ed., *The Soviet Union and East Europe into the 80's: Multidisciplinary Perspectives* (Oakville, Ont.: Mosaic Press, 1978).
2. This and other comparisons with East European countries are based, in part, on Z. Fallenbuchl, E. Neuberger, and L. Tyson, "East European Reactions to International Commodity Inflation," Joint Economic Committee of Congress Compendium, 1977.
3. An example best illustrates how the administrative link between domestic and world market prices operates: in a 1973 social agreement on prices of nonferrous metals and products, it was decided that domestic prices would be set equal to average world futures prices quoted during the past six months, evaluated at the official exchange rate, and increased by 3 percent because of tariff protection. See Ivo Karli, "Neki aktuelni problemi sistema i politike cijena," *Ekonomski pregled* 8-9 (1974):603-32.
4. The role of devaluation, as well as other more technical questions connected with the impact of world inflation on Yugoslavia, are discussed in our paper, "Can a Rise in Import Prices Be Inflationary and Deflationary: The Case of Yugoslavia," Stony Brook Working Paper No. 175, April 1977.
5. Federal price control agencies have jurisdiction over major agricultural product prices, most industrial prices, and rail freight rates; republics control electricity rates, rail and bus rates, and construction materials; communes control rents, community utilities, and retail food prices. Thus, it is the federal and republican control agencies that determine the effectiveness of the propagation mechanism and the impact of increases in wholesale prices of imports on prices of all other goods.
6. This argument is summarized in Marcus Miller, "Can a Rise in Import Prices Be Inflationary and Deflationary? Economists and U.K. Inflation, 1973-74," *American Economic Review* (September 1976):507-08.
7. See Neuberger and Tyson, "Rise in Import Prices."
8. Although the enterprise members' freedom to decide on enterprise income distribution is a key feature of the Yugoslav doctrine of self-management, this freedom has been circumscribed in various ways all along. Since 1971 a type of incomes' policy has been developed. It consists of social agreements that con-

strain the distribution of income between personal incomes and enterprise savings. These agreements are not primarily aimed at controlling the absolute level of wages but at setting limits to acceptable interenterprise wage differentials. However, because the overall rate of wage inflation is partly dependent on the efforts of workers in low-wage enterprises to catch up with labor earnings in high-wage enterprises, these agreements have probably moderated aggregate wage inflation as well.

9. J. R. Hicks, "What is Wrong With Monetarism," *Lloyds Bank Review* (October 1975):1–13.

10. This does not mean that we should expect all members of the enterprise to have the same objectives and that no conflict may arise between different groups of workers or between the blue-collar workers and the manager and his staff. See E. Neuberger and E. James, "The Yugoslav Self-Managed Enterprise: A Systemic Approach," in Morris Bornstein, ed., *Plan and Market: Economic Reform in Eastern Europe* (New Haven, Conn.: Yale University Press, 1973).

11. M. Sekulic and M. Babic, "Uvozna zavisnost Jugoslavenske privrede i efekti povencanja uvoznih cena," *Ekonomski pregled* 5–6 (1975):347–65.

12. Ibid., p. 363.

13. In fact, to the extent necessary, the Yugoslavs made special efforts to counteract the contradictionary effects on the money supply of the loss of foreign exchange reserves caused by the balance of payments deficit. As argued in our paper and as cited in note 4, they also had to try to offset the real income loss due to the deterioration in the terms of trade.

14. Turnover taxes are a relatively small component of retail prices in Yugoslavia as compared to other East European economies — about 12.5 percent on average. Their small magnitude and the policy goal of reducing the use of taxes and subsidies to influence relative price precluded the use of reductions of turnover taxes as a major containment policy, as was the case in other East European economies.

15. A net inflow of 50,000 workers is reported in the Yugoslav Federal Planning Office document, "Analytical Basis for the Documents of the Social Plan of Yugoslavia for the Period of 1976–1980." A. Antic cites a figure of 100,000 workers in "Yugoslavia on the Way to Economic Recovery," *Radio Free Europe Background Report,* no. 229, (November 9, 1976):5.

8 THE EVOLUTION OF AGRICULTURAL TECHNOLOGY IN THE PEOPLE'S REPUBLIC OF CHINA, 1957–1976

Thomas Wiens

Until very recently, few China specialists would have disagreed with the observation that the People's Republic of China was failing to generate a sustained positive rate of increase in productivity in its agricultural sector. However, this idea has become untenable now that U.S. analysts have accepted the reality of an annual harvest growth rate of about 2.1 percent in food grains and 2.8 percent in cotton since 1957, the peak year before the Great Leap Forward, despite a slight decline in total cultivated acreage.[1] In view of this turnabout, the question arises as to whether success is due to a change in technological policies or to greater interest in carrying them out and improved means of doing so.

Not surprisingly, the answer is that it is due to a combination of both factors. The technological reforms promoted under the rubric of the "Eight-Character Charter," which still defines the path of agricultural development, were first enunciated by Mao Tse-tung in 1958, but they can be traced

This research was partially supported by a grant from the Social Science Research Council, Joint Committee on Contemporary China. The author is indebted to Professor Motonosuke Amano and Professor Shigeru Ishikawa for providing invaluable access to materials in their possession, and to Professor Shinichi Ichimura for use of the facilities of the Southeast Asian Research Institute at Kyoto University.

to earlier discussion and debate and ultimately to advice from Soviet experts. The charter took soil improvement (especially deep plowing) as its base; heavy fertilizer use, irrigation, drainage, and work on seed selection as prerequisites; and scientific dense planting as its "main theme" — supported by plant protection from blight and harmful insects, careful field work, and improvement of farming tools.[2] Yet the elements of the charter that received emphasis, as well as the specific means of implementation, changed significantly and decisively after the Great Leap Forward, resulting in rapid growth that began little more than a decade ago.

Many aspects of the evolving Chinese agricultural technology have been discussed in both the popular and the scholarly literature, although the institutional and economic policies that facilitate the adoption of this technology have received most emphasis.[3] However, foreign observers have generally been handicapped by some combination of (1) limited agronomic knowledge, (2) a perspective biased by Western agricultural experience, (3) unfamiliarity with the environmental and economic constraints affecting Chinese technological policies, and (4) ignorance of the way in which these policies have evolved historically. By focusing in depth on a number of significant elements of Chinese technology that are not well understood in the West, I hope to provide a more multidimensional insight into its development. Five of the eight components of the Eight-Character Charter will be touched on in this process.

The discussion will be in concrete, rather than abstract, terms in order to show clearly the elements of continuity and discontinuity in decisions to promote or ignore particular practices or innovations, as well as the economic and environmental reasons for the initial choices and for changes in policy. An attempt will be made to evaluate the technical soundness and potential significance of innovations, and where policy errors are indicated, the reasons why they were made will be considered. Finally, to a certain extent, developments in Chinese agricultural technology will be compared or contrasted with those occurring elsewhere in Asia.

IMPROVED SEEDS

Because of the complex interrelationships among all factors contributing to the improvement of productivity in agriculture, it is difficult to isolate one factor as more important than others. Nevertheless, in the aftermath of the "Green Revolution," it is common to treat the development and diffusion of improved seeds as the sine qua non of a sustained increase in land productivity,[4] especially in view of the examples of successful long-term productivity provided by Japan and the United States.

The rate of growth and the timing of the contribution of seed improvement to agricultural development are constrained in three ways:

1. If the process depends on the traditional method of seed selection, it is limited by the natural rate of genetic mutation and by the thoroughness of the attention that farmers and researchers devote to selection. Scientific hybridization and other artificial methods can direct and greatly speed up the process of achieving a desirable genetic combination, although selection continues to be important in determining appropriate biological parents and refining and maintaining the characteristics of subsequent generations.

2. Hybridization requires decisions about breeding objectives since there may be many characteristics that need improvement and only one or two characteristics may be served by a given crossing. Vague objectives, such as "yield improvement," will not suffice as guidelines, since yields depend on a variety of plant and environmental characteristics. The appropriate objectives are not necessarily the most obvious, and much time may be wasted in pursuing ill-chosen ones.

3. From initial crossing through stabilization of characteristics, local trials, multiplication, and distribution, a number of years are required — twelve or thirteen in Japanese rice breeding, including three years for distribution.[5] While there are ways of reducing this time lag, a too hasty program courts disaster.

The Chinese seed-breeding program initially suffered under each of these limitations. From the start, breeders were under party pressure to achieve rapid high-yield breakthroughs.[6] Thus, they inevitably relied on combinations of farmer selection, products of Republican-period experimental stations, and imported varieties. For example, of ninety-five improved rice varieties that were distributed in south China before 1959, only 20 percent were products of post-1949 breeding by professional agronomists; and 40 percent of the improved varieties distributed in north China were Korean or Japanese imports.[7]

The diffusion of improved varieties required the development of an extensive network of experimental stations, which occurred in parallel with the cooperative movement and reached the level of about one station per eight thousand households in 1956.[8] Centralized direction and organization of these institutions apparently were not formalized until 1957, when the Academy of Agricultural Sciences was established in Peking under the Ministry of Agriculture.[9] Because of the time required for institutional and technological developments, varieties that were developed experimentally after 1949 received widespread distribution only from 1958 on.

The primary weaknesses of existing varieties of Chinese seeds included a relative lack of responsiveness to the use of fertilizer and water and inadequate disease resistance (although minimal yields were maintained when they were subject to crop diseases). Overcoming these weaknesses became the primary objective of seed development.[10] However, because of the weakness of the Chinese plant-hybridization program in the 1950s, initial successes were limited.

Two of the four most widely planted improved varieties in this period were of foreign origin (an Italian wheat and an American cotton variety).[11] However, foreign varieties did not always prove to be superior under conditions in China, and thus wholesale borrowing was not feasible. In general, certain foreign varieties proved valuable because of their resistance to particular diseases (and thus as breeding stock) and in other instances were hardier than local varieties (they did not lodge under conditions of high wind or rain and high fertilizer use). On the other hand, some of the more spectacular foreign developments were not widely applicable — high-yielding tropical wheat because of its excessive sunlight requirements[12] and Japanese varieties of glutinous rice because of their preference for a cool climate or high altitudes, their need for a long growing season, and their lack of yield superiority except under conditions of unusually high fertilizer use.[13]

Local selection of superior strains, on the other hand, proved moderately effective for some crops, such as rice, but not for others. Locally selected varieties of wheat, in particular, had relatively small scope for application elsewhere. As a result, and because of a pronounced bias in selection and experimental cultivation toward high-yield varieties that required heavy fertilizer and water use,[14] greatest benefits of seed development in the 1950s were concentrated in areas of central and south China, where agricultural technology was already advanced.

Work on hybridization began in the early 1950s, but a breakthrough was not achieved until 1956 when rice breeders in Kwangtung realized that they had been pursuing the wrong breeding objectives. Because they knew that the key to increasing fertilizer response was to strengthen the stalk of the plant (to enable it to bear the burden of more and heavier tassels and grains), their initial approach in choosing parent stock was to select strains that had tall and strong stalks, large tassels, and large grains. After observing the lodging resistance of a glutinous dwarf Champa rice variety from Kwangsi and the practice some farmers followed of deliberate stunting through fertilizer and water control, the breeders apparently became convinced that exceptionally short, not tall, stalks should be the key breeding objective.[15]

The first Chinese crossing of a dwarf with a high-yielding variety in production use was accomplished in 1956. In that same year, a nonglutinous dwarf was selected from an improved conventional variety. A third variety was developed from a crossing in 1958.[16] Distribution for full production of these and other dwarf rice varieties began in 1964 and was expanded rapidly thereafter. With adequate fertilizer and water supplies, they offered yields of 6.3 or more tons per hectare[17] and, as second-crop rice, more than 4.5 tons per hectare in production.[18] In this respect and others, these varieties were the equal of the IR-8 dwarf rice developed in the Phillipines (released in 1966), which launched the "Green Revolution" elsewhere in Asia. Like the IR-8 dwarf rice, these varieties were initally weak in resistance to some diseases and were clearly superior to the best local varieties only on middle-fertility land with sufficient fertilizer use.[19] Unlike the IR-8 dwarf rice, however, their growing period — 110 to 115 days — was short enough to make them usable in double-cropped rice areas.[20]

The success of the new rice varieties proved to be an important stimulus to plant-breeding work, including hybridization of other crops. There is substantial evidence of achievement — in particular, of recent distribution of fertilizer-responsive, irrigated, high-yield wheat varieties, some of partly foreign parentage.[21] Something must be said about measures taken to reduce the time lag between initial hybridization and production, which initially was eight to ten years: (1) The six to seven years required to stabilize characteristics of hybrid seeds was reduced to three to four years by multiple cropping. This required adjustment of the cropping schedule to permit the replanting of seeds in successive crop seasons and special techniques to allow for differences in sunlight hours required for early and late crops (including the use of special rooms that could be darkened and black plastic film for shading). Hothouse breeding in winter was used to facilitate a third crop. To maximize the seed-multiplication rate, sparse planting, high fertilizer use, and continuous, repeated harvesting were employed. (2) Equivalent production facilities were set up at widely distributed research stations, which were closely supervised by the main institutes. The more advanced stations were given seed before complete stabilization had been achieved, and the less advanced were given seed later. In both cases, the tasks of these stations were to determine local adaptability and production characteristics, to perform continued selection, and eventually to undertake seed reproduction — again, in the shortest possible time.[22] These methods were first developed in the south, but they have been replicated in the north — for example, by flying the seeds to temperate Hainan Island for a second, winter crop.

By such methods, the Chinese have succeeded in cutting the time lag between breeding and distribution to levels well below those elsewhere without courting disaster by premature distribution. However, the need to stabilize characteristics imposes a lower limit to this time lag under conventional seed-breeding methods. The importance of this problem is reflected in the major research effort that has been underway since 1966 in search of means of immediate stabilization. Although the process developed is still experimental, several new varieties of rice, wheat, and tobacco that required only two generations for complete stabilization have been released for testing.[23] The prospects thus seem good for virtual elimination of the constraint on the rate of increase in productivity imposed by time requirements in seed development.

FERTILIZER USE

As noted above, improved seeds have had high average and marginal rates of response to fertilizer applications. As such seeds have become available, the need to generate new sources of fertility has become more urgent. Thus, research and extension programs have continuously sought to improve the use and efficiency of existing fertilizer sources, while the production of chemical fertilizer has received increasing priority in industrial development. Since the rapid growth of the latter is well known, I will consider here the practical innovations in plant and animal husbandry that have made possible an equally remarkable expansion of organic fertilizers.

The initial level of organic fertilizer use was high, comparable to the roughly 50 kilograms per hectare of nitrogen from organic sources that Japanese farmers used in the early part of this century (but with a higher proportion from animal manure).[24] However, in Japan, as elsewhere, the use of organic fertilizer subsequently declined as a result of the increased availability of chemical fertilizers and the replacement of animal labor with machines, which led to decreased supplies of barnyard manure. In contrast, China appears to have expanded the nutrient supply from organic sources by about 41 percent between 1957 and 1971, which accounted for about 56 percent of the total increase in production, despite a rapid increase in chemical fertilizer supply.[25]

The reasons for the emphasis on organic fertilizer growth are quite straightforward. With a cultivated area as large as that of China, it was impossible in the short term to expect increased supplies of chemical fertilizers to satisfy demands for higher levels of nutrient application. Moreover, long-term intensive farming requires organic fertilizers to restore and preserve soil conditioning. In addition to organic material and nitrogen, animal and green manures are particularly high in potassium and phosphate content relative to plant requirements. Hence, their use permits concentration on nitrogenous chemical production.[26] Phosphates, if applied to green-manure crops rather than used directly, generate their own weight in additional (fixed) nitrogen (a method called "turning the small into the large"). Finally, manure is a by-product of animal husbandry, the expansion of which is also desirable for meat production.

On the other hand, dependence on organic fertilizer has three distinct disadvantages: (1) With organic fertilizers, it is difficult to obtain nutrient proportions that match plant requirements. Since release rates are slow, it is impossible to ensure concentrated release at appropriate periods of plant growth.[27] (2) Overall, at least 20 percent of total agricultural labor time (often 30 to 50 percent) was spent in collecting, transporting, and applying organic fertilizers, which made their use both inconvenient and expensive in areas where there was a seasonal labor shortage. Use of chemical fertilizers, which have a far higher potency, drastically cuts this cost.[28] (3) Sources of organic fertilizer are involved in a symbiotic relationship with the overall level of agricultural productivity because of land-use competition and the successive dependence of manure supplies on numbers of animals, feed supplies, and (closing the circle) fertilizer availability. It is difficult to break out of this "vicious circle" to higher levels of organic-fertilizer supply.[29]

Chinese policymakers have attempted, with some success, to overcome or minimize these disadvantages. First, the use of organic fertilizers has been confined largely to base dressings, which are applied during plowing and before sowing; chemical fertilizer, in small amounts, has been recommended for use mainly as top dressing at appropriate stages of plant growth, even in areas with responsive varieties.[30] To ensure that chemical fertilizer would not be substituted for organic, the price of the former has been kept relatively high. For example, ammonium sulphate sold for about 0.34 yuan per kilogram in 1955, and only slightly less in 1964.[31] The average cost of equivalent manure (including all costs of collection, transport, and application) was found to be about two-thirds of these figures, with marginal costs only 40 percent and declining.[32] Since most of the "cost" of organic fertilizers simultaneously represents income to members of production units, the incentive to substitute chemical for organic sources has indeed been low.

This policy has been directly contrary to the policies of other Asian countries known for intensive fertilizer use (and to American advice on agricultural development). For example, the ratio of the price of ammonium sulphate to that of rice has only recently fallen to nearly 1.0 in China, whereas in Japan it was about 0.33 in 1960, and in Taiwan it fell from 1.2 in 1950 to 0.53 in 1972.[33] Yet there is no indication of a lack of peasant demand for chemical fertilizers in China at current levels of production, probably because their purchase as a supplementary nutrient source imposes a far smaller burden on peasant incomes than it does in other countries where organic fertilizer has been abandoned.

Various methods have been promoted to reduce the impact of the labor cost of organic fertilizer use. These include confining animals to pens (to reduce collecting costs) and delivering manures to the fields well in advance of plowing (to reduce the opportunity cost of labor).[34] Where labor has been a serious constraint, green manure has been recommended, since the labor cost lies only in the sowing.[35] The job of collecting manure generally falls to wives and children, who are rewarded with cash payments (rather than work points). Thus, with low opportunity-cost labor and adequate cash incentives, the labor burden has become bearable, although this may change as further development raises the unit value of labor.

These measures, however, do not remove the difficulty of breaking out of the "vicious circle." In the final analysis, such a breakthrough requires increasing the number of pigs per acre, or per capita, since the pig was (by 1965) the largest and most efficient source of fertilizer (green-manure crops were used more efficiently in pig feeding than directly).[36] Yet, despite the care taken to avoid the destruction of livestock, such as accompanied forced collectivization in the Soviet Union, the Chinese were slow to find a mix of policies that would favor growth of the animal stock. To reverse the declining trend of the pig stock through mid-1956, more was required than official condemnation of local tendencies toward "excessive communalization."[37]

On the basis of available data, it is not possible to be certain which policies or innovations proved crucial. However, the extent of success can be documented. Numbers of live pigs (118 million at mid-1957) rose rapidly, then fell (paralleling the harvest figures of the Great Leap), but recovered so rapidly that record numbers could be claimed for 1964. By 1972 the midyear stock had reached about 260 million — 120 percent more than in 1957, even though the 1972 food-grains harvest was only some 30 percent larger.[38] This success must be credited to some combination of increased feed, better incentives, and improved husbandry.[39]

Feed availability was clearly a prerequisite for increased animal husbandry, and yet the amount of food grains usable as feed was essentially the residual after quota sales, taxes, seed, and human food were deducted from total supply. The elasticity of per capita feed consumption with respect to per capita grain supply in China could be as high as three to four, but there is no reason to believe that the per capita grain supply increased between 1957 and 1972.[40] Although during this period the state returned some part of quota grain as an incentive for animal raising, that return came at the expense of urban consumption, stocks, and exports and cannot explain a growth rate of animal stock that is much above that of total grain production.[41] However, the decreasing relative burden on the feed supply caused by the *labor* animal stock could have permitted a growth of as much as 60 percent in the pig stock, with no increase in the proportion of total supply that was used as feed. Labor animals, which can consume nearly six times as much grain per head as pigs, grew in numbers by only 14 percent over the period.[42]

The remaining growth must be attributed to a reduction in dependence on fine feeds (grain, millings, oilseed cakes, potatoes, etc.) and an increase in consumption of coarse fodder (straw, stalks, etc.) and green fodder (grasses, wild vegetables, squashes, etc.) While the authorities were promoting this substitution in the mid-1950s, peasant resistance was initially high. Techniques for increasing both the digestibility and the nutritional effectiveness of coarse and green fodders were not fully researched or well known to cadres and peasants, nor were they accessible in the absence of processing machinery in the countryside. Moreover, the incentive structure did not favor this reform. Initially, payment for manure was often in work points at rates that reflected neither the marginal productivity nor the cost of equivalent chemical fertilizers. (The value of nutrient was potentially more than one-third of the sale price of a fattened pig, enough to spell the difference between profit and loss.)[43] Without cash payments for manure, adequate processing facilities, and ready sources of green fodder, the marginal value product of labor expended in fodder collection seemed too far below the average wage-point value to justify peasant effort.[44] Hence, peasants, understandably relied on grain as much as possible and limited the number of pigs raised accordingly.

These obstacles apparently were overcome in the 1960s through policies designed to shift the processing industry from the cities to the communes and to increase the cultivation of green manures that could also be used as fodder.[45] Important factors included the production and distribution on a large scale of simple milling and shredding machinery, multipurpose engines and motors, and extensive rural electrification.[46] Systems for developing and improving fodder supplies were researched and widely publicized. These systems typically involved the use of scrap land, ponds, and seasonably fallow land to grow sources of fodder, which were to be ground up, mixed with small amounts of carbohydrate, and fermented for use as feed.[47] Finally, the consistent advice of "specialists" that adequate incentives be provided seems to have been implemented and to have survived the Cultural Revolution.[48] However, the availability of low opportunity-cost female and child labor remains today as crucial to reliance on coarse and green fodders as it is to reliance on organic fertilizers.

IRRIGATION AND WATER CONTROL

The essence of China's problem with water resources is an unhappy contradiction of climate and geography. Only 11 percent of China's area is cultivated; of that 11 percent, more than half, and by far the best half in terms of soil quality and terrain, is located in north China, whereas south China has largely mountainous terrain and leached, acid soils. But south China, with a warm climate and a long growing season, also has the heaviest rainfall and about two-thirds of the surface flow. Because more than half of the country's rainfall is concentrated in two or three summer months, spring droughts and summer floods are a perennial problem. Annual fluctuations in rainfall are quite severe, especially in the north. (In the interior, the ratio of largest to smallest annual rainfall is two or three to one, or more; in the northeast and northwest, it is as much as ten to one.) Natural disasters therefore tend to be much more severe in the north — drought because of a lack of surface-water sources and a fluctuating water table that makes shallow wells an unreliable water source; flood because of a severe erosion problem in the denuded loess soils of the northwest, which has led to a buildup of the bed of the Yellow River to a level well above that of the north China plains, and because of a lack of storage area for runoff during the flood season.

As a result of the drought problem, irrigation requirements for secure yields in dry farming in the north are not substantially lower than they are for paddy farming in the south.[49] Yet the securely irrigated area of the pre-Liberation period was overwhelmingly concentrated in south China, giving that area a share of total production that was out of proportion to its cultivated area and land quality.

It is not surprising that the extension of water resources to nonirrigated or poorly irrigated areas should have been the linchpin of the post-Liberation strategy for agricultural development. As the irrigated area grew, it was possible to substitute high-yielding crops and to extend multiple cropping, employing improved seeds, more fertilizer, and intensive cultivation techniques to great effect. While this strategy implied a concentration of water-resource investment on the areas north of the Yangtse, where high-cost, large-scale programs were required, it was initially believed that returns to such investments would be relatively high.[50]

Initial emphasis, however, was required on problems of flood control and waterlogging, especially in the Yellow, Hai, and Huai river basins. Dikes and embankments needed to be repaired, restored, or newly built, and drainage in the low-lying areas adjacent to rivers needed to be improved. Roughly 70 percent of state capital construction funds in water conservancy during the First Five-Year Plan was spent on these tasks, and only 20 percent on irrigation. Some work, however, was multipurpose, and local labor and funds were devoted largely to extending irrigation. By late 1957 it was felt that these problems were basically under control, and attention turned to irrigation.[51]

This judgment was premature, as the large floods from 1959 to 1961 proved.[52] It was later admitted that of the 27 million hectares subject to flood in the Hai and Huai basins, only half had been "basically" protected by the work through 1959 and that in north China as a whole, flood control was generally at a level of protection against floods occurring once in five to ten years and at twice this level in a minority of areas.[53] Furthermore, the potential seriousness of the problem of waterlogging had been greatly underestimated.

Large increases in irrigated area, along with improvements in the quality of existing systems, were also claimed during the period of the First Five-Year Plan. The most significant gains were in the north, where sixteen of the eighteen identifiable large reservoirs completed before 1959 are located. However, most irrigation gains were the product of small-scale works, notably the digging in 1956 of 4.6 million wells, about 40 percent of which were of "good quality."[54] While these wells were effective during short dry spells, Chinese well-drilling and pump technology was not yet capable of extensive construction of deep wells (i.e., over twenty meters in depth).[55]

With Soviet assistance, by 1958 an expanding Chinese technical cadre had completed draft plans for major multipurpose water-control projects on the northern river systems. These plans may initially have been relatively modest in conception, but in the ensuing discussion, amidst the fever of the Great Leap Forward, growing pressure was apparently exerted by local-level cadres who were anxious for quick breakthroughs. As a result, the plans quickly became hugely ambitious and unrealistic. At their height, the plans for the Yellow River system alone included twenty dams on the main stream and ninety large and medium dams on tributaries in the middle and upper reaches (the northwest), providing for the irrigation and electrification of 5.7 million hectares (roughly double the 1957 irrigated area).[56] In the lower reaches, where dams were less suitable because of terrain, long-run plans called for the development of an extensive network of interconnected water courses, linking the Yellow River with the Hai, Huai, and Yangtze rivers and providing for both irrigation and transportation on a scale comparable to that of the network of watercourses in Kiangsu and Chekiang. For Hopei, Honan, Shantung, Anhwei, and Kiangsu, 100 percent irrigation was targeted, and the canal excavation in the lower reaches was to be made deep enough to absorb flood runoff, as well as to provide for irrigation. However, the entire water resources of the Yellow River and its tributaries could not meet the projected demands for irrigation in the lower reaches, except at a very thin level. Consequently, the plans called for diversion of water from the Han (a tributary of the Yangtse) and from the Yangtse itself to the Yellow River system.[57]

The first-stage construction work on the Yellow River system began in 1958 and continued through 1959. It included the construction of some sixty water gates and extensive major and subsidiary channels on the banks of the lower reaches and the concomitant development of irrigation systems in the Huai basin of northern Anhwei and Kiangsu. Of the immense increase claimed in irrigated acreage — 32 million hectares in 1958 — the five provinces benefiting from these projects (Hopei, Honan, Shantung, Kiangsu, and Anhwei) accounted for 56 percent.[58] However, not long thereafter, work was stopped on many of the incomplete projects, the overall plans were shelved, and most of the claimed increase in irrigation "evaporated," probably because many areas had been ordered to stop irrigation.[59] Since this meant abandoning hopes for rapid extension to the north of securely irrigated acreage and high-yield crops, such as paddy rice, and thereby forced a revamping of the entire agricultural development strategy, the reasons for the halt deserve careful examination.

In some part, the abandonment of many major projects was due to substitution of small local projects. This substitution reflected not only the victory of Maoist development strategy, but also a shortage of cement and steel, which could meet only 20 to 30 percent of the demands for dam construction.[60] Small local dams could use earth and rock fill, if necessary with a concrete core or facing.[61] Thus, they could also serve as the first market for the new, small-scale, rural cement and steel production.[62] The growing demand for irrigation water (and retention of runoff in local storage facilities) reduced the electricity-generating potential and thus the economic justification of some planned dams below original levels.[63] The policy of simultaneous and uncoordinated development of major and minor facilities on main rivers and tributaries, which exploited the mass enthusiasm of the moment, was replaced by a more rational development policy.[64] The Soviet withdrawal of technical and material aid also doomed some major projects, and the large-scale floods of 1959 to 1961 may have clinched matters by forcing a return to the earlier emphasis on flood prevention, at the expense of irrigation and electricity generation.

As if the above factors were not devastating enough, two fatal technical errors were made, which more careful and extensive study might have prevented. First, the major factor that historically had precluded extensive irrigation in the Yellow River basin was the extraordinary silt content of the river, which has led to an elevation of the bed, the silting of irrigation channels, and consequently to frequent and devastating floods. Soviet and Chinese planners and engineers proposed to deal with the problem both by afforestation in the northwest and by construction of a series of dams from San Men Gorge upstream, which was expected to drastically reduce the silt content downstream.[65]

The afforestation program ran well behind schedule (and today remains far from complete), probably because the northwest is underpopulated and the *local* benefits of afforestation were not sufficient incentive to mobilize the necessary local labor.[66] Construction of the San Men dam was nevertheless completed in October 1960, but the effects on silt content in the lower reaches of the river were not significant, apparently because the scouring of banks and beds *below* San Men Gorge allowed the river to pick up large quantities of silt again. Silt thus continued to clog irrigation works in the lower reaches, which had been constructed on the assumption that this problem would be solved. Consequently, at least one major intake and many smaller channels failed to take in water.[67] Moreover, the continued buildup in the riverbed, canals, and irrigation channels "became a causative factor in the large floods" of 1959 to 1961.[68]

Second, the serious potential for waterlogging and salinization does not seem to have been foreseen, largely because data on the level of the water table in the various areas that were to benefit from irrigation were insufficient. Only in discussing the long-run plans for the diversion of water from the Han and Yangtse rivers into the Yellow River system was it noted that "there will be the possibility of great increases in ground water in Hopei and Anhwei." Hence, systematic study of the problem was advised.[69] But the explosive growth of irrigation in this area during 1958 and 1959, combined with the effects of the floods of 1959 to 1961, led to rapid and drastic elevation of the water table and thus to potential or actual salinization of large areas of cultivated land.[70]

It is not clear how far this process had gone before a decision was made to stop further extension of irrigation in the Yellow River basin and to halt irrigation in some areas where it had already been under way. By late 1959, official policy had shifted from an emphasis on storage to an emphasis on drainage as a way of protecting against waterlogging and salinization.[71] By late 1962, some areas had been ordered to stop irrigation, and emphasis had shifted to curing, which was attempted only for *newly* salinized land.[72]

Moreover, salinization had been elevated from a relatively minor problem in the 1950s to third rank among the four most serious problems of north China's agriculture (the others being drought, flooding, and silting) and was cited as the *main* obstacle to a rapid expansion of irrigation.[73] If the claimed 1958 increase in irrigated area of 15 million hectares for Honan, Hopei, and Shantung actually occurred, it was short-lived; as recently as 1972, only 3.2 million hectares of irrigated area were claimed for the entire Yellow River basin, of which only .5 million hectares represented waterworks along the banks of the river.[74]

The failure of the surface water schemes for the north China plain left two other options for this region, at least in the intermediate run: direct treatment of the drainage problem or reliance on subsurface water sources. The former approach was inevitably slow and difficult; the terrain is flat, and both surface flow and groundwater must be drained off. It required deep subsurface channels and drainage pipes under the fields. In addition, low-lying fields had to be elevated by employing the dual-purpose traditional methods of removing silt from irrigation channels and rivers and piling it onto fields. The process required vast amounts of slack-season labor, and peasants accustomed to dry-field cultivation in drought-stricken areas had first to be persuaded that there was good reason to invest considerable effort in allowing hard-won irrigation water to "drain away."[75] Despite the motivation inspired by the Tachai model and related campaigns, the achievements seem small compared to earlier hopes; only 100,000 hectares along the Yellow River were so improved between 1957 and 1972, "salinized or poor quality land thus converted into high-yielding paddy or wheat land."[76]

The second option, on the other hand, proved to be an important means of rapidly increasing the scope of irrigation in the north China plain. Surveys in the mid-1960s first determined that reliable, deep-strata water resources existed in this area.[77] The use of subsurface water for irrigation posed less danger than did the use of surface water, since the former only replaced what it had removed from groundwater levels. What was required were cheap and efficient pumps and drilling technologies. Large-scale production of submersible pumps designed for wells that are more than thirty meters deep seems to have begun in the late 1960s. (Increasing rural electrification also played a role.)[78] On the other hand, the well-drilling technology that was used was "improved traditional" — that is, human-powered, but with components of steel plate, pipe, and cable. (About 324 labor days per well sunk in soft soil were compressed into one week of continuous labor.) Well linings were made of local handicraft-factory products (such as ceramic, cement, bamboo, sorghum rope, and paper) and were installed in an ingenious fashion.[79] This "package" of product and process, which combined minimal, but essential, inputs from modern industry, maximum use of local and partially handicrafted products and labor, and systematized and innovative techniques, epitomizes the "bootstrap" mode of rural technological improvement that has been promoted since the Great Leap.

Moreover, it was successful. More than 1 million such tubewells were installed in north China, accounting for about 7 million hectares of irrigated land — about 70 percent of the increase in irrigated acreage since 1957.[80] Chinese studies suggest that, even in the absense of other improvements, such land yields about 70 percent more in years of drought and 10 to 20 percent more in wet years.[81] Far more important in the long run, irrigation opens up opportunities for a full-scale transformation of local agricultural technology.

MECHANIZATION

The optimal pace and forms of farm mechanization have been the subject of considerable controversy since the inception of the People's Republic, although the issue remained largely academic until the production capacity of the machine-building industry reached significant levels (after the Great Leap Forward). On the one hand, mechanized farming as practiced in the Soviet Union or the United States symbolized "modernity" and the elimination of the distinction in technique and psychology between farm and factory labor.[82] On the other hand, introducing machinery at an early stage of agricultural development might save labor without concomitant increases, or even with a decrease, in land or capital productivity. It was accepted as a general principle that China should develop and produce machinery that would contribute to all three measures of productivity (i.e., labor savings and land and capital productivity) and that labor-saving machinery should be introduced only where released labor could be used profitably to intensify cultivation, open or improve land, repair waterworks, or increase sideline activities.[83]

Of a variety of mechanizable farming activities, plowing offered the greatest potential for economically justifiable innovation. It has been argued that improvements in the traditional Japanese plow made late in the Meiji period were a prerequisite to the "takeoff" in fertilizer usage that contributed so much to subsequent growth in Japanese agricultural productivity.[84] The significant improvement in the Japanese case was due to the increased depth of plowing (permitting better developed root systems and thus more fertilizer-absorption capacity and less tendency to lodge). In the

Chinese multiple-cropping regimen, the potential labor savings were equally significant because of the time pressures on the labor supply in short period during which harvesting, plowing, and sowing or transplanting had to be done successively.[85]

The traditional Chinese plow, like its Japanese counterpart, was light, small, simply constructed, and cheap owing to its minimum metal requirement (12 yuan for dry field; 4.67 yuan for paddy plow). However, it required considerable human and animal effort, plowed to an average depth of only four to five inches, and did not turn over the soil well. Beginning in the early 1950s, the Chinese began producing and distributing on a large scale various improved traditional plows, characterized by enlarged share and moldboard and, on some dry-field plows, the addition of a guide-wheel. These implements increased average plowing depth to six and a half inches and reduced significantly the labor requirement per hectare (by 40 percent for dry field and 17 percent for paddy), but at the expense of a substantial increase in unit cost (to 21.70 yuan for dry field and 14.84 for paddy plows).[86] Still, the investment was small relative to the value of labor savings, and these plows were evidently well received.

While the improved traditional plow was a product of handicraft industry, modern industry showed its willingness to "serve agriculture" by producing large numbers of double-wheel, double-share (DWDS) plows, which were copies of Soviet and Polish models best suited to dry-field cultivation, but adaptable to paddy conditions.[87] This animal-powered, all-metal implement was far more costly than traditional or improved plows (initially 90 yuan).[88] Yet, even if one accepts advertised capabilities, it is not clear that the DWDS plow was superior to the improved plow, except in working difficult or unbroken soils where its greater weight counted in its favor. The depth of plowing was comparable, if more even; the greater breadth of furrow (and hence speed) was offset by the larger pulling requirement — two or three animals, as opposed to one or two for the improved traditional plow.[89] Still, in plains areas with well-arranged fields and adequate numbers of labor animals (or a shortage of human labor), the greater speed of plowing and the durability of the implement were advantageous. Moreover, continuous price reductions (to 61.50 yuan in 1956 and 27.30 yuan in 1974)[90] expanded the market, and the fact that the DWDS plow is still produced today attests to its ultimate profitability to the purchasers in north China.

Nevertheless, promotion of the same plow for use in paddy cultivation in south China proved to be one of the major blunders of Chinese agrotechnical policy. Between 1956 and 1958, vast numbers of DWDS plows were produced for this purpose, but rice-growing peasants reacted negatively to them. Inventories at distribution centers piled up, and many plows that were sold were later returned unused. In fact, the 40 percent price reduction in 1956 was a direct reaction to the surplus stock. (Ironically, this reduction accounts for much of the improved "terms of trade" of the peasantry during the First Five-Year Plan).[91] While this mistake in policy has commonly been attributed to blind "commandism" or technical stupidity, these explanations will not suffice.

There were strong political reasons for promoting the DWDS plow. The policy of rapid promotion of cooperatives from 1956 on made it necessary to demonstrate to the peasants that the collective organization could improve their livelihoods substantially. Such a demonstration could be accomplished through the use of the large-scale collective labor force, as in the irrigation projects discussed above, or through the use of a larger accumulation of funds to make more expensive capital equipment accessible for the first time. At the time, the DWDS plow was virtually the only expensive capital item that could be produced and distributed in quantity (tractor production began only in 1958). Thus, if benefits could be demonstrated, there was reason to produce and promote this implement.

Experiments in paddy cultivation in 1954 and 1955 did convince the leadership that the DWDS plow could be beneficial, but there were problems in extrapolating from experimental to field conditions: (1) The traditional paddy plow required one buffalo, whereas the DWDS plow required two. Animals had to be trained to "cooperate," and plowmen had to be trained to manage them. (2) In theory, the DWDS plow required less pulling power than did two traditional plows, but this was not the case in practice. Pulling requirements could be reduced by modifying the DWDS plow, but initially these modifications were left to the purchasers to make. (3) Under actual field conditions, paddy fields proved too short for efficient use of the DWDS plow, and the paths between them too narrow to transport the plow. It was optimistically assumed that cooperativization would induce peasants to modify these conditions, but the costs involved apparently were not considered. (4) Efficiency in handling the plow improved with use and training; thus, plowmen who were new to the implement were discouraged when they could not reach the rated speed of plowing. (5) The economic efficiency of DWDS plows was predicated on labor shortages that were expected to result from a rapid expansion of multiple-cropping and fertilizer-collection techniques. This expansion was not realized in the short run.[92] (6) Without modification, the DWDS plow could be used only on a hardpan paddy — not in mountainous areas, terraced fields, muddy (i.e., marshy) fields, or areas where animals were scarce. This eliminated its usage in many areas — for example, some 55 percent of the cultivated acreage in Chekiang. (7) The experimental results indicated increases in yield of more than 14 percent over the yield of traditional plows, but in large-scale comparisons under field conditions the average increase fell to 5 percent.[93]

Although many of these problems could have been eliminated eventually, it is still true that the DWDS plow offered at best only limited labor savings[94] and a *decreased* (although more even) depth of plowing compared to the improved paddy plow, despite the much higher cost of the former. These factors, in combination with the loss (or decreased strength) of animals and shortages of steel as the Great Leap ended in disaster, probably doomed the promotion of this implement for paddy use. By the time recovery was complete, China was in a position to move to a more advanced stage of mechanization of rice cultivation.

In view of the high opportunity cost of maintaining or expanding the animal labor stock (in terms of grain or meat consumption sacrificed), the direction of advance could only be toward the use of tractors, but at first such a plan did not seem feasible for paddy cultivation. To be sure, tractors with 25 to 30 horsepower could be modified for use with reasonable efficiency in hardpan paddy fields if the field size was enlarged to about two-thirds of a hectare per plot.[95] However, these conditions, as well as cost considerations, restricted the tractor's applicability to a small percentage of the acreage in the mountainous south.

By the late 1950s, Japan, in response to similar needs, was producing and distributing rotary power tillers, and China was quick to test their applicability. The initial conclusion was negative, even though labor productivity was three times as great as when the traditional plow was used, the quality of work was considerably higher (one pass being equivalent to one plowing and two harrowings by a traditional plow), and the time-utilization rate was quite high regardless of the size of the field. The reason for the rejection was clear; increased plowing depth was considered crucial to the yield-increasing strategy of the Chinese, as enshrined in the Eight-Character Charter, and the power tiller cultivated to a depth of only five inches on an average — just slightly better than the traditional paddy plow and worse than the improved paddy plow (four to five and six and one half inches, respectively).[96]

Attitudes toward the power tiller changed in the 1960s, however, and by 1966 production was being rapidly increased; indeed, the spread of the power tiller has been the most notable feature in China's use of the tractor ever since.[97] The policy reversal reflected a further emphasis on multiple cropping in the south, even at the cost of loss of yields resulting from reduced depth of plowing.[98] Double or triple cropping of rice created an overwhelming labor-time constraint, which made economical not only the power tiller but also, in a few areas, the mechanical transplanter — an indigenous innovation that also saves labor time without directly contributing much to yields.[99] The change in attitude toward the power tiller should not be seen as a correction of a previously erroneous policy. Rather, it should be regarded as part of a program that included the development of seeds with shorter growing seasons, an increase in fertilizer supplies, and improvement of water control and organizational techniques. This program relaxed the set of constraints that had limited the expansion of multiple cropping in the 1950s.

IMPROVED TECHNIQUES

Of all the agricultural practices recommended by the Eight-Character Charter, the only one that represented a break with trends in technique elsewhere in Asia was the promotion of "scientific dense planting." It has been described as the charter's "main theme."[100] While many other aspects of improved technique have proven more important in the long run, the origins, evolution, and eventual fate of this innovation are particularly illuminating to our topic.

The emphasis on greater plant density as a yield-improving technique may derive from Soviet advice and, more specifically, from the theories of Lysenko. Lysenko believed in the lack of intraspecies competition and the advantage of numbers when one species is in competition with another (e.g., crops against weeds). Thus, he argued for dense planting. Although in the Soviet Union the method and its most famous application (to tree planting for shelter belts) were attacked as failures in 1954, these attacks were suppressed by political supporters of Lysenko.[101]

Emphasis on increased plant density in China cannot be explained entirely by Lysenkian Soviet advice, however. Chinese experiments did establish that increased density, in conjunction with deep plowing, not only increased yields but also significantly raised the marginal response to nitrogen applications (with *existing* seed varieties).[102] The explanation was roughly that deeper plowing and increased fertilizer applications made greater vertical root development possible, thereby permitting closer planting without the decrease in yields that would otherwise result.

Unfortunately, as in the Soviet Union, this change in technique captured the imagination of political cadres, who appreciated the analogy between the "collectivist nature" *(ch'un-t'i-hsing)* of plants and the process of communalization; the apparent refutation of the "bourgeois" law of diminishing returns; and the seeming requirements of only labor and additional seed to implement this reform. In the fever of the Great Leap, the reform was pushed on reluctant peasants with the same "excesses" that caused the debacle in local irrigation work and accompanied the ill-conceived promotion of the DWDS plow.[103] For example, the traditional rice-planting density in the province of Kwangtung was less than 1.5 million seedlings per hectare and differed little from traditional standards elsewhere in Asia.[104] However, by 1958 this traditional density had been increased by about 50 percent, and with the specification of the Eight-Character Charter in time for the fall planting, density reached 6 million to 7.5 million seedlings per hectare. In some localities, density was even higher. For 1959 the Kwangtung Central Committee advocated a further increase to 12 million to 15 million seedlings per hectare.[105]

A severe economic loss was clearly the only result of these "excesses." According to one postmortem, an increase in seedling density from 2.3 million to 7.5 million per hectare did increase yields, but only by 180 kilograms.[106] However, the increased yield was almost canceled by the increased seed requirement of 150 kilograms. Moreover, additional land had to be reserved for seedbeds (at the expense of both preceding and current crops); added labor was required for preparation, transplanting, and care; and heavier applications of fertilizer were also needed.[107]

With the experts again in command, promotion of "scientific dense planting" was subtly modified to a "reasonable range of density" (*ho-li mi-chih*) and de-emphasized. Had the course of Chinese agrotechnical development followed that of other Asian countries, recommended density could then have been expected to decrease. For example, in Japan there was "a gradual tendency for the density of planting rice . . . to decrease as the quantity of fertilizers used . . . increased and as rice varieties of a more prolific type [became] common."[108] In other words, seed selection and cultivation in Japan emphasized the development of plants bearing a maximum number of tillers (grain-bearing offshoots of the main stalk) per seedling. This trend naturally saved both seedbed area and labor expended in transplanting. Thus, by the 1950s, standard density in Japanese rice cultivation was down to only .84 million seedlings per hectare.[109] Improved row-planting methods in the Phillipines were said to reduce density to .99 million per hectare, and experiments with IR-8 seed in western Pakistan showed that a density of .87 million per hectare gave highest yields.[110]

However, in the mid-1960s Chinese experts were still recommending densities between 2.25 million and 3.75 million seedlings per hectare for rice, citing studies documenting that the point of maximum yields lay within this range.[111] In 1974 a delegation of U.S. plant scientists was surprised to observe densities far higher than were favored elsewhere.[112] In response to the excesses of the Great Leap, Chinese agronomists have given the question of optimal density careful and extensive study; thus, the difference in technique is likely to be enduring.

Several reasons may be cited for the greater density levels promoted in Chinese cultivation. First, in attempting to explain decreases in yield resulting from excessive density, the Chinese discovered that the major problems were a reduction in the amount of light reaching the plants and reduced air circulation, which affected the microclimate. Optimal spacings, row arrangements, and timings of fertilizer application were found to reduce the impact of these problems and to permit higher density levels.[113] Second, contrary to previous doctrine but in accordance with findings abroad, Chinese research concluded that density should be inversely proportionate to fertilizer use (because with low fertilizer use, it is necessary to rely on the main stalk and to neglect subordinate spikes). However, "high fertilizer use" justifying sparse planting was considered to be something on the order of 225 kilograms of nitrogen per crop hectare from all sources, far above average levels of application anywhere in the world. Hence, these findings do not really explain the difference between Chinese and foreign density levels. Third, cold climates in the north and double or triple cropping in the south have dictated a fast maturation process, which has meant reliance on the main head (which can develop faster if subordinate heads are suppressed). In these circumstances — which differ significantly from those elsewhere in Asia — dense planting is optimal.[114] Finally, and somewhat speculatively, seed selection and hybridization have been carried out in the People's Republic of China with high yield *under dense planting* as a major objective. It is not unlikely that the seeds thus developed would respond differently to higher levels of planting density than those developed under different objectives.

CONCLUSION

This discussion has done scant justice to the rich materials available on the transformation of agricultural technology in China over the past decades. However, having followed the evolution of a few key elements of that technology from weakness to strength, the reader should now at least sense the complexity of the Chinese strategy for improving productivity in agriculture. As Professor Ishikawa has pointed out, this strategy can best be summarized as:

1. Utilizing as much as possible the local resources for agricultural inputs (designated as "traditional" inputs in contrast to "modern" inputs).
2. Economizing as much as possible on modern input (here defined as the inputs produced with the use of nonfarm resources).
3. Researching and developing scientific methods for productivity increase on the basis of traditional inputs or a combination of traditional and modern inputs.[115]

This strategy and the corollary tenets of the Eight-Character Charter have been the central themes of Chinese policy since the mid-1950s. Within this framework, China has groped for means of implementation that are suitable to its environmental and economic conditions. In the first stage of the search, some characteristics of the Soviet model were adopted — namely, an emphasis on large-scale, multipurpose water control projects, heavy tractors, and other European-style machinery; a Lysenkian faith in deep plowing and dense planting; and a relatively unproductive research program. More recently, features of the Japanese and Taiwanese technological models have been ascendant, including an emphasis on the development of hybrid seeds, intensive fertilizer use, power tillers, and other small machines, as well as a well-organized research and extension network. These parallels should not be overdrawn. In part, they represent regional focuses and changes in emphasis and timing.

It is also difficult to generalize in abstract terms about what is unique to the evolving elements of Chinese agricultural technology. For most specific elements, parallels or precedents can be found in the experiences of other countries. Nevertheless, China at least was unusually successful in implementing the following aspects of its technological program and unique in combining these into a single program and time period:

1. Rapid, indigenous development of superior seeds with unique suitability to a multiple-cropping regimen.
2. Implementation of means of decreasing the time lag between initial hybridization and final distribution of improved seeds.
3. Preservation and enlargement of organic fertilizer use, in parallel with the rapid growth of chemical fertilizer supplies.
4. Substantial enlargement of production of animal protein, partly through grain-saving feeding techniques, despite stagnant per capita grain supplies.
5. Rapid expansion of tubewell irrigation through an innovative combination of factory and handicraft technology and labor-intensive installation techniques.

In implementing these improvements and others that I have ignored because of lack of space, China has apparently found a program that can exploit most fully all its limited resources. On the one hand, by emphasizing multiple cropping, it has sought to maximize both land productivity and the utilization of its rural labor force. On the other hand, by emphasizing the combined use of improved traditional and modern handicraft and factory-produced machinery and implements, it has sought rapid enlargement of capital contribution to agriculture production.

Although China has shown an impressive capacity for increasing its agricultural productivity over the last two decades, optimism about the future must be guarded. Development has been very uneven across regions and among localities, suggesting a strong potential for further gains. However, laggard areas in general have poorer land and poorer water resources, which will require higher per-hectare investment costs if a reasonable rate of growth is to be maintained. Moreover, the fundamental problems of silting and waterlogging in the north remain unsolved. And since productivity growth has barely kept pace with population growth, the success of population-control policies is crucial if living standards are to be raised.

NOTES

1. The percentages were computed for the period between 1957 and 1973. If computations are based on five-year averages (between 1951–1955 or 1956–1960 and 1971–1975), average annual growth rates appear substantially higher. See U.S. Department of Agriculture, Economic Research Service, *The Agricultural Situation in the P.R.C. and Other Communist Asian Countries,* Foreign Agricultural Economic Report No. 124 (Washington, D.C.: U.S. Department of Agriculture, 1976), p. 63.
2. See Shahid Burki, *A Study of Chinese Communes* (Cambridge, Mass.: Harvard University Press, 1969), p. 4; Asakawa Kenji, "Four Reforms in Chinese Agriculture," *Chugoku Kenkyu Geppo* [Chinese Studies Monthly], no. 154 (January 30, 1961), trans. JPRS 9,209, p. 42.
3. These are well covered in Benedict Stavis, *Making Green Revolution* (Ithaca, N.Y.: Cornell University Press, 1974).
4. The spread of improved seeds had been econometrically shown to contribute to productivity growth in Japanese agriculture far more than does fertilizer use. See Yujiro Hayami and Saburo Yamada, "Agricultural Productivity at the Beginning of Industrialization," in K. Okhawa et al., eds., *Agriculture and Economic Growth: Japan's Experience* (Princeton, N.J.: Princeton University Press, 1970), pp. 14–16.
5. Matsubayashi Minoru et al., eds., *Theory and Practice of Growing Rice* (Tokyo: Fuji Press, 1968), pp. 69–72, 75.

6. Chiang Yin-sung, "Keng-tan 'kui-hua-ch'ou' ti shih-yen shih-fan ho t'ui-kuang ti tiao-ch'a pao-kao," *Chung-kuo Nung-pao,* September 1957, p. 27.

7. Ting Ying, *Chung-kuo shui-tao tsai-p'ei hsüeh* [Study of chinese paddy rice cultivation], (Peking, 1961), pp. 257–61, 269–74, 277–78, 282–84, 288–90.

8. See Nai-ruenn Chen, *Chinese Economic Statistics* (Chicago: Aldine, 1967), Table 5.101, p. 369, and Table 5.104, p. 370.

9. Burki, op. cit., p. 48.

10. Po Mu-hua, "Wo-kuo nung-tso-wu ti p'in-chung tzu-yüan," *People's Daily,* December 11, 1962.

11. Ts'ai Hsü, "Tso-wu yü-chung chi liang-chung fan-yü chung ti jo-kan wen-t'i," *People's Daily,* October 9, 1962

12. Po Mu-hua, op. cit.

13. Ting Ying, ed., *Tao-tso k'o'hsüeh lun-wen hsüan-chi* (Peking, 1959), p. 13; Chiang Yin-sung, op. cit., pp. 27–28.

14. Ts'ai Hsü, op. cit.

15. Kwangtung Provincial Academy of Agricultural Sciences, "Principals Experience in the Breeding of Dwarfed Paddy Rice," *People's Daily,* December 11, 1964, trans. JPRS 28,507.

16. Li Mei-sheng, "T'ui-kuang shui-tao ai-kan p'in-chung ying chu-i ti chi-ko wen-t'i," *Chung-kuo Nung-pao,* February 1965, p. 16; Paddy Rice Scientific Technique Group, Academy of Agricultural Science, "Kwang-ch'ang-ai ho chen-ch'u-ai ti p'in-chung t'e-hsing ho tsai-p'ei chi-shu tsung-chieh," *Chung-kuo Nung-yeh K'o-hsüeh,* January 1966, pp. 28–30.

17. Li Mei-sheng, op. cit., p. 15.

18. Chekiang People's Press, eds., *Nung-yeh sheng-ch'an hsüeh-hsi tsu-liao* (Hangchou: Chekiang People's Press, 1965), pp. 13, 16, 20.

19. The superiority became visible at nitrogen application levels exceeding 75 kilograms per hectare. Li Mei-sheng, op. cit., p. 15.

20. The Plant Science Delegation of the National Academy of Sciences to the People's Republic of China was told that IR-8 was tested shortly after its release but was rejected largely because of its long growing period. See their *Trip Report* (Washington, D. C.: 1975), p. 53.

21. These wheat varieties probably account for yield gains for that crop of nearly 40 percent between 1965 and 1972, and more of late. See Thomas B. Wiens, "Agricultural Statistics in the P.R.C.," unpublished manuscript, 1976, p. 53. Periodicals and books brought back by recent delegations to China show a multiplicity of new hybrids of wheat and other crops in the distribution stage, including many double crosses. Parentage cited includes Mexican, Korean, Italian, and other foreign stock. High-yielding (6 to 7 tons per hectare) semi-dwarf wheat varieties are currently in experimental use in the north and northwest. See Chiao Hung-chang, "Hsiao-mai kao-ch'an hsin-ching-yen," *Chung-kuo Nung-yeh K'o-hsüeh* 1 (January 1976): 25–28.

22. Kwangtung Provincial Academy, op. cit., pp. 32–34. The functions of various levels of seed-breeding stations are identical with the Japanese system. See Matsubayashi Minoru et al., op. cit., p. 30.

23. The process is based on the pollen culture of anthers taken from Fl hybrids. For description, see Plant Science Delegation, *Trip Report,* pp. 125-27; *Kuang-ming Jih-pao,* December 9, 1975.

24. Shigeru Ishikawa and Kazushi Ohkawa, "Significance of Japan's Experience — Technological Changes in Agricultural Production and Changes in Agrarian Structure," in Japan Economic Research Center (JERC), *Agriculture and Economic Development: Structural Readjustment in Asian Perspective* (Tokyo: JERC, 1972), p. 146; Shigeru Ishikawa, *Factors Affecting China's Agriculture in the Coming Decade* (Tokyo: Institute of Asian Economic Affairs, 1967), Table 12, pp. 60-61 (mimeographed).

25. Wiens, op. cit., Table 18, p. 59. Total nutrient per cultivated hectare in 1971, including N, P_2O_2, and K_2O, was about 195 kilograms; nitrogen alone, about 93 kilograms (or roughly 65 per sown hectare), compared to 50 in 1957.

26. Ch'en Shang-chin, "Kuan-yü ching-chi yu-hsiao shih-yung hua-hsüeh fei-liao ti shang-ch'üeh," *People's Daily,* December 24, 1963.

27. Ibid.; Ch'en En-feng, "Wu-chi-fei-liao tui nung-yeh sheng-ch'an ti tso-yung," *People's Daily,* August 27, 1963.

28. Ting I et al., "Kuan-yü fa-chan hua-hsüeh fei-liao wen-t'i ti shen-t'ao," *People's Daily,* November 15, 1962. See also Yen Jui-chen, "Kuan-yü t'i-kao fei-liao ching-chi hsiao-yü ti chi-ko wen-t'i," *Ching-chi Yen-chiu* 6 (1964):34.

29. Ibid., p. 27.

30. Paddy Rice Scientific Technique Group, Academy of Agricultural Sciences, "1965 nan-fang shui-tao feng-ch'an tsai-p'ei chi-shu ch'u-pu tsung-chieh," *Chungkuo Nung-yeh K'o-hsueh* 2 (1966):18-19.

31. Government of India, Ministry of Food and Agriculture, *Report of the Indian Delegation to China on Agricultural Planning and Techniques* (New Delhi, 1959), p. 126; Yen, op. cit., p. 29.

32. I Ts'ai and Wang Pi-chang, "Ts'ung Hai-ch'eng kao-liang yang-pan-t'ien k'an t'i-kao shih-fei ching-chi hsiao-kuo ti t'u-ching," *Ching-chi Yen-chiu* 4 (1965):42-46.

33. Japanese wholesale prices from "The Oriental Economist," *Japan Economic Yearbook,* 1961, p. 178 (a 10 percent retail/wholesale margin has been assumed); Taiwan barter ratios from H.Y. Chen et al., "Rice Policies of Taiwan," *Food Research Institute Studies* 14, no. 4 (1975):412-13. Recent evidence indicates that the ratio of the purchasing price of wheat or rice to the retail price of ammonium sulphate has risen to nearly 1.0. See Stavis, op. cit., pp. 124-25; *Peking Review* 32-33 (August 9, 1976):26; unpublished notes of the Wheat Delegation of the National Academy of Sciences.

34. Yen, op cit., p. 35.

35. Ibid., p. 29.

36. Ibid., p. 33.

37. Liu Jui-lung, "Ch'üan-kuo yang-chu chung-tien hsien tso-t'an-hui tsung-chieh pao-kao," *Chungkuo Nung-pao,* November 1957, pp. 1-3. See also Kenneth Walker, *Planning in Chinese Agriculture* (Chicago: Aldine, 1965).

38. Wiens, op. cit., pp. 25-26, 146; Chiang I-chen, "Fa-chan Tachai ching-shen,

cheng-ch'ü nung-yeh ch'üan-mien ti keng-ta ti feng-shou," *Chungkuo Nung-pao,* February 1965, p. 2.

39. Ishikawa, op. cit., pp. 16–17.
40. Wiens, op. cit., pp. 65–66.
41. Yen, op. cit., p. 43.
42. Ibid.; Wiens, op. cit., p. 146. The calculation assumes food grains consumption of roughly 360 kilograms per year for pigs, 2,000 kilograms per year for work animals, and an annual flow/stock ratio of 2.0 for pigs; these figures are close to those found in several Chinese sources.
43. At 31–32 yuan per pig of 50 kilogram average slaughter weight, from Liaoning Province Statistical Bureau, "Tui wan-ch'eng sheng-chu sheng-ch'an chi-hua ti chi-tien chien-i," *T'ung-chi Kung-tso* 4 (1957):22; 7.2 kilograms annual nitrogen content of manure, if fully utilized, worth 10–11 yuan if derived from chemical sources, from Teng Ching-chung, "The Methods of Calculating Livestock Standard Units," *Ti-li-hsüeh Tsu-liao* 4 (June 1959), trans. JPRS 38,917; plus the value of other nutrients and organic matter, which has not been computed.
44. Liaoning Shenyang County Statistical Bureau, "Kuan-yü 1957-nien sheng-chu sheng-ch'an wen-t'i ti ch'u-pu fen-hsi," *T'ung-chi Yen-chiu* 7 (1958):33.
45. The key policy decisions were made in 1957. Liu Jui-lung, op. cit., pp. 3–4.
46. See, for example, the cover of *Nung-yeh Chi-shu,* April 1966, and p. 30. See also Stavis, op. cit., pp. 52–54 on electrification.
47. For a model example of this technology, see Yü Tsung-chün, "Li-yung ch'ing, ts'u ssu-liao tuo-yang chu, yang hao-chu," *Nung-yeh Chi-shu* 2 (1966):30–33.
48. For discussion of the recent role of the private economy, see Jack Chen, *A Year in Upper Felicity* (New York: Macmillan, 1973), pp. 160–63.
49. The discussion of the irrigation problem in north and south China is based on Ministry of Agriculture, People's Republic of China, *Nung-t'ien Shui-li* (Peking, 1963), pp. 7, 27.
50. For example, the proposal for the Hui River project anticipated a payoff period of less than three years. See *Chungkuo Shui-li* 4 (1957):22.
51. Ishikawa, op. cit., pp. 50–51, especially note 63.
52. Tojin Sha, ed., *Ajia no Yume* [Dream of Asia], (Tokyo: Tojin Sha, 1964), trans. JPRS 32,681, p. 53.
53. Su Tsung-sung, "Wei hua-pei p'ing-yüan fa-chan nung-yeh sheng-ch'an 'ch'u ssu-hai'," *People's Daily,* December 18, 1962.
54. Central Intelligence Agency, *The Program for Water Conservancy in Communist China* (Washington, D. C., 1962), p. 14.
55. Ministry of Agriculture, op. cit., pp. 31–33, 41–42.
56. Tojin Sha, op. cit., pp. 60–61.
57. Ibid., pp. 75–77, 79, 87, 90.
58. Central Intelligence Agency, op. cit., pp. 38–39; *Ninmin Chugoku* 6 (1973):23.

59. Hsiung Yi, "Hua-pei p'ing-yuan t'u-jang yen-hsien-hua ti fang-chih," *People's Daily,* December 18, 1962; Su Tsung-sung, op. cit.; Wiens, op. cit., Table G-3, p. 144.
60. Tojin Sha, op. cit., p. 164.
61. Ministry of Agriculture, op. cit., pp. 30-31.
62. Central Intelligence Agency, op. cit., p. 11.
63. Tojin Sha, op. cit., p. 63.
64. Su Tsung-sung, op. cit.
65. Tojin Sha, op. cit., p. 83. For the history of the problem, see Joseph Needham, *Science and Civilization in China,* vol. 4:3, pp. 232-45.
66. Su Tsung-sung, op. cit.; *Ninmin Chugoku,* op. cit., p. 22. As a result, the useful life span of the San Men dam was reduced.
67. Su Tsung-sung, op. cit.
68. Tojin Sha, op. cit., p. 53.
69. Ibid., p. 79.
70. Egypt, also with Soviet aid, has unfortunately repeated the Chinese error in its Aswan project but has not yet faced the full consequences. See the *Wall Street Journal,* September 24, 1976.
71. Ho Chi-feng, "Shih-nien-lai wo-kuo nung-t'ien shui-li chien-she ti hui-huang ch'eng-chiu," *Shui-li Shui-tien Chien-she* 18 (1959):16-17.
72. Hsiung Yi, op. cit.
73. Compare Ministry of Agriculture, Propaganda Bureau, eds., *Nung-yeh sheng-ch'an chi-shu chi-pen chih-shih vol. 14: Tu-jang* (Peking, 1956), pp. 22-23, 26-28, with Su Tsung-sung, op. cit.
74. *Ninmin Chugoku,* op. cit., p. 23.
75. Hsiung Yi, op. cit.
76. Ninmin Chugoku, op. cit., p. 23.
77. Jack Chen, op. cit., pp. 209-212.
78. The state of pump technology through 1965 is described in Ministry of Agriculture (1963), op. cit., pp. 31-71; see also *Chieh-fang Jih-pao,* July 20, 1965.
79. The well-drilling process and technology are well described in Jack Chen, op. cit., pp. 215-20.
80. Wiens, op. cit., pp. 57-58.
81. Liu Pai-t'ao, "Basic Research on the Economic Efficiency of Irrigation," *Ching-chi Yen-chiu* 8 (1964):30.
82. Chinese admiration for mechanized farming is well reflected in William Hinton, *Iron Oxen* (New York: Vintage Books, 1970).
83. Hsiang Te, "Wo-kuo nung-yeh chi-chieh-hua wen-t'i ti t'an-t'ao" *People's Daily,* July 2, 1963.
84. Takekazu Ogura, ed., *Agricultural Development in Modern Japan* (Tokyo: Fuji, 1967), p. 370.
85. For further discussion, see Kenneth Walker, "Organization of Agricultural Production," in A. Eckstein, W. Galenson, and T.C. Liu, eds., *Economic Trends in Communist China* (Chicago: Aldine, 1968), pp. 405-13.

86. Price averages, descriptions, and technical characteristics of plows tabulated by the author from Ministry of Agriculture, People's Republic of China, *Nung-chü T'u-p'u* (Peking, 1958), and 2nd Ministry of Light Industry, Agricultural Implements Bureau, *Nung-yeh Chi-chü Ts'ung-shu,* vol. 1 (Peking, 1966). On improved implements, see Amano Motonosuke, "Daiyakushin ki no nogu," *Ajia Keizai* 14: 12 (1973).

87. Ministry of Agriculture (1958), op. cit., pp. 25–27.

88. Central Intelligence Agency, *Prices of Machinery and Equipment in the P.R.C.* (Washington, D. C.: 1975), p. 14.

89. Claims in 1957 indicated labor savings of 28 percent or more, but 1964 materials indicate no labor savings (human plus animal) at a ratio of animal-to-human labor cost of 3:1. See Ministry of Agriculture, *Nung-yeh Chi-chü* (Peking, 1964), p. 40. An article in *People's Daily,* June 16, 1958, indicated that the DWDS plow could not plow much more deeply than traditional plows with only two animals or weak ones.

90. Central Intelligence Agency (1975), op. cit., p. 14.

91. See *People's Daily,* October 7, 1955, and February 5, 1958.

92. *People's Daily,* February 5, 1958.

93. Ibid.; *People's Daily,* January 26, 1958.

94. My calculations imply none at all, at the 3:1 animal-to-human cost ratio, based on figures in Ting Ying (1961), op. cit., p. 632.

95. Ibid., pp. 626–27.

96. Ibid., p. 628; Matsubayashi Minoru et al., op. cit., pp. 382–85. Moreover, power tillers were restricted to hardpan paddy fields.

97. Central Intelligence Agency, *Production of Machinery and Equipment in the P.R.C.* (Washington, D.C., 1975), p. 10.

98. However, plowing with animals once a year could still be practiced.

99. The first transplanter was invented by a Hunan peasant youth in 1958; models approved for widespread manufacture in 1960 were experiment station products, however. At best, these machines improved slightly on yields through more consistency in density, orderliness, and depth of transplanting. See Ting Ying (1961), op. cit., pp. 638–42. Transplanting has not yet been mechanized in Japan, probably because limited multiple cropping imposes no serious time constraint.

100. Asakawa Kenji, op. cit., p. 43.

101. Loren Graham, *Science and Philosophy in the Soviet Union* (New York: Knopf, 1972), pp. 237–39. Lysenkian doctrine reached China in the early 1950s, where, as in the Soviet Union, it was used to attack theoretical research and promote practical research inspired by advanced peasant practices. See Fang Ts'ui-nung, "Nung-yeh k'o-hsüeh kung-tso-che wei nung-yeh sheng-ch'an fu-wu ti tao-lu," *Hsin Chien She* 3 (1954):18.

102. See Ting Ying (1961), op. cit., pp. 369, 372, for results demonstrating these points. Existing seed varieties presumably had low tillering rates.

103. The volume of propaganda "refuting" local opinions concerning dense planting is a good indication of the extent of peasant resistence. See Kenneth

Walker (1968), op. cit., p. 421; Ministry of Agriculture, Foodgrains Production Bureau, *1958-nien nung-tso-wu mi-chih ching-yen* (Peking, 1961).

104. Ibid., p. 5. Density in the Phillipines was traditionally about 1.3 million seedlings per hectare (from unpublished materials of the IRRI). According to data in Ma Chien-yu, "The Group Concept in Agricultural Production" (March 23, 1961), trans. JPRS 9,398, .66 kilograms of seed produce around 10,000 seedlings.

105. Ministry of Agriculture, Foodgrains Production Bureau, op. cit., p. 5.

106. Effective ears in the amount of 2.85 million resulted from 2.25 million seedlings, at 64.24 grains per ear; 7.5 million seedlings led to 5.85 million ears, but only 32.58 grains per ear and with a 10 percent decrease in weight per grain.

107. Ma Chien-yu, op. cit.

108. Takane Matsuo, *Rice and Rice Cultivation in Japan* (Tokyo: Ministry of Agriculture and Forestry, Government of Japan, 1959), p. 127.

109. Ibid., pp. 127, 164.

110. The Phillipines datum is from IRRI materials (1968); the Pakistan datum from Agricultural Department, Government of West Pakistan, *Annual Report on Accelerated Rice Research Program* (1966), Table 7, p. 31.

111. Ministry of Agriculture, People's Republic of China, *Shui-tao Tsai-p'ei* (Peking, 1965), p. 30; T'ang P'ei-sung, "Ts'ung chih-wu ti kuang-neng li-yung hsiao-lu k'an t'i-kao tan-wei mien-chi ch'an-liang," *People's Daily,* November 12, 1963.

112. Plant Science Delegation, National Academy of Sciences, op. cit., p. 45.

113. Ministry of Agriculture, People's Republic of China, *Nung-yeh Ch'i-hsiang* (Peking, 1963), pp. 24–25.

114. Kuo I-hsien, "Ts'ung ch'ün-t'i chieh-kou t'an-t'ao shui-tao kao-ch'an kui-lü," *People's Daily,* April 9, 1963.

115. Shigeru Ishikawa, "Agrarian Reform and Its Productivity Effect—Implication of the Chinese Patterns," in *The Structure and Development in Asian Economies* (Institute of Economic Research, Hitotsubashi University, Paper No. 10, September 1968).

9 POLITICAL LEADERSHIP AND PERSONNEL POLICY IN ROMANIA:

Continuity and Change, 1965–1976

Mary Ellen Fischer

Most Western scholars agree that a distinguishing feature of communist political systems is the high concentration of influence in the hands of the "men at the top." This is particularly true in Romania where, as Kenneth Jowitt has noted, Ceausescu is attempting to develop "his personal role to the point where the Party cannot check, divert, or delay his policies." Andrzej Korbonski has argued that "this concept of leadership . . . provides at least a partial explanation of the process of change in that country."[1] The personalities and priorities of Ceausescu and those around him certainly are important inputs into the political process. Of course, no political system can be fully understood by studying only its leaders. However, information about these individuals can provide insight into the nature of the political decision-making process in which they participate.

Most data in this study come from the author's own personnel files compiled from *Scinteia,* the Romanian Communist party's daily newspaper. In addition, the Romanian research division of Radio Free Europe has excellent archieves on the entire Romanian political elite, and the biographical newspaper index at Radio Free Europe was an invaluable aid in preparing the present study. Finally, the above sources have been supplemented by twelve months of residence in Romania from 1973 to 1975, and I would like to thank IREX and the Romanian Ministry of Education for that opportunity.

210

The study of such elites — not only the small group of individuals in the highest party leadership, but also those broader categories of political and economic decision makers that can now be analyzed on the basis of increasingly available data — has been, and remains, a productive area for scholars.[2]

Although the comparative study of communist elites has expanded in recent years, the leaders of the Romanian Communist party (RCP) have been virtually ignored in such comparisons. This void is certainly not due to the ineptness or low profile of the Romanian party leadership. Indeed, discussions of the Romanians' now famous "independent" foreign policy invariably include praise for the perspicacity of their diplomacy. And President Ceausescu himself has become one of the most widely known communist leaders, partly because of his many trips abroad and partly because of his own populist style. The problem in studying the Romanian leadership is lack of information; secrecy in Romania regarding party matters is an obsession that extends beyond the decision-making process to biographical and career data on those involved. Information on the Romanian elite is consistent only in its inconsistency or inadequacy.[3]

There are some exceptions to this discouraging situation. Excellent analyses are available on the very top leaders in the pre-1965 period.[4] In addition, several brief biographies of Ceausescu have been commissioned by the Romanian government.[5] Still, knowledge about the present leadership group surrounding Ceausescu remains scanty. This paper will partially fill that void by describing the 1974 Executive Committee and comparing its members with those of the Gheorghiu-Dej Politburo. This discussion will be followed by an analysis of the personnel policies that enabled Ceausescu to gain and maintain his control within the RCP. The first section will essentially compare two small groups of leaders to see how the criteria for membership in the top party organ changed between 1965 and 1974. The rest of the paper will look at a larger number of individuals, including the local party officials who played such an important role in Ceausescu's rise to power.

Many of the conclusions will inevitably be speculative. Given the secrecy of internal party affairs, uncertainty in research of this sort is inherent. A party official's sector of responsibility must often be deduced from his participation in certain types of meetings and receptions. An individual's status must be inferred from press reports or, all too frequently, after the fact of his dismissal. Major officials usually confine their public statements to the current party line already expressed by Ceausescu, and so their own opinions remain unknown. Nevertheless, a close examination of personnel patterns in Romania over the last decade — shifts in such objective characteristics as age, ethnicity, and career pattern, as well as the timing and location of promotions — indicates both change and continuity in the style and content of political leadership.

THE GHEORGHIU-DEJ AND
CEAUSESCU LEADERSHIP GROUPS

A comparison of the Romanian leadership at the death of Gheorghe Gheorghiu-Dej in March 1965 with the Ceausescu group as it had evolved by the Eleventh Party Congress in November 1974 is particularly revealing. Both Gheorghiu-Dej and Ceausescu presided over radical personnel changes following their accessions to power. Gheorghiu-Dej had essentially completed this process of change as early as 1952; a few demotions took place in 1957, but from 1957 to 1965 the Politburo remained virtually unchanged. Only after Gheorghiu-Dej's death and Ceausescu's election as First Secretary did a similar turnover in personnel take place. The timing of the turnovers and the subsequent supremacy of the party leader indicate that in both cases the leader determined the selection of top political personnel. No individual could be a member of the highest party body without the acquiescence, if not the active support, of the leader.[6] Hence, the change over time in the background and experience of those promoted to the highest decision-making level reveals the priorities and preferences of this top individual and has important implications for policy formulation and content within the RCP.

In early 1965, the Romanian party leadership was quite diverse. Only eight of the fifteen men discussed here could be defined unequivocally as ethnic Romanians.[7] Six of the fifteen had lived for years in the Soviet Union and were considered to have close ties to that country. Eight members of the group claimed to be from worker or peasant families, several admitted a bourgeois background, and the social origins of the rest are unclear. About half of the men had received some form of higher education. As a whole, then, the Politburo was certainly not homogeneous in ethnic, social, or educational background, and the extensive connections with the U.S.S.R. were not what might be expected of a group of Romanian "nationalists."

In terms of background characteristics, there were in fact *two* distinguishable groups within the 1965 leadership. Gheorghiu-Dej, Nicolae Ceausescu, Chivu Stoica, Gheorghe Apostol, and Alexandru Draghici were all ethnic Romanians of proletarian or peasant background, with no formal education, and all had spent the war years in Romanian prisons. In contrast, Emil Bodnaras, Petre Borila, Dumitru Coliu, Leonte Rautu, and

Leonte Salajan were not ethnic Romanians, had some higher education, and had spent the war in the Soviet Union.[8] The remaining five men do not fit smoothly into either category. These two groups reflect the dichotomy present in the communist party leaderships throughout Eastern Europe in the postwar years, the "home communists" and the "Soviet communists."[9] However, it is perhaps surprising that this division existed in Romania as late as 1965. By that time, the COMECON dispute with Moscow had ostensibly been decided in the Romanians' favor, and a major factor contributing to the Romanians' success was the unity of the RCP leadership around Gheorghiu-Dej. The leaders were united, but this unity was not the result of ethnic or social homogeneity.

In fact, the Romanian leadership under Gheorgiu-Dej was as a whole homogeneous in only two respects: longevity in office and prewar illegal communist activity. Of the nine full members of the Politburo, five had been members before 1952,[10] two joined in 1952, and the two relative latecomers, Ceausescu and Draghici, became members in 1955. Thirteen of the fifteen were Central Committee members by 1948. All but two were RCP members by 1936,[11] and eight had spent long years in prison in Romania. The remaining five escaped into exile in the U.S.S.R. Bodnaras managed to experience both prison and exile.

These two common background characteristics of the party leadership indicate the bases of group unity and the priorities of the First Secretary in selecting his close associates: (1) personal loyalty to Gheorgiu-Dej, demonstrated by long years of service with him, and (2) a deep commitment to Marxist revolutionary activity, proven by imprisonment or exile. These bonds were strong enough to maintain group solidarity in the face of ethnic diversity and Soviet pressure. The attitude of most of these men toward the U.S.S.R. must at one time have been positive. After all, during the illegal days, the Communist party of the Soviet Union was their only outside source of support, and it was the Soviet Army that established the RCP in power.[12] At the same time, however, they were probably a bit wary of blindly following Soviet advice. The prewar RCP had not always found the COMINTERN line to be advantageous in Romania,[13] and postwar economic exploitation by the Russians, who regarded Romania as an enemy combatant, was extremely hard on an already devastated economy.[14]

Nevertheless, the Romanian communist leaders adopted the Soviet model of economic development[15] — including the priority development of heavy industry and the policy of industrial protectionism[16] — with resulting hardships on the population. The correctness of the model had been convincingly demonstrated to the Romanians by the Soviets in the victory over Germany. Once the Romanian leaders reaffirmed the Soviet model in their industrialization plans announced in 1958, they were forced by subsequent Soviet opposition to become "nationalist" and "anti-Soviet." In other words, the Soviet leaders themselves opposed Romanian emulation of the industrialization plan laid down by the U.S.S.R. under Stalin. Ironically enough, the Romanians' admiration for Soviet economic success and desire to follow the Soviet path brought them into direct conflict with the Soviet leadership. The dispute between Romania and the U.S.S.R. in COMECON during the early 1960s should therefore be viewed not so much as a nationalist controversy between Russians and Romanians, but more as a quarrel among dedicated Marxists over the correct path of socialist development for Romania.[17]

In this context, the division of the 1965 Politburo into "home" and "Soviet" groups becomes less relevant. The entire Romanian leadership was caught between the conflicting demands of economic integration within the Soviet bloc and emulation of the Soviet domestic model with its emphasis on heavy industry. Those individuals with the closest ties to the U.S.S.R. may have been the most offended by the Soviet refusal to sanction Romanian emulation. The dispute with COMECON therefore acted to unify the Romanian leadership, rather than to split it into its component parts. From the Romanian viewpoint, both national aspirations and socialist economic development demanded the same line of policy: heavy industrialization. The crucial formative experience of the Romanian Politburo proved to be the long years of service to the Romanian revolution and to Gheorghiu-Dej, enabling the group to remain united despite the diverse ethnic, social, educational, and political backgrounds of the individual members.

The two dominant characteristics of the Gheorghiu-Dej leadership — longevity in office and prewar party activity — were no longer typical of the Executive Committee in November 1974.[18] Only two important figures remained from the March 1965 Politburo: Ceausescu and Bodnaras, and the latter has since died.[19] However, ten men had been at least candidate members of the Executive Committee since its formation in 1965, indicating that the new group was establishing its own tradition of longevity. Aside from Ceausescu and Bodnaras, only seven had a record of prewar party activity,[20] and most did not even become full members of the Central Committee until the 1960s (see Tables 1 and 2). Another bond had, however, appeared within the group: ethnicity. Seventeen of the twenty-three were ethnically Romanian; again excluding Bodnaras, there were two Hungarians, two Jews, and one Bulgarian from the Dobrudja. Moreover, only one person (aside from Bodnaras) had lived for any extensive length of time in the Soviet Union.[21]

Table 1. Party Seniority of 1974 Executive Committee		Table 2. Central Committee Seniority of 1974 Executive Committee	
Date Joined RCP	*No.*	*Date First Elected CC Member*	*No.*
Pre-1939	9	1944–1948	3[a]
1944	1	1952	1[b]
1945	4	1954–1955	3
1946	1	1960	5
1947	1	1965	5
1945–1947[a]	6	1969	3
1953	1	1972	3
Total full members	23	Total full members	23

[a]Exact date is unknown.   [a]Bodnaras, Rautu, Voitec.
                                         [b]Ceausescu.

There were also age and educational differences between the Gheorghiu-Dej and Ceausescu groups. Ceausescu, born in 1918, had been the youngest member of the 1965 Politburo; by 1974 he was one of the oldest on the Executive Committee (see Table 3). The educational backgrounds of the new leaders reportedly were better than those of the earlier group. Sixteen had received a higher education; nine of them had specialized in technical or scientific areas and had become economic administrators; the rest tended toward careers in culture or education. Those without a formal higher education (including Ceausescu) rose in the party apparatus after the war and evidently studied at party schools during their careers. By 1974, then, the RCP leadership was composed predominantly of ethnic Romanians, most of whom had joined the party after the war, had lived all their lives in Romania, and had received some higher education.

    One brief disgression must be added here; the "Romanianization" of the Executive Committee should be interpreted as the result of the political maturation of the party within Romania, rather than as a policy of conscious discrimination on the part of Ceausescu against minority groups. The country's population is 88 percent ethnically Romanian, and the unusual prewar situation of the RCP, when it appealed mostly to minority intellectuals and a tiny portion of the incipient industrial working class, has ended. The RCP has become the governing party and, as such, reflects the ethnic composition of the population. Although this change was not reflected at the highest levels of the party until the personnel turnover following

Table 3.   1965 and 1974 Leadership Groups: Dates of Birth

Date of Birth	1965	1974
1900–1905	4	2
1906–1910	4	2
1911–1915	5	1
1916–1920	2	4
1921–1925	0	5[a]
1926–1930	0	8[b]
1931–1935	0	1

[a]Two are estimated.
[b]Three are estimated.

Ceausescu's accession, it was evident much earlier in the ethnic membership figures for the party as a whole. Ceausescu has certainly not excluded ethnic minorities from the leadership group. His intensely nationalistic statements always define "Romanian" according to *state* boundaries and specifically include the "cohabiting nationalities" as Romanian citizens. Just as ethnicity was not an infallible guide to policy tendencies in the Gheorghiu-Dej group, the current Romanianization of the leadership *in itself* does not demonstrate intolerance toward ethnic minorities. Instead, it indicates the maturity of the RCP, its development from a revolutionary to a ruling party. The *content* of nationality policies must be judged separately.[22]

Despite the relative homogeneity of the 1974 RCP leadership, three different groups may be distinguished according to education and career pattern. First, there were the party administrators, with little or no formal higher education, who had moved up through the local party apparatus or the Union of Communist Youth; Gheorghe Pana, Virgil Trofin, Iosif Uglar, and Ceausescu himself could be considered as part of this group. Then there were the well-educated technical specialists, who often began their careers in the state hierarchy, moving laterally into high party positions after demonstrating their expertise in industrial or financial administration; Emil Draganescu, Gheorghe Oprea, and Ion Patan exemplified this route to the top. Finally, there were the more broadly educated cultural specialists, such as Paul Niculescu, Dumitru Popescu, and Cornel Burtica; they had all held the position of Central Committee Secretary with responsibilities for culture, education, and/or propaganda.

The 1974 leadership was more homogeneous than the Politburo of 1965. The prewar dichotomy between Romanian workers and minority intellectuals had largely disappeared, and even the postwar split between "home" communists and the "exile" group no longer existed. Diversity did remain, but it was no longer the diversity resulting from persecution and geographical separation that had characterized the RCP in its earlier years and had left a deep imprint upon the leadership for two decades after the war. Rather, it was a diversity in educational preparation and career pattern, reflecting the needs of a ruling party for administrators with a variety of skills.

CEAUSESCU'S LEADERSHIP

It might be assumed that the maturation and Romanianization of the RCP leadership would reinforce "nationalist" and "anti-Soviet" tendencies within the ruling group. Ceausescu's policies so far would support such an assumption, but, again, such a prediction is not valid merely on the basis of ethnicity. The major conclusion that *can* be drawn from this new "Romanian" leadership is more relevant for domestic than for foreign policy; for the first time, the RCP, under Ceausescu, has the opportunity to become more acceptable in the eyes of the population as an indigenous political movement. Ceausescu and his supporters may finally be able to dissociate themselves from unpopular RCP policies of the past, particularly toward the Soviet Union and Romanian border areas, and concentrate on building the legitimacy of the regime through economic development and successes in foreign policy. The educational and career backgrounds of the new men — their extensive experience in administrative and technical problem solving and diplomacy — would seem to bode well for both of these goals. So far, however, popular acceptance of party policies has been largely limited to the area of foreign policy.

The major difficulty in domestic policy lies in the priorities of Ceausescu himself. His intense patriotism, seconded by most Romanians, includes a strong belief in the need for extremely rapid economic development. In his view, such development necessitates high investment and low consumption, a combination not favored by the average citizen. Yet the priority given to industrial development, despite its unpopularity, remains publicly unchallenged within the country. This unquestioned acceptance is the result of another major characteristic of the leadership turnover in the post-1965 era: each of the personnel changes mentioned above has enhanced Ceausescu's personal power within the political system.

Ceausescu is now the only important figure remaining from the Gheorghiu-Dej group; the others are clearly his juniors in the party hierarchy, both by revolutionary generation and by service at the top level. His offices and honors have proliferated rapidly. In March 1974 the position "President of the Republic" was created especially for Ceausescu, and he was sworn into office with a presidential sash and mace, both reminiscent of past Romanian royalty. At the Eleventh Party Congress in November 1974, the suggestion was made that he be elected Secretary General for life; Ceausescu himself refused the honor, but the extreme adulation accorded to him has been one of the most distinctive features of recent Romanian politics. His speeches decide priorities and goals, as well as organizational methods for implementing them. No Romanian official delivers a report without referring to Ceausescu's political insight and leadership as the main source of inspiration and guidance. Successes are attributed to Ceausescu, failures to organizations that have not carried out his suggestions correctly. He is, by all public indications, the dominant personality in Romania.

It is clear that the period after 1965 witnessed a change in personal power at the apex of the Romanian political system. However, the question still remains: How did Ceausescu bring about such a change, and, perhaps more important, what are the implications of his techniques for the future of Romanian politics? Although the content of his policies — economic, cultural, and diplomatic — has obviously played a role in his rise to power, this brief discussion will concentrate on personnel tactics: When and from where did this new leadership group around Ceausescu emerge? The absence of reliable information forces us to make several assumptions: Ceausescu's present power and the evident loyalty of those around him lead to the conclusion that he himself had a great deal of control over personnel policy in the 1960s and, more particularly, that those who have continued to rise within the political system have done so with his support. Let us look first at the Executive Committee itself and examine exactly when and how the personnel turnover at this highest level occurred. Then we will go on to lower levels within the party, specifically to the regional organs, to explore the location and timing of promotions to these bodies, and to the Central Committee apparatus and higher party organs in Bucharest.

THE EXECUTIVE COMMITTEE

The Ninth Congress of the RCP in 1965 replaced the nine-member Politburo with a seven-member Presidium and an Executive Committee of fifteen full members and ten candidate members. Ceausescu claimed that the Presidium would be small enough to allow "collective" decision making on a daily basis and so would prevent one individual (*unul singur*) from concentrating executive decisions in his own hands.[23] However, since seven of the nine Politburo members formed the new Presidium, this "collective" organ was almost as unwieldy as the Politburo had been.[24] Indeed, this first reorganization set the pattern of personnel change for the next two and a half years: promotions rather than demotions. Between July 1965 and December 1967, the three top party organs — the Presidium, the Executive Committee, and the Secretariat — did not lose a single member.[25] Instead, each was increased in size, evidently to assure Ceausescu of a majority in all three. The crucial demotions began only after the Party Conference of December 1967, when Ceausescu became Chairman of the Council of State as well as party leader. By the Tenth Party Congress in August 1969, over half of the Presidium members and almost half of the Secretariat and Executive Committee members had resigned or been excluded in disgrace. During this eighteen-month period, a new party leadership was formed around Ceausescu.

Table 4 illustrates the personnel turnover that occurred between 1965 and 1976 by dividing the Executive Committee into three groups — the old Politburo contingent, the new men elected in 1965, and those subsequently elected — and showing the varying size of each group over time. The table indicates that the periods of radical change were those of the Party Con-

Table 4. Membership Composition of the RCP Executive Committee, 1965-1976

Year[a]	Pre-1965 Leaders	Elected 1965	Elected Post-1965	Total Membership[b]
1965	13	12	0	25
1966	12	12	2	26
1967	12	12	4	28
1968	8	12	6	26
1969	5	12	15	32
1970	6	12	15	33
1971	6	12	19	37
1972	6	12	20	38
1973	6	12	23	41
1974	6	8	22	36
1975	5	8	22	35
1976	4	8	27	39

[a]Figures given are for the end of each year except for 1969 (after August Party Congress) and 1976 (as of July).
[b]Includes full and candidate members of the Executive Committee.

gresses: 1965, 1968–1969, and 1974. Aside from these years, the composition of the Executive Committee has been quite stable. The "retirement" of the old Politburo members took place in 1968 and 1969: thirteen of the fifteen in the Gheorghiu-Dej group were elected to the Executive Committee in 1965, but only five remained by the end of August 1969.[26] Twelve new faces appeared in 1965, and the same twelve continued in office until 1974. In fact, out of twenty-seven new members elected between 1965 and 1969, not one was demoted until April 1972, when Dumitru Popa was removed for "serious shortcomings" in his work as First Secretary of Bucharest.[27] Ceausescu had, then, brought in a new group of leaders who continued to serve with him for an extended period of time. The composition of that stable group of twelve is particularly revealing: seven had been Regional First Secretaries, and three more had spent many years in the Central Committee apparatus in Bucharest. Apparently only one man, who moved in laterally from the state hierarchy, had a technical higher education.[28]

Ceausescu's personnel tactics can be divided into two distinct periods. The 1965–1969 era was characterized by *promotion* of new individuals into the top leadership. This is clear from Table 4, as is the elimination of the pre-1965 leaders in 1968 and 1969. The second period, after 1969, has been one of *circulation* of offices: individuals have been moved back and forth between the Secretariat and the Council of Ministers, while others have been shifted from Bucharest to regional posts or the reverse. This circulation of personnel from one high office to another is perfectly illustrated by the career of Virgil Trofin. Trofin was a Central Committee Secretary from 1965 until 1971, when he was elected head of the trade unions. A year later he became a vice-chairman of the Council of Ministers and Minister of Internal Trade, but in 1974 he returned to "party work" as First Secretary of Brasov, the county second only to Bucharest in industrial production.

This horizontal circulation of top officials has for the most part left the composition of the Executive Committee unchanged. Trofin, for example, was promoted to that body in 1967 and has remained there ever since. The circulation has, however, caused extensive alterations in the Council of Ministers. For example, of twenty-three ministers and ten other officials with ministerial rank in 1969, only five remained unchanged in 1973, and about a third of the offices changed hands more than once during those four years. The major party administrative body, the Secretariat, also underwent extensive changes: Ceausescu's service there began in 1965, but only one other man, Dumitru Popescu, was still a Secretary in 1976. A total of twenty-one men served as party Secretaries from 1969 to 1976, and at least half of these individuals also spent time on the Council of Ministers.

The other type of elite circulation — the interchange of cadres between Bucharest and outlying areas — was specifically advocated by Ceausescu at a Central Committee Plenum in February 1971 in order to "strengthen the ties between the leading organs and the masses" and to "combat excessive centralism." Two members of the Executive Committee, Constantin Dragan and Vasile Vilcu, and a Central Committee section chief, Andre Cervencovici, immediately "expressed the wish to be sent to work in local Party organs" and were elected county First Secretaries.[29] At least eleven more changes in the next two years involved this circulation of cadres between central and local offices, and the trend has continued.

The second major personnel turnover since 1965 occurred in 1974, along with an extensive reorganization of the top party bodies. Nine of the thirty-nine individuals promoted to the Executive Committee after the death of Gheorghiu-Dej were not reelected by the November Party Congress, including four of that stable group of twelve who had served with Ceausescu since 1965.[30] In addition, the nine-member Presidium, which had remained almost unchanged since 1969, was abolished in favor of a Buro, and the Executive Committee was renamed the Political Executive Committee. When the composition of the Buro was announced in March 1974, it was to be a large body of both party and state officials. However, when actually elected after the November Congress, the Buro had only five members: Ceausescu, Manea Manescu (who had replaced Maurer as chairman of the Council of Ministers the preceding March), and three men who were first elected to the Executive Committee at that same Congress: Gheorghe Oprea, Ion Patan, and Stefan Andrei. Here at last was the small "collective" decision-making body that Ceausescu had advocated in 1965, but all of the other members were clearly his juniors and owed their election to his personal support. This Buro would present even less of a potential challenge to Ceausescu's authority than did the Presidium, whose members were beginning to achieve senior status in the party. Indeed, the Buro seemed most likely to be a small council of advisers to the president, rather than an organ independent of that office.[31]

Ostensibly, the Buro is to be merely an administrative organ, carrying out the policy decisions of the Political Executive Committee (emphasized by moving the word *political* from the Buro to the Executive Committee). It is true that membership in the Buro is not even mentioned in press reports of its members' activities; status is still accorded on the basis of Political Executive Committee membership. But the latter is a large and unwieldy body, and whether the Buro will in fact be the subordinate organ remains unclear. What *is* clear is that Ceausescu has continued to reshuffle personnel. No individual has been allowed to administer a given office long enough to establish a base of support from which to challenge the president; and if the Presidium and Executive Committee have appeared potentially strong enough to question his ideas, Ceausescu has found a way to eliminate or circumvent these relatively stable and senior party bodies. What seems to have evolved in Romania is a strong presidential system where Ceausescu is the prime mover and where there are no periodic electoral challenges to question his personnel or policy decisions.[32]

LOCAL PARTY ORGANS:
CEAUSESCU'S EARLY POWER BASE?

Ceausescu's personnel policy at the highest levels of power divides into two distinct periods of *promotion* and then *circulation* of cadres. These tactics have allowed him to gain and maintain control over the RCP and the entire Romanian political system. However, the question still remains: What sources of support did he have in 1965 that enabled him to begin this process? Did he control the party apparatus in outlying regions? Did he promote the incumbents to Bucharest in order to establish his personal control at the highest level? And if so, is it possible to ascertain exactly when he began to control cadre appointments throughout the party? An examination of the subsequent careers of those men who were regional First Secretaries during the 1950s and 1960s yields partial answers to these vital questions.

Ceausescu became a Central Committee Secretary in April 1954. Reportedly, he was responsible for organizations and cadres under Gheorghiu-Dej. If that is the case, then he must have had some influence over appointments to the posts of regional First Secretaries during the period before 1965. Table 5 shows the number of these men appointed each year from 1952 to 1967 and what happened to them between 1965 and 1969, the period of the personnel turnover following Ceausescu's accession — that is, in relation to the position held by each man in 1965 (which may or may not by then have been regional First Secretary), the table indicates whether his 1969 post was higher, lower, or comparable in status.[33] Unfortunately, the data before 1958 are incomplete; however, most promotions are likely to be included here since those individuals would be in this author's personnel files. Note that a move to the Central Committee apparatus or a high state position in Bucharest was considered a promotion; continuing in the region as county First Secretary or being appointed to a minor state position in Bucharest was regarded as comparable; and only officials who were relegated to a minor local position, removed in disgrace, or who simply dropped out of public office were considered demoted.

Table 5.   1965–1969 Status Change of Officials Appointed Regional First
Secretaries between 1952 and 1967

Year Appointed	1965–1969 Status Change			Total Appointed
	Higher	Lower	Comparable	
1952	1	1	0	2
1953	0	1	1	2
1954	2	1	0	3
1955	1	1	0	2
1956	2	4	1	7
1957	0	0	0	0
1958	2	0	0	2
1959	2	1	0	3
1960	1	1	1	3
1961	2	0	0	2
1962	2	0	0	2
1963	0	0	1	1
1964	3	0	0	3
1965	4	2	2	8
1966	3	0	0	3
1967	1	0	0	1
	26	12	6	44

The most striking aspect of Table 5 is that eight of the twelve demoted
between 1965 and 1969 were appointed as regional First Secretaries before
1957, while twenty of the twenty-six promoted between 1965 and 1969
gained their regional posts after 1957.[34] Table 6 groups the data more effectively. If we assume that Ceausescu had an important influence over status
change from 1965 to 1969 and connect this influence to the appointment of
regional First Secretaries, we can distinguish three periods in the pre-1965
era: 1952 through 1957, when many officials became regional First Secretaries, the majority of whom were demoted between 1965 and 1969; a transition period from 1958 through 1960, when Ceausescu strongly influenced
the choice of regional First Secretary and later promoted most of those so
appointed; and finally 1961 through 1964, when Ceausescu evidently controlled the selection of top regional personnel and later promoted almost all
of these men to Bucharest. Of course, we cannot conclude that Ceausescu
determined their original appointments merely because he later promoted
them. However, considering the personal control that he established over
the political system between 1965 and 1969, he must at least have developed
a favorable working relationship with these men in the pre-1965 period and

Table 6.   1965–1969 Status Change of Officials Appointed Regional First
Secretaries between 1952 and 1967

| Year | 1965–1969 Status Change | | | Total |
Appointed	Higher	Lower	Comparable	Appointed
1952–1957	6	8	2	16
1958–1960	5	2	1	8
1961–1964	7	0	1	8
1965–1967	8	2	2	12
	26	12	6	44

approved their subsequent rise in status. And it seems reasonable to conclude that he also influenced the original selection of many of them. This
conclusion is reinforced by the figures for the mid-1960s: out of sixteen men
who were regional First Secretaries in 1965, eleven had moved into the top
party organs or the Central Committee apparatus by 1969, while the other
five all continued as county First Secretaries.

The situation was complicated somewhat by the administrative-terri-
torial reorganization of 1968, when the two tiers of sixteen regions and 150
districts were replaced by a single level of forty counties. Extensive changes
had been made in the regional offices by that time. Between July 1965 and
December 1967, there was a 50 percent turnover rate in regional First Secretaries, but only one change involved a demotion, and that individual had
been promoted after 1965 and apparently proved incompetent in his new
position.[35] Seven regional First Secretaries were promoted to Bucharest,
two to the Executive Committee, two to posts with ministerial status, and
three to the Central Committee apparatus.[36] The 1968 reorganization
brought further changes: twelve of the sixteen regional First Secretaries
were put in charge of counties, and the remaining four were promoted to
Bucharest.[37] It could be argued that the move from regional to county official — from being one of sixteen to one of forty — was in itself a demotion; however, each county First Secretary simultaneously became chairman
of the county People's Council, at least softening the blow.

The policy of continuity or promotion of these local officials was to continue until 1971. Of the forty county First Secretaries elected in February
1968 (this includes thirty-nine counties plus the municipality of Bucharest),
thirty-three were still in office three years later. Three were removed in
December 1968, evidently in disgrace; the other four, however, were promoted to Bucharest. In summary, out of a total of fifty-nine men who held

the post of regional or county First Secretary between 1965 and 1971, only four were demoted, and fifteen went on to higher offices. In 1971 a new personnel policy — the regular interchange between Bucharest and the counties — was announced at the February Plenum. Nineteen changes were made among the county First Secretaries from 1971 through 1973, and thirteen of these involved "interchange" with Bucharest. Just as Ceausescu had previously used the regional and county party officials as a pool from which to bring new faces to the capital (in his period of promoting cadres), he was now using party posts in outlying areas to "circulate" personnel.

The data do, therefore, provide at least partial answers to the questions posed at the beginning of this section. Ceausescu certainly did promote regional party officials to Bucharest as part of his personnel tactics. He promoted individuals who had been in office before 1965, which indicates that they were willing to support him, possibly because of his responsibility for their original appointments. Finally, there seems to be a significant difference in the subsequent careers of those appointed before and after 1957, and so that is possibly the key year when Ceausescu began to influence personnel decisions.[38]

Of course, the regional First Secretaries were not Ceausescu's only power base within the political system. After the war he had been in charge of the Union of Communist Youth (UCY) and later supervised it from the Secretariat; from 1950 to 1954 he served as head of the Armed Forces Political Directorate; and he had most recently (and for the longest period of time) worked in the Central Committee apparatus in Bucharest. But let us look once more at that original group of twelve who were promoted in 1965 and remained in the top leadership until 1974. Seven of them had been regional Secretaries during their careers; two had worked at the Central Committee in Bucharest since the mid-1950s; another had been a longtime UCY official; and only two had moved over from the state hierarchy, one a specialist in agriculture and the other in heavy industry. This group could be considered a microcosm of Ceausescu's sources of support in 1965.

At this point, the changes that occurred in 1974 appear to be significant, perhaps as part of a pattern that has only recently become discernible: four of those twelve men were not reelected to the Executive Committee at the Eleventh Party Congress, and all four were in the group of previous First Secretaries. Of course, the changes are examples of Ceausescu's frequent shifts in personnel that prevent any individuals from seriously challenging his authority. But is it not also conceivable that the regional party apparatus is no longer so vital a source of personnel for the RCP leadership? If we compare the Executive Committees as elected by the Tenth and Eleventh Party Congresses, both held after Ceausescu became the dominant figure in

Table 7. Early Careers of 1969 and 1974 Executive Committee Members

	Regional/County First Secretary	Central Committee Apparatus or UCY	State Hierarchy	Total
1969 Executive Committee	16 (59%)	6 (22%)	5 (19%)	27 (100%)
1974 Executive Committee	11 (32%)	11 (32%)	12 (36%)	34 (100%)

Note: Excluded from the 1969 members are Ceausescu and the other holdovers from the Gheorghiu-Dej Politburo: Bodnaras, Maurer, Rautu, and Voitec. Excluded from the 1974 group are Ceausescu, Rautu, Voitec, Elena Ceausescu, and Lina Ciobanu; it seems more accurate to omit Ceausescu's wife, whose career is irrelevant, and the other woman elected with her as part of an ostensible effort to promote women. The women would have increased the number of the second and third 1974 groups (Central Committee or UCY and state hierarchy) by one each.

the political system, we find a major difference in the composition of these two groups: the percentage of individuals who began their careers as local party officials was sharply reduced (see Table 7). The composition of the new Buro was even more of a contrast: only Ceausescu and Stefan Andrei had party backgrounds, the latter in the Union of Communist Youth and Central Committee apparatus; Manescu, Oprea, and Patan were all state technicians.[39] If we look at incoming members to the Executive Committee between 1965 and 1976, the trend toward state officials is also clear (see Table 8).

Table 8. Early Careers of New Executive Committee Members by Year of Election, 1965-1976

Year Elected	Regional/County First Secretary	Central Committee Apparatus or UCY	State Hierarchy	Total New Members
1965	7	3	2	12
1966-1969	10	2	3	15
1970-1971	4	3	0	7
1972-1973	0	2	5	7
1974	1	1	3	5
1975	0	0	0	0
1976	2	0	3	5

The evidence in Tables 7 and 8 seems to indicate a new pattern in personnel promotions in recent years: the increased inclusion of state officials in
the highest party bodies. Certainly this development reflects the need of the
political system for technical input into the decision-making process. However, it also reflects Ceausescu's control over the state hierarchy. The circulation of cadres since 1969 has not only brought state technicians into the
top party organs but has also placed many of Ceausescu's original supporters in high state positions. Ceausescu has called for the unification of party
and state and, as part of this campaign, has created many joint party-state
committees and commissions. He has also tied the two hierarchies together
at various levels by entrusting the same official with party and state responsibilities. One person is both county First Secretary and chairman of the
county People's Council. The party Secretary for culture or agriculture or
economic planning in each county also directly administers the respective
government office at that level. Viewed in this context, the addition of government administrators to the party Executive Committee is a reflection of
the unification of party and state. But in the context of Ceausescu's past
personnel policies, the influx of state officials reflects a broadening of his
sources of personal support to include the state apparatus, and not merely a
growing need for technical expertise.

Certainly the circulation of officials reveals an arbitrary hand making
cadre decisions. The spectacular rise of certain party and state personnel
(Gheorghe Pana, Oprea, Patan, to name but a few) and the unusual shifts
in career patterns (Niculescu's moves from the Ministry of Education to the
committee overseeing the distribution of consumer goods and then to the
Ministry of Finance is but one example; Trofin's checkered career is
another) indicate that personality factors — particularly the personal relationship with the party leader — may play a more important role in an individual's career than expertise. Nevertheless, the changing composition
of the Executive Committee *has* increased the technical expertise of its
deliberations and reduced the proportion of relatively less educated party
administrators.

CONCLUSION

Given the composition of the new Executive Committee and the patterns of
personnel change that have emerged since Ceausescu's accession, what can
we conclude about the nature of political leadership in Romania? First,
there has clearly been a total turnover of personnel at the highest levels; the
individuals who served for so many years under Gheorghiu-Dej have been
replaced by a new generation promoted into power largely in the Ceausescu

era. The patterns of personnel change — first promotion and then circulation of elites — make it obvious that the current supremacy of Ceausescu
within the leadership has not been merely fortuitous. Rather Ceausescu
used his position in the Secretariat to promote his supporters within the
party and more recently has circulated these individuals from office to
office to maintain his own control. By uniting the party and state hierarchies at various levels and moving his own supporters into the state
apparatus, he has extended his influence into that organization and has
brought more and more state officials into the top party bodies.

There are some encouraging signs in the patterns of leadership change
that have appeared since 1965. Perhaps the most positive sign is the increased number of technicians included in top administrative and planning
decisions. However, the arbitrary nature of so many recent personnel decisions and the radical shifts in career patterns indicate a less favorable type
of continuity in the nature of Romanian political leadership. The personalization of political power is as strong as ever; only the individual at the top
has changed. Ceausescu is still using some of his original appointees as
troubleshooters, sending them, regardless of expertise, into emergency sectors when a crisis threatens.[40] Even the promotion of technical experts
reflects this personalization of power very clearly; the sudden rise and fall
of Oprea and of Draganescu, respectively, show that good personal relations with Ceausescu himself — including unquestioning support for his
ideas and policies — are as much a prerequisite to high office as technical
expertise.

The implications to be drawn from post-1965 leadership patterns regarding the nature of political decision making in Romania therefore center on
the personality of one man. This personalization of power represents a clear
continuity in the political system. There have been important changes that
may become significant in the long run. The participation of technicians at
the highest levels of decision making *should,* for example, improve the quality of those decisions; the Romanianization, and hence potential legitimation, of the party leadership *could* decrease the need for coercion — *if* economic priorities were to become more palatable to the population and *if*
policies toward the national minorities were not to become more harsh.
(Unfortunately, both of these prerequisites are highly questionable.) The
immediate future of Romanian politics, however, depends upon the personality and priorities of Ceausescu. While it is certainly possible that he
will become too arbitrary for his supporters or lose his skill in personnel and
policy matters, there are no visible signs of either development at present. It
seems likely, therefore, that personalized political decision making will continue to characterize the form and content of Romanian politics, along with
rapid economic development at the expense of the consumer and an activist

foreign policy aimed at maximizing national independence and flexibility. These have been, and continue to be, Ceausescu's priorities. The combination has worked very well for him personally in the past, and, barring an unforeseen crisis, these same priorities will probably continue to dominate Romanian policies, just as Ceausescu dominates the political system.

NOTES

1. Jowitt's statement appeared in his article "Political Innovation in Romania," *Survey* 20, no. 4 (1974):148. It was also quoted by Korbonski when he made his assertion in "The Change to Change in Eastern Europe," in Jan F. Triska and Paul M. Cocks, *Political Development in Eastern Europe* (New York: Praeger, 1977), p. 20.

2. For a discussion of the importance and methodology of comparative elite studies in communist systems, see the introduction and conclusion by William A. Welsh in Carl Beck et al., *Comparative Communist Political Leadership* (New York: McKay, 1973), pp. 1–42, 298–308. The extent to which power is concentrated in different communist systems; the nature, unity, and goals of the ruling elites (technocrats or *apparatchiks*); and the degree and meaning of mass "participation" in political decisions have all become matters for debate among scholars. This is not the place to document the history of these various debates. However, for an elaboration of this author's views on internal party organization and the elite-mass relationship in Romania, see her "Participatory Reforms and Political Development in Romania," in Triska and Cocks, *Political Development in Eastern Europe,* pp. 217–37.

3. Recent studies on comparative communist leaderships stress the inadequacy of data on Romania. See, for example, the comments in R. Barry Farrell, *Political Leadership in Eastern Europe and the Soviet Union* (Chicago: Aldine, 1970), pp. 89, 160. Romania is not mentioned in Beck et al., *Comparative Communist Political Leadership.* There is no biographical handbook for parliamentary deputies, such as exists for the U.S.S.R. *Dictionar enciclopedic romin,* 3 vols. (Bucharest, 1962–1966), and *Mic dictionar enciclopedic* (Bucharest: Editura Enciclopedica Romina, 1972) include some biographical information on the highest leaders: date of birth and party membership, but not education or complete career data.

4. One example is the now out-of-date article by D. A. Tomasic, "The Rumanian Communist Leadership," *Slavic Review* 20 (October 1961):477–94. See also Ghita Ionescu, *Communism in Rumania, 1944–1962* (New York: Oxford University Press, 1964); Kenneth Jowitt, *Revolutionary Breakthroughs and National Development: The Case of Romania, 1944–65* (Berkeley: University of California Press, 1971). Several works by Stephen Fischer-Galati, particularly *The New Rumania* (Cambridge, Mass.: M.I.T. Press, 1967), also contain information on the Romanian leadership. However, all of these studies focus on the pre-1965 period, as well as on the very top group.

5. See Michel-P. Hamelet, *Nicolae Ceausescu: Présentation, choix de textes, apercu historique, documents photographiques* (Paris: Seghers, 1971); Donald Catchlove, *Romania's Ceausescu* (London: Abacus, 1972); *Omagiu Tovarasului Nicolae Ceausescu* (Bucharest: Editura Politica, 1973). The last is an enormous, illustrated volume published in honor of his fifty-fifth birthday.

6. This does not imply that the party leader at either time had absolute control. As far as we can tell, Gheorghiu-Dej had few limits to his personal power; he was severely criticized by Ceausescu in 1968 for arbitrarily usurping the functions of the Politburo (see, for example, Ceausescu's speech to the Bucharest party organization, *Scinteia*, April 28, 1968). Ceausescu evidently has done the same, but it is impossible to know the extent of his power. The dangers of political prediction are obvious, as Khrushchev's abrupt departure in 1964 illustrated. An individual may become too confident, producing "harebrained" schemes and forcing his colleagues to take the drastic step of removing him.

7. Included are the nine full members of the Politburo, the five candidate members, and the one Central Committee Secretary, Mihai Dalea, not on the Politburo. Ethnicity, except in the case of Jews, is defined in terms of mother tongue.

8. The location of Bodnaras and Salajan during the war is not completely certain. At present, the Romanians claim that both were in Romania, but most sources indicate otherwise.

9. The distinction between a "home communist" and a "Soviet communist" is usually considered to be the location of the individual during World War II: at home, often in prison, or in the Soviet Union. It is frequently asserted that Gheorghiu-Dej purged the "Soviet" group in 1951 and 1952; Ana Pauker and Vasile Luca were indeed ousted then, but others remained.

10. One of these men, Ion Gheorghe Maurer, lost the position he held from 1952 to 1960.

11. The two exceptions were Mihai Dalea, who joined during the war, and Stefan Voitec, who had been a Socialist during the 1930s and played an important role in uniting the Socialist party with the communists in 1948.

12. Romanian accounts still give the U.S.S.R. credit for creating the "favorable international conditions" that allowed the RCP to overthrow the Antonescu regime. See the official *Histoire de la Roumanie* by Miron Constantinescu et al. (Paris: Horvath, 1970; originally published as *Istoria Romaniei*, Bucharest, 1970), p. 361. The more recent *Pages from the History of the Romanian Army* (Bibliotheca Historica Romaniae, Monograph XV, Centre for Military Research and Theory Studies and Research, Bucharest: Editura Academiei and Editura Militara, 1975) attributes the favorable conditions to "the victories of the anti-Hitler coalition and . . . the impetus of resistance movements in the countries occupied by fascists." More emphasis is thus given to domestic opposition, but still "the decisive event was the Soviet offensive." See pp. 206–07.

13. For examples, see Ionescu's discussion of the prewar RCP in *Communism in Rumania,* especially pp. 10–28, 40–46, 58–61.

14. See Nicholas Spulber, *The Economics of Communist Eastern Europe* (London: Wiley, 1957), pp. 35ff., 78, 172ff., 190ff., 202ff., 213ff.; John Michael Montias, *Economic Development in Communist Rumania* (Cambridge, Mass.: M.I.T. Press, 1967), pp. 16–23, 187–88; Ionescu, *Communism in Rumania,* pp. 90–92, 112–13, 137–38. Ironically enough, Gheorghiu-Dej himself had carried out these reparation payments as Minister of National Economy.

15. For an excellent discussion of the Romanians' emulation of the Soviet model, see Jowitt, *Revolutionary Breakthroughs,* pp. 100–02, 178–82.

16. There is a fascinating note on the Romanian national background for these protectionist policies in Montias, *Economic Development,* pp. 195–96.

17. In a sense, then, it was a continuation of the quarrels within the COMINTERN.

18. The group discussed here consists of the twenty-three full members of the Executive Committee elected by the Eleventh Party Congress in November 1974. Information on these individuals comes from the *Mic dictionar enciclopedic* (Bucharest: Editura Enciclopedica Romina, 1972), the Romanian press, and this author's visual impressions at the Congress (age, for example).

19. Bodnaras's obituary appeared in *Scinteia* on January 25, 1976. Two additional members of the 1974 Executive Committee had been candidate members of the Gheorghiu-Dej Politburo, but one was Stefan Voitec, the old Socialist whose position had long been titular, and the other was Leonte Rautu, who remained on the Executive Committee after losing his important cultural posts. He had been reduced to rector of the Stefan Gheorghiu Higher Party Academy.

20. These included Rautu, Voitec, and Ceausescu's wife, Elena, leaving only four others.

21. This was Gheorghe Radulescu, educated at the Tashkent Planning Institute.

22. For a more detailed discussion of the status of the major national minorities in Romania, see this author's "Nation and Nationality in Romania," in George W. Simmonds, ed., *Nationalism in the USSR and Eastern Europe in the Era of Brezhnev and Kosygin* (Detroit: University of Detroit Press, 1977), pp. 504–21. The analysis of political, economic, and cultural indicators leads to the conclusion that official regime policies have not been significantly more disadvantageous for the minorities than for other citizens of Romania. Recent reports to the contrary are disturbing. See, for example, Eric Bourne, *Christian Science Monitor,* February 8, May 2, and May 25, 1978; Michael Dobbs, *Guardian,* March 12, 1978; *Radio Free Europe Research,* Romanian Situation Reports/4, 5, 6, 7 (February 16 and 25, March 9 and 17, 1978); Amnesty International, *Romania* (New York: Amnesty International, 1978). The data presented in these sources do indeed suggest discrimination; however, the Romanianization of the party leadership *in itself* does not.

23. *Congresul al IX-lea al PCR* (Bucharest: Editura Politica, 1966), p. 732.

24. The two members of the Politburo who did *not* make it to the Presidium, Petre Borila and Alexandru Moghioros, *were* elected to the Executive Committee. Both were rumored to be sick, and both died within a few years; so their reduction in status was at least partly due to natural causes.

25. Leonte Salajan, Minister of Defense, who died in 1966 of a "serious digestive hemorrhage," was the one exception. His death led to the abrupt dismissal of the Minister of Health for the "grave deficiencies" in his ministry revealed by errors in the treatment of Salajan (*Scinteia*, August 25, 29, and 30, 1966).

26. The two not elected in 1965 were Gheorghiu-Dej himself and Mihai Dalea, who did continue as Central Committee Secretary and finally was elected a candidate member of the Executive Committee in 1970. The five remaining after 1969 were Ceausescu; Maurer, the chairman of the Council of Ministers, who retired in March 1974; Bodnaras, who retained his high office until his death in January 1976; and Rautu and Voitec (see note 19).

27. *Scinteia*, April 19, 1972.

28. This was Gheorghe Radulescu (see note 21). Others, however, were well educated — Niculescu and Lupu, for example — and Berghianu had received advanced party training in economics. Nevertheless, the educational background of this group presents a sharp contrast to the subsequent promotion of technical specialists, such as Manescu, Oprea, and Patan.

29. *Scinteia*, February 18, 1971, p. 1.

30. The four who lost out were Maxim Berghianu, Petre Blajovici, Florea Danalache, and Constantin Dragan, all former regional First Secretaries.

31. The additional members elected to the Buro in early 1977 merely reinforce this conclusion. They include Cornel Burtica, a cultural specialist who rose to prominence in the late 1960s; Elena Ceausescu, wife of the president; Gheorghe Radulescu (see note 21); and Ilie Verdet, one of Ceausescu's closest associates, brought into the top party leadership immediately after the death of Gheorghiu-Dej. Both Burtica and Verdet reportedly are related to Ceausescu. The Buro had reached that magic figure of nine members, which for so long characterized both Gheorghiu-Dej's Politburo and Ceausescu's Presidium. Other shifts made at the same time involved major changes throughout the local party apparatus and in the Council of Ministers. See *Scinteia,* January 26, 1977, pp. 1–2.

32. The RCP did recently introduce multicandidate elections, but unfortunately little room for choice was allowed to (or exercised by) the voters. See this author's "Participatory Reforms and Political Development in Romania" (note 2).

33. If appointed as regional First Secretary in 1966 or 1967, that year is taken as the starting point.

34. $X^2 = 4.96, p < .05$. Of course, age would also have been a factor.

35. This was Ion Voina, who lost his post in Brasov after only one year.

36. Maxim Berghianu and Vasile Vilcu; Ion Stanescu and Virgil Cazacu; Stefan Matei, Aldea Militaru, and Gheorghe Rosu. An eighth man, Victor Bolojan, temporarily disappeared, possibly also to the Central Committee apparatus, and turned up in 1968 as a county First Secretary.

37. Ion Carcei, Vasile Potop, Gheorghe Calin, and Constantin Mindreanu.

38. That is also the year in which Miron Constantinescu lost his position in the Secretariat; evidently Ceausescu took over his responsibilities for cadres.

Ceausescu did bring him back into the leadership after 1965, and even to the Secretariat from 1972 until his death in July 1974. However, in 1961 Ceausescu attacked him viciously for his activities as Central Committee Secretary in the 1950s; this was at the Central Committee Plenum that described in detail the errors of those purged in 1957. For Ceausescu's speech, see *Scinteia,* December 13, 1961, p. 2. He described Constantinescu as a man devoid of scruples, a careerist, who conducted the Central Committee organizational section without regard for party regulations.

39. The members added in January 1977 balance this somewhat: Verdet did begin his career in the local party apparatus, and Burtica, the one cultural specialist on the Buro, rose in the student and communist youth organizations.

40. It is difficult to distinguish between the use of troubleshooters, on the one hand, and demotions or "circulation" of supporters, on the other, but surely the careers of Niculescu, Trofin, Cioara, Pana, and Verdet all reveal a bit of both.

III HUMAN WELFARE

10 KANTOROVICH AND PRODUCTION PLANNING

Edward Ames

In the past forty years, economics has become an applied science, and to a degree that one would have been foolhardy to predict. Two main tendencies have been discernible, each with its own basic theory and quantitative method. One of these, which is macroeconomic in concept, springs from Keynes's *General Theory of Employment, Interest and Money* (1935) and the responses of Keynes's critics. The quantitative methodology of this macroeconomic work is based on the work of Koopmans and his associates on simultaneous equations estimation. It is beyond the scope of this paper.

The other main branch of applied economics springs from the independent work of Kantorovich (1939) and von Neumann (1944). This work was in concept microeconomic, though it is not limited to small economic units in its application. It makes no separation in principle between the underlying theory and the quantitative procedures used in numerical work, and in this respect it is more coherent than the first branch. This paper is concerned with the second branch, most particularly with Kantorovich's contribution to it. We shall make a somewhat artificial distinction between *opti-*

I am indebted to A.I. Katsenelinboigin, former associate of Kantorovich, for very helpful comments on an earlier draft of this paper.

mal planning (which is the name Kantorovich gave his method) and *linear programming* (which is the conventional designation in the Western world for von Neumann's contribution). When we wish to speak of the two jointly, we shall refer to *linear economics*. This more general term will also be taken to include the important and closely related *input-output* of Leontief and *activity analysis* of Koopmans.[1]

Kantorovich's work arose immediately from a consulting problem in which he was asked to find a way to decide which of a number of different grades of plywood should be produced on each of a number of different machines. The inspiration for von Neumann's work was the strategy involved in two-person games. Schumpeter told his students that von Neumann and his colleagues used to "match pennies" to see who would pay for the coffee at their Viennese cafe and that von Neumann's work may have arisen from the practical concern of avoiding the payment of unnecessary coffee bills. Whether this story is true or not, linear programming was almost at once applied to a variety of practical managerial problems. The two lines of work, in any event, have been extensively used, and new professions (typically called operations research in the West) that combine applied mathematics and economic theory have emerged in a way hitherto unexperienced in economies. The methodology has proved strong enough to be extended (in areas called convex and dynamic programming, optimal control theory, etc.) to a wide variety of pure and applied subject matter (the latter being not necessarily economic).

Kantorovich's contribution to the history of linear economics is somewhat hard to explain precisely. His 1939 paper formulated a basic problem and presented a computational technique for solving it. This procedure is, however, based on a branch of mathematics (functional analysis) in which the problem does not seem altogether straightforward. The problem had been formulated earlier by von Neumann (in 1928). By 1944 von Neumann could present it and show its solvability in a different branch of mathematics (linear algebra and topology), which is the branch in which the problem is today considered rightfully to belong.[2] Numerical procedures based on von Neumann's approach first became practical in 1948 when Dantzig presented the simplex method for solving a great many such problems. Even though the von Neumann-Dantzig methods came later than Kantorovich's, they became much more widely used.[3] This wider application was partly because they were simpler in concept and partly because U.S. computer technology developed quicker than Soviet technology. In addition, it was partly because Kantorovich's methods were little known in the West; language barriers and the lack of contact between Soviet and Western scholars were supplemented by official Soviet mistrust (on ideological grounds) of optimal planning. By 1956 when the Soviet Communist Party Congress recognized the importance and usefulness of this new science, Western linear economics, based on von Neumann's version of the subject, had acquired a great deal of practice through application, and Kantorovich's part in inventing it had become a piece of mainly forgotten history.

For this reason, Western economists tend to consider Kantorovich from a misleading point of view. The decision of the 1956 Communist Party Congress ended a twenty-five-year period in which the party considered analytical economics to be a dangerous, if not treasonable, activity.[4] Over this period, hardly any Soviet work was done in this area. Kantorovich, Novozhilov, and Lur'e are almost the only names one can mention. Westerners tend to attribute to Kantorovich the leadership in the effort to change party attitudes and therefore to consider him a successful (and praiseworthy) academic politician. In fact, the effort to "legalize" economic research was led by Nemchinov, who is not himself a major contributor to analytical economics. The effort at legitimation was successful mainly because the political leadership of the country felt a need to improve practical planning methods; and Kantorovich had the only procedures that could be adapted to modern computer technology. Nevertheless, Western economists tend to think of Kantorovich in political terms because of the indisputable fact that certain aspects of his procedures were politically unacceptable in the U.S.S.R. from 1939 until 1956.[5]

The reference to computer technology in the last paragraph points to a final difficulty facing anyone who wishes to assess the significance of Kantorovich-von Neumann methods. These methods were invented at about the same time as the digital computer. If there were no computers, Kantorovich-von Neumann methods might be, for all practical purposes, unusable except in very simple problems. On the other hand, computers would have been simply a research aid if Kantorovich-von Neumann methods had not permitted them to be used to solve management problems. Historians of science and technology have before them the fascinating problem of evaluating the importance of Kantorovich and von Neumann in creating a commercial demand for digital computers and in inducing technological advance in this (by now very large) industry. Historians of economic thought may ponder whether the flow of resources into research on the Kantorovich-von Neumann inventions would have taken place if there had been no computers that could handle the numerical work involved in solving practical managerial problems.

Given these cautionary remarks, one can proceed with an exposition of Kantorovich's system. In the next section, we will present a formulation of what Kantorovich calls the *fundamental problem of production planning*.

This problem will be presented in the format of Koopmans's activity analysis, which is the format used in 1957 by Kantorovich himself. Although the problem was originally considered to be a problem in plant management, it can be regarded as a problem at any level of economic management. Indeed, it is a special case of Tinbergen's central planning model. Because (in a different notation) Kantorovich presented this model in 1939, it clearly antedates Tinbergen's work of the 1950s. It can nevertheless serve to illuminate some of the special features of Soviet (as distinct from Western) views of the planning process.

In particular, one may use Kantorovich's formulation of optimal planning as a starting point for the consideration of some problems of centralization in large economies. After presenting the fundamental problem of production planning, we will discuss such problems in a way designed to relate the concept of centralization to the computation of optimal plans.

THE FUNDAMENTAL PROBLEM OF PRODUCTION PLANNING

The fundamental problem of production planning, as formulated by Kantorovich,[6] is that of deciding on the rates at which productive activities are to be employed so that total output, to be measured in a specified way, may be as great as possible. It is also required that certain specified kinds of output reach some specified minimal levels and that certain specified kinds of resource use do not rise above specified levels. In what follows, activities are designated by superscripts $1, \ldots, m$, and goods and services are designated by subscripts $1, \ldots, n$. Thus, the *number* a_i^j stands for the quantity of good i associated with activity j.[7] This number will be positive if process j produces good i and negative if it uses good i. (If $a_i^j = 0$, good i is neither produced nor used in process j.)

Thus, activity j may be completely characterized by the quantities of goods $1, \ldots, n$ that it makes and uses, and one may write

$$A^j = (a_1^j, a_2^j, \ldots, a_n^j) \qquad (j = 1, \ldots, m).$$

The numbers a_i^j are referred to as components of A^j. There are a number of postulates made about the activities:[8]

1.   Not all the components of A^j are positive. If they were, it would be possible to produce without using any resources.
2.   Not all the components of A^j are negative. If they were, the activity in question would represent pure waste of resources.

3. It is possible to operate an activity at any non-negative rate. That is to say, if A^j is an activity, then for h^j 0, there is an activity

$$h^j A^j = (h^j a^j_1, h^j a^j_2, \ldots, h^j a^j_n).$$

This postulate involves constant returns to scale. It is evidently open to various economic objections, to which we shall have occasion to return.

4. If activities A^j and A^r are feasible, there is an activity

$$A^j + A^r = (a^j_1 + a^r_1, a^j_2 + a^r_2, \ldots, a^j_n + a^r_n),$$

which can be interpreted as the simultaneous operation of A^j and A^r. It is quite possible for a^j_i and a^r_i to be of opposite sign. This would be the case if good i is produced by one activity and used by the other — that is, if good i is an intermediate product.

5. No activity is reversible. That is, if A^j is an activity,

$$-A^j + (-a^j_1, -a^j_2, \ldots, -a^j_n)$$

is *not* an activity. (One does not return coal into the ground nor decompose automobiles into metal, paint, cloth, and rubber.)

There are various technical questions to be resolved, but it is possible to decompose a collection of activities into *basic* activities so that everything the manager can do can be represented as some sum

$$h^1 A^1 + h^2 A^2 + \ldots + h^m A^m$$

of the basic activities $A^1 \ldots A^m$, all of which are to be operated at appropriate rates $h^1, h^2, \ldots, h^r$. The decision involved is the selection of an

$$h = (h^1, h^2, \ldots, h^r)$$

where all the h^j are greater than zero or (if some activities are not to be used at all) equal to zero.

Now suppose that the manager is required to produce at least b_i units of good i (b_i then is positive). If each activity A^j is used at some rate h^j, one will have a total output of good i

$$a^1_i h^1 + a^2_i h^2 + \ldots + a^m_i h^m \geq b_i.$$

(This does not mean that every a^j_i must be positive, but only that the sum is positive.) Alternatively, if good i is a resource used by the process and b_i is the maximum amount of this resource that may be used, then resources are designated by negative numbers, and one has total use of good i

$$a^1_i h^1 + a^2_i h^2 + \ldots + a^m_i h^m \geq -b_i,$$

which is essentially (apart from the sign on the right side) the same inequality as the preceding one. Let us suppose that goods 1,2, . . ., k are affected by such restrictions.

The manager is now given an *assortment plan;* that is to say, he is told to produce goods $(k + 1)$, $(k + 2)$, . . ., n in fixed proportions and to produce as many of these as he can. An *assortment bundle* is the collection $(q_{k + 1}, q_{k + 2}, \ldots, q_n)$, where $q_r > 0$ is the number of goods of type r $(r = (k + 1), \ldots, n)$ included in each assortment bundle. If the manager produces μ such bundles, then his output of assortment-plan goods is the collection

$$(\mu q_{k + 1}, \mu q_{k + 2}, \ldots, \mu q_n).$$

Moreover, for $r = (k + 1), \ldots, n$ it will be the case that

$$a_r^1 h^1 + a_r^2 h^2 + \ldots + a_r^m h^r \geq q_r \mu.$$

(There may be a strict inequality, $>$, here if it turns out to be useful for the manager to make some excess of good r even if it has to be "thrown away" because it does not fit into a "bundle." If such waste can be avoided, an equality would hold.) This statement is equivalent to

$$a_r^1 h^1 + a_r^2 h^2 + \ldots + a_r^m h^r - q_r \mu \geq 0.$$

In discussing this "fundamental problem of production planning," Kantorovich proves the following theorem:

A plan $h = (h_1, \ldots, h_r)$ is optimal if, and only if, multipliers $c_1, \ldots, c_h$ (objectively determined evaluations) exist so that

$$c_i \geq 0 \qquad (i = 1, \ldots, n)$$
$$\text{Max } c_j > 0 \qquad (j = (k + 1), \ldots, n)$$

(valuations are non-negative and at least one of the products included in the assortment plan has a positive valuation);

$$\sum c_i a_i^s \leq 0 \qquad (s = 1, \ldots, r)$$

(for every activity the valuation of the product cannot exceed the valuation of the factors used);

$$\sum c_i a_i^s = 0 \text{ if } h_i > 0$$

(for the activities used, the valuation of the product equals the valuation of the factors used);

$$c_i = 0 \text{ if relation } i \text{ is a strict inequality } (1 \leq i \leq n)$$

(for factors of production that do not limit production and for products produced in excess of the requirements of the production plan, the respective valuations are equal to zero).

The Western linear programmer uses the term *shadow price* in place of Kantorovich's *objectively determined evaluation*. Kantorovich's terminology seeks to avoid confusion between his concepts and those of traditional Soviet political economy. The ideological arguments enshrouding Soviet discussions of price and value were of major importance in the tentative and limited acceptance of optimal planning within the Soviet Union. They have been considered elsewhere, however, and need no further evaluation here.[9] Rather, Kantorovich's model will be considered from an economic point of view, using linear programming theory.

One of the fundamental propositions of linear programming is that problems may be defined in pairs. In an economic context, one problem (called *primal*) has to do with quantities of goods and services to be produced or used in production. The second problem (called *dual*) has to do with income and expenditures. The pair can thus be interpreted in terms of the same kind of duality that relates output to income in a set of social accounts, such as the gross national income and product accounts. Formally, the linear programming technique applies this duality principle to "small" problems (such as those of a single enterprise or industry), as well as to "big" problems (such as those of an entire economy). The basic assumption is that income and expenditures are generated if, and only if, production of goods and services takes place.

In a *linear* production process, there are neither economies nor diseconomies of scale. Economists have found all theorizing difficult when there are economies of scale (this would be a *concave* programming problem, and these present mathematical, as well as economic, difficulties.) "Standard" economies work well if there are decreasing returns to scale. This corresponds to *convex* programming, an extension of linear programming. (Convex programming is technically more difficult than linear programming, and thus it is natural to start with linear production.)

A pair of linear programming problems (primal and dual) formulates a pair of objectives for the economic unit (enterprise, industry, or economy) in question. In the primal problem something is to be minimized, and in the dual problem, something else is to be maximized. These optimization objectives are subject to the data of the problem, which constrain the ability of the optimizer to do what he wishes. Moreover, it is not necessarily possible to choose independently the objectives of the primal and dual problems. One gains an understanding of the substance of a linear programming problem by examining simultaneously the primal and dual parts to the problem.

Kantorovich's fundamental problem of production planning is equivalent to a (primal and dual) pair of linear programming problems. There are activities $A^1, \ldots, A^m$, with $A^j = (a_1^j, \ldots, a_n^j)$ as formulated above. In linear programming terms, the *primal problem* is to select the intensities $h_1, \ldots, h_r$ with which the activities are used in such a way as to maximize μ, the number of bundles of assortment-plan goods:

$$
\left.
\begin{aligned}
a_1^1 h_1 + \ldots + a_1^r h_r &\geq b_1 \\
\text{------------------------------------} \\
a_k^1 h_1 + \ldots + a_k^r h_r &\geq b_k
\end{aligned}
\right\}
\begin{aligned}
&b_i \text{ is a } \textit{fixed} \text{ resource constraint} \\
&\text{or output requirement.}
\end{aligned}
$$

$$
\left.
\begin{aligned}
a_{k+1}^1 h_1 + \ldots + a_{k+1}^r h_r & \\
- q_{k+1}\mu &\geq 0 \\
\text{------------------------------------} \\
a_n^1 h_1 + \ldots + a_n^r h_r & \\
- q_n\mu &\geq 0
\end{aligned}
\right\}
\begin{aligned}
&q_i \text{ is a coefficient of the assort-} \\
&\text{ment plan for good } i.
\end{aligned}
$$

$$-\mu = v(\text{Min}).$$ Maximizing μ is the same as minimizing $(-\mu)$.

The *dual problem* is to select non-negative shadow prices $c_1, \ldots, c_n$ for the various goods in such a way as to maximize

$$\sum_1^k b_k c_k:$$

$$
\left.
\begin{aligned}
a_1^1 c_1 + \ldots + a_k^1 c_k & \\
+ a_{k+1}^1 c_{k+1} + \ldots + a_n^1 c_n &\leq 0 \\
\text{------------------------------------} \\
a_1^r c_1 + \ldots + a_k^r c_k & \\
+ a_{k+1}^r c_{k+1} + \ldots + a_n^r c_n &\leq 0
\end{aligned}
\right\}
\begin{aligned}
&\text{Expenditure of activities} \\
&1, \ldots, r \text{ must be as great} \\
&\text{as income.}
\end{aligned}
$$

$$-q_{k+1} c_{k+1} - \ldots - q_n c_n \leq -1$$ The cost (in shadow prices) of a bundle of assortment-plan goods equals 1.

$$b_1 c_1 + \ldots + b_k c_k = z(\text{Max}).$$ The shadow prices must maximize the valuation of the fixed resource and output requirements.

Kantorovich's own formulation of the "fundamental problem" takes elements of the primal and dual problems given here, combining them in a manner somewhat different from that used in the West.[10] Substantively, however, there is no difference between his problems and those presented here.

For further reference, readers should note that relation i ($i = 1, 2,$ etc.) of one problem contains the coefficients that appear in the i-th column of terms in the other problem. The coefficients that appear in the objective function (the final relation) of one problem appear to the right of the inequalities in the other problem. Knowing one problem, one easily constructs the other; but if one needs special restrictions on both problems, some special ingenuity is needed in the construction of both.

Disregarding the computational problem of finding the numerical values of the solutions of this pair of problems, the theory of linear programming says a number of interesting things about the solutions:[11]

1. v(Min) $= z$(Max); that is, at the optimum,

    $$-\mu = b_1 c_1 + \ldots + b_k c_k.$$

    The number of bundles of assortment-plan goods is equal to the negative of the sum of the fixed constraints, valued at their shadow prices. If it were possible to increase the amount of resource i by one unit, then μ would be increased by c_i units.[12] Thus, the shadow price of good $i(c_i)$ measures the value of additional resources of type i. (This is the reason for using the term *shadow price* in this problem.) This value is measured in bundles.

2. Whenever relation i in one of these problems is a strict inequality (given optimal values of the variables of the system), then variable i of the other problem will have optimal value zero, and conversely. Therefore:

    a) If any assortment-plan goods are produced ($\mu \neq 0$), then relation $r + 1$ of the dual is an equality:

    $$q_{k+1} c_{k+1} + \ldots + q_n c_n = 1.$$

    Thus the cost of a bundle of assortment-plan goods is one.

    b) If any activity (relations $1, \ldots, r$ of the dual problem) fails to cover its cost, that activity will not be used.

    c) If output of any good (relations $1, \ldots, n$ of the primal problem) is in excess of requirements, its shadow price will be zero.

If one could identify the shadow prices of this model, even approximately, with the prices in actual Soviet business transactions, condition 2.*b* would say that industries that fail to cover their production costs should not be subsidized. It also suggests that the services of land and means of production should in principle have non-zero prices. Traditional Soviet price policy has involved the subsidization of many industries; and classical Stalinist economics regarded rental and interest payments as "capitalistic." Thus there have been ideological problems with this result. Likewise, condition 2.c seems to say that a manager whose output is above plan should receive a bonus only if all other managers produce above plan (for only in the second case are more bundles of assortment-plan bundles produced; "unfinished" bundles are of no use). Such a policy would violate the time-honored Soviet system of rewards for above-plan production.

Kantorovich has not sought to identify shadow prices with actual Soviet prices or to advocate that actual prices be adjusted to the structure of shadow prices. (Part of the reason he did not do so was that his work concerned "small" units, such as plants or ministries, and not the entire economy.) The interpretations available for the shadow prices are:

1. The value of one bundle of assortment-plan goods is 1.
2. The maximum number of bundles of assortment-plan goods equals the sum of the fixed constraints upon the primal system, valued at their respective shadow prices.
3. The individual shadow price of the i-th good measures the number of additional bundles that could be produced if an additional unit of the i-th resource became available.

These interpretations provide planners with useful information without being immediately connectable to any administrative price-setting calculations.

The solution to the primal problem has an immediate economic interpretation (and the Soviet government has always talked as if maximizing output were an important objective). But the maximand of the dual problem, namely,

$$b_1 c_1 + \ldots + b_k c_k = z \text{ (Max)},$$

has no immediately appealing interpretation. It says merely that (shadow) prices should be set to make the fixed resources as inexpensive as possible and the outputs for which fixed requirements exist as expensive as possible. This maximand certainly lacks intuitive appeal, but it is an inescapable dual to the intuitively appealing maximand of Kantorovich's primal problem.

Nothing in this formulation of Kantorovich's problem specifies that the "manager," who is to calculate the optimal plan h, is managing a single department of a factory, an entire factory, the factories of a ministry, or an entire economy. In this respect the problem is a general economic question. The manager (whoever he may be) receives an assortment plan ($q_{k+1}, \ldots, q_n$) from outside. This situation is empirically verifiable for Soviet institutions. In particular, the State Planning Commission receives its instructions from the heads of the Soviet government and Communist party.

Western literature on central planning has been based on the analysis of Frisch and Tinbergen. They have modeled a central planner as one who maximizes the welfare of the head of government, subject to constraints imposed by the workings of the economic process. They divide economic variables into three sets: $y = (y_1, \ldots, y_r)$, a collection of (target) variables, over which the government has preferences; $x = (x_1, \ldots, x_s)$ a collection of (instrumental) variables, which the planner can control directly; and $z = (z_1, \ldots, z_u)$ a collection of (exogenous) variables, which also affect the values of target variables. If the economic process can be represented by some system

$$y = F(x,z)$$

and the preferences of the planner are represented by a utility function $U(y)$, then the planner has the problem of selecting such a collection x^* of instruments that $U(y^*) = U(F(x^*,z))$ is as great as possible.

It can be shown that when the economy is represented by a system of inequalities that is exactly like that of Kantorovich's primal problem (except that the terms $(-q_r \mu)$ are omitted) and when the head of government has the utility function

$$U(y) = \text{Min} \left(\frac{x_{k+1}}{q_{k+1}}, \ldots, \frac{x_n}{q_n} \right),$$

then Tinbergen's central planner would make exactly the same choices as Kantorovich's. In this sense, Kantorovich in 1939 had formulated and solved a problem that Frisch and Tinbergen did not present and solve until the 1950s.

The Kantorovich hypothesis about the planning process is influenced by the realities of classical Soviet economic procedures in two respects. First, the preferences of the government (as embodied in the assortment plan) are very rigid. It is not generally possible to "compensate" the government for having less of one good by giving it more of another. (Marginal rates of substitution, i.e., trade-offs, are all zero or infinite.) In contemporary Western economics (notably that of Theil), trade-offs are always possible. Second, the constraints in Kantorovich's system are entirely specified by a production technology (the a_i^j), by resource limitations, and by minimal output requirements (the b_i). The typical Western planning model usually assumes that the constraints are imposed by macroeconomic and/or monetary processes, having to do directly with rates of unemployment and inflation and only secondarily with the technology of production.

Western economists, however, cannot object to the fact that Kantorovich has defined a planning problem in which the institutional assumptions differ from those that they themselves would make. These assumptions may well be appropriate to the Soviet setting in which Kantorovich's planning is always assumed to take place.

There are various empirical objections to the use of this model as applied to the Soviet Union. These objections take into account that Soviet enterprise managers appear to have various incentives besides maximizing output and that Soviet central planners also seem to have goals (including some related to income distribution) that seem quite distinct from those assumed in the model. Another set of objections arises from the fact that actual behavior of enterprises always differs in some degree from planned behavior. There exists a body of theoretical work aimed at explaining the difference between plans and performance in the Soviet type of system. These objections seem plausible, but they do not decrease the value of Kantorovich's model as a first approximation. In effect, they merely invite the theorist to make a more complicated model, in which various qualifications to familiar results will be registered.

In fact, some aspects of the practice of optimal planning are more flexible (and interesting) than the mathematical problem itself suggests. The practice takes advantage of the speed of the digital computer to do something that at first sight seems strange. The optimal planner is able (once his data have been compiled) to prepare several different "variants" of a proposed plan for submission to higher authority. Each variant shows the plan that would be adopted, given a particular assortment plan. In other words, the planner invites the head of government to select among a number of proposed assortment plans.

Frisch considered the problem of finding out the utility function of a head of government, and he devised an interview technique for doing so. The procedure involved identifying the variables of concern and then investigating marginal rates of substitution. Frisch's procedure required that the subject consider and evaluate situations that the latter might consider impossible of achievement; Frisch observed that government leaders had to be specially conditioned before they were willing to talk about impossible states of the world, even though it was mathematically desirable that they do so.

By presenting a collection of "variants" to a head of government, the optimal planner may be able to bypass one of the difficulties of the interview technique. If the head of government believes that the optimal planning technique involves no gross errors, he will also believe that each proposed plan is feasible; he will then be able to concentrate on the comparison of the states of the economy implied by each and to decide which he likes best. Implicitly, then, the "plan-variant" procedure replicates Frisch's interview procedure.

In discussing central planning, Frisch comments on "parliaments" in a way that could perhaps be applied to Soviet Politburos (about whose actual deliberations, of course, we know nothing). Frisch says that parliaments devote far too much attention to the discussion of particular proposed governmental actions. Such discussions become involved in "econometric questions" (how the economy actually works), which are highly technical and not necessarily within the competence of the officials in question. According to Frisch, it would be better for parliaments to spend their time clarifying their preferences (what they would most like to have happen), leaving the choice of the technical methods to be used to attain those objectives to the experts.

If Soviet government leaders were willing to accept the computations of optimal planners and to concentrate their efforts on selecting the assortment plan that gave them a most preferred state of the economy, they would, in effect, be following the procedure recommended by Frisch. To do so, however, they would have to accept a model of the economic process that they might not fully understand. They would also have to have confidence that optimal planners were indeed disinterestedly trying to help the government achieve its own objectives. These requirements are hard to meet given the suspicion with which Marxists, and practical people in general, have traditionally viewed economic theory.

OPTIMAL PLANNING AND THE SOVIET ECONOMY

Modern computer technology has altered everyone's perspective on the nature of "easy" and "difficult" numerical problems. The speed at which arithmetical operations can be performed has made solvable many problems that formerly could not be handled at all. On the other hand, this situation has raised new problems, both at the mathematical and the substantive levels.

As long as Soviet planning relied on pencil, paper, the desk calculator, and the abacus, the extent to which the "human element" might intervene at various levels of the planning process remained uncertain. Because of the volume of "paper work" in the system, higher officials had no effective way of knowing the extent to which their subordinates were efficient and obedient in the preparation of instructions to lower officials. Computers, however, are loyal, obedient, and tireless servants. On the other hand, they are completely lacking in initiative and, in some respects, are downright stupid.

Once Soviet leadership had become convinced that optimal planning (and its later extensions) provided potentially useful instruments, the next question naturally would be the scale on which they should be used. In principle, one can imagine computers so large and powerful that they could plan the smallest details of the most insignificant enterprise. It is natural, therefore, to consider how Kantorovich's procedures might be expanded to encompass all the economic life of a large economy, such as the Soviet Union's.

As an empirical matter, Frisch found that individual government officials appeared to be interested in fifteen to twenty economic variables. Some of these variables were unlikely to change materially in any short period, and so the number of variables that policy could actually affect was on the order of ten. (This was the case because the officials were interested in such macroeconomic indexes as the price level, the unemployment rate, and the current balance of payments position). Indeed, the entire Frisch-Tinbergen planning scheme involves the assumption that most of the economy is nongovernmental; the purpose of government is to correct for a small number of undesirable macroeconomic tendencies (which, however, are individually important).

In contrast, in the present state of the art, the optimal planner deals with systems of 500 to 600 variables. In principle, then, a head of government would have to construct an assortment plan involving this many variables. The objective of optimal planners is evidently to expand their calculations to a point where they encompass the entire economy, in full detail. The achievement of this objective requires a great deal of data (not now available) and computers far larger than present ones. It is interesting, however, to consider the magnitude of the problem involved.

As of 1970, the State Planning Commission prepared plans for about 1,500 variables; other agencies also prepared plans for enterprises in their jurisdictions. It is estimated that a total of about 15,000 plans were being prepared. On the other hand, the "nomenclature," or official list of all goods and services, is said variously to have included 12 million to 20 million entries.

A rule of thumb often used in computer circles says that the capacity of computers increases by a factor of 100 per decade. In optimal planning problems, the data involved varies roughly with the square of the number of variables (because the number of bits of data needed varies with the product of the number of activities times the goods appearing in each activity vector). Thus, the number of *variables* that can be handled by a computer should increase by a factor of $\sqrt{100} = 10$ per decade. It will therefore take about fifty years before optimal planners can hope to plan the entire Soviet nomenclature. This is not a negligible period, but it is short enough for us to conclude that it will become *feasible* (which is not necessarily the same as *desirable*) to do all Soviet planning by computer in the foreseeable future.

To use Kantorovich's procedure (in its original form) for such universal planning, it would be necessary for the head of some future Soviet government to write down the composition of a bundle of assortment-plan goods, containing literally millions of goods. Given the timing mentioned in the preceding paragraph, this leader may now be in his cradle. If present Western leaders care about only fifteen to twenty variables, they are very different from this hypothetical infant in the detail with which they can perceive economic events. Yet if one is to take seriously the possibility of applying Kantorovich's model in any literal sense to a universal Soviet plan, one must suppose a quite unprecedented command of detail on the part of future Soviet leadership.

Administratively speaking, an official who has "too much to do" delegates tasks to subordinates. If possible, the superior tries to make the subordinates do what he would do if he were going to perform those tasks himself. To delegate work means, among other things, to divide up a large task into smaller ones. The less interdependence among the smaller tasks, the easier the delegation.

Somewhat the same situation exists in computer technology. In 1961 Dantzig and Wolfe proposed a technique by which a given computer could handle larger programs by dividing them into subprograms that could be handled separately and "pulled together" at the very last stage.[13] The development of this proposal has been referred to as *decentralization* or *devolution,* terms of administrative origin. Thus, at least metaphorically, if Kantorovich has prepared a model of the Soviet planning process, the Dantzig-Wolfe modification (which has influenced Soviet thought) can perhaps be regarded as a model of a "multilevel" hierarchical planning process.

When applied to Kantorovich's problem, the Dantzig-Wolfe procedure assigns activities to several subprograms, each of which has an appropriate segment of the assortment plan. The optimal solutions to each subprogram form a cone. Given a collection of such optimal cones, there is a master program to select one vector from each cone in such a way as to provide an optimal plan for the entire program. (In this manner, the State Planning Commission will "coordinate" the draft proposals of the various ministries.)

The computer programmer's standard for evaluating the Dantzig-Wolfe procedure is simple: does it generate the same plan that a single-stage Kantorovich procedure would generate, if the computer were large enough to solve the problem by that method? To ensure that this will happen, (1) the fixed constraints (the b_i of Kantorovich's model) must be the same in the two procedures; (2) the same sets of activities must appear in the two procedures; (3) the same assortment plan must hold for the two procedures; and (4) there must be neither economies nor diseconomies of scale. (This last requirement will not be discussed since only linear processes are relevant to the present work.)

An economist relating planning problems to the Dantzig-Wolfe procedure would find certain critical points at which this particular metaphor may fail. Some (though not all) of the fixed constraints are of administrative origin. For instance, although the size of the labor force may be a physical datum, its allocation among ministries may be fixed only in an administrative sense. The operation of dividing a program into subprograms may be much less neutral than that of dividing an economy into "ministries," and the collection of fixed constraints may (in economic terms) be altered by the subdivision.

Second, in a linear program, it should not matter which activities are assigned to which subprograms. The administrative analogue to this assignment, however, involves assigning factories (and sometimes technological processes) to ministries. As a consequence, factories might be reshuffled without correspondingly changing the fixed constraints on the system, altering the productivity of an economic system, because such reorganization would almost necessarily violate the Dantzig-Wolfe assumptions.

Third, if separate ministries (subprograms) are free to generate their own assortment plans, there is no assurance that these will be the same as those generated for a comprehensive program of the Kantorovich type. That is to say, ministries may not have the same utility functions as the head of government. If a major difficulty about the universal Kantorovich model is that the head of government cannot "know enough" to make an assortment plan for the economy, then there is no way to prove that he can get what he most wants by allowing his subordinates to generate their own assortment subplans.

For a variety of reasons, therefore, the analogy between Soviet planning and solutions and the Kantorovich model appears to break down in the presence of a hierarchical governmental structure. There are severe economic difficulties in associating the Dantzig-Wolfe procedure with such structures. Indeed, a consideration of the probable span of attention of Soviet economic leadership casts doubt upon the use of the Kantorovich procedure as a positive model of the Soviet economy (though *not* as a normative instrument for the Soviet leadership.)

If the individual Soviet leader has on the order of 15 to 20 variables under his attention (as does his Western counterpart), the present optimal planning model (of 500 to 600 variables) has an assortment plan whose elements are the solution to some collective choice problem and are not derivable from a utility function. In other words, a number of individuals must be involved in the preparation of an assortment plan. Welfare economics has dealt extensively with the theoretical problems of "social utility functions," and it is doubtful that they are useful artifacts. If they are not, then the Frisch-Tinbergen model is inapplicable to Soviet conditions, and Kantorovich's "fundamental problem" cannot be interpreted in terms of this model.

As long as Kantorovich's central planner can regard the assortment plan as a collection of numbers printed out by a black box called "the Soviet government," optimal plans can be generated. The economist who is looking for a model of Soviet social choice may be unwilling, however, to treat "the Soviet government" as a black box about which nothing is known except that it does not maximize utility. Similarly, if Soviet planning is to be modeled as a multilevel process, the Dantzig-Wolfe procedure does not necessarily provide a model for it: the assortment plans governing the "ministerial" subprograms and the "central" program are not necessarily the same. It is therefore not meaningful to ask (as computer programmers naturally would) whether "decentralized" programs yield the same results as "centralized" programs.

These comments, it should be noted, are not based upon any assertion that there will be conflicts of interest among Soviet ministries (though these are not excluded). Rather, the argument relies upon the assertion that planning processes of the Kantorovich type, which involve millions of separate goods, are beyond the comprehension of individuals and thus that a theory of social choice is needed to explain the formation and coordination of (sectoral) assortment plans.

Tinbergen has advanced the view that Eastern economies (in particular the Soviet economy) will tend to become more like Western (developed) economies. He justifies this forecast by saying that market mechanisms do quickly and effectively what planners can only do slowly and at considerable cost; he believes it reasonable to assume that Soviet planners will eventually become more tolerant of market processes than they have been in the past.

The correctness of Tinbergen's view is not self-evident. The achievements of linear economics generally, and of optimal planning in particular, are sufficiently striking to make another forecast defensible at the present time. If multistage programming methods are not regarded simply as a device for increasing the effective capacity of computers, but, rather, are seen as a first step in the development of a second-generation theory of planning, the Eastern economy need not converge toward the Western in order to retain efficiency. A precise formulation and solution to this new problem is not yet in sight. If it were, it might not be acceptable to Soviet leadership.

CONCLUSION

In this review, attention has been centered on Kantorovich's production planning procedure and its relation to the theories of economic policy and systems. Other aspects of his work have been neglected, most notably that which relates to economic growth. Even so, it has been possible to note the close connections existing among optimal planning, activity analysis, and linear programming. These, together with input-output, are collectively the main new feature of twentieth-century economics. Collectively, the linear economists have revolutionized many aspects of the management of individual enterprises, formulated an impressive collection of new mathematical and scientific problems, and foreshadowed a methodology for controlling entire economies. This methodology does not yet exist because limitations on computation techniques are still unresolved. For the U.S.S.R., the resolution of the computational problems is contingent on the resolution of organizational problems having to do with the distribution of power at various administrative levels. Curiously enough, Kantorovich's procedures, so long resisted by the Soviet leadership, imply a concentration of power in the hands of a leader. In this sense, they are far more "centralized" and even "autocratic" than one would expect of someone whose work was for so long viewed as suspect by the Soviet government.

ADDENDUM: KANTOROVICH'S CONTRIBUTION TO THE DEVELOPMENT OF APPLIED MATHEMATICS

The most complicated numerical problem presented in Kantorovich's 1939 paper was the following: Given eight machines and five kinds of output, construct work schedules assigning the time of each machine to the various kinds of goods in such a way as to maximize total output. Since about 1870, economists had given a great deal of attention to abstract production processes, but they were quite unable to solve a problem as simple as Kantorovich's (a problem much simpler than that facing many enterprises in 1870).

Kantorovich has traced his methods back to Monge (1746–1818), while von Neumann traced his to the work of Farkas and Minkowsky (around 1900). Hicks and Samuelson, who in the 1940s developed the production theory now most used by academic economics, used methods of Lagrange (1736–1813). In one sense, then, contemporary economics, both theoretical and applied, "presents nothing new." To say this, however, is to miss the point of the achievement of this group of writers. By way of analogy, one of the important achievements of twentieth-century mathematics was the clarification of the structure of real numbers. A milestone in this work was the analysis of Peano of the natural numbers $(0,1,2,3, \ldots)$; he stated axiomatically what it means to count, an activity of man since prehistoric times.

Kantorovich and von Neumann realized that certain "bits and pieces" of mathematics could be assembled into a new structure, which could be used to solve a wide variety of managerial problems. The individual pieces were to some extent known, but the structure and its economic application were quite new. Moreover, once the standard linear programming problem had been formulated clearly, it turned out to be very closely related to a variety of special topics in other parts of mathematics and economics.

Consider, for example, planners who must maximize output over a period of time (rather than at a single moment) or who must reach a particular level of output as quickly as possible. Their problems can now be formulated in terms of optimal control models. The methods they employ were part of a rather obscure special case in the calculus of variations until the 1950s and were (for practical purposes) reinvented by people used to Kantorovich-von Neumann methods. In their new environment, they were no longer obscure special cases, but natural parts of a coherent body of thought. In effect, optimal control theory specifies that Kantorovich-von Neumann solutions hold at every instant of some period of time. This theory is more stringent than the original, but it is clearly related to it.

In military and political life, the longer a person's title is, the more important he is. In mathematics, however, the more obscure a subject is, the more adjectives one must use to describe it. The methods discussed in this paper were considered, as recently as 1950, to pertain to "pointed polyhedral convex cones"; currently they are referred to as the "theory of convex sets." The loss of two adjectives marks a substantial increase in the perceived importance of the subject.

The rise in the status of convex sets as a mathematical subject clearly is in part due to its demonstrated usefulness. In all major industrial countries, operations research methods have been successfully applied to a considerable range of management problems. In their application of economics, the professions involved have begun to attain the status that engineers have long enjoyed in applying physics and chemistry to management problems. Kantorovich-von Neumann methods are fundamental to those applied disciplines and have therefore been the object of intense applied research.

In addition, however, the theory of convex sets has led to a reorientation of a good many purely intellectual problems. In presenting Kantorovich's problem, this paper has relied (as did Kantorovich's own 1957 book) on Koopmans's axiomatization of production theory; this is one of a number of presentations of problems of general economic equilibrium in an axiomatic manner. These presentations, while relatively abstract, are in many respects more appealing intuitively than the methods previously available.

One finds in contemporary economic thought a representation of the connection between output and income, and between the quantities of goods produced and their prices, a duality relation that is fundamentally the relation illustrated in the primal-dual linear programming problem presented above. Kantorovich's 1939 proof that optimal plans (representing the quantities of goods produced in an economy) are associated with "objectively determined evaluations," now customarily called "shadow prices" (measuring the gain to the economy of a lifting of economic constraints and, in particular, the value of a bundle of assortment-plan goods) is a fundamental clarification of economic concepts. Although the idea had been partially formulated in various ways before Kantorovich, its central importance to economics had not. By extension, it now becomes available to a number of ostensibly noneconomic disciplines in which constrained optimization problems exist.

This is not an occasion for discussing the technical advances made in the theory of convex sets over the past thirty years. It is sufficient to point out the sense in which Kantorovich's work has made a fundamental clarification of economic ideas — a clarification that has given him a major place in the development of economics.

NOTES

1. The major work of J.R. Hicks (*Value and Capital*) and P.A. Samuelson (*Foundations of Economic Analysis*) is perhaps wrongly neglected in this statement. Our emphasis results from the fact that applications of economics to managerial problems at all levels relied very heavily on linear economics,

which from the start was oriented to numerical work. The Hicks-Samuelson methodology is, from a theoretical point of view, more general than that discussed here, and it is mathematically equivalent in many cases.

2. There are mathematical antecedents to all this work. Hicks and Samuelson trace their methods to Lagrange, while Kantorovich traces his to Monge (both in the eighteenth century). von Neumann traces his ideas back to Minkowsky and Farkas (around 1900). The importance of the antecedent work to economic (and computational) problems, however, was obviously not realized until the work of Kantorovich and von Neumann appeared.

3. G. B. Dantzig, *Linear Programming and Extensions*, chapter 2, gives a history of linear programming in the West, which suggests that Kantorovich's work was not important to Western development of this technique. Even so, it represents a remarkable achievement.

4. M. Ellman (*Soviet Planning Today* and *Planning Problems in the U.S.S.R.*) and A. Zauberman (*The Mathematical Revolution in Soviet Economics* and *Mathematical Theory in Soviet Planning*) give accounts of the situation in Soviet economics after 1930.

5. T. C. Koopmans, "Mathematical Methods of Organizing Planning Production," gives Kantorovich credit for temporal priority over von Neumann. A. Charnes and W.W. Cooper, "On Some Works of Kantorovich, Koopmans and Others," have challenged this claim. Kantorovich and von Neumann evidently met in 1935, before Kantorovich became interested in these questions; neither knew of the other's interest in the subject. Certainly their work was independent.

6. This is Problem D in the appendix of L.V. Kantorovich, *The Best Use of Economic Resources*. By concentrating on production planning, we leave out Kantorovich's contribution to economic growth. (Readers are referred to Zauberman, *Mathematical Revolution*.) Our focus omits, among other things, Kantorovich's treatment of interest and rent. These subjects led to a great deal of discussion among Soviet economists, but are familiar to Western readers.

7. It is obviously a tedious technical matter to put together lists of all the materials, labor, and machine requirements associated with complicated production processes.

8. The postulates of activity analysis are discussed at length by T.C. Koopmans in *Activity Analysis of Production and Allocation*. Methodologically, there is a major difference between Koopmans and Kantorovich. The former is interested in efficient production: an activity A is efficient if there is no other activity A' that can produce more goods than A, using given resources, or produce exactly as much as A, using fewer resources. Kantorovich is interested in a single efficient activity (defined by the assortment plan). The set of all possible assortment plans defines the set of all efficient activities. In a competitive economy, there is no assortment plan, and that is why Koopmans's problem is formulated differently from Kantorovich's.

9. See Ellman, *Soviet Planning* and *Planning Problems;* Zauberman, *Mathematical Revolution* and *Mathematical Theory*.

10. Kantorovich's theorem, cited at the beginning of this section, seems to assert that the evaluations are feasible, not that they are optimal solutions to the dual linear programming problem. Korbut, in V.S. Nemchinov, ed., *The Use of Mathematics in Economics,* p. 359, asserts that Kantorovich's method of computing the evaluations is equivalent to a method of Dantzig (*Linear Programming,* chapter 30) and others for the simultaneous solution of the primal and dual linear programming problems. We have not found a proof of the assertion, but do not require it since a solution to the dual program is of necessity feasible.

11. Dantzig, *Linear Programming,* chapters 5, 6.

12. In this discussion we disregard an important practical aspect of the linear programming model. If one imagines that the assortment plan is gradually changed, the h_i change gradually. The c_i may remain constant, but they may also change abruptly (discontinuously). These points of change correspond to "edges" of the convex cone of feasible solutions. There is no assurance that for some given assortment plan an optimal solution will not happen to occur at such an "edge." If it does, the reasoning of this paragraph will not be possible.

13. G. B. Dantzig and P. Wolfe, "The Decomposition Algorithm for Linear Programming."

BIBLIOGRAPHY

Ames, E. *Soviet Economic Processes.* Homewood, Ill.: Irwin, 1965.

Ames, E., and E. Neuberger. "Frisch and Tinbergen on Central Planning." *Journal of Comparative Economics* 1, no. 2 (June 1977).

Barone, E. "The Ministry of Production in the Collectivist State," *Giornale degli economisti,* (1905). Translated in F.A. von Hayek, ed., *Collectivist Economic Planning.* London: Routledge, 1935.

Charnes A., and W.W. Cooper. "On Some Works of Kantorovich, Koopmans and Others." *Management Science* 8 (April 1962):246–62 (with comment by Koopmans).

Dantzig, G. B. *Linear Programming and Extensions.* Princeton, N.J.: Princeton University Press. 1963.

Dantzig, G. B., and P. Wolfe. "The Decomposition Algorithm for Linear Programming." *Econometrica* 29 (October 1961).

Davis, H.T. *The Analysis of Economic Time Series.* Bloomington, Ind.: Principia, 1941.

_____. *The Theory of Econometrics.* Bloomington, Ind.: Principia, 1941.

Ellman, M. *Soviet Planning Today: Proposals for an Optimally Functioning Economic System.* Cambridge: Cambridge University Press, 1971.

_____. *Planning Problems in the U.S.S.R.* Cambridge: Cambridge University Press, 1973.

Gale, D. *The Theory of Linear Economic Models.* New York: McGraw-Hill, 1960.

Hardt, J. P., et al., eds. *Mathematics and Computers in Soviet Economic Planning.* New Haven, Conn.: Yale University Press, 1967.

Hicks, J. R. *Value and Capital.* London: Oxford University Press, 1939.

Kantorovich, L. V. *Mathematical Methods of Organizing and Planning Production* (1939). Translated in *Management Science* 6 (July 1960):366–422 and in Nemchinov, *Use of Mathematics.*

_____. *The Best Use of Economic Resources.* Cambridge, Mass.: Harvard University Press, 1965.

Koopmans, T. C. "A Note about Kantorovich's Paper, 'Mathematical Methods of Organizing and Planning Production.' " *Management Science* 6 (July 1960): 363–65.

_____, ed. *Statistical Inference in Dynamic Economic Models.* New York: Wiley, 1950.

_____, ed. *Activity Analysis of Production and Allocation.* New York: Wiley, 1951.

Kuhn, H. W., and A. W. Tucker, eds. "Linear Inequalities and Related Systems." *Annals of Mathematical Study* 38 (1956).

Lange, O. "On the Economic Theory of Socialism." In B. E. Lippencott, ed., *On the Economic Theory of Socialism.* Minneapolis: University of Minnesota Press, 1938.

Montias, J. M. "Soviet Optimizing Models for Multiperiod Planning 1967." In Hardt et al., *Mathematics and Computers.*

Nemchinov, V. S., ed. *The Use of Mathematics in Economics.* Translated by A. Nove. Cambridge, Mass.: M.I.T. Press, 1964.

Samuelson, P. A. *Foundations of Economic Analysis.* Cambridge, Mass.: Harvard University Press, 1948.

Schultz, H. *The Theory and Measurement of Demand.* Chicago: University of Chicago Press, 1938.

Theil, H. *Optimal Decision Rules for Government and Industry.* Amsterdam: North Holland, 1952.

von Neumann, J., and O. Morgenstern. *The Theory of Games and Economic Behavior.* Princeton, N.J.: Princeton University Press, 1944.

Ward, B. *Linear Programming and Soviet Planning,* 1967. In Hardt et al., *Mathematics and Computers.*

Zauberman, A. *The Mathematical Revolution in Soviet Economics.* London: Oxford University Press, 1975.

_____. *Mathematical Theory in Soviet Planning: Concepts, Methods, Techniques.* Cambridge: Cambridge University Press, 1976.

11 THE THEORY AND PRACTICE OF SELF-MANAGEMENT:
An American Perspective

Jaroslav Vanek,
with the assistance of Christopher Gunn

I have promised to prepare a paper on the theory and practice of self-management. But after reflecting on the task, I have realized that I have already produced considerable writing on the general theory, general practice, and implementation of self-management and that perhaps it would be more desirable to give this analysis a more particular orientation. Writing for the American audience, I would like to cast my subject as much as possible in the context of the American experience. Thus, for example, in discussing the theory of self-management, I intend to present it as much as possible in the context of categories and thought best known to us in the United States. In discussing problems of implementation, I will concentrate on problems in the American institutional and legal setting.

In addition to concentrating on the American context, I would like to give my discussion another broad orientation. I assume that my audience is not a restricted one of specialists in any particular field. Rather, I take it to be an audience concerned not only with the narrowly defined problem of self-management, but also with the potential or actual significance of self-management for the life of our nation in general. I have done a good deal of thinking about these broader issues over the past several years but have never expressed them in any systematic manner. I use this opportunity to do so. For this reason, my presentation will no doubt strike the audience as rather nonconformist, perhaps even shocking. I am convinced of the truth of what I have to say, and although these thoughts may shock the reader I cannot refrain from voicing them.

DEFINITIONS OF SELF-MANAGEMENT

The question of what self-management is, or what a self-managed economy or system would be like, can be answered in two different ways. First, the definition can be comparative, referring to similarities or differences with other systems. Second, the definition can be operational and descriptive, indicating what the different characteristics are, how the system works, and so on. We will concentrate first on the broad comparative definition.

Self-management as an economic system is often incorrectly thought of as some form of compromise or point of convergence between the major world systems, characterized by the American system on the one hand and the Soviet on the other. This is a fundamental misconception. The American and Soviet economic systems are a good deal closer to each other than either of the two is to the self-managed economy. The first two are both capitalistic, while the last is humanistic. The two are capitalistic because in both of them the owners — in the American economic system, private owners; in the Soviet, the state — exercise control over the enterprise and the economy in general and appropriate the enterprise's products. By contrast, in the labor-managed or self-managed economy, power of control and management and the right of appropriation belong to the working community.

To use a historical parallel, capitalism with its control and management coming from (or appointed from) the outside is comparable to our colonial days. By contrast, self-management is comparable to the last two hundred years of national independence during which those who have belonged to the nation have exercised their rights of self-determination and, if they wished, self-management.

In this comparative view of self-management, one other significant distinction must be drawn. Under the heading of self-managment or self-managed systems, two major categories should be distinguished. The first, often referred to as *workers' management,* emerges from the Marxian tradition and is represented by the important case of the Yugoslav economy. The second, perhaps best described by the term *labor management,* is non-Marxian in its origins and can be associated with Western, and specifically American, economic thought. Both alternatives are of the humanistic, rather than the capitalistic, variety. But their distinction turns around the question of remuneration of capital. In the worker-managed form, typified by the Yugoslav alternative, all net income of enterprises belongs and is assignable to the working community. In the labor-managed alternative, the working community hires capital and is always expected to remunerate it by some appropriate scarcity-reflecting rent, whether the capital comes from external sources or from the income of the working community.[1]

The operational definition of self-management can be traced to the work of Phillippe-Joseph-Baptiste Buchez, who in 1831, seventeen years before Marx and Engels's *Manifesto,* was the first to write of the concept of self-management. Buchez, a historian of the French Revolution, can best be described politically as a Christian socialist. His idea of self-management grew from his historical and philosophical work, and he spoke of his new form as the "republic in the workshop."[2] To this day, that characterization is probably the most correct one; a self-managed enterprise can be thought of as a republic of equals — equals in the democratic exercise of power, although obviously different in the skills that they bring together in the common endeavor of the enterprise. As in a political democracy, the ways in which decisions are made depend on the significance of the issues and on the size of the decision-making unit. As in a political democracy, important distinctions should be made between current or parliamentary decision making and more fundamental and lasting constitutional decisions. An example of a very important constitutional decision, better termed a *statute decision* in the case of the enterprise, is the decision on income distribution. Two sets of forces are inputs into such a decision — on the one hand, forces of relative scarcity of skills, as in a capitalist economy; on the other, forces of collegiality and empathy, which are unlike the forces in a capitalist economy. Income distribution is consistently more equitable in self-managed organizations than in traditional capitalist organizations. Without any doubt, this factor serves to diminish class antagonisms.

Passing now from individual enterprises to the economy as a whole, it can be said that in the broadest sense a labor-managed economy is a decentralized market economy. By this, however, we should not understand that values determined by markets are automatically accepted. Rather, society may exercise its democratic sovereign right to control external economies or diseconomies, monopoly power, or any other pathology of market forces. In fact, in a longer perspective, it can be expected that self-management in the world will be moving in the direction of less and less market determination and more and more determination of values founded on principles of justice and equity.

WILL SELF-MANAGEMENT WORK?

The standard critique of self-management is that although such a system has considerable human and social advantages, we must pay for these advantages with losses in economic efficiency and performance. More modern and far more scientific work indicates that this position is much too conservative and unfavorable to democracy and self-determination in the economic sphere. Some of this evidence is contained in the study *Work in America*.[3] Other evidence in the American experience (such as the plywood cooperatives in the American Northwest) points to reorganized capitalist firms that could not make it under the old order but that have been successful as democratic organizations. Probably the most positive Western experience is that of the hundred or so worker-managed firms in Mondragon, where growth has averaged 30 percent per year in the past decade and where other indicators of performance are equally impressive.[4]

On the macroeconomic level, the evidence is equally positive.[5] Systematic theoretical work strongly supports the thesis of the superior productive and human efficiency of self-management.[6] Probably the most comprehensive study to date is one that analyzes the performance of seventy national economies, including those of the United States and Yugoslavia.[7] This study indicates, especially for the *labor-managed* subcategory of self-management, a very strong comparative advantage for the democratic solution. Also of note is Professor Melman's study examining the performance of kibbutz cooperatives in Israel, which generally tells the same favorable story.[8] A large number of positive sociological results are brought together by Paul Blumberg, who finds strong evidence of increased satisfaction in work arrived at through increased worker participation.[9]

In summary — to tell what in a full treatment would require many more pages — self-management and democratic organization of an economy can be expected to perform very well not only in terms of a happier and fuller life for the working communities, but also in terms of physical performance and productivity. This will be especially true where capital scarcity is recognized and services of capital (whether private, public, or belonging to the workers) are appropriately remunerated. A systematically more equitable income distribution is a further major asset of the democratic solution.

PROBLEMS OF IMPLEMENTATION

Another study of many pages — and a very interesting one — could be written on why self-management, if it is so efficient, has not become the prevalent form of economic organization in the world. The reasons are most diverse and include political, economic, and other factors. First, it must be recognized that established orders and systems always develop their own maintenance and self-preservation mechanisms. Second, there is the fact that only some among the many possible forms of economic democracy are very effective. These two factors, combined with human ignorance and absence of an economic theory of the system (such theory has been developed only very recently), were more than sufficient to arrest the spread of democracy from the political to the economic domain.

For those of us in the United States, there are many concrete and very specifically American problems of implementation that would have to be resolved before democracy could truly pass through the factory gates. Nothing but a sketch is possible within the confines of this paper. First of all, both theory and experience teach us that the self-management sector of economy needs a supporting structure.[10] Its role is multifarious and includes funding (even if capital is generated by the firms involved), technical assistance, education, and technology development. The Federation for Economic Democracy, a national nonprofit organization, was begun for this purpose.[11] For the moment, it is not much more than a grain of sand in a sea.

Another American problem is that we do not have appropriate legal forms for self-management. Other forms, such as cooperatives, nonprofit corporations, for-profit corporations, and trusts, are being borrowed and adapted, but they are far from ideal.

A financial and institutional problem to be overcome is somewhat more technical and less conspicuous. Like any enterprise, the self-managed firm needs to raise funds in a way that allows the sharing of risks between the enterprise and the lender or provider of funds. In capitalist firms, this is done through shares of common stock. But because profit is not objectively defined in the democratic enterprise, shares of common stock under self-management are a contradiction in terms. Power of control, by definition, cannot belong to capital; thus the need for a new debt instrument that will allow return to vary with risk and performance. And such a need calls forth the need for a capital market acquainted with debt instruments. The problems are similar when it comes to any questions requiring professional expertise, whether pertaining to legal, accounting, brokerage, or organizational matters. Bankers to whom we go for credit to finance a self-managed enterprise are puzzled by organizations whose primary objective is not generation of profit for capital investors.

Another problem of implementation of self-management in the United States concerns the role of labor unions. Quite obviously, introducing democratic organizations into the American enterprise is unthinkable without facing the question of labor unions, their historical role and their present function in the American economy. The problem is a very difficult one and cannot be circumvented. Without full support of the labor unions, full democratization of our economy is hardly possible. Labor unions have been the legitimate tool of organization and protection of the worker in America. In a self-managed system this role would continue and gradually be broadened, liberating workers from the labor contract and ultimately fostering the free association of workers as producers.

Unions are in a unique position to facilitate this transformation by serving as a supporting structure for self-managed firms. A gradual process of transformation could find unions providing the following services:

1. Self-management, unlike capitalism, places emphasis on the working person. Its implementation will require gradual, liberating human transformation through education, training, and a dialogue among workers. Revision of training, apprenticeships, and professional education to emphasize cooperative learning within the work place will be necessary. Experimentation with working models and pilot projects can be added to existing union educational programs.

2. A period of need for funding of democratic forms of work organization is upon us. Unions can help raise funds for job preservation through worker takeover of viable firms closed because of supposed "underprofitability."

3. Involvement with managerial and technical groups will be essential to the transitional period. While continuing the traditional collective bargaining relationship, unions can gradually seek positive collaboration of managerial talent to serve new common goals.

4. Self-management will require new technologies that are efficient in terms of the humanization of work organization, in addition to being efficient in terms of productivity. Unions are in a position to contribute to the development of such technologies for the use of all their members' firms.

5. When unattainable within an enterprise, resolution of grievances could be accomplished by union-sponsored arbitration committees.

6. The actual creation of new self-managed firms could be within the scope of union activities. There is substantial need for this now, particularly in areas where plant closings have left large numbers of union members unemployed. Participation in the community of workers of the self-managed firm created by union members could presuppose union membership, providing a vital vehicle for growth for the union. The need for creation of firms will no doubt grow in importance as capitalist firms move their production units abroad or to lower-wage regions of this country.

SELF-MANAGEMENT AS A STRATEGY FOR FULL EMPLOYMENT AND NATIONAL REUNIFICATION

Having outlined the major problems of implementation of self-management in the United States, let us now consider why self-management is essential for solving the problems besetting our nation. It so happens that because democracy is the essence of self-management and because democracy is also the cornerstone of our political system, self-management fits the needs of the nation, especially needs now emerging on the horizon.

Unemployment has plagued our economy ever since World War II, and the problem has been becoming more acute over time. Given the enormous wage differentials between the United States and the developing countries, together with our multinational corporations' search for maximum profit at lowest cost, the unemployment problem, if anything, will grow worse. In this context, self-management offers a powerful remedy. Even if a profit-oriented corporation loses interest in continuing its operations in a particular activity in a particular geographic area, the working community may not lose interest. Especially in small towns, self-management and workers' ownership, sometimes combined with local community participation, can help. There are now dozens of instances of worker and community takeover of "divested" firms, and these acts of worker and community initiative fit the thrust of self-management, even if the end results are not always democratically managed.[12] However, for this to happen, we need supporting, rather than obstructive, state and national legislation, and obviously a broader understanding of the potentials of self-management as well.

In an extensive critical evaluation of Congressman Hawkins's proposed full employment legislation (now the Humphrey-Hawkins bill), I took precisely this position.[13] The main thrust of the legislation at present is to call for creation of public jobs and other government-designed stopgap measures. But this thrust in my view is contrary to American beliefs; it constitutes too much ineffectual government interference and too little decentralization and self-reliance. By contrast, self-management not only relies on local initiatives and devolution of power, but also develops cooperation and group entrepreneurship as it fosters self-confidence and useful educational exposure. This would seem to me most salutary in a period when, if anything, we experience increased individualization, social fragmentation, and neglect of others.

This last point deserves elaboration. Class divisions, alienation, discrimination of all kinds, inability to understand others, fragmentation of society, and the labor-management conflict are probably the most critical problems of our society. Many of them are directly related to conditions of work, and others are indirectly related. Self-management — in which all individuals in the enterprise act as a single democratic community composed of blue- and white-collar workers of both sexes, all colors, all religious beliefs, with equal power and equal right to a portion of total income — would certainly improve at least some of these conditions; it could hardly worsen any.

THE EDUCATIONAL AND ECOLOGICAL DIMENSIONS

Some of the problems noted in the last paragraph are perpetuated, if not accentuated, by our educational system. This fact emerges quite clearly from the writings of some of our more alert experts on pedagogy.[14] Our schools and the whole educational system are quite detached from reality and from real living and working experiences. Abstract learning that never reaches a real context is usually fast forgotten. We can all look into our past many years of learning and see how much of what we have learned has actually stayed with us; what has been sealed in by practical experience is what seems to remain. Many claim that our communication and educational systems are too much geared to the needs of business and industry, including the need for passive consumers, and insufficiently oriented toward formation of complete, critically conscious human beings. We cannot even guess the distortional effects of most of our television and advertising; their fruits may be fully recognizable only over generations.

Two important and well-established notions related to self-management bear on all this. First, whenever democracy exists in the place of work, the human needs of the working community — not just the need for profit or income — suddenly come to the surface. Among these human needs, education figures prominently. With its power of self-determination and decision making, the self-managed working community attends to such needs in far greater measure than does the average capitalist enterprise. Moreover, these needs are attended to in the context of real working experiences, which, as we have noted already, lead to more lasting and solid learning.

The second point is that the activities of self-management in its purest form really are a dialogue, more or less structured within the working community; and that dialogue is a learning and educational experience in itself, teaching tolerance and the value of community and democracy. As the participants form their collective preferences through dialogue, they learn about their enterprise and its overall environment, and about human nature and effective decision making.

In addition, because the education gained through self-management is based on real life experiences, there is far less danger that it could go astray. Indeed, if we are too much detached from real life and work in our teaching and theorizing, there is a considerable danger that we will lose vision of reality or that we will become irrelevant. Moreover, education related to self-management adapts much more directly and immediately to changing conditions, and this in turn becomes a considerable asset in a period when technology, attitudes, and human relations keep changing at an ever-increasing rate.

Self-management and democracy in the work place are also likely to deal far more effectively with a whole number of ecological problems and externalities than do capitalist enterprises. Only a sketch and a few examples can be given here, but the reader certainly will think of others. As a general rule, a working person prefers to work on high quality, rather than low quality, products. He or she takes a greater pride and can more easily identify with products of lasting quality than with the often imperfect results of assembly-line mass production. Such preferences would no doubt be reflected in the selection of things to be produced under self-management. This means that per ton of steel, coal, or copper — and even per unit of fuel — we would have more output, and output of far better quality, as measured in use value. In a self-managed economy, we would drive cars and buses of better quality far longer, thus economizing on natural resources and energy and even reducing air pollution through lower gross production requirements.

Another example of environmental benefits under self-management would result from the decision makers being a part of the community where the firm is located. Decisions to control pollution of the environment would rest with the worker-managers, whose families and neighbors would actually be affected by their decisions, and not with corporate officers thousands of miles away. At the least, a judicious evaluation of pollution's opportunity costs in terms of income or output would be made by those who have to breathe or drink or look at the pollution.

Both theory and practice indicate that under self-management there would be less high-pressure advertising and less production and selling of unnecessary goods.[15] Thus, there would not only be less air pollution, but also less mind pollution, commercial distortion of human values, and even interruptions of television programs! Our values might also change in positive ways, but that subject would take us into the the realm of philosophy and is beyond the scope of the present paper.

THE OVERALL DOMESTIC SIGNIFICANCE

Most Americans believe that the United States Constitution, with its guarantees of democracy and fundamental rights, is the best in the world; the same is claimed for our free capitalist system. Indeed, both have worked well for many Americans. Yet there seems to be a basic contradiction between the two, with the first implying equality and self-determination and the second implying inequality and external control by stockholders who do not belong to the working community but who profit from that community's work. It is for this reason that the capitalist system is under considerable strain in the world and that the American people are beginning to have doubts about its ability to survive.[16]

As I see it, the resolution of the contradiction of the dilemma is the following: It can be said that our overall political economic and social system is a beautiful edifice, but it is only half an edifice, and if it is to survive, it must be completed. Completion requires the extension of the political democracy and political rights to economic democracy and economic rights in the fullest sense. Without such an extension, the half edifice will inevitably crumble.

Although it constitutes a revolutionary change, such a transformation need not be violent and could be brought about gradually during the coming generation. Above all, this type of change requires an educational process, a national dialogue leading to the creation of new legislation and new institutions.

THE INTERNATIONAL SIGNIFICANCE

If the contradiction between democracy and free-market capitalism is subdued and not quite perceptible in the United States, it is flagrantly apparent abroad, especially in the poor countries. And it is because of this contradiction, rather than because the developing countries are evil or ill-advised, that for many years the United States has been in the position of being a leader of the minority within the United Nations. Votes of 120 or 140 to 1, 2, or 5 have led our delegate to the United Nations — an intelligent person — to refer to a "tyranny of the majority," when this tyranny is precisely what we call democracy in our domestic politics.

The essence of the situation is this: In any poor country with very scarce natural and capital resources relative to labor and population, the capitalist order, with a free competitive labor market, must lead to subsistence living conditions bordering on starvation for the large majority of the population. If true democracy were practiced under these conditions, capitalism would always naturally be suppressed and replaced by some form of socialist economy based on planning and nonmarket income distribution. Thus, if one wants to preserve capitalism in these countries, one must use repression and must support dictatorial regimes. Because we preach both democracy and capitalism, we are facing an unsolvable dilemma in our relations with foreign countries, especially with the developing nations. A choice must be made between one of the two in shaping our foreign policy, and we invariably have chosen capitalism — presumably to offer a fertile ground for our multinational corporations — to the detriment of democracy and human rights. Without exception, our closest friends and allies among the developing nations are, or have been, dictatorial and repressive regimes, within which our multinationals and our economic creed thrive.

In this complex world situation, a democratic system based on self-management and on the consistent application of democracy and fundamental rights in both the political and economic spheres offers concrete solutions. With self-management, wages and incomes are no longer determined by competition in the labor market. Rather, they are determined by the value of the product, by rules of income distribution adopted by the enterprise, or by the economy as a whole. Under self-management, those who work exercise control over the technology that they use and over their work organization. This control is exceedingly important since one of the key reasons for low incomes and wages in developing countries is the application of foreign capital-intensive technology and foreign organization of work. Both stand in the way of more complete employment of labor.

At present, the developing world looking at us sees not the greatest nation on earth, as President Carter would like to have it, but a nation with a split personality. The completion of our democratic edifice at home (at least a gradual completion) and a true and fully consistent support of democracy and human rights abroad constitute the only road to world leadership for our nation. It is also a road of return to social sanity and a defense system far more efficacious than any system of atomic arms or intercontinental ballistic missiles. The world in which our grandchildren will live will be either a world of extreme right or extreme left dictatorial and repressive regimes or a humane world based on justice and respect among people. No nation in the world is in a better position than the United States to influence the outcome. However, we should not take the second alternative for granted. In fact, if we continue on our current path, it is the first that will prevail.

NOTES

1. A notable example of the self-managed alternative is Mondragon, Spain, a community of linked enterprises in the Basque country of northern Spain. This constantly growing industrial community of over 10,000 workers pays a return on all capital utilized, is fully democratically managed, and places a strong emphasis on the education and development of its own craftsmen and managers.

See R. Oakeshott, "Mondragon: Spain's Oasis of Democracy," in J. Vanek, ed., *Self-Management: Economic Liberation of Man* (London: Penguin Books, 1975), pp. 290–96.

2. See Vanek, *Self-Management,* p. 16.
3. *Work in America: Report of the Special Task Force to the Secretary of Health, Education and Welfare* (Cambridge, Mass.: M.I.T. Press, 1973).
4. Oakeshott, "Mondragon," pp. 290–96.
5. B. Balassa and T. J. Bertrand, "Growth Performance of Eastern European Economies and Comparable Western European Countries," in Vanek, *Self-Management,* pp. 339–51.
6. J. Vanek, *The General Theory of Labor Managed Market Economies* (Ithaca, N.Y.: Cornell University Press, 1970).
7. J. Vanek, "Self-Management, Workers Management and Labour Management in Theory and Practice: A Comparative Study," Cornell Department of Economics, Working Paper No. 119, July 1976.
8. S. Melman, "Industrial Efficiency under Managerial versus Cooperative Decision-Making," in Horvat, Markovic, and Supek, eds., *Self-Governing Socialism,* vol. 2 (White Plains, N.Y.: International Arts and Science Press, 1975).
9. P. Blumberg, *Industrial Democracy: The Sociology of Participation* (Constable, 1968).
10. Vanek, *General Theory,* chapters 14, 15. "Mondragon" provides an excellent example of such a supporting structure. See Oakeshott, "Mondragon."
11. For futher elaboration, see Ithaca Work Group, *Implementing Democracy in the Workplace: A Handbook for Worker Cooperatives and Self-Management,* forthcoming.
12. A successful example is Library Bureau, Inc., in Herkimer, N.Y., which was taken over by workers and community leaders after Sperry Rand announced that it would close the plant. A forthcoming paper by William F. Whyte of the New York State School of Industrial and Labor Relations at Cornell University will discuss this and similar cases.
13. Correspondence of January 8 and 16, 1975. Reprinted in the *Newsletter* of the Association for Economic Democracy, no. 11, February–March, 1975.
14. S. Bowles and H. Gintis, *Schooling in Capitalist America: Educational Reform and the Contradictions of Economic Life* (New York: Basic Books, 1976); Martin Carnoy, *Schooling in a Corporate Society* (New York: McKay, 1975).
15. J. Vanek and A. Steinherr, "Sales Promotion in Labor-Managed versus Capitalist Economies," in J. Vanek, ed, *The Labor-Managed Economy: Essays* (Ithaca, N.Y.: Cornell University Press, 1977).
16. For example, a 1975 survey conducted for the People's Bicentennial Commission by Peter D. Hart Research Associates polled a cross section of adult Americans, with the following results: When asked if they believed the capitalist economic system was improving, in decline, or neither, 23 percent responded that it was improving; 34 percent responded that it was in decline; 30 percent responded that it was neither improving nor in decline; and 14 percent

expressed no opinion. When asked how they felt about changing the current economic system, 41 percent responded in favor of making major adjustments and trying alternatives not tried before; 37 percent favored minor changes; 17 percent opted for allowing the system to straighten itself out; and 5 percent were unsure. Respondents were also asked about the kind of firm or company for which they would most like to work. Given the following choices, the results were: 66 percent would prefer to work for an employee-owned and controlled company; 20 percent preferred the idea of working for an investor-owned company; 8 percent indicated preference for a company owned by the government; and 6 percent were unsure. The complete survey appears in Jeremy Rifkin, *Own Your Own Job* (New York: Bantam Books, 1977).

12 DECENTRALIZED ECONOMIC CONTROL IN THE SOVIET UNION AND MAOIST CHINA:
One-Man Rule versus Collective Self-Management

Steven Rosefielde and Henry Latané

Socialists of diverse persuasions have long agreed that when socialism is finally triumphant, it will usher in an era of material and spiritual plenty. All workers will achieve a high standard of living, none will want, and interpersonal relations will be suffused with a collectivist ethos in which the full development of the individual is predicated on the full development of the community at large.

Before this high stage of socialism is realized, however, developing nations must decide whether to stress material or ethical means for the construction of socialist societies. Influenced by Engels, most Marxists have tended to believe that the material conditions for socialism had to be established before socialist ethics could become potent. Direct appeals to conscience seemed too idealistic, too impractical to revolutionary realists, especially those familar with the experience of War Communism in which moral zealotry contributed to material ruin and was repudiated by Lenin as "infantile leftism."

After half a century of Soviet rule, many socialists, observing that the establishment of the material conditions for socialism does not necessarily produce a humane society, have had second thoughts about Engels's strategy. Mao Tse-tung in particular took the view that any attempt to build a socialist society with methods that stress material incentives must necessarily result in bureaucratic counterrevolution. To avoid this danger in China, Mao launched the Great Proletarian Cultural Revolution with the intention of making "Redness," rather than "expertness," the founding principle of socialist construction. "Redness" implies an ethical commitment to a set of collectivist values that make community interest superior to individual concerns. Workers are enjoined to "fight self," renouncing egoism, avarice, and arrogance in favor of service to the collective and to society as a whole. Mao contended that through altruism and self-sacrifice and through collective and cooperative action, the material foundation for full socialism could be built without bureaucratic administration and control. In effect, Mao stands Engels on his head by making communist morality the sine qua non of a material development that does not compromise socialist principle.

This is a very provocative viewpoint, and it is not surprising that the Maoist approach has gained more and more adherents.[1] However, in the rush to defend the old Engels orthodoxy or to champion the insurgent doctrine of Mao, most students of comparative socialism have overlooked the systems implications of Mao's views.

How precisely does communist morality affect material production? Does it insure full employment of labor and capital? Does it assist in directing primary and intermediate factors to their most effective uses? Does it eliminate potential conflicts among local, regional, and national priorities? Does it foster technological progress? These are very fundamental issues for the comparative analysis of economic systems. Not only do they bear on organization, efficiency, and growth potential, but they also allow us to perceive deeper implications of Maoist theory that illuminate the issue of moral versus material priorities.

STRUCTURAL SIMILARITIES OF THE CHINESE AND SOVIET ECONOMIC SYSTEMS

In trying to come to grips with Maoist theory, it should always be kept clearly in mind that the organization of the Chinese economy, even during the Great Proletarian Cultural Revolution, has been more similar to the Soviet system than dissimilar.[2] In the absence of competitive markets, both economies rely extensively on central and regional planning to assure macroeconomic and microeconomic coordination. Both employ ministerial bureaucracies to insure that firms that operate on an independent cost-accounting basis properly execute the plan. In both countries, the means of production are publicly owned; foreign trade is a state monopoly; prices are administratively determined according to average labor production costs; and turnover taxes are levied on wholesale and retail production, the proceeds of which are used to finance state expenditures and investment.

These similarities are not accidental. They reflect a common need for alternative structures of economic control to replace the automatic adjustment mechanisms of the market. Without such structures, economic activity would lack overall coherence. Local conditions would completely determine the level and composition of production, regardless of interindustrial requirements, social need, or national priorities.

The need for control structures does not, however, determine their exact character. For example, Chinese planning has been and remains far more decentralized than Soviet planning. Only 25 percent of Chinese production during the early 1970s was centrally planned and concentrated in basic industries, such as petroleum, steel, communication, transportation, construction, and trade. Most light industrial activity is planned regionally, as is agriculture. While funds for heavy industrial investment are disbursed centrally, regional investment is for the most part internally generated. In general, Chinese planning is less comprehensive and sophisticated than Soviet planning. Fewer products are planned, computational methods are cruder, and control is more diffuse.

Nowhere is this point better illustrated than in the principle of direct links. Instead of trying, as the Soviets do, to separate buyers and sellers through the wholesale network, the Chinese encourage direct contacts. The central Chinese planners inform the relevant ministries of their basic goals. The ministries then establish targets that are directly negotiated with the largest and most advanced firms. These firms then subcontract to smaller independent enterprises without further state supervision. At every level, the principle of direct links implies that only the interests of the main contracting parties are given serious consideration, it being presumed that more ambitious attempts at global coordination are superfluous in view of the relative backwardness of the Chinese economy.

From the systems standpoint, what appears to differentiate the Soviet and Chinese apparatuses of economic control is not so much alternative approaches to planning as the degree to which the priorities of the planners are consistently transmitted through the control structure. With the Chinese statistical base being embryonic, transportation and communication poor, and computational facilities inadequate, effective decision making has sensibly devolved from the center to more peripheral agencies. Formally, this implies that Chinese planners cannot enforce their decisions on other agents in the economic system as effectively as the Soviets can. If the Soviet control system can be conveniently described as a command model, then the Chinese control system might aptly be understood as a primitive variant in which the command structure is underdeveloped and is effective only over a very circumscribed domain of decision making.

DECENTRALIZATION IN ADMINISTRATIVELY PLANNED ECONOMIES

The characterization of the Soviet control system as a command model is useful up to a point. However, it is misleading insofar as it gives the impression that the Soviet command structure is efficient. As is well known, Soviet planners do not set production targets for the more than ten million goods currently manufactured in the Soviet Union. Typically, only some two thousand composite goods are determined centrally, and even these are not optimized in any meaningful technical sense.[3] Official plans sent to the ministries cannot really be disaggregated into operational supply directives because input supplies are contingent on decisions made at the ministerial and enterprise level regarding the precise composition of produced goods. As a consequence, commands transmitted through the control structure are almost never consistent with production possibilities and thus are frequently inoperative from the viewpoint of their ultimate recipients, the managers of Soviet enterprises.[4]

Although the Soviets do not emphasize the point, the very principle of managerial incentives determined by independent cost accounting (*khozraschyot*) testifies to the inadequacy of the command principle.[5] Instead of simply instructing managers to obey commands, the Soviets have developed an elaborate bonus system to establish effective priorities in the face of inconsistent orders and unreliable supples.[6] The critical determinant of managerial behavior under these circumstances is the exact nature of the rules that govern the bonus. If, for example, total output is the key success indicator, then managers will select the output mix that provides the highest measure of physical production. If profit is the key indicator, managers will use official accounting prices to maximize revenue and minimize input cost.

In theory, discretion of this sort does not pose a control problem because officials in the state wholesale system determine the interenterprise flow of intermediate goods to avoid allocations inconsistent with central directives. Similarly, through its control over financial flows, the bank insures that firms do not acquire resources, including labor, in volumes that exceed their ability to pay.

These checks have some force, but it is difficult to imagine that they solve the problem of effective material supply. To really determine a rational flow of intermediate goods among enterprises, supply functionaries would have to know prevailing enterprise production possibilities, as well as the precise mix of goods required by society. Short of "computopia," information of either sort cannot be obtained independently; thus, the supply agencies are forced to rely on the enterprises themselves for guidance on input needs and output supply. The requisite information is obtained in two steps. First, enterprises forward output supply projections to ministries as part of the annual plan formation. Then, much later, enterprises send requests for input supplies to the material technical supply agency. These requests specify the exact input bill desired within the quota constraints for funded goods established by Gosplan and the ministries.[7] It can be anticipated that in this process managers will seek to obtain the most valuable (in terms of real productivity) input mix possible for each class of funded good allocated to them.

Upon receipt of the enterprise supply requests, the ministries aggregate them and begin negotiations for their acquisition from the supply agencies of other ministries. It is in each ministry's interest to supply external purchasers with an input bundle that is relatively easy to produce and to obtain in exchange inputs that precisely meet the requirements identified by its own enterprises.[8] Since the result of this negotiation process is the signing of legally binding production and supply contracts between individual firms, ministerial supply agencies must protect the interests of their enterprises as much as possible.[9] This is achieved through informal discussions with enterprise managers to determine what can and cannot be feasibly supplied to other ministries.

In all cases, note that what counts for the parties involved is not the production of a socially optimal output mix, but the achievement of those targets likely to maximize managerial bonuses. Although enterprise managers attain their ends at arm's length, this by no means diminishes the fact that it is the managers' preferences and not the planners' that determine the actual composition of production. The supply agencies as representatives of state authority do not possess an independent method of assessing social needs. Without this capacity, the material technical supply system cannot function as an effective instrument of rational state control, and so an independent role for managerial decision making is assured. Moreover, managerial independence is bolstered by the failures of the Soviet administrative planning system itself. As shortages develop and delays occur, managers must either personally or through their *tolkachi* (expediters) enter into direct relations with their contractors. Production plans, assortment plans, and supply schedules are revised by direct negotiation, further enhancing the effective decision-making power of managers. These arrangements are, of course, sanctioned only informally, but formal arrangements would simply put the burden on the ministerial supply agencies or the courts, which in the final analysis would have to rely on information provided by the enterprise for any adjudication.[10]

Thus, while nominally subordinated to the planning system, enterprise managers have enormous power in specifying their input needs and determining the composition of goods actually produced. Moreover, this discretionary authority is not accidental. In the absence of comprehensive optimal planning and automatic market adjustment processes, effective decision-making responsibility necessarily devolves to those most knowledgeable about the production possibilities of the basic units of social production — unless, of course, higher authorities are willing to accept the consequences of their uninformed and arbitrary decisions. Since it is not in the interest of the ministries to reduce the productivity of enterprises under their jurisdiction merely for the sake of caprice, it is erroneous to perceive the material technical supply system as a surrogate form of optimal planning providing the rational direction that Gosplan itself fails to effectuate.[11] As a consequence, managerial control over the Soviet economic system is far more profound than is usually recognized, governed largely by the vagaries of prevailing material incentives embodied in the bonus system.[12]

ONE-MAN RULE VERSUS COLLECTIVE SELF-MANAGEMENT

Precisely because the limitations of the command concept are seldom appreciated, comparisons of the Maoist and Soviet systems are often perceived in a warped perspective. Instead of focusing on the organization and control of the enterprise, attention is deflected to the more general issue of centralized and decentralized planning. However, once it is realized that both the Maoist and Soviet economies are operationally decentralized, this confusion is easily overcome. It immediately becomes clear that what differentiates the two systems is not their disposition toward planning, but their philosophy of decentralized managerial control.

Critically significant here are the respective attitudes of the two systems toward accountability and toward the fundamental distinction between individual and collective responsibility. On this crucial issue, which decisively affects enterprise organization and control, the Soviets and Maoists hold totally antithetic views. For their part, the Soviets adhere to the principle of individual accountability, or one-man rule (*edinonachalie*), in which every participant in the enterprise is responsible for a clearly defined task assigned by a superior who, in turn, is subordinated to the ultimate source of authority, the enterprise manager.[13] If anything goes wrong under this system, it is a relatively simple matter to identify the responsible party and take appropriate corrective action. If a worker is careless, he is chastised by the foreman. If the work unit underfulfills its quota, the foreman is reprimanded. If equipment malfunctions, the specialists are rebuked, and so on, up to the manager, whose performance is evaluated by his superiors in the ministerial hierarchy. At every step, individual accountability facilitates control and permits a clear delineation of authority in the enterprise.

In the Soviet view, one-man rule also fosters efficiency through a scientific division of labor that assigns workers to tasks according to their aptitude.[14] Manually gifted individuals are given manual work assignments and are paid on a piecework basis. Laborers with specialized skills are given jobs in their specializations, while those with engineering or managerial abilities are made responsible for coordinating productive activity, maximizing efficiency, and promoting the interests of the entire enterprise.[15]

From the Soviet standpoint, individual accountability is therefore synonymous with scientific rationality. The organization of the enterprise is not arbitrary or tyrannical; it is based on scientific imperative. To achieve optimal efficiency, the enterprise must be organized technocratically, with each individual performing the task for which he is best suited. The individual is accountable to his superiors who, in turn, are fully responsible for their own actions.[16] At every step, functionally desirable behavior is encouraged through a "judicious" mix of incentives and punishments. To reinforce the workers' "natural" socialist impulses and the moral admonitions of the party, material incentives in the form of differential piece rates and bonuses are employed to encourage socially advantageous behavior. Although there is always some danger of abuse, the established norms in principle provide the requisite incentives without promoting significant socioeconomic differentiation on the basis of ability or privilege. Since the state controls both prices and basic wage-rate structure, there is merit in the Soviet position on material incentives. Bonuses and above-norm piece rates are not, in fact, the primary source of social differentiation in Soviet society.[17] The principles of organization and control employed by the Soviet enterprise must therefore be seen as a coherent and consistent whole, combining individual accountability with a reward system designed to achieve optimal efficiency at minimum cost.

Without rejecting the virtues of either science or efficiency, the Chinese during the Great Proletarian Cultural Revolution chose to organize their enterprises according to an entirely different conception, substituting collective accountability for individual accountability. Instead of making individuals solely responsible for the tasks they perform, supervised by appropriate authorities in a hierarchical chain of command and rewarded with material incentives, the Chinese insisted on the principle of group responsibility. Although the concept of *edinonachalie* is appealing in the abstract, in practice the performance of any individual will depend in part on the performance of his coworkers. For example, if managers ineffectively organize the production process, if engineers fail to utilize the technological potential of existing capital, and if foremen misallocate production tasks, the performance of individual workers must necessarily suffer for reasons entirely beyond their control.

Realizing that individual accountability may well have dysfunctional consequences, especially under conditions of extreme economic backwardness, the Chinese have adopted a system of decentralized managerial control that combines collective accountability with collective supervision. Mao first established the fundamental principles of Chinese enterprise organization in 1960 in the "Charter of the Anshan Iron and Steel Company." After that date and continuing through the first year of Chairman Hua's rule, these principles were taken as guides in running state-owned enterprises. The charter is very short. It states:

1. Keep politics firmly in command.
2. Strengthen party leadership.
3. Launch vigorous mass movements.
4. Institute the system of cadre participation in productive labor and worker participation in management; reform irrational and outdated rules; insure close cooperation among workers, cadres, and technicians.
5. Go full steam ahead with technical innovations and the technical revolution.[18]

The first three articles are general exhortations urging workers to embrace, promote, and defend the objectives of the proletarian revolution against antisocialist forces wherever they might arise. The fourth and fifth articles are more substantive. They define the rules governing enterprise organization, all of which entail the principle of collective responsibility. Party cadre, technicians, and managers cannot stand above the workers. Cadre must participate in productive labor, and all laborers must participate in management. More generally, the enterprise was to be run on the basis of workers' self-management in which specialists, party officials, and workers jointly determine collective tasks and responsibilities in accord with revolutionary priorities established by the party leadership. Implementation of these collectively determined objectives was to be achieved through collective self-supervision. Instead of depending on authority, control was to be realized through a process of perpetual group criticism in which individual policies and actions that infringe upon the consensus view of collective purpose were to be subjected to collective censure. Material incentives, which play such a prominent role in the Soviet managerial system, were redundant in this context. The successes of the enterprise were conceived to be collective successes that could not be attributed preferentially to individual members of the working collective.

Thus, the essence of the Maoist approach to decentralized managerial organization and control clearly lies in the substitution of collective accountability for individual accountability. It is from this innovation that all the distinctive characteristics of Maoist economics flow. Collective accountability destroys the justification for authoritarian control. It repudiates the notion that expertise by itself constitutes an adequate reason for accepting the technical, managerial, or moral precepts of technicians, managers, and cadre, unchecked by the direct experience of the workers. Moreover, collective accountability renders material rewards and incentives superfluous since by definition all members contribute equally to the collective effort. In short, collective responsibility required Maoist enterprises to be organized in a manner that made workers the equals of the technocrats by counterposing their practical knowledge and revolutionary morality with the special skills of professional experts.[19]

From the standpoint of scientific management, it is difficult to distinguish the a priori superiority of either the Maoist or Soviet approaches to decentralized managerial control. Neither approach repudiates efficiency or the necessity of increased material production. Both claim that their enterprise organization overcomes deficiencies inherent in other systems, and both ignore their own deficiencies.

WORK, MORALITY, AND HUMAN WELFARE

In attempting to come to terms with the issue of systems merit, it is important to recognize that mechanistic descriptions of enterprise organization and control constitute an inadequate basis for comprehensively appraising the actual performance of the Maoist-Chinese and Soviet economic systems. Such descriptions overlook the direct socio-psychological costs and benefits associated with alternative strategies of decentralized management.

Socialist theoreticians have long understood that work benefits society in numerous ways. In addition to providing material goods for consumption and investment, work can be a profoundly creative experience that enables people to recognize and realize their full human potential. For example, Karl Marx often stressed the liberating character of socialist labor in which manual and intellectual mastery of the primitive forces of nature, coupled with the deep satisfaction of cooperative enterprise, effectively eliminates alienation, allowing socialist workers to attain levels of self-awareness and communal consciousness unknown under capitalism.[20]

Although different authors have different conceptions of the exact character of the nonmaterial benefits derived from productive socialist labòr, there can be no doubt that work can provide the working class with substantial psychological benefits. The question then arises whether the quantity and quality of these benefits are sensitive to alternative forms of enterprise organization. Both the Soviets and the Chinese appear to believe that enterprise organization and control do affect workers' psychological well-being. In the Soviet view, the nonmaterial benefits of work are maximized when productive labor is organized according to the principle of individual accountability. Each worker, within his circumscribed area of specialization, is encouraged to develop his abilities to the fullest, without overstepping the boundaries of his competence. Instead of being frustrated by his inability to solve problems that are beyond his capability, the creative potential of each worker is stimulated by the success he achieves within his specialization. Although Soviet workers are aware of the constraints imposed by individual accountability, they see them as a necessary part of rational enterprise organization that enables every worker to participate according to his ability in a manner that does not compromise the efficiency of the whole. Soviet workers do, of course, discuss and contribute to policy formation of a general sort through their union representatives, but this is not the basic source of psychological satisfaction derived from socialist labor. The really profound psychic benefits come from mastering one's specialization in an economic environment known to be scientifically rational.

In contrast to this orderly, thoroughly Hegelian vision of worker psychology under Soviet socialism in which the contemplative proletariat savors the objective correctness of Soviet enterprise organization, the Maoists have an entirely different conceptualization based on collective accountability. In the Maoist view, specialization does not determine the limits of worker participation. Every individual possesses hidden talents and abilities. By collectively discussing and analyzing problems of every sort, workers discover their creative potential, expand their competence in multifaceted ways, and develop the confidence necessary to transform their ideas into realities. Moreover, precisely because enterprise management is cooperative, workers become schooled in communitarian ethics, which enables them to fight egoism and other forms of antisocialist conduct. Just as in the writings of the revolutionary syndicalist George Sorel, Chinese workers are perceived as heroes of productive labor, creating true communist morality and consciousness through cooperative self-management.[21]

Instead of accepting the existing order, Maoist workers strive to transform it, to create socialism from below — socialism by the proletariat, not over the proletariat. Material efficiency in this perspective becomes a subsidiary concern. The psychological benefits of collective self-management are portrayed as being so great that material production becomes merely an adjunct to the direct creation of a socialist commonwealth.

Although characterizations of this sort have tremendous romantic appeal, a cautious attitude is warranted in evaluating their objective content. Both the Soviets and the Maoists vehemently repudiate each other's description of the conditions and consequences of work in their respective systems. For their part, the Maoists contend that enterprise organization and control in the Soviet Union are not socialist at all. They see Soviet material incentives, individual self-seeking, profit maximizing, authoritarianism, and the very principle of functional accountability as manifestations of state capitalism. The Maoists assert that Soviet workers, instead of being autonomous and self-limiting agents in a rational socialist economic order, are cogs in a bureaucratic apparatus who, lacking all but the meagerest outlets for their creative needs, are thoroughly repressed and alienated. In consequence, the Maoists believe that the Soviet system is statically and dynamically inefficient, that it is slowly strangling itself in bureaucracy and privilege, and that it will inevitably lead to economic crisis.

The Soviets are no more sanguine about Chinese reality during the Great Proletarian Cultural Revolution. For them, all the talk about revolutionary morality is empty petit-bourgeois rhetoric — the traditional preaching of anarcho-syndicalism. In the Soviet opinion, the Chinese, faced with the problem of building a scientific socialist order on insecure foundations, have reverted to the precepts of peasant anarchism. Collective self-management, instead of being a progressive method of enterprise organization and control, is merely an expression of the bankruptcy of Maoist socialism and the victory of infantile leftism. As a consequence, the Soviets forecast a breakdown in economic production, followed perhaps by a return to progressive technocratic ways.

The gaps between the self-perceptions of the Maoists and Soviets and between their antagonistic perceptions of each other are virtually unbridgeable. The only point of agreement appears to be the negative conclusion that the economic system of the adversary is unsocialist and prone to crisis. Who is right?

COMPARATIVE ECONOMIC PERFORMANCE

Since theory does not provide the answers we seek to the question of how enterprise organization and control affect the comparative merits of the Maoist and Soviet economic systems, an empirical survey of comparative performance may be illuminating. It must be immediately acknowledged that the economic and sociological data available are limited, especially data from China, which makes it impossible to apply modern econometric techniques to the evaluation of comparative merit. Nonetheless, some suggestive quantitative observations can be made. First and foremost, it must be recognized that both systems appear to have performed reasonably well over the long term, providing steadily improved standards of per capita industrial and agricultural production. Table 1 presents comparative data on postwar per capita production substantiating this success; it also reveals that the Chinese have outperformed the Soviets in industry but not in agriculture.

This evidence does not, however, provide an effective perception of the dynamic properties of these economies. Table 2 reveals periodic tendencies in gross industrial production concealed by the per capita growth aggregates. From average quinquennial compound rates of growth, it appears that Soviet industrial growth has slowly but steadily decelerated from 12.7 to 8.2 percent. Moreover, for the period from 1976 through 1980, the official Soviet Tenth Five-Year Plan anticipates a further decline to only 6.5 percent.[22] Thus, while the long-term performance of the Soviet industrial sector has been robust, average long-period rates appear to be camouflaging a significant deterioration in the effectiveness of the Soviet economic system.

Many hypotheses have been advanced to explain postwar retardation in Soviet industrial growth. Although differing in emphasis, most explanations stress two fundamental problems: a low elasticity of capital-labor substitution (capital can be substituted for labor only with difficulty) and inadequate technical progress. Both these causes can be related in some degree to the managerial system employed by the Soviets. Responsibility for technological innovation in the Soviet Union is centralized in research institutes. This approach has the advantage of allowing the Soviets to concentrate

Table 1.   Postwar per Capita Production in the Soviet Union and China, 1950-1976 (Average Annual Compound Rates of Growth)

	Industry[a]	Agriculture[b]
U.S.S.R.	8.1%	2.1%
China	9.6-10.5%	1.1-2.0%
		(0.3-1.2%)[c]

[a]Industrial growth rates cover the period from 1950 through 1976. Chinese data prepared at the CIA by Robert Field are reported in Arthur Ashbrook, "China: Shift of Economic Gears in Mid-1970's," in U.S. Congress, Joint Economic Committee, *Chinese Economy post-Mao* (Washington, D.C., November 1977), p. 231. These gross value data are discussed in Central Intelligence Agency, "The Gross Value of Industrial Output in the People's Republic of China: 1965-77" (Washington, D.C., June 1978), and in Robert Field, Nicholas Lardy, and John Emerson, "Provincial Industrial Output in the People's Republic of China: 1949-75," Foreign Economic Report No. 12 (Washington, D.C.: U.S. Department of Commerce, 1976). An alternative value added series can be found in Central Intelligence Agency, "China: Economic Indicators" (Washington, D.C., October 1977), and in Robert Field, "Industrial Production in the People's Republic of China: 1949-74," in U.S. Congress, Joint Economic Committee, *China: A Reassessment of the Economy* (Washington, D.C., 1975), p. 149. The gross value data are employed to calculate the per capita growth rates shown above. Allowance has been made for alternative rates of population growth (see note b). The Soviet data are taken from various issues of *Narkhoz SSSR*, weighted by 1966 final demand shares derived from the 1966 Soviet input-output table. The rate computed in this manner corresponds closely with the official figure found in *Narkhoz za 60 Let*, p. 168. Population growth has been subtracted from the underlying physical growth rate.

[b]Agricultural growth rates pertain to the period from 1953 through 1976. The Chinese figures are derived from Ashbrook, "China: Shift of Economic Gears," p. 231, lines 8 and 14. Cf. John S. Aird, "Population Growth in the People's Republic of China," in U.S. Congress, Joint Economic Committee, *Chinese Economy post-Mao* (Washington, D.C., November 1977), pp. 439-75. The lower rate of per capita agricultural growth reported above uses Ashbrook's population growth rate of 2.2 percent per annum; the higher rate uses Colin Clark's estimate of 1.3 percent per annum. See Colin Clark, "Economic Development in Communist China," *Journal of Political Economy* 84, no. 2 (1976): 259. Chinese population statistics are particularly controversial. Agricultural growth for the Soviets covers the period 1950-1976 and was derived from *Narkhoz za 60 Let*, 1977, pp. 7, 275. Soviet agricultural statistics are subject to considerable distortion, but the time trend shown here should be reasonably reliable.

[c]Chinese per capita agricultural growth rates are very sensitive to the year in which the series begins. The estimates in parentheses shown above use 1953 instead of 1950 as the base year. According to the *Wall Street Journal* (June 28, 1979, p. 15), the Chinese, for the first time in twenty years, have published a detailed statistical handbook on their national economy; it covers 1978 and includes a population estimate of 958 million as of December 1978. This implies that the lower estimates of per capita Chinese growth (9.6 percent for industry, 0.3 percent to 1.1 percent for agriculture) are more accurate than the higher estimates shown above.

Table 2.   Soviet and Chinese Industrial Production Trends (Average Rates of Growth)

U.S.S.R.		China	
1950–1955	12.7%	1950–1953	30.2%
1955–1960	10.6	1953–1957	13.4
1960–1965	8.9	1957–1960	22.0
1965–1970	9.0	1960–1961	− 42.3
1970–1975	8.2	1961–1966	17.2
		1966–1967	− 12.7
		1967–1973	13.6
		1973–1976	4.8

Source: See Table 1. Official Soviet data indicate an even sharper rate of decline. For the period 1970–1975, the official industrial growth rate is 7.4 percent. See *Narkhoz za 60 Let*, p. 168. The CIA's estimate of Soviet industrial growth is lower still. See Rush Greenslade, "The Real Gross National Product of the USSR," in U.S. Congress, Joint Economic Committee, *Soviet Economy in a New Perspective* (Washington, D.C., 1976), p. 271.

their scientific talent and of facilitating the broad dissemination of new inventions. Its major disadvantage is the separation of invention from a clear perception of need at the enterprise level. Judging from the record, this disadvantage has been important. Despite a sharply declining rate of industrial manpower growth, new inventions do not appear to economize labor any more effectively than the old technology.[23] As a consequence, with the low historical elasticity of Soviet factor substitution, the marginal productivity of capital has continued to fall, and so the Soviets have obtained steadily less output from each ruble of new investment. Similarly, abstracting from the problem of factor proportions, the rate of neutral Soviet industrial technical progress (approximately 3 percent per annum) has been modest in comparison with the possibilities for technological borrowing from the West.

There is some evidence suggesting that technological progress is accelerating in the Soviet economy. On the whole, however, it appears that the Soviet preference for centralizing innovation, while decentralizing managerial enterprise control, has through its rigidity contributed to the retardation of postwar Soviet industrial growth.[24] Whereas authoritarian management motivated by material incentives and guided by an administrative planning network was once a powerful engine for economic growth, today it seems that this same system is not flexible enough to cope with the changing economic environment in an adequate manner.

The historical record places the Chinese experience in a very different light. As Table 2 demonstrates, Chinese industrial growth has been erratic, exhibiting prodigious rates of growth that have been followed by disastrous setbacks. Unlike the Soviet example, the Chinese experience shows no clear secular tendency that can be attributed to the system of economic management. High rates of growth have been achieved in periods characterized by very different managerial control philosophies, which makes it is impossible to seriously infer that industrial performance depends systematically on "expertness" or "Redness." Nonetheless, it is especially interesting to note that in the period following the Cultural Revolution when decentralized workers' self-management was most fully implemented (1967–1973), industrial development proceeded vigorously and was uninterrupted by the breakdowns that had accompanied previous spurts. Only during the succession struggle associated with the rise of the "gang of four" when centralized political control began to disintegrate (1974–1976) did the industrial growth rate falter, declining to 4.7 percent per annum.[25] While this impressive record does not prove that moral incentives are superior to material incentives, it does demonstrate convincingly that industrial growth and decentralized workers' self-management are compatible.[26]

THE ROLE OF MANAGEMENT IN CHINESE AND SOVIET ECONOMIC DEVELOPMENT: UNACKNOWLEDGED CAUSALITY

Although it would be premature to attempt a definitive evaluation of the long-term comparative merit of the Maoist and Soviet economic systems, the actual growth performance of both economies clearly falsifies the assertion that either system is unworkable. How can their successes be explained? Should we accept the Soviet and Maoist descriptions of how their enterprises are organized and run? Should we surmise that the Maoist and Soviet systems each embody a distinct conception of scientific managerial rationality and that both are reasonably efficient?

In our opinion, such inferences are unwarranted. There is simply too much plausibility in each adversary's critique of the other to take their positive pronouncements at face value. On the one hand, it is hard to avoid the conclusion that control in the Soviet enterprise is authoritarian and arbitrary in a sense that refutes the scientific rationality of its overall operation. On the other hand, it is difficult to believe that a process of permanent,and often adversative, negotiation between workers, cadre, technicians, and managers constitutes a sufficient basis for efficient enterprise decision making at the same time that it promotes the communist morality of hero workers.

But if it is accepted that the imagery of managerial practice is too self-serving, how can the undeniable economic successes of these systems be explained under conditions of decentralized managerial control?

In our opinion, the hidden mechanisms of Soviet and Chinese economic progress can be best understood by identifying the areas of their greatest success, assessing whether these successes correspond with enunciated party priorities, and determining how the enterprise control apparatus is designed to achieve those ends. This is not an especially difficult task. Tables 1 and 2 provide the necessary clues. Rapid economic growth has been the cardinal objective of both economic systems for more than two decades.[27] Although other economic objectives, such as quality, assortment, consumption, and equity, have been given some attention, when the trade-offs have been evaluated, growth has always been given the first priority. Certainly party doctrine makes it crystal clear that rapid economic development is desired in its own right, as well as for the purpose of catching up with and overtaking the economic achievements of the advanced capitalist nations. Therefore, the first step toward understanding how decentralized managerial control works in China and the Soviet Union is to recognize that, above all else, both systems are designed for the mobilization of productive resources in an effort to maximize the long-run rate of economic development.

Since both systems emphasize resource mobilization, the role and organization of enterprise production in the Maoist Chinese and Soviet economies exhibit important similarities. First and foremost, the level of aggregate national industrial investment is determined not by the enterprise, but by the state.[28] Neither Soviet managers nor self-managing Chinese workers' collectives have any significant discretion in the allocation of investable funds, which are absorbed through the turnover tax system and vested in the state budget. In this way, the party leadership retains firm control over the aggregate volume and structure of investment within the framework of the total productive effort.

Second, central manipulation of prices and wages encourages managers in both systems to utilize fully all the capital and labor they can acquire. Wages and prices are set so that the revenue generated from the sale of produced goods, including subsidies where applicable, almost always exceeds the wage bill. Managers rarely have to be concerned that increased levels of production will cause losses by raising marginal costs above marginal revenue. They never have to fear insolvency. As a result, enterprise success is measured directly in terms of the physical volume of production (or indirectly through nominal profit), regardless of real factor cost. This constitutes an enormous stimulus for full- and over full-capacity utilization and is an important factor contributing to rapid economic development.[29]

Third, material and moral incentives are used to reinforce the incentives created by price controls. By linking managerial bonuses, piece rates, and progressive piece rates primarily to the volume of production and by continuously exhorting workers to recognize their moral responsibility to labor unstintingly for society and the revolution, the entire enterprise is mobilized to maximize the physical volume of output. Although important differences exist in the motivational devices employed by the Soviets and the Maoists, both rely on material and moral incentives as basic mechanisms of labor mobilization. Even the Great Proletarian Cultural Revolution did not change matters fundamentally in this regard. Rather than relinquishing material incentives as a method of rewarding enterprises that fulfill their production targets, the Maoists altered the character of material incentives. Instead of dispensing bonuses on a preferential basis to individual managers and workers, they distributed bonuses equally to all members of the self-managing collective, in accord with the principle of collective accountability. In this way, while bonuses were eliminated for individual achievement, they were preserved as a collective inducement to maximize the volume of physical production and as a collective mechanism of social mobilization.[30]

Resource mobilization models are not, however, without their disadvantages, and it is here that the differences between the Chinese and Soviet approaches become especially significant. As we pointed out earlier, central planners can neither compute opportunity costs nor control the actual mix of goods produced in a manner that efficiently satisfies interindustrial need. Confronted with the task of maximizing output with inputs that often are of the wrong type or are supplied in the wrong proportions, managers invariably attempt to satisfy plan targets by adulterating quality and providing an assortment of products they know to be socially suboptimal, confident that the center will not discover their deceit. Machinations of this sort cause two types of economic loss. First, they diminish the real value of final consumption and, second, they retard economic growth by forcing enterprises to employ inefficient input mixes.

These microeconomic irrationalities are not accidental. They are the necessary consequence of promoting full-capacity utilization by fixing prices so that revenues exceed cost regardless either of the assortment of goods produced or of the level of enterprise activity.[31] As such, they cannot be eliminated in any simple way. The best the party leadership can do is to adopt policies that mitigate the aggregate loss in the absence of an automatic market adjustment mechanism. The traditional strategy adopted by the Soviets has been to employ special bonus incentives that encourage managers to economize scarce inputs, produce a reasonable product assortment, and insure minimum quality standards, especially for high technology producer durables.[32] Similarly, wage rates have been differentiated and progressive piece rates employed to encourage rational utilization of scarce labor skills.

Given the fundamental intractability of the problem, Soviet experience with material incentives has, if anything, been better than one might have reasonably anticipated. Wherever qualitative factors can be reduced to simple engineering norms, a wide assortment of goods of surprisingly good quality are actually produced.[33] Consumer goods, of course, are notoriously bad, and the diffusion of technology is widely recognized as an endemic problem. Nonetheless, in broad perspective, material incentives have contributed importantly to the coherence of an economic system that lacks a viable mechanism for linking social demand with social supply cost.

For many years the Chinese, like the Soviets, seemed satisfied to employ material incentives to mitigate the worst distortions of the social mobilization model. With the advent of the Cultural Revolution, the situation changed radically. Material incentives based on individual merit were comprehensively eliminated. Bonuses, prizes, progressive piece rates, and even piece rates themselves were widely repudiated and replaced by moral incentives.

On first consideration, the elimination of material incentives that help determine assortment and quality might appear to be a bold and dangerous action. Can moral incentives really form the basis for rational microeconomic decision making? Can collaborative discussions between managers, technicians, cadre, and workers really enable the enterprise to assess the most efficient utilization of labor, level of voluntary labor effort, conditions of employment, production routine, technological alternatives, and product assortment and quality? More generally, how can the moral precepts embodied in "Redness" serve as the criteria for resolving questions of engineering and efficiency?

Since no direct correspondence is known to exist between communist moral norms and opportunity costs, most economists would reject the notion that "Redness" can serve as an adequate substitute for material incentives in the microeconomic decision-making process. This judgment, although undoubtedly correct, misperceives the true situation. First, it should be realized that the Maoist repudiation of material incentives did not extend to the wage structure itself. Wages for managers, technicians, cadre, and workers continued to be differentiated.[34] Only the bonus component of labor remuneration was changed and made more egalitarian. Similarly, it is not altogether clear that the Maoists eliminated bonus incentives pertaining to quality and assortment. Just as in the case of aggregate production, only the inegalitarian distribution of these rewards appears to have been eliminated. Third, regardless of whether assortment incentives were in force, it should not be forgotten that the old price system was preserved. No matter who was empowered to make microeconomic decisions in the enterprise, the advantages of choosing one product mix over another were influenced by the effect that official prices had on net revenue and attainable levels of aggregate output. Thus, upon close scrutiny, it appears that the real effect of "Redness" and moral incentives was to transfer decision-making responsibility from individual experts to the collective as a whole, while retaining conventional norms of economic efficiency.

This was not an unreasonable approach, especially when it is remembered that official prices are average cost labor value prices, which at the microeconomic level bear little systematic relationship to marginal costs. Since these prices cannot be relied upon as indicators of social value, they cannot serve as an effective device for mitigating the deficiencies of the basic resource mobilization model. As a consequence, little damage and great benefit may be derived from making the moral conscience of the collective responsible for determining product mixes that satisfy the spirit, as well as the letter, of assigned production tasks. Whereas an individual manager might be tempted to produce a socially undesirable output assortment in order to earn his bonus, individual members of the collective might be less blatant, fearing denunciation and criticism. Making the group responsible could, of course, have negative consequences as well. Since choosing an optimal assortment is likely to be a contentious undertaking, the collective might take the path of least resistance by paying lip service to quality and assortment, while concentrating on maximizing the volume of output regardless of its effect on social welfare.

The tremendous emphasis placed on communist morality — on "Redness," "fight self," and "serve the people" — was surely intended to counteract any possible distortions of the collectives' decision-making responsibility. Whether Mao's morality campaigns were successful in this regard is difficult to assess. It does seem clear, however, that the operational effects of moral incentives on enterprise organization and control were less drastic than they are often made to appear. Material incentives and economic rationality did not really disappear; they were merely reformed and rendered consistent with the principle of collective accountability. Undoubtedly, the Maoists placed, and still do place, more importance on communist morality and cooperation than the Soviets do. The Maoists also appear to have been willing to allow more latitude to individual worker collectives in interpreting precisely what constitutes communist morality. This represents a critical difference from the human point of view insofar as workers' participation infused with "Redness" transforms the psychological effect of work; however, it must be strongly emphasized that the basic function of the enterprise in the traditional social mobilization model remained largely unaltered. The enterprise continued to serve as a device for maximizing the volume of output at the expense of other microeconomic objectives, only partially mitigated by the structure of material reward and moral exhortation. Since the Soviet Union routinely saturates its workers with appeals to socialist duty, it must be concluded that the only essential contribution of the Cultural Revolution to the practice of economic mobilization has been the principle of collective accountability.

Is this really a momentous contribution, or is it merely ideological pyrotechnics? In our view, there are two good reasons for believing that the Maoist contribution in the limited sense described above (i.e., collective accountability) is substantial. First and foremost, the fact cannot be ignored that the Soviet system is repressive and totalitarian. Even if worker self-management predicated on communist morality is only an illusion and even if worker participation is merely a method of self-surveillance,[35] the Maoists have successfully raised the issue of the quality of human relations under socialism and have shown empirically that economic mobilization can be effectively achieved without one-man rule. Moreover, to the extent that worker participation has genuinely evoked creative interaction within the enterprise, has mitigated microeconomic distortion, and has directly enhanced the psychological well-being of the Chinese working masses, the Maoist contribution has been substantial, pointing to the objective possibility of achieving socialist ends within the framework of a resource mobilization model.

Second, the material success of labor self-management suggests that developing nations may avoid the pernicious consequences of social stratification that envenom social relations and threaten social cohesion by vesting economic accountability with the working collective and moving toward an egalitarian distribution of income. Whether these benefits were outweighed by other factors during the Great Proletarian Cultural Revolution is difficult to assess. Regardless of the actual balance of costs and benefits, however, the principle appears sufficiently meritorious to us to justify the assertion that the Maoists have made a fundamental contribution to the theory of economic mobilization.

CONCLUSION

Does the Maoist economic system offer a viable alternative to the Soviet approach to the construction of socialism, facilitating development without sacrificing social welfare? We have attempted to analyze this crucial question in a systems perspective by identifying precisely how the Soviet and Maoist economies differ from one another. We have argued that both systems are much more decentralized than is commonly recognized, that they are organized primarily to achieve rapid economic development through a strategy of resource mobilization, and that decentralized managerial control is the critical factor governing economic performance, given the prevailing central allocation of investable funds. In addition, we have demonstrated that the principles of microeconomic control in Soviet and Maoist Chinese enterprises also are more similar than is widely supposed. Both systems use material and moral incentives to induce managers to maximize the physical volume of enterprise output and to mitigate the economic distortion engendered by the economic mobilization model.

Despite these similarities, the Maoist system appears to have introduced one element that could, at least in principle, transform the totalitarian character of the Soviet system along socialist humanist lines: collective self-management. By repudiating the concept of individual accountability and replacing it with collective accountability, the Maoists were able, to a considerable degree, to make managers, technicians, cadre, and workers relatively coequal participants in controlling the enterprise. Income inequality and destructive individualism were substantially reduced by eliminating bonus incentives and piece rates. To the extent that the dual process of income leveling and joint responsibility promoted genuine cooperation and assisted workers in achieving higher moral consciousness, it appears that the Maoist system succeeded in infusing socialist humanist ends into a model that up to the present has placed production above socialist purpose. That this was accomplished, even in a very limited degree, without any perceptible diminution in the rate of Chinese economic development is probably the essence of the Maoist contribution, for it demonstrates that economic mobilization models need not exhibit all the unacceptable totalitarian attributes of the Soviet system.

It goes without saying that the Maoist model may not be superior under all circumstances. Totalitarian control mechanisms can take many forms, and it is always possible that collective control may merely constitute an alternative form of oppression. Moreover, for developed countries with high per capita consumption, it is questionable whether social mobilization models make any sense at all. But these are broader themes. Suffice it to say, then, that from a systems standpoint the Maoist model may well be more promising than the Soviet model in combining socialist purpose with the imperative of rapid economic development, despite the policy reversals that occured after Mao's death. Whether practice would follow theory is, of course, an open question, which, in our opinion, cannot be prejudged.[36]

NOTES

1. The most comprehensive and cogent defense of the Maoist approach to socialist construction is found in Charles Bettelheim, *Class Struggles in Russia 1917-1923.* Also see Mao Tse-tung, *A Critique of Soviet Economics.*
2. For a systems comparison that differs from the one put forward here, see Thomas Rawski, "China's Industrial System." Other interpretations of interest are E. L. Wheelwright and Bruce McFarlane, *The Chinese Road to Socialism;* Harry Magdoff, "China: Contrasts with the USSR"; Dwight Perkins, "Industrial Planning and Management"; Yuan-li Wu, "Planning, Management and Economic Development in Communist China."
3. This figure (2,000) is a useful approximation, but it is only that. From 1953 to 1959, the number of "funded" goods formally planned by Gosplan declined from 2,100 to 135. In 1971 the figure was 277. This reduction has diminished the burden on the Council of Ministers, which is responsible for approving "funded" material balances. However, the overall scale of Gosplan's task has not changed proportionally since in addition to planning "funded" goods, it must compile a great many "planned" commodities. Indeed, in 1968 the total number of products compiled by Gosplan was only slightly less than 2,000, including 400 "funded" and 1,569 "planned" goods. It should also be noted that Gosplan is not the only agency with authority to establish material balances. The State Committee on Supply (*Gosnabs*), the All-Union Supply Administrations (*Soiuzglavsnabsbyty*), the territorial Supply Administrations, and the ministries all share in the process that encompasses another 14,343 material balances, bringing the grand total to 16,312. Although some sources suggest that at times more than 50,000 balances have been compiled, the exact number is not crucial to the main thrust of the argument being developed here, which stresses the gap between the centrally planned balances and the total number of different goods produced in the U.S.S.R. See Joseph S. Berliner, *The Innovation Decision in Soviet Industry,* p. 64; Paul Gregory and Robert Stuart, *Soviet Economic Structure and Performance,* pp. 125-26.
4. For a general discussion of the recursive properties of the Soviet planning system, see Michael Manove, "A Model of Soviet-Type Economic Planning" and "Non-Price Rationing of Intermediate Goods in Centrally Planned Economies."
5. In his seminal article "Notes for a Theory of the Command Economy," Gregory Grossman distinguished carefully between command in an efficiency sense

and command as a mechanism for achieving crude material balance. *Khozras-chyot* does not invalidate the command principle in this second sense, which is the one stressed by Grossman. Also note that our discussion does not deal with the latest reforms. For an evaluation of recent changes, which as usual have changed little, see Gregory Grossman, "An Economy at Middle Age."

6. An appreciation of how the bonus system operates in practice is effectively demonstrated in Berliner, *Innovation Decision*, pp. 399–550.

7. For a more complete discussion of the material technical supply system that provides details of the general procedures described above, see Berliner, ibid., pp. 63–92.

8. As a consequence of the 1965 reform, bonuses were tied to sales, rather than to the gross value of output. This is an important change in principle; however, in the chronic sellers' market that prevails in the U.S.S.R., it is difficult for buyers to refuse delivery unless goods are manifestly unacceptable. See Berliner, ibid., pp. 209–24.

9. The institutionalization of the ministry enterprise support system is notorious and is summarized by the expression *krugovaia poruka*, which Berliner loosely, but aptly, translates as *family circle*. See Joseph S. Berliner, *Factory and Managers in the USSR*, pp. 259–63.

10. Gregory Grossman has been kind enough to supply us with references supporting our interpretation of the contracting process. Those interested in further details may wish to know that a dissertation on the subject is being written under Professor Grossman's direction. Also see P. E. Orlovskii, ed., *Uridicheskii spravochnik khozyaistvennika*, pp. 150–53; V. S. Kurotchenko, ed., *Spravochnik po material'no-tekhnicheskomy snabzheniu i sbyty*; and a recent editorial by the Gosplan official, V. Rzheshevskii, "S ychetom postavok."

11. Cf. Herbert Levine, "The Centralized Planning of Supply in Soviet Industry." Levine is unclear about how interministerial supply negotiations generate legally binding supply contracts between firms. Also see Alec Nove, *The Soviet Economy*, 2nd ed. For additional details concerning Soviet planning practice, see Michael Ellman, *Soviet Planning Today*. On contracting and quality issues, see Martin Spechler, "Decentralizing the Soviet Economy."

12. Most specialists today take the position that the Soviet economy is centralized. Although they acknowledge that managers have some independent decision-making authority, it is argued that directives issued by Gosplan, Gosnab, and the ministries circumscribe managerial action and effectively control enterprise activity. This attitude can largely be attributed to Gregory Grossman, whose seminal article "Notes For a Theory of the Command Economy" helped clarify many ambiguities latent in the term *control*. Grossman made a sharp distinction between control appraised from the standpoint of efficiency and control as a means of achieving balance (pp. 101–03). The former, which is a market-equilibrium criterion, was dismissed as inapplicable under Soviet conditions; the latter, which simply requires that all available supplies be inventoried and allocated (regardless of opportunity costs and commodity-substitution possibilities), was identified as the linchpin of Soviet practice. Therefore,

in Grossman's conception command was restricted to the notion that through the compilation of material balances, planners could establish the parameters of managerial discretion, without the further implication that material balances determined the exact bill of goods produced.

Up to this point, there is no contradiction between Grossman's position and the one elaborated in this paper; there is only a difference in how the term *control* should be interpreted. In our interpretation, control is vested in the hands of those whose actions concretely determine the mix of goods produced, especially in interindustrial transactions in which the decisions of producers condition the production possibilities of purchasers. In Grossman's view, control rests with those who establish the main contours of economic policy, rather than with the managers who implement directives as expediency dictates. Our interpretation has the advantage of focusing attention on how different managerial practices alter the way in which any particular command model (in Grossman's sense) operates. This, as we shall see, greatly illuminates the fundamental difference between the Chinese and Soviet economic systems. Grossman's interpretation is useful for identifying the distinguishing characteristics of economic systems that have similar managerial philosophies but different degrees of bureaucratic supervision.

On one issue, however, there seems to be an important substantive difference — the degree of managerial discretion. Grossman appears to argue that managers have very limited discretionary authority. He writes, "So understood, khozraschet is a system that is well devised to control the behavior of managers in a command economy where a certain minimal amount of devolution of power to them is inevitable, and where further, the managers' goals and values do not necessarily coincide with official ones" (p. 117). Perhaps Grossman only means to say here that judged from the standpoint of the planners' general objectives ("enforcement of the regime's values," "resource mobility on a large scale, especially in emerging situations," "concentrating scarce skills and talents at the top," and "maintaining balance"), the range of managerial discretion is severely circumscribed (p. 115). Unfortunately, however, his word has too often been taken at face value to mean that the center controls the economy through the command mechanism in regard not only to balance but to all other economic criteria as well. This is patently untrue, as the testimony of specialists on Soviet management makes clear. David Granick, for example, repeatedly stresses the enormous decision-making independence of Soviet managers in *Management of the Industrial Firm in the USSR* and in *Red Executive*. Berliner sustains this judgment in *Factory and Managers* and, obviously uneasy with the "command" theory dominating current thinking, writes in *Innovation Decision:*

The location of the center of decision making in the central planning apparatus has never provided a fully satisfactory explanation of how resources actually do get allocated in the Soviet economy. The great mass of familiar evidence about managerial maneuverability within and around the planned magnitudes is a perpetual denial of the view that when one has explained what Moscow decides, one has explained it all. . . . Hence, in seeking to explain the process of resource allocation in the early period, the notion of the centralized "command economy," as it was named by Gregory Grossman, provided a successful explanatory model. But we have now approached a time when the model explains less about how the system really operates than one designed to explain the joint behavior of planners and enterprises. [pp. 15, 18]

Berliner is still a bit ambivalent, but as the preceding passages make clear, the approach taken in this paper, while unorthodox, is consistent not only with logic, but also with expert opinion and what appears to be an emerging reevaluation of the utility of command theory as a vehicle for understanding the behavior of alternative nonmarket economic systems.

Cf. Alexander Eckstein, "The Chinese Development Model."

13. Berliner, *Factory and Managers*, pp. 15–16.

14. For a full description of Soviet wage policies, see Abram Bergson, *The Structure of Soviet Wage*; Leonard Kirsch, *Soviet Wages*.

15. Harry Braverman correctly attributes the adoption of this mode of labor organization to Lenin who openly embraced Taylorism as a superlative model of "scientific management." Despite Lenin's authority, however, Braverman argues that Taylorism is fundamentally a bourgeois conception incompatible with either socialism or true science. He writes, "In practice, Soviet industrialization imitated the capitalist model; and as industrialization advanced the structure lost its provisional character and the Soviet Union settled down to an organization of labor differing only in details from that of capitalist countries, so that the Soviet working population bears all the stigmata of the Western working classes." See Harry Braverman, *Labor and Monopoly Capital*, p. 12.

16. However, this principle, which has been the dominant one, does not imply that the trade unions have not had some influence in representing workers' interests at the enterprise level or that Communist party officials do not intervene from time to time. The Soviet system has overlapping control structures. Nonetheless, trade union and local party interference in production decision making is decidedly a secondary phenomenon precisely because it obscures accountability. See Granick, *Management of the Industrial Firm*, pp. 203–61; Berliner, *Factory and Managers*, pp. 264–78; Mary McAuley, *Labor Disputes in Soviet Russia 1957–1965*; Emily Clark Brown, *Soviet Trade Unions and Labor Relations*.

17. Murray Yanowitch, "The Soviet Income Revolution" and "Trends in Soviet Occupational Wage Differentials"; Peter Wiles and Stefan Markowski, "Income Distribution under Communism and Capitalism"; Peter Wiles, *Distribution of Income*; Kirsch, *Soviet Wages*.

18. *Peking Weekly*, April 16, 1976, p. 21. One of the authors attempted to get a fuller statement of the charter while in Peking in May 1976, but was told that this was all. It was written as a directive on the report of the Iron and Steel Company. Perhaps we will get more detail when Mao's collected works for the period are published.

19. The most effective study of collective accountability as it is practiced in China

today can be found in Charles Bettelheim, *Cultural Revolution and Industrial Organization in China*. On the general subject of labor self-management, see Jaroslav Vanek, *The General Theory of Labor Managed Market Economics* and *The Labor-Managed Economy*. See also Jaroslav Vanek, ed., *Self-Management*.

Other useful sources on the Chinese economic system are Alexander Eckstein, *China's Economic Development* and *Communist China's Economic Growth and Foreign Trade*; Kang Chao, *The Rate and Pattern of Industrial Growth in Communist China*; T. C. Liu and K. C. Yeh, *The Economy of the Chinese Mainland*; Walter Galenson and Ta-Chung Liu, eds., *Economic Trends in Communist China*; James Pao, "A Current Appraisal of China's Economic Strategies"; Perkins, *Market Control and Planning*; Paul Sweezy, "China: Contrasts with Capitalism"; Magdoff, "China: Contrasts with the USSR"; John Gurley, "The Formation of Mao's Economic Strategy, 1927-1949"; Wheelwright and McFarlane, *Chinese Road to Socialism*; Jan Prybyla, *The Political Economy of Communist China*; Wu, *Economy of Communist China*; Subramanian Swamy, *Economic Growth in China and India, 1952-1970*; U.S. Congress, Joint Economic Committee, *China: An Economic Assessment*.

20. Karl Marx, *The Economic and Philosophic Manuscripts of 1844*, pp. 114-15, and *The Grundrisse*, p. 142. Cf. Karl Marx, *Capital*, vol. 1, pp. 422-25. Apart from scattered and terse references to the humanizing potential of socialist work, Marx never elaborated a rigorous theory of communist labor. His early statements cited above (circa 1844 and 1857) are imbued with a romantic, universalizing naturalism that by contemporary philosophic standards must be considered dubious, or worse. After 1858, perhaps sensing the treacherous ground upon which his vision of communist utopia was based, Marx sidestepped the problem, concentrating on a critique of capitalism in which the virtues of socialism could be perceived as the antithesis of degenerate capitalist social relations. Therefore, in attributing Maoist doctrine to Marx, it should be recognized that Marx's own attitude toward socialist labor can be neither unequivocally ascertained nor restated in a rigorous, scientifically testable form.

21. George Sorel, *Reflections on Violence*, pp. 242-45. For a typical example of this theme in the Chinese context, see Wheelwright and McFarlane, *Chinese Road to Socialism*. See also Mao Tse-tung, *A Critique of Soviet Economics*, pp. 84-85, 119.

22. *Materialy XXV s"ezda KPSS*, p. 124.

23. For a comprehensive analysis of the innovation process in the Soviet Union with special emphasis on organizational and managerial issues, see Berliner, *Innovation Decision*; David Granick, *Soviet Introduction of New Technology*.

24. Steven Rosefielde and Knox Lovell, "The Impact of Adjusted Factor Cost Valuation on the CES Interpretation of Postwar Soviet Economic Growth." This paper analyzes the state of the art in production function studies of the Soviet economy and provides a comprehensive bibliography. Also see Berliner, ibid; Granick, ibid.

25. Arthur Ashbrook, "China: Shift of Economic Gears in Mid-1970's," pp. 212–14. A sharp distinction needs to be drawn between political turmoil and the efficacy of collective self-management. Field, McGlynn, and Abnett present some suggestive regional data on the relationship between political disruption and industrial production, which they imply bear on the global viability of Maoism. Their data, however, capture the effect of collective self-management very obliquely and, as their own Table A–1 indicates, are extremely sensitive to the definition of the variable that measures political stability. See Robert Field, Kathleen McGlynn, and William Abnett, "Political Conflict and Industrial Growth in China: 1965–77," p. 265. Needless to say, the possibility that the slowdown from 1974 to 1976 is attributable to the Maoist strategy of enterprise management cannot be rejected without further study.

26. A strong tendency exists in the semiofficial U.S. government literature to dissociate the Maoist economic achievements from the Maoist strategy of industrial control. See U. S. Congress, Joint Economic Committee, *China: A Reassessment of the Economy* (July 1975) and *Chinese Economy post-Mao* (November 1977). An analysis of the aggregate impact of technical progress on Chinese growth analogous to our discussion of the Soviet Union has been omitted because from a statistical standpoint Chinese data are too incomplete to allow for the necessary calculations. The Chinese, of course, claim that their technology strategy emphasizing local innovation is very effective, the cornerstone of their rapid economic development, but this claim unfortunately cannot yet be tested. For a concise statement of Chinese technology, see Bettelheim, *Cultural Revolution*, pp. 83–89.

27. Profitability and "saleability" have recently become important elements in managerial bonus functions. However, these changes should not be taken to mean that rapid economic growth is no longer a cardinal objective of Soviet policymakers. Under Soviet conditions, in which all factor and commodity prices are fixed by the state and profit margins are built into the price formation process, profits are not linked effectively to marginal costs. Given the range of feasible outputs that any enterprise could produce at a specific moment in time, it is extremely unlikely that production would be curtailed because marginal cost had become equal to marginal revenue. The real purpose of profitability is not to restrict output to profitable levels, but to assist managers in discovering socially preferred output mixes.

28. Some decentralized investment does take place in the Soviet Union, but it is relatively unimportant. See Berliner, *Innovation Decision*, pp. 181–90.

29. The counterpart of this strategy under capitalism occurs when central authorities freeze wages but allow prices to rise so that profitable operation is almost guaranteed. For a more detailed discussion of decentralized control, see Steven Rosefielde, "Was the Soviet Union Affected by the International Economic Disturbances of the 1970's?"

30. Although a careful reading of the available literature reveals that material incentives played an important role under Mao long before the ascendency of Hua and Teng, the revelations of the post-Mao leadership have thrown pro-Maoist intellectuals into considerable turmoil. For a Marxist perspective on the

implications of material incentives in China before and after Mao, see Charles Bettelhéim, "The Great Leap Backward," pp. 37–130; Neil Burton, "In Defense of the New Regime"; Paul Sweezy and Harry Magdoff, "China: New Theories for Old"; J. Chen et al., "China since Mao." With regard to the older literature, see Carl Riskin, "Workers' Incentives in Chinese Industry"; Jan Prybyla, "A Note on Incomes and Prices in China."

31.   For a discussion of Soviet price formation and accounting profits, see Berliner, *Innovation Decision*, pp. 237–54.

32.   For a discussion of various bonus schemes devised by the Soviets for controlling managerial behavior, see Berliner, ibid., pp. 277–542.

33.   Martin Spechler, "The Pattern of Technological Achievement in the Soviet Enterprise."

34.   Riskin, "Workers' Incentives," pp. 216–22.

35.   It is erroneous to suppose that moral incentives and collective self-management are necessarily progressive. Collective control can also be a mechanism of extreme oppression. Soviet experience with collective "management" provides a concrete, if more sinister, example of how moral incentives can be transformed into instruments of material control.

    A few passages from Alexander Solzhenitsyn's *Gulag Archipelago* (vol. 2, pp. 17, 118) are illuminating:

Oh, without the brigade one could still somehow manage to survive the camp! Without the brigade you are an individual, you yourself choose your own line of conduct. Without the brigade you can at least die proudly, but in the brigade the only way they allow you even to die is in humiliation, on your belly. From the chief, from the camp foreman, from the jailer, from the convoy guard, from all of them you can hide and catch a moment of rest; you can ease up a bit here on hauling, shirk a bit there on lifting. But from *the driving belts*, from your comrades in the brigade, there is neither a hiding place, nor salvation, nor mercy. You cannot *not want* to work. You cannot, conscious of being a political, prefer death from hunger to work. No! Once you have been marched outside the compound, once you have been registered as going out to work, everything the brigade does today will be divided not by twenty-five, but by twenty-six, and because of you the entire brigade's percentage of norm will fall from 123 to 119, which makes the difference between the ration allotted record breakers and ordinary rations, and everyone will lose a millet cake and three and a half ounces of bread. And that is why your comrades keep watch on you better than any jailers! And the brigade's leader's fist will punish you far more effectively than the whole People's Commissariat of Internal Affairs.

    Now that is what *spontaneous initiative in re-education* means! That is *psychological enrichment of the personality by the collective*! . . .

    . . . (And for those who find it hard to imagine, well, this sort of thing took place in freedom too. And in China.)

Corroboration of Solzhenitsyn's allusion to China can be found in the excesses of moral zealotry described in William Hinton, "Hundred Day War."

36.   An excellent Marxist appraisal of the prospects for achieving a genuine socialist economic system in China can be found in Paul Sweezy, "Theory and Practice in the Mao Period."

BIBLIOGRAPHY

Aird, J. S. "Population Growth in the People's Republic of China." In U.S. Congress, Joint Economic Committee, *Chinese Economy post-Mao*. Washington, D.C., November 1977.

Ashbrook, A. "China: Shift of Economic Gears in Mid-1970's." In U.S. Congress, Joint Economic Committee, *Chinese Economy post-Mao*. Washington, D.C., November 1977.

Bergson, A. *The Structure of Soviet Wage*. Cambridge, Mass.: Harvard University Press, 1944.

Berliner, J. S. *Factory and Managers in the USSR*. Cambridge, Mass.: Harvard University Press, 1957.

_____. *The Innovation Decision in Soviet Industry*. Cambridge, Mass.: M.I.T. Press, 1976.

Bernardo, R. *Popular Management and Pay in China*. Quezon City: University of the Philippines Press, 1977.

Bettelheim, C. *Class Struggles in Russia 1917–1923*. New York: Monthly Review Press, 1974.

_____. *Cultural Revolution and Industrial Organization in China*. New York: Monthly Review Press, 1974.

_____. "The Great Leap Backward." *Monthly Review* 30, no. 3 (July–August 1978):37–130.

Braverman, H. *Labor and Monopoly Capital: The Degradation of Work in the Twentieth Century*. New York: Monthly Review Press, 1974.

Brown, E. C. *Soviet Trade Unions and Labor Relations*. Cambridge, Mass.: Harvard University Press, 1965.

Burton, N. "In Defense of the New Regime." *Monthly Review* 30, no. 3 (July–August 1978):9–36.

Central Intelligence Agency. "China: Economic Indicators." Washington, D.C., October 1977.

_____. "The Gross Value of Industrial Output in the People's Republic of China: 1965–77." Washington, D.C., June 1978.

Chao, K. *The Rate and Pattern of Industrial Growth in Communist China*. Ann Arbor: University of Michigan Press, 1965.

Chen, J., et al. "China since Mao." *Monthly Review* 31, no. 1 (May 1979):21–60.

Clark, C. "Economic Development in Communist China." *Journal of Political Economy* 84, no. 2 (1976).

Eckstein, A. *Communist China's Economic Growth and Foreign Trade*. New York: McGraw-Hill, 1966.

_____. *China's Economic Development*. Ann Arbor: University of Michigan Press, 1975.

_____. "The Chinese Development Model." In U.S. Congress, Joint Economic Committee, *Chinese Economy post-Mao*. Washington, D.C., November 1977.

Ellman, M. *Soviet Planning Today*. London: Cambridge University Press, 1971.

Field, R. "Industrial Production in the People's Republic of China: 1949–74." In

U.S. Congress, Joint Economic Committee, *China: A Reassessment of the Economy*. Washington, D.C., 1975.

Field, R., N. Lardy, and J. Emerson. "Provincial Industrial Output in the People's Republic of China: 1949–75," *Foriegn Economic Report* No. 12. Washington, D.C.: U.S. Department of Commerce, 1976.

Field, R., K. McGlynn, and W. Abnett. "Political Conflict and Industrial Growth in China: 1965–77." In U.S. Congress, Joint Economic Committee, *Chinese Economy post-Mao*. Washington, D.C., November 1977.

Galenson, W., and T. Liu, eds. *Economic Trends in Communist China*. Chicago: Aldine, 1968.

Granick, D. *Management of the Industrial Firm in the USSR*. New York: Columbia University Press, 1954.

_____. *Red Executive*. New York: Doubleday, 1969.

_____. *Soviet Introduction of New Technology: A Depiction of the Process*. Menlo Park, Calif.: Stanford Research Institute, 1975.

Greenslade, R. "The Real Gross National Product of the USSR." In U.S. Congress, Joint Economic Committee, *Soviet Economy in a New Perspective*. Washington, D.C., 1976.

Gregory, P., and R. Stuart. *Soviet Economic Structure and Performance*. New York: Harper & Row, 1974.

Grossman, G. "Notes for a Theory of the Command Economy." *Soviet Studies* 15, no. 2 (October 1963):101–22.

_____. "An Economy at Middle Age." *Problems of Communism* (March 1976):18–33.

Gurley, J. "The Formation of Mao's Economic Strategy, 1927–1949." *Monthly Review* 27, no. 3 (July–August 1975):58–132.

Hinton, W. "Hundred Day War: The Cultural Revolution of Tsinghua University." *Monthly Review* (July–August 1972).

Kirsch, L. *Soviet Wages*. Cambridge, Mass.: M.I.T. Press, 1972.

Kurotchenko, V. S., ed. *Spravochnik po material'no-technicheskomy snabzheniu i sbyty*. Moscow: Ekonomika, 1976.

Levine, H. "The Centralized Planning of Supply in Soviet Industry." In U.S. Congress, Joint Economic Committee, *Comparisons of the United States and Soviet Economies*. Washington, D.C., 1959.

Liu, T. C., and K. C. Yeh. *The Economy of the Chinese Mainland: National Income and Economic Development 1933–1956*. Princeton, N.J.: Princeton University Press, 1965.

McAuley, M. *Labor Disputes in Soviet Russia 1957–1965*. Oxford: Clarendon Press, 1969.

Magdoff, H. "China: Contrasts with the USSR." *Monthly Review* 27, no. 3 (July–August 1975):12–57.

Manove, M. "A Model of Soviet-Type Economic Planning." *American Economic Review* 61, no. 3, part 1 (June 1971):390–406.

_____. "Non-Price Rationing of Intermediate Goods in Centrally Planned Economies." *Econometrica* 41 (September 1973):829–52.

Mao Tse-tung. *A Critique of Soviet Economics*. New York: Monthly Review Press, 1977.

Marx, K. *Capital*, vol. 1, New York: New World, 1967.

———. *The Economic and Philosophic Manuscripts of 1844*. New York: New World, 1971.

———. *The Grundrisse*. New York: Harper & Row, 1971.

Materialy XXV s"ezda KPSS. Moscow: Politizdat, 1976.

Nove, A. *The Soviet Economy*, 2nd ed. New York: Praeger, 1969.

Orlovskii, P. E., ed. *Uridicheskii spravochnik khozyaistvennika*. Moscow: Moscow University Press, 1963.

Pao, J. "A Current Appraisal of China's Economic Strategies." *Association for Comparative Economic Systems Bulletin* 18, no. 4 (Winter 1976):3–34.

Peking Weekly. April 16, 1976, p. 21.

Perkins, D. *Market Control and Planning in Communist China*. Cambridge, Mass.: Harvard University Press, 1965.

———. "Industrial Planning and Management." In Galenson and Liu, *Economic Trends*.

Prybyla, J. *The Political Economy of Communist China*. Scranton, Pa.: International, 1970.

———. "A Note on Incomes and Prices in China." *Asia Survey* (March 1975).

Rawski, T. "China's Industrial System." In U.S. Congress, Joint Economic Committee, *China: A Reassessment of the Economy*.

Riskin, C. "Workers' Incentives in Chinese Industry." In U.S. Congress Joint Economic Committee, *China: A Reassessment of the Economy*.

Rosefielde, S. "Was the Soviet Union Affected by the International Economic Disturbances of the 1970's?" In E. Neuberger and L. Tyson, eds., *Transmission and Response: Impact of International Economic Disturbances on the Soviet Union and Eastern Europe*. Elmsford, N.Y.: Pergamon Press, forthcoming (1980).

Rosefielde, S., and C. A. K. Lovell. "The Impact of Adjusted Factor Cost Valuation on the CES Interpretation of Postwar Soviet Economic Growth." *Economica* 44 (November 1977):391–92.

Rzheshevskii, V. "S ychetom postavok." *Sotsialisticheskaia Industria* 5, no. 3 (1977).

Solzhenitsyn, A. *The Gulag Archipelago*, vol. 2. New York: Harper & Row, 1975.

Sorel, G. *Reflections on Violence*. London: Collier Macmillan, 1970.

Spechler, M. "Decentralizing the Soviet Economy: Legal Regulation of Price and Quality." *Soviet Studies* (October 1970):222–54.

———. "The Pattern of Technological Achievement in the Soviet Enterprise." *Association for Comparative Economic Systems Bulletin* 17, no. 1 (Summer 1975):63–87.

Swamy, S. *Economic Growth in China and India, 1952–1970*. Chicago: University of Chicago Press, 1973.

Sweezy, P. "China: Contrasts with Capitalism," *Monthly Review* 27, no. 3 (July–August 1975):1–11.

———. "Theory and Practice in the Mao Period." *Monthly Review* 28, no. 28 (February 1977):1-12.

———. "Paul Sweezy Replies." *Monthly Review* 29 (May 1977):13-19.

Sweezy, P., and H. Magdoff. "China: New Theories for Old." *Monthly Review* 31, no. 1 (May 1979):1-19.

U.S. Congress, Joint Economic Committee. *China: An Economic Assessment.* Washington, D.C., 1972.

———. *China: A Reassessment of the Economy.* Washington, D.C., 1975.

Vanek, J. *The General Theory of Labor Managed Market Economics.* Ithaca, N.Y.: Cornell University Press, 1970.

———. *The Labor-Managed Economy: Essays.* Ithaca, N.Y.: Cornell University Press, 1977.

———, ed. *Self-Management: Economic Liberation of Man.* London: Penguin Books, 1975.

Wheelwright, E. L., and B. McFarlane. *The Chinese Road to Socialism.* New York: Monthly Review Press, 1970.

Wiles, P. *Distribution of Income: East and West.* Amsterdam: North Holland, 1974.

Wiles, P., and S. Markowski. "Income Distribution under Communism and Capitalism." *Soviet Studies* 22, nos. 3 and 4 (January, April 1971):344-69, 487-511.

Wu, Y. *The Economy of Communist China.* New York: Praeger, 1965.

———. "Planning, Management and Economic Development in Communist China." In U.S. Congress, Joint Economic Committee, *An Economic Profile of Mainland China.* New York: Praeger, 1968.

Yanowitch, M. "Trends in Soviet Occupatonal Wage Differentials." *Industrial and Labor Relations Review* 14, no. 2 (1960):166-91.

———. "The Soviet Income Revolution." *Slavic Review* 22, no. 4 (December 1963):683-97.

13 MORALITY AND PRAGMATISM IN THE SUPERPOWER RELATIONSHIP

Dimitri Simes and Aileen Masterson

Three years of intensive efforts to affect human rights in the Soviet Union have not been spent in vain. It appears that both the Carter administration and the American public have gradually developed a greater understanding of the problem of human rights in the context of the U.S.-Soviet relationship, as well as a more sophisticated approach toward that problem. The administration has learned that the public pursuit of its human rights campaign had a spillover effect on other issues with the Soviet Union and that human rights cannot be divorced from the overall framework of U.S.-Soviet relations. Similarly, the focus of American popular attention has shifted somewhat from such topics as the Helsinki Agreements and the Jackson-Vanik Amendment to questions of military and strategic balance, defense spending, and arms limitation; and human rights has become one factor among many that influence public opinion toward the Soviet Union. American understanding of the Soviet regime and its dissenters has deepened and matured, as has our understanding of human rights in general and its place among the concerns of American foreign policy.

This paper is based in some parts on Dimitri K. Simes's article "Human Rights and Détente," *Proceedings of the Academy of Political Sciences* 33, no. 1 (1978).

Needless to say, an appreciation of the complexities involved in handling the problem of human rights in no way diminishes the importance of the issue as an American concern. The topic of human rights is a constant reminder to the United States of the differences between this country and the Soviet Union, both in systems of government and in basic standards. The popular skepticism about American values prevalent in the Vietnam and Watergate era has now evolved into a more mature realization that while we cannot apply our values wholesale to every situation in every country, the United States must stand for something more important than its own material prosperity and narrowly defined security and that it has a responsibility to articulate the fundamental tenets of Western civilization. Similarly, the Kissinger concept of a pragmatic foreign policy in which American national interest is almost an exclusive criterion and President Carter's original foreign policy based on unattainably high ideals have been synthesized and tempered into a blend of idealism and realism that assesses our own influence and objectives in the complex and contradictory international environment.

This greater self-knowledge is accompanied by a clearer American perception of the grim reality and staying power of Soviet repression. The hope that détente might transform Russian society into a more open one is now gone. Any dreams of converting the Soviet Union to our beliefs through greater exposure to the Western world are shattered. Although a particular change in the international environment or application of a certain diplomatic tool may prove helpful in alleviating specific cases of violations of human rights, the nature of the Soviet regime itself is not likely to be altered under any pressure we can currently apply. Recognizing that only limited achievements in promoting human rights can be secured through leverage provided by the U.S.-Soviet relationship, Washington is confronted with the unpleasant, but unavoidable, task of conducting business as usual and cooperating on many issues with those very Soviet authorities whose behavior it finds so distasteful.

The past few years have also taught both the administration and the American people much about the differences between Soviet and American perceptions of human rights in general and attitudes toward dissent in particular. We are becoming aware that to assess the Russian reaction to the dissidents, it is necessary to examine the background — both historical and current — against which the Soviet regime and, more generally, Russian authoritarianism view dissent. Only then can we understand the feelings of the Soviet authorities and the Russian people toward the dissident movement and comprehend the full variety of views within the opposition itself.

HUMAN RIGHTS IN THE SOVIET CONTEXT

To appreciate the complexity of dealing with human rights in the Soviet context, it is important to remember that the traditional Russian attitude toward individual liberties differs greatly from the ideals of Anglo-Saxon civilization. In Russia, rights of citizens have always been considered secondary to the interests of the state. Anarchy resulting from unlimited freedom was more feared than abuses of power. Collectivism, rather than individualism, was a dominant force in Russian political philosophy even before the Revolution.

Russians have never lived under a truly democratic government. The short period after the collapse of the tsarist regime and before the Bolshevik takeover was not so much a democratic interlude as it was an intensive struggle between different authoritarian forces. Significantly, while both the Bolsheviks and their right-wing autocratic opponents managed to develop impressive popular constituencies during the civil war, the moderate liberal elements found themselves almost totally isolated and failed to display any real muscle.

Dissidents capable of courageously protesting Soviet repression frequently display remarkable intolerance of even minor disagreement. According to George Kennan:

> Our experiences with Soviet defectors had shown us that however such people might hate their Soviet masters, their ideas about democracy were primitive and curious in the extreme, consisting often only of the expectation that they would be permitted and encouraged by us to line their recent political adversaries up against the wall with a ruthlessness no smaller than that to which they professed to be reacting, after which they would continue to rule, with our help, by their own brand of dictatorship.[1]

Surely most, if not all, modern Soviet dissenters would be outraged at any suggestion that there are similarities between their perceptions of democracy and those of the Kremlin. Yet there are strong indications that such similarites do exist. Examples of the dissidents' autocratic thinking range from their attitudes toward repression outside the Soviet borders to bitter debates among themselves. Alexander Solzhenitsyn, for instance, had warm words for Franco's rule in Spain. According to *Kontinent,* an influential émigré journal, there are no political prisoners in Greece and Chile. This statement was made while the Greek Black Colonels were still in power.[2] Solzhenitsyn clearly prefers authoritarian rule as long as its leaders accept "their responsibility before God and their own conscience," a kind of authoritarianism with a human face.[3] Outraged by repression in the Soviet

Union, Solzhenitsyn is unhappy about the "surplus" of freedom in the
West. The Soviet dissidents often seem incapable of political compromise.
When the Medvedev brothers, two well-known liberal Marxists, challenged
a common view of the opposition community regarding the wisdom of
indiscriminate Western pressure on the Kremlin, they were called traitors
and even agents of the KGB. The intolerance evident in some dissident writings raises disturbing questions about the strength of their commitment to
democratic ideals.

A similar intolerance manifests itself in the publications of the Soviet
émigré community about dissidents with whom they disagree ideologically.
Despite the fact that these journals are theoretically devoted to encouraging
resistance to the oppressive Soviet regime, their criticism of other émigrés
and dissidents still in the Soviet Union is sometimes more intense than their
criticism of the Soviet Union. Reading the bitter polemics of modern
émigrés, one cannot help being struck by their similarity to Lenin's poison-
ous attacks against other factions of the Russian revolutionary movement
before the tsar's resignation. The spectrum of views among the émigrés goes
from the "Slavophile," or nationalist-religious, perspective of Solzhenitsyn
and *Kontinent* to the Marxist beliefs of the Medvedevs. This range of views
is perhaps explained by Ludmilla Alexeyeva's comment that "clannishness
of nationalities and differences in philosophies that were blunted in the
Soviet Union because of common vulnerability in the face of an aggressive
regime become much sharper in emigration, and divergencies in opinion become quite substantial."[4] With such a diversity of views, disagreement is
bound to occur, but it is the bitterness of the vendettas and the use of such
charges as "KGB agent" and "Soviet spy" that indicate a failure to accept
the concept of a plurality of views, as well as a lack of commitment to such
Western ideals as free speech and political tolerance. As Abraham
Brumberg points out in his analysis of émigré infighting in Paris, the issue
"is not the absence of unanimity; it is the inability to 'agree to disagree.' "[5]

Needless to say, the dissident movement includes quite a few individuals
whose perceptions of democracy seem close to the traditional Western view.
Andrei Sakharov is a case in point, as are Andrei Sinyavsky and Ludmilla
Alexeyeva. However, one must wonder whether these liberals represent a
mainstream of dissident thinking. Even more important is a serious doubt
about whether these liberal dissidents can rally public support in a society
that has had little opportunity to develop a taste for freedom and that for
centuries has accepted repression as a way of life.[6]

Obviously, the fact that some dissidents are undemocratic does not mean
that repression directed against them is any more justified than if they were
devoted supporters of Western liberal values; neither does it mean that they

do not deserve the sympathy and encouragement of the West. What the strength of authoritarian views among the dissident and émigré communities does mean is that in trying to change repressive Soviet practices, the West is dealing not just with the Kremlin, but also with the power of Russian autocratic tradition and the prevailing philosophy of Soviet society. To a degree, that philosophy is shared even by those brave people who oppose the regime.

CONTINUITY AND CHANGE IN SOVIET REPRESSION

To understand the reaction of Soviet leaders and the general Russian population as well, it is important to remember that from their perspective, the status of human rights in the U.S.S.R. is probably better today, and definitely not worse, than it ever has been. The Soviet elite is probably particularly bitter about Western involvement with dissidents because it feels that the Soviet Union was slowly, but gradually, moving in a direction of greater respect for human rights. Soviet progress in this field is far from satisfactory. The entire system is based on violence and lack of freedom, and Western standards of tolerance and humanity are widely disregarded by Soviet authorities. Still, one could argue that Soviet citizens today enjoy more freedom than have citizens in any other period of Soviet history, including the period of the celebrated Khrushchev thaw. Yet, simultaneously, violations of human rights in the Soviet Union are receiving more publicity in the West than ever before. As George Kennan has observed, "Compared with what existed forty years ago, what we have before us today, unjust and uncalled for as it may appear in our eyes, is progress. And yet it is the object of Western press attention and Western protests on a scale far more extensive than were the much greater excesses of the Stalin period."[7]

Of course, one should not hasten to applaud the Kremlin for ending the mass slaughter of Soviet subjects. The Soviet regime still relies on deceit and coercion. People are still dismissed from their jobs, sent to the Gulag Archipelago, and confined to mental institutions for speaking their minds. And if the number of political prisoners is currently in the thousands rather than in the millions, this is scarcely a reason to praise the Soviet human rights performance. The Soviet Union remains a despotic and closed society.

Encouraging changes have taken place in the Soviet Union, however, and these should be noted. First, in contrast to the events of the Stalin era, today almost nobody is arrested under political charges without cause. This is not to say that the persecution of dissidents is in any sense justified, but at least the dissidents can feel that their arrests are related to an expression of their beliefs. Second, real dissident activity, though rarely a violation of the law, is required before the state brings criminal charges, whereas under Stalin, and even under Khrushchev, an innocent political joke was punished with long-term sentences. Contrary to earlier practices, private dissent is tacitly tolerated. Third, even public debates on many subjects, except particularly sensitive ones, are allowed in the mass media, especially in professional journals, as long as their participants do not question the foundations of the system and are willing to pay lip service to the official ideology. True, there were debates ranging from genetics to linguistics even in Stalin's time, but they were usually settled by police methods. Today, the authorities rely more on the professional judgment of their experts, avoiding direct interference in their arguments except in extreme circumstances.

Fourth, the growing stratification of Soviet society has made an entire segment of the population (the elite) almost totally immune from political persecution. Under Stalin, political conflicts led to the destruction of numerous officials. Under Khrushchev, executions and imprisonment were replaced with political purges and the public humiliation of opponents. Since Khrushchev's dismissal, however, the price of losing a power struggle has been considerably lower. Careers are still destroyed, but this is not unusual in any society. Significantly, top Soviet officeholders are now allowed to retire honorably with comfortable pensions. If they have not reached retirement age at the time of their dismissal, they are shifted to minor, but relatively prestigious, positions that entitle them to continue receiving the special benefits reserved for the elite. To be stripped of elite status is today almost unknown. Even prominent dissenters like Andrei Sakharov have not been expelled from the Soviet Academy of Sciences, and they are still entitled to special benefits that membership in the Soviet scientific body accords them.[8] Egalitarian sensibilities may be offended by the privileges enjoyed by important Soviet citizens. Yet it should be remembered that throughout history, rights for all citizens usually emerged initially as privileges for some. In this sense, the fact that at least one Soviet stratum has gained relative security and freedom is not altogether a negative development.

Fifth, the material standards of the masses have improved considerably. The regime is still unwilling to undertake a major reallocation of resources in favor of the Soviet consumer, and consumer expectations are rising faster than the Soviet ability to satisfy them. Nonetheless, Soviet people today have a better diet, are better dressed and housed, and have more consumer durables than in the past.

Sixth, the right to privacy has been strengthened. The authorities are currently much less involved in dictating to the people what clothes they should wear, what hairstyles are appropriate, and what sexual standards should be observed. This is not a minor matter in the everyday life of Soviet citizens who remember the early 1960s when, under Khrushchev, bands of young hoodlums, sporting arm bands of the voluntary police, publicly cut citizens' clothing and long hair if they did not correspond to the official standards of good taste and decency. Furthermore, in an important break with previous tradition, party committees are now increasingly reluctant to discuss such private matters as adultery and premarital sex.

Seventh, in the 1970s, more than 180,000 Soviet citizens were allowed to emigrate. Certainly the right to leave the country is still far from being assured. Emigration is essentially limited to minorities, primarily Jews and Germans, who have homelands outside the Soviet Union, and to those whose dissident activities have given the authorities reason to be eager to be rid of them. Even representatives of these groups are frequently harassed or denied exit visas under the false pretext that they have access to state secrets or because of objections from parents and other relatives. Nevertheless, for the first time since the 1920s a mass departure from what is supposed to be a socialist paradise has become a reality in Soviet life. While it is possible that this development is a tactic designed by the authorities to remove a troublesome and embarrassing sector of the population, it is significant that the regime has advanced to the point of tacitly admitting that such dissatisfaction exists. True, this emigration has occurred under strong international pressure, but it is probable that in the past no such pressure would have worked. For emigration to be treated as a feasible response to domestic and foreign demands required the degree of pragmatism and tolerance that has characterized the Brezhnev era.

If all this is true, why do so many Westerners tend to believe that the Brezhnev era has taken a step backward from the Khrushchev renaissance? One reason is the emergence of dissent that has highlighted the deficiencies in the Soviet system without placing them in a historical perspective. Also, the Brezhnev regime, having adopted a much more conservative style of leadership, does not inspire the excitement of the Khrushchev era. There is no sense of movement and no promise, even if unjustified, of better days. Brezhnev and his associates do not pay tribute to de-Stalinization, although there is no evidence that they ever seriously intended to return to Stalin's practices. Still, the lack of publicity about Stalin's crimes raises suspicions in the minds of many Soviet intellectuals. Finally, the Brezhnev-dominated leadership is not particularly favorable to the Soviet intelligentsia. The incomes of average intellectuals are rising, but not quite as rapidly as those of workers and collective farmers, on the one hand, and the elite, on the other. Furthermore, while there is more freedom of scientific discussion, the creative and artistic processes — ideologically sensitive and considered unessential for production purposes — are still severely limited. The recent prosecution of those associated with the magazine *Metropol,* a journal founded to challenge government controls on artistic experimentation, highlights the Kremlin's continuing unwillingness to allow greater freedom in the spread of ideas. It is in these areas that no progress has been made since the Khrushchev era. Before making value judgments, however, one should remember that Khrushchev's de-Stalinization crusade and the accompanying thaw with the intellectual community were a matter of political tactics and, in a way, a tool in the purge of his political opponents — who were not necessarily any more sympathetic to Stalin than Khrushchev himself.

To understand the relatively indifferent, and sometimes hostile, attitude toward the dissident movement among even liberal segments of the Soviet elite and upper-middle class, one should be aware of the fundamental differences between Stalinist blind terror and the ugly, but still limited, repression of the Brezhnev years. First of all, political methods are no longer used to solve disputes among Soviet officialdom, as they were under Stalin. Equally important, as was suggested above, is that persecution is no longer indiscriminate and, on the contrary, is carefully directed against real dissenters. Finally, the whole magnitude of repression under Khrushchev and Brezhnev is, of course, incomparable to the repression that occurred under Stalin. As a matter of fact, there is a certain fallacy in the argument that the dissidents have failed to gain greater sympathy among the wider strata of the population because of harsh responses by the authorities. If anything, the Soviet dissident movement was born in the mid-1960s, when there was a strong perception of an imminent threat of neo-Stalinism. As Alexander Solzhenitsyn still believes, "An abrupt return to Stalinism headed by the 'iron Shurik' Shelepin was in the making."[9] He attributes the arrests of Sinyavsky and Daniel to the influence of Shelepin and his supporters and suggests that they were planning to arrest about one thousand intellectuals in Moscow alone. According to Solzhenitsyn, "Shelepin's power would mean my immediate demise."[10] The same account of a resurgence of Stalinism is provided by some other Soviet dissidents.[11]

In short, many members of the Soviet liberal intelligentsia, including some members of the elite, were willing to risk a great deal to block what they perceived as a return to Stalinism. However, quite a few of these people would not necessarily accept smaller risks in order to challenge the milder and more discriminating repression practiced by Brezhnev and his associates.

CHANGES IN U.S. PERCEPTIONS OF THE DISSIDENTS

The past few years have also done much to change our own perceptions of the Soviet dissidents. In the early days of Western fascination with the Soviet human rights movement, rational discussion of Soviet dissent was an extremely difficult task because of the enormous emotional involvement of many Western observers with the Soviet opposition. Objective attempts by some students of Soviet society to evaluate the political philosophy, personal values, and tactics of the dissidents frequently met with strong disapproval and even hints that those who, with whatever intentions, expressed less than total admiration of the dissidents were doing the KGB's work. As a result, the study of Soviet dissent was dominated by scholars who perceived themselves not only as students of an important political phenomenon, but also as active allies of those fighting against Soviet authoritarianism. Serious analytical studies of the Soviet opposition are becoming more prevalent, however, and the real complexity of the situation is becoming increasingly evident.

The older model of Soviet dissent among Western students of Soviet affairs assumed that although protestors might argue among themselves, and commit minor tactical errors, as a rule their objectives were extremely noble, reasonable, and worthy of unquestionable support. For instance, according to Leonard Shapiro, "Of course, Solzhenitsyn is not on the side of anyone or anything — except truth, justice and freedom under the law."[12] Perceptions of truth, justice, and freedom vary from one individual to another, however, and the dichotomy between Solzhenitsyn's ideas on freedom and those of the Western liberal tradition has become increasingly clear and widely perceived, especially in light of his 1978 speech at Harvard's commencement ceremonies. In fact, Solzhenitsyn is now recognized as the leading exponent of the nationalist-religious or nationalist-patriotic school of ideology, which espouses a renunciation of Marxism and internationalism and a return to Russian orthodoxy.[13] Even more extreme views were publicized in the Soviet Union by the *samizdat* journal *Veche* (until its closing by the Soviet authorities), whose goal was, in the words of its editor Vladimir Osipov, to "safeguard the people, particularly the youth, from cosmopolitan corruption."[14] While many of the liberal dissidents, such as Sakharov, disagree with the nationalist-religious emphasis on Russian nationalism, which is usually coupled with anti-Zionism (frequently a code word for anti-Semitism), they cannot deny that some of those beliefs apparently have considerable appeal for some sectors of the Soviet population.

Among many analysts, there is also a growing realization that Solzhenitsyn, as extreme as he now appears to us in light of his condemnation of

Western practices and values, may actually be a moderate by comparison with some of his Slavophile colleagues and certainly is by comparison with those supporters of the antiregime right wing who advocate the liberation of Russia from the "Kremlin Zionists." According to Michael Meerson-Aksenov, "For these extreme trends of nationalist-patriotism, even *Veche* and the works of the Solzhenitsyn are playing into the hands of cosmopolitanism and 'World Zionism.' "[15]

It is becoming increasingly clear that although much is known about some of the pro-Western dissidents who see foreign reporters in Moscow as their main channel of communication and hope for the future, the Soviet opposition movement also encompasses other groups on both the left and right. Members of these groups, while persistent in opposing official controls, hold views that are as incompatible with Western values in some respects as are those of current Soviet leaders. Information about such groups can be quite difficult for the Western observer to obtain, and even when it is obtainable, it is difficult to verify and interpret because of the lack of first-hand contacts.

There are good explanations for the pro-dissident bias in Western studies, such as the traditional American sympathy for the underdog and respect for the courage of individuals standing against an enormous system of suppression. There is also a natural confusion between enemies of one's enemies and one's friends. However, as the example of Iran illustrates, opposition to a common enemy, such as the Shah, did not make Khomeini and Bakhtiar friends, and the Soviet opposition includes similar allies in adversity who share only the adversity.[16]

Another problem with the American understanding of Soviet dissidents stems from the ambiguity of the word *dissidents*. The word is used to cover individuals concerned with publicizing and attempting to change the political nature of the regime, as well as those whose goal is simply to leave the Soviet Union to escape religious or ethnic discrimination. Obviously, *dissidents* as used here does not mean everyone who opposes some particular official policy and is striving for reforms, but only those who are alienated enough from the system to work outside the official framework.

DISSIDENT GOALS

By the very act of going outside the system, the dissidents challenge the fundamentals of the regime. In the late 1960s, when the dissident movement emerged as a political phenomenon, the situation was quite different. Many protesters felt that their views and those of the regime were not irreconcilable and hoped to find a common language with Soviet officialdom. In most cases, such hopes have ceased to exist, and opposition to particular policies has been replaced by rejection of the regime.[17] Certainly the Soviet authorities, with their constant tendency to overreact and perceive even moderate public criticism channeled through other than officially approved avenues as a threat to the very survival of the system, are the first to blame for the increasing radicalization of dissent. Whatever the reason, the gap between the Soviet elite and the mainstream of the opposition movement appears at this stage to be unbridgeable.

Having become disillusioned about the possibility of either having a constructive dialogue with the regime or attracting any serious political constituency within the Soviet Union, dissidents adopted appeals to foreign groups and even foreign governments as their main tactic. Leading dissidents admit that without the support of the West their movement could not survive. Soviet officials, in turn, charge that protesters are paid agents of anti-Soviet forces and even of intelligence agencies that are committed to undermining the Soviet system. Undoubtedly, with very few exceptions, alleged connections between dissenters and the Central Intelligence Agency are unfounded. Nevertheless, strong links between the Soviet opposition movement and foreign groups hostile to the Kremlin are difficult to deny. The fact that such links are usually based on a similarity of objectives and not on any formal arrangements is an important legal difference. However, as far as the Soviet regime is concerned, political dissenters represent a Western fifth column in the Soviet Union. It is partly for this reason that the Kremlin interprets even the most cautious and indirect American involvement on behalf of the dissidents as unwarranted interference in Soviet affairs and as a questioning of the very legitimacy of the regime.

There are Soviet dissident groups whose disagreement with the system is of a less fundamental nature. This is especially true among ethnic movements, such as those of the Jews and the Volga Germans, who are interested primarily in leaving the country, not in changing Soviet society. Significantly, in this field the regime was willing — admittedly under strong international pressure — to grant concessions and to allow thousands of applicants the right to move to nations of their choice. Western involvement with emigration movements hardly pleases the Soviet authorities, but they do not necessarily perceive it as a threat to the survival of the regime. Prominent activists of the Jewish emigration movement, despite obvious harassment, have nonetheless been treated more mildly than dissidents striving for domestic change. Typically, the most dramatic recent case of prosecution of a

Jewish activist, Anatoli Shcharansky, involved not just participation in the emigration movement, but membership in the Helsinki monitoring movement as well.[18]

In sum, the mainstream of the Soviet dissident movement has gone beyond the advocacy of introducing an element of law and humanity into Soviet official practices. With some obvious exceptions (such as the liberal Marxist Medvedev brothers, on the one hand, and the National Bolshevik Gennady Shimanov, on the other), the dissidents tend to be in opposition to the regime itself, and partial reforms leaving the foundation of the system intact will not satisfy them. It is probably for this reason that the movement has achieved so little success with the Soviet middle class, which, more or less satisfied with its own standard of living and thus with the regime, sees the dissidents as radicalized, unreasonable, and unsatisfiable. The Soviet elite, in turn, feels that the protestors are questioning the legitimacy of its rule, since the political controls they oppose are considered essential for the preservation of the existing order.

U.S. POLICY CONSIDERATIONS

Clearly the United States has learned much about the difficulty of developing and maintaining a workable approach toward the human rights issue within the framework of the U.S.-Soviet relationship. For instance, the debate that has existed over the Jackson-Vanik Amendment from the time of its introduction to the present day bears witness to the difficulty of putting America's concern into legislative terms without destroying the tenor of U.S.-Soviet relations. A direct single-issue linkage between the Soviet human rights performance and American concessions on trade credits and trading status entails a risk that we may lose our economic leverage in the conduct of our overall policy toward the Soviet Union. Furthermore, the provisions made to ensure consistently good Soviet human rights performance — Soviet assurances on emigration made to the president — strike the Soviets as humiliating and unworthy treatment of one world power by another.

Moreover, the Kremlin is very sensitive to any indication that Washington is granting Peking preferential treatment. If China is granted most favored nation status and access to Export-Import Bank credits without similar benefits being awarded to the Soviet Union, one may predict a great bitterness not only in the narrow circle of Kremlin gerontocrats, but also among the Soviet elite in general, despite the fact that China, unlike the Soviet Union, is willing to satisfy the requirements of the 1974 Trade Act by providing assurances about its emigration performance. There is little doubt that from the Soviet standpoint, the Chinese record on human rights is unimpressive, and the Soviets would inevitably perceive Chinese assurances as a convenient technicality allowing the United States to give preferential treatment to Moscow's bitterest enemy. The fact that Senator Jackson, who is viewed in the Soviet Union as the archenemy of détente, is simultaneously a major spokesman for a rapprochment with China (a rapprochment that includes providing China with trade benefits) only reinforces the impression within Soviet official circles that the U.S. human rights campaigns are an integral part of a realpolitik, anti-Soviet outlook.

On the other hand, there is also the danger that if human rights are not specifically addressed in some form of legislation, the policy of "quiet diplomacy" (i.e., dealing with individual cases on an ad hoc basis) will degenerate into "silent nondiplomacy," with human rights issues being shuffled aside in the face of ever-present "other priorities." This risk is particularly acute at present, with our concern for strategic and military balance looming so large that we have subordinated practically all other issues to the single issue of SALT and defense spending. It is necessary to keep the broader relationship between the United States and the Soviet Union in mind, with all its complexity and competing factors, rather than focusing on each troublesome aspect in succession as a new toy or new scare that is more important than all the others.

Furthermore, our concern with human rights should not be a matter of political convenience in which we use the dissidents as symbols to support greater defense spending or fewer concessions to the U.S.S.R. As a forum for his pre-Vienna summit charge that the Carter administration was conducting a Munich-like policy of appeasement, Senator Jackson selected a meeting of the Coalition for a Democratic Majority to give freedom awards to two Soviet dissidents. One of the two, Vladimir Maximov, speaking at another gathering in Washington several days earlier, proclaimed himself a monarchist. As the editor of *Kontinent*, he was also responsible for bitter attacks on those questioning the repressive practices of the Greek Black Colonels and the Chilean junta. One may only suspect that whatever the motives of the sponsors of the meeting and Senator Jackson may have been, the Soviets probably considered the whole event an example of using the dissidents to torpedo the entire U.S.-Soviet relationship and SALT in particular.[19]

Of course, any American attention, particularly official attention, to human rights issues in the Soviet Union is bound to cause displeasure in the Kremlin. This should not, however, prohibit the United States from voicing its humanitarian concerns and adhering to the fundamental values of Western civilization. Moscow operates in a subtle international environment, and one should not exaggerate the role of emotional anger in Soviet foreign policy formulation. Moreover, providing the Kremlin with veto power over an important and legitimate dimension of American diplomacy would indeed amount to moral appeasement. The real issue is not whether the United States should pursue the issue of human rights in its relationship with the Soviet Union; the nature of American domestic politics, on the one hand, and the nature of Soviet authoritarianism, on the other, virtually guarantee that Soviet repression will remain on the superpower agenda. The problem is finding the right balance between the pragmatic necessities of the U.S.-Soviet relationship and the more humanitarian imperative of our moral concerns. Inevitably there will be a danger of one of the two extremes — total subordination of human rights to geopolitics or the launching of messianic crusades. In addition, as noted earlier, there is the possibility of a mixture of the two, a kind of "moralpolitik" in which the issue of human rights acquires the function of a major political weapon in the great power rivalry.

Our argument should not be misconstrued. All differences notwithstanding, an assertive pursuit of human rights may be both morally and politically beneficial for the United States, and it is unfair and indeed unwise always to demand immediate results from every administration's human rights initiatives. The fundamental caveat on human rights diplomacy, however, is that in the long run its effect depends mainly upon the perception of those to whom the policies are addressed. It will certainly not have the desired effect if its recipients feel as if they are being treated as cruel barbarians or, even worse, primitive tribesmen obliged to follow uninvited advice from Washington. A respect for human rights should include a degree of understanding for local traditions and prides. It should also incorporate the realization that it is extremely difficult to promote morality with a gun. Sometimes a very heavy gun may work, but not a relatively small stick, such as the one that constitutes the limited leverage the United States possesses over the Soviets in the area of the human rights.

NOTES

1. George F. Kennan, *Memoirs, 1950–1953,* vol. 2, (Boston: Little, Brown, 1972), pp. 96–97.
2. *Kontinent,* no. 2 (1975):468–69.
3. Alexander Solzhenitsyn, *Iz-pod glyb: sbornik statei* (Paris: YMCA Press, 1974), p. 26.

4. Ludmilla Alexeyeva, "The Human Rights Movement in the USSR," *Survey* (Autumn 1977–78):80.
5. Abraham Brumberg, "Moscow on the Seine," *New Leader* (May 21, 1979):6.
6. As a recent article by Soviet dissident Victor Nekipelov suggests, the resurgence of pictures of Stalin in the homes and vehicles of many Soviet citizens may indicate that a significant sector of the population professes a desire for even stronger leadership and authoritarian control than the Brezhnev regime provides. While this trend may be more of an expression of dissatisfaction with the current regime than an indication of real desire to return to Stalinism, it is clear that part of the Soviet general public misses Stalin more than it does Khrushchev. See Victor Nekipelov, essay from *Kontinent,* reprinted in the *New York Times,* August 14, 1979.
7. George F. Kennan, *The Cloud of Danger: Current Realities of American Foreign Policy* (Boston: Little, Brown, 1977), p. 214.
8. Significantly, Benjamin Levitch remained a member of the academy until that organization limited its membership to Soviet citizens, thus automatically excluding Levitch who had ceased to be a Soviet citizen upon his emigration.
9. Alexander Solzhenitsyn, *Bodalsya telenok s dubom* (Paris: YMCA Press, 1975), p. 112.
10. Ibid., p. 127.
11. See Nekipelov's essay reprinted in the *New York Times,* August 14, 1979.
12. Leonard Shapiro, "Some Afterthoughts on Solzhenitsyn," *Russian Review* 33 (October 1974):417.
13. Obviously, the nationalist-religious views on Marxism find little favor with such liberal Marxist dissidents as Roy Medvedev, who had sharp criticism for the journal *Kontinent,* frequently a forum for Solzhenitsyn and some other more radical dissidents who perceive a foreign-invented Marxism as the major source of Russian ills. Medvedvev wrote: "This journal is dedicated not to the East but to the West, and its main task is the debunking of Marxism and Socialism in the eyes of the Western intelligentsia and youth." See Roy Medvedev, "Questions Which Alarm Everyone," *Dvadsatsy vek* 1 (London, 1976), p. 25.
14. Quoted in Michael Meerson-Aksenov's introduction to "The Debate over the National Renaissance in Rûssia" in M. Meerson-Akensov and Boris Shragin, eds., *The Political, Social and Religious Thought of Russian 'Samizdat' — An Anthology* (Belmont Calif., 1977), p. 348.
15. Ibid., pp. 350–51.
16. The parallel between the Iranian and Soviet situations is still more striking when one considers the prevalence of strong religious-nationalist sentiments even among dissidents whose own religious views are far from Russian Orthodoxy. For example, Aleksandr Ginzburg, in a recent Radio Liberty interview, replied to a question about his wishes for Russia's future: "I would like to see a Christianized Russia . . . but I cannot imagine the form of this government." *Radio Liberty Bulletin* 22 (June 1979).

17. In this connection, see Ludmilla Alexeyeva's comment on the Jewish refus-niks' failure to cooperate with the human rights movement in its early days for fear of losing the possibility of emigration by associating with those opposing the system. As she notes, the reverse proved true; those who agitated the most against the system were released first. See Alexeyeva, "Human Rights Movement."

18. This is not to suggest that Shcharansky does not deserve strong international support. Not only does all the available evidence indicate that the official charge of treason is without foundation, but also the whole trial had simul-taneously strong anti-Semitic and anti-American overtones.

19. Of course, Solzhenitsyn's exposure of Soviet brutality did indeed play an im-portant role in changing the American public's perception of the Soviet Union and in creating a far more cautious, if not more hostile, attitude toward the U.S.S.R. This attitude may not only be well deserved by Soviet officialdom, but possibly also responds well to the needs of U.S. foreign policy. However, it is hardly realistic to expect that the Soviet elite would be grateful to their own citizens who made a major contribution to foreign policy change detrimental to the interests of the regime.

CLOSING OBSERVATIONS

Communist development during the preceding six decades has been very uneven. On the one hand, the political economic structures that have been created function more effectively than many scholars would have supposed. These structures have enabled communist societies to adopt factor-intensive industrialization strategies that have eradicated some aspects of their earlier economic backwardness.[1] Industrial production in the East has grown rapidly and in the not too distant future could eclipse the production capacity of the West.

On the other hand, the successes of communism in industry have not been matched in other areas. Per capita consumption, which was extremely low by international standards a half century ago, remains comparatively low today.[2] Human welfare, which declined to appalling levels under Stalin, has improved to a degree, but the gains of the recent past hardly seem secure and could easily be undone.[3]

The explanations for this uneven performance have been, and remain, disputable. It appears reasonably certain, however, that the seige mentality that permeated the communist bloc until well into the 1950s importantly influenced the pattern of communist industrialization and the measures taken to ensure its success.[4] Industrialization was not sought merely for its own

321

sake, nor was it sought just to provide consumers with an increased standard of living; rather, it was perceived to a significant extent as the sine qua non of proletarian self-defense.[5] Industrialization and military procurement were the dominant themes in the Stalinist era, and, rightly or wrongly, they had the effect of subordinating socialist construction to the imperative of survival.[6]

As the external justification for the communist seige mentality waned in the 1960s, one might have supposed that priorities would have gradually shifted away from defense toward building the humane society for which so many sacrifices had seemingly been made in vain. Some small advances of this sort were made, but world communist defense expenditures were in no way curtailed. Despite the rhetoric of the "thaw," "peaceful coexistence," and "détente," the communists — primarily the Soviets — chose to accelerate their defense effort.

The consequences of this decision are now apparent and have been documented in this volume. For the first time in history, the communist world has attained military ascendancy. By and large, it has done so without departing from the patterns of the past, but at significant cost to its primary ideological objective, the construction of a humane communist society.

Achieving superiority and maintaining it are, however, two entirely separate matters. To sustain its military ascendancy, the communist bloc will have to bear an enormous cost. Its newly acquired military preeminence is the outcome of a policy decision to allocate resources disproportionately to defense and is not attributable to the superior efficiency of communist political economy.[7] For these reasons, the communists cannot maintain their ascendancy and at the same time transfer resources to improve domestic human welfare. Nor can communist leaders significantly alter prevailing political-economic structures without threatening the elite consensus that supports their present military posture.

World communism is therefore at a crossroads in a very profound sense. For six decades it has evaded the task of building a society that authentically embodies the human ideals affirmed by Marx and Engels. This evasion may have had some material or psychological justification during Stalin's reign. To a lesser degree, the same arguments could be said to hold as long as the "correlation of forces" inclined toward the capitalist camp. But now that the military balance has tipped the other way, how can the behavior of the communist world be explained?[8]

The essays in this volume do not provide an answer to that question. They were not designed to do so. Instead, they have served a less ambitious, but nonetheless important, function. They have given us a better understanding of why communist military ascendancy is a landmark event. Not only has the recent change in the "correlation of forces" ruptured the international status quo; it has also created a situation in which it will become increasingly difficult for the communist world to reconcile its pursuit of power with its manifest failure to achieve a humane communist society. The obverse side of communist military ascendancy, given the unevenness of communist development, appears to be a severe intensification of the fundamental contradictions of communism. A communist legitimation crisis of substantial dimensions seems to be in the making as a direct consequence of a one-sided success, and if the world survives, it will be fascinating to observe whether communist idealism can really triumph over the destructive logos of Stalinism.

NOTES

1. Abram Bergson, *Productivity and the Social System — The USSR and the West* (Cambridge, Mass.: Harvard University Press, 1978); Steven Rosefielde, "The First Great Leap Forward Reconsidered: The Lessons of Solzhenitsyn's *Gulag Archipelago*," *Slavic Review,* forthcoming (December 1980).
2. Bergson, *Productivity and the Social System.*
3. Rosefielde, "First Great Leap Forward."
4. Ibid.
5. Alec Nove, *An Economic History of the USSR* (London: Allen Lane, 1969), p. 188: "It was then [1931] that [Stalin] made the justly famous prophecy: 'We are fifty or a hundred years behind the advanced countries. We must make good this distance in ten years. Either we do so, or we shall go under.' 1941 was ten years away."
6. Rosefielde, "First Great Leap Forward." I have argued elsewhere that this is a false dichotomy. Survival would have been better assured if Stalin had followed a saner approach to industrialization.
7. Bergson, "Productivity and the Social System."
8. The communists will probably attempt to resolve this dilemma by denying it. They will contend that human welfare is already high and is improving as their political economies steadily progress from socialism to higher stages of communism; and they will explain that military preeminence is needed to support the emancipation of the oppressed everywhere from the capitalist yoke. This, after all, has been their official position for fifty years. However, not all explanations are convincing. The dilemma posed in the text cannot be invalidated by assertions that are palpably false. Communist military successes are visible; their fabled humanistic accomplishments are not. The pretences of the weak may be winked at, but the same indulgence is seldom accorded to the strong.

BIOGRAPHICAL SKETCHES
OF CONTRIBUTORS

1. Patrick Parker: Chairman of the National Security Affairs Program, Naval Postgraduate School, Monterey, Calif.; Professor of Business Administration, University of California, Berkeley; President of Hickok Belt Corporation; Assistant Secretary of Defense for Intelligence under Nixon and Ford; currently holding numerous positions on various special defense panels.
2. Steven Rosefielde: Associate Professor of Economics, University of North Carolina, Chapel Hill; author of *Soviet International Trade in Heckscher-Ohlin Perspective* and *Economic Welfare and the Economics of Soviet Socialism* (forthcoming), as well as *Underestimating the Soviet Military Threat: The CIA's Direct Cost Estimating Effort 1960-1975* and numerous scholarly articles.
3. William Lee: Independent Defense Analyst, formerly with the CIA and SRI; author of *The Estimation of Soviet Defense Expenditures for 1955-1975: An Unconventional Approach* and numerous other pieces.
4. Jiri Valenta: Assistant Professor and Coordinator of Soviet and East European Studies, Department of National Security Affairs, U.S. Naval Postgraduate School, Monterey, Calif.; author of *The Soviet Intervention in Czechoslavakia: Anatomy of a Decision* and numerous scholarly articles; coeditor of the forthcoming volumes *Eurocommunism between East and West* and *Communist Countries' Involvement in Africa*.

5. James Leutze: Professor of History, University of North Carolina, Chapel Hill; Director of the Curriculum on Peace, War and Defense, University of North Carolina; author of *The London Journal of General Raymond E. Lee* and *Bargaining for Supremacy: Anglo-American Naval Collaboration, 1937–1941* (for which he was awarded the Bernath Prize for Distinguished Publication in Foreign Policy), as well as *Admiral Thomas C. Hart: A Different Kind of Victory.*

6. Gur Ofer: Professor of Economics, Hebrew University, Jerusalem; author of *The Soviet Service Sector* and numerous scholarly articles.

7. Egon Neuberger; Professor of Economics, State University of New York, Stonybrook; author of *International Trade and Central Planning* and *Comparative Economic Systems,* as well as numerous articles; coeditor, *Transmission and Response: Impact of International Economic Disturbances on the Soviet Union and Eastern Europe.*

8. Laura Tyson: Assistant Professor of Economics, University of California, Berkeley; author of numerous articles on Yugoslavia; coeditor, *Transmission and Response: Impact of International Economic Disturbances on the Soviet Union and Eastern Europe.*

9. Thomas Wiens: Senior Research Analyst on China, Mathematica, Inc., Betheseda, Md.; former Assistant Professor at the University of Oregon.

10. Mary Ellen Fischer: Associate Professor of Political Science, Skidmore College; author of many articles on Romanian politics.

11. Edward Ames: Professor of Economics, State University of New York, Stonybrook; author of *Soviet Economic Processes* and *Macroeconomics,* as well as numerous scholarly articles.

12. Jaroslav Vanek: Professor of Economics, Cornell University; author of *The General Theory of Labor Managed Markets* and *Self Management,* as well as *The Labor Managed Economy* and numerous other books and articles on socialist economics.

13. Christopher Gunn: Lecturer in Economics, Hobart College.

14. Henry Latané: Professor of Economics and Business Administration, University of North Carolina, Chapel Hill; author of *Security Analysis and Portfolio Management* and numerous scholarly articles.

15. Dimitri Simes: Professor of Political Science, Georgetown Institute for Strategic Studies; managing editor of the monthly newsletter *Soviet Report.*

16. Aileen Masterson: Research Assistant, Center for Strategic and International Studies, Washington D.C.; editorial associate of the monthly newsletter *Soviet Report.*

INDEX